Wives, Husbands, and Lovers

Wives, Husbands, and Lovers

MARRIAGE AND SEXUALITY IN HONG KONG, TAIWAN, AND URBAN CHINA

Edited by Deborah S. Davis and Sara L. Friedman

Stanford University Press
Stanford, California

Stanford University Press
Stanford, California

Printed in the United States of America on acid-free, archival-quality paper

Library of Congress Cataloging-in-Publication Data

Wives, husbands, and lovers : marriage and sexuality in Hong Kong, Taiwan, and urban China / edited by Deborah S. Davis and Sara L. Friedman.
    pages cm
    Includes bibliographical references and index.
    ISBN 978-0-8047-9062-8 (cloth : alk. paper) —
    ISBN 978-0-8047-9184-7 (pbk. : alk. paper)
    1. Marriage—China. 2. Marriage—China—Hong Kong. 3. Marriage—Taiwan.
4. Sex—China. 5. Sex—China—Hong Kong. 6. Sex—Taiwan. 7. China—Social conditions—1949- 8. Hong Kong (China)—Social conditions. 9. Taiwan—Social conditions—1975- I. Davis, Deborah, editor of compilation. II. Friedman, Sara, editor of compilation.
    HQ684.W58 2014
    306.810951—dc23

                                                                2013043604

ISBN 978-0-8047-9185-4 (electronic)

Published in Asia, Australia and New Zealand by Hong Kong University Press
The University of Hong Kong, Pokfulam, Hong Kong

www.hkupress.org
ISBN 978-988-8208-41-2

Typeset by Thompson Type in 10/14 Minion

ACKNOWLEDGMENTS

The chapters in this book were first presented in July 2011 at a conference hosted by the Hong Kong Institute for the Humanities and Social Sciences at the University of Hong Kong. We thank Francis Cheng, Venus Lee, Natalie Wong, and Emily Yip for their excellent logistical support and good cheer that made the conference such a pleasure to organize and attend. As we progressed toward publication, we benefited greatly from close readings of individual chapters by Steven Harrell, Yu Li, Athena Liu, and Mark Selden. John Palmer, Michael Duckworth, and the anonymous reviewers for Hong Kong University Press and Stanford University Press provided valuable comments and critiques that strengthened the coherence of the volume. Stacy Wagner's early support at Stanford University Press was essential, and we thank her for seamlessly managing our editorial transition. For her expert guidance throughout the review and publication process, we are immensely grateful to our Stanford editor, Michelle Lipinski. Lastly, we acknowledge our gratitude to Helen Siu and Angela Leung, founding and current Directors of HKIHSS, for their unstinting intellectual encouragement and generous provision of a publication subvention.

Deborah Davis and Sara Friedman
September 2013

CONTENTS

FIGURES AND TABLES

CONTRIBUTORS

Yong Cai, Associate Professor, Department of Sociology, University of North Carolina

Deborah S. Davis, Professor of Sociology, Yale University

John Nguyet Erni, Professor, Department of Humanities and Creative Writing, Hong Kong Baptist University

James Farrer, Professor of Sociology and Global Studies, Sophia University, Japan

Sara L. Friedman, Associate Professor of Anthropology and Gender Studies, Indiana University

Petula Sik Ying Ho, Associate Professor, Department of Social Work and Social Administration, Hong Kong University

Grace Shu-chin Kuo, Associate Professor of Law, National Cheng Kung University, Taiwan

Yu-sheng Liu, Postdoctoral Fellow, Center for Survey Research, Academia Sinica, Taiwan

Hsiu-hua Shen, Associate Professor, The Institute of Sociology, National Tsing-hua University, Taiwan

Peidong Sun, Associate Professor, Department of History, Fudan University, Shanghai, PRC

Kwok-fai Ting, Professor of Sociology, The Chinese University of Hong Kong, Hong Kong

Wang Feng, Professor of Sociology, University of California, Irvine

Ruoh-rong Yu, Research Fellow and Executive Director, Center for Survey
Research, Research Center for Humanities and Social Sciences, Academia
Sinica, Taiwan

Jun Zhang, Research Assistant Professor, The Hong Kong Institute for the Humanities and Social Sciences, University of Hong Kong, Hong Kong

Wives, Husbands, and Lovers

1 DEINSTITUTIONALIZING MARRIAGE AND SEXUALITY

Deborah S. Davis and Sara L. Friedman

ON NOVEMBER 6, 2010, CHEN WEI-YI, a thirty-year-old Taiwanese woman, married herself in an elaborate Taipei wedding ceremony in the wake of an online publicity campaign that attracted thousands of comments about the pressure on single women to marry before age thirty.[1] Two years later, Hunan television broadcast a thirty-eight-episode soap opera entitled "Dutch Treat Marriage" that parodied the efforts of newly married couples in the People's Republic of China (PRC) to clearly demarcate spousal finances.[2] Later in 2012, the BBC circulated a sensational story about Cecil Chao, a never-married Hong Kong shipping tycoon, who was offering £40 million to "any man able to woo and marry his lesbian daughter who had already married her partner in France."[3]

Media representations such as these titillate a broad public precisely because they resonate with more general anxieties about the fate of marriage in contemporary Taiwan, Hong Kong, and the PRC. Marriage in these three societies is changing so rapidly that young and old alike often struggle to come to terms with new sexual mores, the erosion of traditional gender norms, and growing rates of marital infidelity and divorce. To marry oneself, as Chen Wei-yi did, might first appear as a bizarre twist on normative heterosexual marriage, but her act underscores the persistent centrality of the institution of marriage and the multiple ways that contemporary marriages differ from those of the past. Similarly, for those who do marry, changing expectations of marital roles and obligations challenge long-standing definitions of the good husband or the proper wife. Carefully splitting food and restaurant bills, as did the couple in "Dutch Treat Marriage," pokes fun at these renegotiations, but deciding whose name should be listed on a housing deed or a bank loan is a deadly serious matter.

Anxieties about the status of marriage in Taiwan, China, and Hong Kong today are also intensified by the expanding scope in which marital decisions are made, new family relationships navigated, and disputes resolved. Cecil Chao's efforts to replace his daughter's marriage to another woman in France with a heterosexual marriage, presumably to a man of Chinese descent, points to the distant reaches of this changing scale with regard to both partner choice and geography. Although this volume limits its geographic scope to three Chinese societies in East Asia, it maps the growing intensity of sexual and marital relationships across the borders of these three societies to document the rapidly expanding scale of marital decision making and intimate attachments in the region.

Until the mid-1980s governments in Hong Kong, the PRC, and Taiwan were able to treat marriage and the links between marriage and family formation according to their distinct legal and cultural conventions. Thus, even while sharing a Confucian tradition of patrilineal family formation, each had developed unique legal statutes and quite autonomous economies, and few marriages joined spouses across these jurisdictions. However, as economic integration intensified, ties between Taiwan and the PRC resumed, and Hong Kong became a Special Administrative Region (SAR) of the PRC, cross-border sexual liaisons and marriages increased, and cross-border family ties thickened. In response, individual men and women found themselves searching for partners and entering marriages under different conditions than had their parents or even their older siblings. They faced new opportunities and freedoms but also new anxieties and uncertainties.

Not surprisingly given this context of multifaceted structural and cultural transformation, the case studies in this volume illustrate diverse responses to these new conditions for entering or leaving a marriage and, in some cases, even fundamental changes in the institution of marriage itself. As recently as 1970, it was unusual for a man or woman over the age of thirty in Hong Kong, Taiwan, or the PRC to have never married. Divorce was rare, and homosexual relationships were covert or even criminalized. With the new millennium, however, none of these past generalizations holds true. In fact, marital norms and behaviors have departed so radically from those that had prevailed only a decade earlier that one could say marriages in these three Chinese societies have become "deinstitutionalized."

With the word *deinstitutionalization*, we adopt the terminology of sociologist Andrew Cherlin, who coined the term to identify a process through which previously taken-for-granted assumptions about the propriety of premarital sex, grounds for divorce, or even the necessity of marriage no longer prevail (Cherlin 1978, 2004). In this new environment, individuals have far more freedom to script their lives, but these new freedoms also create new anxieties for both individuals and society about how best to approach and understand marriage. Marriages have always involved conflict, disappointment, and not a small amount of anger, but Cherlin argued that the degree and scope of changes in marital behavior in the United States after 1970 revealed an institution that had become unmoored from earlier sureties. Although Cherlin initially presumed that the changes he observed marked a transition to a new equilibrium, by 2004 he no longer predicted reinstitutionalization around a new set of norms but instead foresaw ever greater variation in marriage, family, and household forms.

Politically and culturally, Hong Kong, Taiwan, and the PRC differ greatly from Cherlin's America. Therefore, we would not expect the process of marital deinstitutionalization to be identical, nor would we presume convergence at some point in the near future. However, there are parallels between the key shifts that Cherlin highlighted in the United States and those emerging recently in these three Chinese societies: a higher age at first marriage, fewer barriers to divorce, declining marital fertility, and greater social acceptance of premarital, extramarital, and same-sex intimate relationships. Many of these trends also replicate shifts observed in Western Europe that demographers such as Ron Lesthaeghe (2010) have defined as a second demographic transition. But whereas Lesthaeghe primarily focused on how changing marital patterns suppressed overall fertility, this volume addresses the multiple ways in which the institution of marriage itself has changed within the context of rapid legal, political, and economic restructuring. Declining fertility is one of our concerns, but it is neither the most important outcome nor the central puzzle.

By locating our study in these three Chinese societies we also offer a comparative, global dimension to existing literature on the deinstitutionalization of intimate life in the United States and Europe. Although we are inspired by Lesthaeghe's insistence that it is cultural values that drive change, we displace his dominant narrative of cultural diffusion from Western settings by tracing new trajectories and potential outcomes that differ in significant ways from those found in Europe and North America. As a consequence, we do not assume that our three societies will display identical patterns even with their shared Confucian heritage. Instead, we pay close attention to how recent political, legal, and cultural histories have diverged across the region, thereby producing significant differences in expectations and experiences. Although each chapter addresses a specific dimension of marriage and sexuality in a single country, it does so with an eye to comparisons both across these three societies and with trends found in other parts of the world. Deinstitutionalization may summarize a global dynamic driven by individuals' pursuit of new possibilities for marital and sexual satisfaction, but the direction of this dynamic and its potential outcomes are by no means universal. Our attention to these three societies, with their shared cultural features and divergent histories, enables us to explore both the roots of change and the multiple possibilities emerging for new marital and sexual futures.

To explain and interpret these changes in marital and sexual mores in contemporary Hong Kong, Taiwan, and China, we first discuss the larger cultural, political, and economic contexts in which couples marry or divorce and in which men and women find intimate or romantic partners. Neither the editors nor any of our contributors presume that a marriage is exclusively a decision of two individuals. Nor do we reduce decisions on whether to marry or divorce to economistic choices intended to maximize individual utility, a perspective Gary Becker adopted when he reasoned that "no person can improve his marriage without making others worse off" (Becker 1991: 108). Rather, our core assumption is that marriage is a complex institution, embedded within a larger system of gendered family and kinship relationships that in turn are embedded within a socially specific economy and polity. Because of these assumptions, our discussion of variation in marital and sexual behavior directly engages questions about how and why boundaries between private and public life shift and under what conditions a society may privilege private over public preferences or distinguish norms for marriage from those for family formation.

Undoubtedly, marriage is an intimate relationship, but because marital status allocates and legitimates societal privileges, rights, resources, and obligations, marriage also is a public institution. For this reason, it is not surprising that Chen Wei-yi chose to hold a public marriage ceremony or that she circulated the news of her wedding widely through social media. In fact, American historian Nancy Cott has argued that for a relationship even to be identified as marriage, it required a certain degree of public recognition and, perhaps more importantly, "state sanction" (Cott 2000: 1–2). Although Chen Wei-yi's ceremony lacked the imprimatur of the state, it made a clear claim for public recognition of her married status.

How do we reconcile this persistent emphasis on public recognition with what legal scholar Jana Singer identifies as a greater preference for "private over public ordering" as the driving force behind increased acceptance of diverse forms of intimacy and family formation (Singer 1992: 1453)? We see this private ordering in the same-sex partner choice of Gigi Chao, daughter of Hong Kong tycoon Cecil Chao, as well as in her father's own lifelong decision never to marry. But Chao's desire to see his daughter married in a heterosexual union suggests that the balance between private and public claims is still quite contested, in part because of deep-seated Confucian patriarchal family values and societal investments in some forms of marriage and family and not others.

Whereas constitutional protection of the right to "the pursuit of happiness" in the United States may provide a moral basis for privileging private over public preferences and for protecting the rights of one spouse or the best interest of the child, what moral logics dominate in Confucian societies with their greater deference to social hierarchy, minimal protection of personal rights, and continued emphasis on the family as a key social institution? Does the emphasis on family ties and obligations explain why our three societies do not display another key feature of marital deinstitutionalization and demographic transition found in the West: the high rates of childbearing outside of marriage? Although we cannot definitively answer that question, in the chapters to follow we show why it is important to distinguish the deinstitutionalization of marriage from the deinstitutionalization of multigenerational family formation. When the distinction between marriage and family is clarified, it becomes quite clear, for example, that increased access to affordable and effective contraception might lower overall fertility rates but have less direct impact on the likelihood of births outside of marriage.[4]

Attuned to these historical and societal specificities, we train a close eye on how negotiations over the balance of private and public ordering take place within families or between spouses and romantic partners, as well as in the courts, the media, and legislative debates. And we ask what this balance and the struggles it provokes teach us about why previously shared expectations about acceptable marital and sexual behaviors have atrophied or even disappeared, while norms of childbearing and intergenerational obligation and reciprocity remain more intact.

Because variation in political, economic, and demographic profiles affects the scope and pace of deinstitutionalization, we first provide an overview of six dimensions of changing marital experience in these three societies: higher age at first marriage, rising percentages of never married, reduced legal barriers to divorce, new norms for sexual intimacy, subreplacement marital fertility, and more frequent cross-border marriage. We then step back from these empirical comparisons to consider the broader question of what the deinstitutionalization of marriage means for both personal and family life in Hong Kong, Taiwan, and urban China today.

POSTPONING MARRIAGE OR REJECTING IT ALTOGETHER?

Historically, marriage in Chinese societies was a familial decision initiated by the parents of a son seeking a daughter-in-law to continue the husband's patriline. Fables of romance and star-crossed lovers certainly flourished in written and oral tales, but in real life young people typically conformed to Confucian expectations of parental obedience and married the mate whom their parents had chosen for them.

Marriage and family formation were sequential and conflated, and every man had the filial obligation to produce offspring within a marriage. Because men outnumbered women and marriage required substantial investments, however, men from poor families risked a future as "bare branches" who never married, whereas rich men often enjoyed the attentions of multiple consorts. By contrast, parents rarely failed to arrange marriages for their daughters, and very few women remained single into adulthood (Hajnal 1953, 1982; Lee and Wang 1999; Wolf and Huang 1980).[5] While the early-twentieth-century upheavals of war and revolution tore apart families and decimated economic and political institutions, marriage rates for women remained high throughout the first half of the century. Thus, not surprisingly, two of the most widely appreciated dividends of China's 1949 Communist revolution were reduced parental control over mate choice and comparable rates of marriage among young men and women regardless of parental wealth.[6]

Traditionally, Chinese parents preferred that their children marry in their teens, and child betrothal was not an uncommon strategy to guarantee continuation of the family line, ensure harmonious intergenerational relations, and reduce expenditures for marriage.[7] After 1950, legal reforms and struc-

Table 1.1. Mean age at first marriage, 1970–2005.

	Hong Kong		Taiwan		China		Shanghai	
	Men	Women	Men	Women	Men	Women	Men	Women
1970	30.2	23.8	24.6	22.6	—	19.7	26.2	23.3
1980	28.7	25.3	25.3	23.9	25.1	22.4	27.0	25.1
1990	29.8	28.0	28.8	26.0	23.8	22.1	25.3	23.3
2000	31.9	29.6	30.5	27.6	25.1	23.3	—	—
2005	33.0	30.3	31.9	29.5	25.7	23.6	26.5	24.1

SOURCES: Jones and Gubhaju (2009), Wang and Zhang (1996: fn 4); figures for Shanghai calculated by Yong Cai from 2005 1 percent Population Change Survey.

tural changes in the economies of Hong Kong, Taiwan, and China reduced the incidence of teenage marriage. Over the subsequent decades, the rapid expansion of secondary and then tertiary education and the proliferation of new occupational choices for women accelerated the shift toward a higher age at first marriage. Thus in Table 1.1 we observe that, overall, between 1970 and 2005, age at first marriage rose steadily for both men and women. However, patterns of change are not uniform across the three jurisdictions. For example, while the average age at first marriage for men in Hong Kong has hovered around thirty for more than three decades, in Taiwan the shift upward toward age thirty comes after 1990, and in China, the average age falls after 1980 before resuming an upward trend nearly a decade later.[8] For women we see a similar pattern of Hong Kong residents experiencing higher average ages than elsewhere and a unique downward turn in China between 1980 and 1990. Moreover, as late as 2005, Chinese men and women, even in the affluent city of Shanghai, married on average several years earlier than their age peers in Hong Kong or Taiwan.

As Yong Cai and Wang Feng explain in Chapter 4, the anomalous decline in age of marriage in China after 1980 derives from the central role of the Chinese government in establishing and enforcing legal and administrative constraints on marriage. Between 1970 and 1980 a nationwide policy of "late marriage" that established minimum ages higher than those prescribed by the Marriage Law had raised the marriage age above what young adults and their parents preferred. Subsequently, as the post-Mao state no longer emphasized delayed marriage as an element of population control policies, couples again married near the legal minimum. Thus, unlike in Taiwan and Hong Kong, where social and economic forces such as the expansion of educational opportunities and the increased employment of young women altered individual preferences, in China state policies were often most decisive (Davis and Harrell 1993).

Because reduced parental control over a child's mate choice is often associated with a higher age at first marriage, rising age at marriage may indicate greater autonomy for married couples. Upward shifts in age, however, do not necessarily indicate that marriage per se is less desirable. Rather, higher average age at first marriage may merely document postponement of a still highly valued status. However, because historically few Chinese married for the first time after age thirty-five, comparing trends in the percentage of those who have never married by their late thirties does provide one metric for evaluating whether marriage is becoming less universal and thus possibly less desirable over time. Moreover, because the majority of both men and women in contemporary Taiwan and Hong Kong complete a postsecondary degree and China's postsecondary completion rates are rapidly approaching this benchmark, comparing rates of marriage among the youngest cohorts of college graduates may also signal dominant trends in the near future rather than reflecting the situation of only a small elite.

The quantitative data in Table 1.2 summarize the changing percentage of never-married college-educated men and women among three different age cohorts: those between the ages of twenty-five and twenty-nine, between thirty and thirty-four, and between thirty-five and thirty-nine for four census years between 1982 and 2005/2010.[9] Overall, there is one story for Hong Kong and Taiwan and another for the PRC. Most simply, the trends document that, in Hong Kong between 1982 and 2005, fewer and fewer college-educated men or women had married by their late thirties. When one looks more closely at this oldest cohort, college-educated women in Hong Kong consistently have been less likely to marry than their male peers. In Taiwan, the trends generally parallel those of Hong Kong, but the rates of never marrying are lower, and the most recent figures (2010) show a convergence in male and female rates. In China, by contrast, the trend is quite different. Virtually all college-educated men and women have married by their late thirties; even in Shanghai, only 9.3 percent of men and 5.3 percent of women in the oldest age group had never married in 2005.

The trends captured in Table 1.2 do not prove that college-educated people in Hong Kong and Taiwan are rejecting marriage altogether. Rather, they indicate that the percentage who have yet to marry by their late thirties has risen dramatically since 1982. Nor do these figures definitively document a clear gender asymmetry whereby marriage is more desirable or possible for college-

Table 1.2. Percentage of never married among college-educated men and women, 1982–2010.

Age	Year	Hong Kong		Taiwan		all PRC		Shanghai	
		Men	Women	Men	Women	Men	Women	Men	Women
25–29	1982	58.3	49.4	65	47	46.6	36	72.9	57.3
	1990	73.6	59.3	78	65	31.3	18.8	61.3	36.2
	2000	83	75.9	85	75	38.2	21.1	57.8	30.9
	2005	87.7	83	—	—	46.9	30	61.3	46.8
	2010	—	—	88	77	—	—	—	—
30–34	1982	33.6	19.6	17	19	7	8.3	20.3	18.5
	1990	34.6	35	28	25	4.3	6	17.6	10.6
	2000	48.1	43.2	39	35	6.2	3.9	20.2	13
	2005	52.2	46.7	—	—	10	5.4	20.8	15.2
	2010	—	—	51	41	—	—	—	—
35–39	1982	8.2	11.4	5	11	1.4	1.8	6.8	4.8
	1990	16.6	21.6	9	15	0.9	2.6	4.5	6.6
	2000	23.6	30.5	15	22	1.6	1.4	9.6	6.1
	2005	27.3	31.3	—	—	2	2.2	9.3	5.3
	2010	—	—	23	24	—	—	—	—

SOURCES: Taiwan figures calculated from census of the Directorate-General of Budget, Accounting and Statistics (DGBAS), with 1980 substituted for 1982 and 2010 substituted for 2005. PRC figures calculated by Yong Cai from census micro samples. Hong Kong figures calculated from 1 percent census samples (1981–1996), 5 percent census samples (2001–2006), Hong Kong Census and Statistic Department 2007a, 2009a, 2009b.

educated men than women. In 2005, 27.3 percent of college-educated Hong Kong men in the oldest cohort had never married; for their female peers it was 31.3 percent. This gap of 4 percent is not trivial, but it is small. In Taiwan in 2010 and in the PRC in 2005, the gap between men and women in their late thirties was virtually nonexistent: a 1 percent difference in Taiwan and 0.2 percent in China. Yet in the public media and in the discourse on "surplus women" in China (Zhang and Sun Chapter 5), one repeatedly finds strong assumptions about the poor marriage prospects of highly educated young women. To address these widely circulating views, we go beyond aggregate rates and turn to our contributors' findings regarding gender asymmetries in the desirability of marriage or satisfaction with the quality of marriages.

Using a 2009 survey, Kwokfai Ting (Chapter 6) found that, although marriage is still highly desired by Hong Kong residents, men and women express different levels of satisfaction with marriage. Overall men reported higher levels of satisfaction than did women, and younger men's satisfaction with their marriage was higher than that of older men. By contrast, levels of satisfaction among women did not vary across birth cohorts. Sikying Ho's interviews

(Chapter 7) with Hong Kong men who have had multiple sexual partners before and during marriage suggest a similar gender asymmetry. Men who openly admit to extramarital relationships describe themselves as respectful of their wives and as better husbands and fathers than their own fathers. Without access to wives' views we cannot know whether the wives of these men share their husbands' portrayals of successful marriages. Ting's findings, however, point to the possibility that marital norms have not kept up with the expectations and desires of Hong Kong women, and Ho's research suggests that Hong Kong men and women may have different understandings of what constitutes a good marriage. Over time, therefore, it is certainly possible that gender-distinct definitions of a good marriage may translate into a different propensity to marry.

Similarly, in Taiwan, our contributors identify norms that seem to make marriage less satisfying for women. However, the trends are not identical with Hong Kong. When comparing attitudes of husbands and wives in three national surveys, Yu and Liu (Chapter 10) find that even when wives work and husbands do not, women perform most of the housework. Moreover, the housework gender gap is most extreme among married women in the youngest cohort between the ages of twenty-five and twenty-nine, who may hold more traditional attitudes than older married women. Similarly in Hsiu-hua Shen's study (Chapter 11) of families in which the Taiwanese husband/father works in China while his wife and children remain in Taiwan, persistent attachment to traditional norms that privilege breadwinning over sexual fidelity allows men the freedom to explore extramarital sexual relationships with Mainland Chinese women while their wives enjoy reduced demands on their household labor but without the same extramarital sexual prerogatives. If such gender asymmetries in expectations of married life continue to grow over time, we may very well observe a similar gap in the appeal of marriage for Taiwanese men and women that we see emerging in Hong Kong. As a consequence, perhaps we should not be surprised that the Internet has yet to feature a male equivalent to Chen Wei-yi and her solo wedding and honeymoon to Australia.

DIVORCE ON DEMAND AND THE SHIFT FROM PUBLIC TO PRIVATE ORDERING

Although imperial Chinese law permitted divorce under certain circumstances, husbands and wives faced very different access to such legal protections. Whereas a man could easily replace his wife with a new spouse or concubine, a woman encountered much higher barriers to marital dissolution. Women themselves could not initiate a divorce lawsuit against their husband or senior conjugal kin; only their natal family could do so on their behalf (a consequence of the Qing code's prohibition of inferiors litigating against legal superiors), and the criteria for granting a divorce were far more rigorous for women than men.[10] By the early twentieth century, Chinese reformers of differing ideological persuasions saw these traditional practices as both symbolic and substantive obstacles to creating a modern Chinese nation, and they drafted marriage laws that made the freedom to divorce part of a larger effort to assert the "equality [of China] among the world of nations" (Tran 2011: 118; see also Glosser 2003; Li and Friedman forthcoming). In practice, however, the new freedom to divorce codified in both the Nationalists' 1931 Civil Code and the Communists' Jiangxi Soviet code was rarely realized, and high barriers to divorce persisted in both urban and rural China (Bernhardt 1994).[11]

Similarly, after the establishment of the PRC, Chinese Communist Party (CCP) leaders acted quickly to promulgate a new Marriage Law that included provisions liberalizing access to divorce.[12] In practice, however, after a brief surge in divorces in the early 1950s, rates declined rapidly as a result of cumbersome and politicized review procedures and societal stigmatization of divorcees (Diamant 2000; Platte 1988). In Hong Kong and Taiwan, divorce also was rare during the three decades after 1950 both because of social stigma and because the state took no initiative to substantially liberalize the grounds for granting divorce. The decade after 1980, however, witnessed a dramatic rise in divorce rates across all three jurisdictions, as the legal barriers to voluntary dissolution of marriage fell and societal attitudes shifted (see Figure 1.1).

In the PRC, reduced legal barriers to divorce followed from a major realignment at the apex of political power after the death of Mao Zedong in 1976. Under Deng Xiaoping, the leadership rejected the extreme politicization of private life that characterized the Maoist decades and moved to draft laws that more clearly defined the rights and legal remedies available to individual citizens. One of the first results of this shift was the promulgation of the 1980 Marriage Law, which permitted divorce solely on the basis of the complete breakdown of affection between husband and wife, even in cases where only one spouse sought to dissolve the marriage. Subsequent revisions to the law in 2001 further reduced obstacles to unilateral divorce, and administrative changes in 2003 cleared the way for marital dissolution even in cases

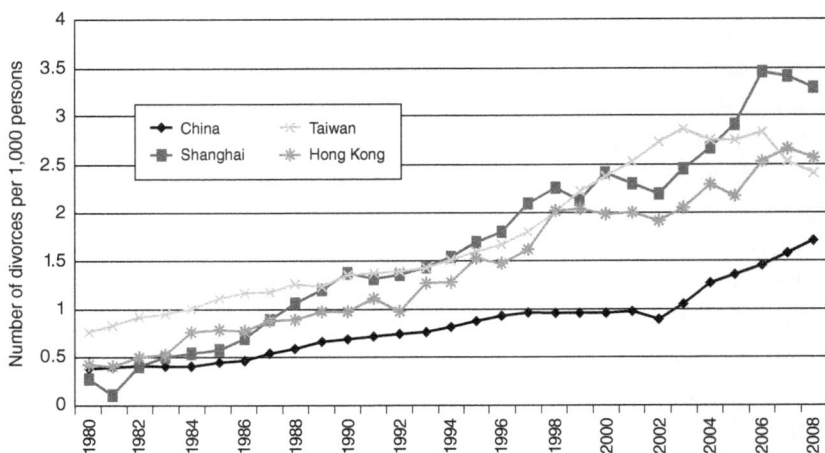

Figure 1.1. Crude divorce rates, 1980–2008.

sources: For Hong Kong, Hong Kong Census and Statistics Department 2007a, 2007b, 2009a, 2009b; for Shanghai, Shanghai Tongji Nianjian 2008; for China, Zhongguo Minzheng Tongji Nianjian 2012; Zhongguo Tongji Nianjian 2012; for Taiwan, Taiwan Department of Household Registration, Ministry of the Interior, "Number and Rates of Birth, Death, Marriage and Divorce, 1981–2012."

in which the petitioner had been accused of blameworthy marital conduct (Davis Chapter 2).

In Taiwan, there were equally fundamental shifts in the laws regulating divorce, but the drivers of change were not the same as in the PRC. Whereas in the PRC a small national elite took the initiative, in Taiwan reforms were spurred by broad political and societal forces. Thus, for example, revisions to Taiwan's divorce laws have been embedded within reforms of the civil and family codes that have introduced greater gender equality into the legal statutes regulating child custody allocation and property rights.[13] Moreover, as Grace Kuo explains in Chapter 9, many of these changes originated from feminist advocacy of divorce as a woman's "right" as well as from broader democratic pressures on Taiwan's Constitutional Court to make family laws conform to constitutionally guaranteed rights to equal protection and treatment under the law. Unlike the top-down legal and administrative shifts that liberalized the Marriage Law in the PRC, in Taiwan a powerful women's movement and democratic political system pushed for legal reforms that remedied certain gender biases in family laws and reduced barriers to divorce.

Nevertheless, despite broad societal and political support for these legal reforms, the 2008 crude divorce rate (CDR) in Taiwan was lower than that in either Hong Kong or PRC cities such as Shanghai.[14] One explanation may be that, although the legal parameters for approving divorce have expanded dramatically, couples in Taiwan must still divorce on the basis of fault. Hence, to fully understand the statistical face of divorce as reflected in numbers such as the CDR, we must look to both legal reforms and broader social transformations (such as those documented in Chapters 9, 10, 11, and 12) to explain why, despite Taiwan's earlier surge in divorce rates, its divorce trajectory and current patterns do not match precisely those in either Hong Kong or urban China.

Hong Kong's route to more liberal divorce law diverges from those both in the PRC and in Taiwan due to its history as a British colony. Prior to 1997, all those who married or divorced in Hong Kong were subject to British colonial law. Until 1971 the colonial government recognized four forms of marriage, but after the adoption of the Marriage Reform Ordinance of 1971, the law no longer tolerated customary marriage, concubinage, or secondary wives, and legal practice in Hong Kong became more closely aligned with that in the United Kingdom. Henceforth, all marriages were to be registered with the Hong Kong government and conform to legal stipulations of monogamy. Courts recognized no-fault unilateral divorce after a separation of five years. In 1992, the government reduced the number of years couples needed to live separately before applying for uncontested divorce from five years to two and strengthened claims for equal division of conjugal property. As legal barriers to divorce fell, no-fault divorce became the norm; by 2009, only 10 percent of divorces were contested in the courts.[15]

Despite variation in the letter of the law and the structure of the judiciaries, courts in all three jurisdictions have adopted a legal logic for granting divorce that privileges private over public preferences, an orientation that scholars first identified as a hallmark of North American and European courts (Cohen 2002; Shanley 2002; Singer 1992). In all three jurisdictions, courts approach marital disputes as a conflict between two individuals and only rarely involve parties other than the two spouses (or in some case minor children) in the proceedings. Thus, even when a contentious relationship with in-laws or financial entanglement with nonkin are central to the breakdown of the marriage, the laws regulating marriage privilege spouses' personal satisfaction and prevent third parties from instigating divorce proceedings.[16]

Beyond courts' new privileging of individual satisfaction and deference to "private ordering" (Cohen 2002: 185), recent legal reforms in all three jurisdictions also point to the privatization of the institution of marriage itself. In making this claim we are not adopting the argument of legal scholars such as

Cass Sunstein and Richard Thaler (2008), who advocate privatization of marriage as a correction to the distortions created when government licensing subsidizes one form of intimacy over another. Rather, we use privatization to identify the trend of states retreating from close supervision of marital discord and increasing legal protection for individual preferences on the grounds that marriage is foremost a private relationship. This trend requires us to balance two dimensions of contemporary marriage and marital regulation. On the one hand, we recognize that marriage performs public functions, and we endorse Nancy Cott's view that the institutionalization and regulation of marriage "facilitate the government's grasp on the populace" (Cott 2000: 1). This public face of marital regulation remains prominent when marriages join spouses across national borders or when groups mobilize to legalize same-sex unions. On the other hand, the recent experiences of men and women seeking divorce in our three jurisdictions document a diminished role for states and judiciaries. In each country, the government no longer routinely privileges social stability, the interests of specific groups, or state policies over the individual civil rights of a husband or wife when adjudicating marital disputes.

SEXUAL INTIMACY: BEFORE, DURING, AND WITHOUT MARRIAGE

As in most societies, men and women in China historically followed gender-distinct sexual scripts. Men were allowed, even encouraged, to gain sexual experience before marriage; by contrast, brides were expected to be virgins on their wedding day. During marriage, wealthy men were free to have multiple partners, even concubines, but women could be divorced for even one adulterous affair. After the death of a spouse, men remarried as quickly as they could afford the cost of a new marriage; widows, by contrast, were to remain chaste, remarrying only in cases of extreme poverty.

In the early twentieth century, gender-distinct sexual norms and expectations came to the forefront of efforts to reform marriage as part of broader initiatives to modernize Chinese society. Reformers across the political spectrum sought to popularize companionate marriage and marital monogamy, and they pushed for legal reforms that would prohibit child betrothals, expand access to divorce, and protect women's right to remarry. New legal codes implemented after the fall of the Qing Empire in 1911 criminalized concubinage as adultery and held both married men and women to expectations of monogamy (Tran 2011). In practice, however, Republican courts did little to enforce restrictions on men's extramarital sexual prerogatives, and gender asymmetries in sexual norms persisted across the region.

Consequential changes came first in the PRC where broad enforcement of the 1950 Marriage Law routinized monogamy and strengthened state regulation of private life. Simultaneously, campaigns to eliminate prostitution dramatically shrunk the commodified sphere of sexual exchange and further restricted sexual relations to the institution of marriage (Hershatter 1997). In this context of close state supervision of intimate relationships, even premarital and extramarital sexual liaisons became politically and socially stigmatized (Evans 1997: 113).

The very different political conditions in Hong Kong and Taiwan after 1949 precluded such direct and comprehensive state regulation of sexual intimacy either within or outside of marriage. Hong Kong mandated monogamy only in 1971, and while organized prostitution was not legal or licensed, brothels openly catered to local and foreign customers. In addition, Hong Kong residents did not face the same political or legal restrictions on sociability and geographic mobility as their PRC counterparts and thus were able to more easily pursue (and if necessary hide from public view) extramarital or nonmarital relationships.

Taiwan's experience took yet another route. The Japanese colonial administration (1895–1945) licensed courtesan houses and brothels and made minimal effort to regulate local marriage practices. In the first years after decolonization, the KMT government attacked the culture of "immorality" inculcated under Japanese rule, but the military retreat of more than one million, mostly young, unmarried men in 1949 led the government to outlaw illicit prostitution while simultaneously "managing" women working in licensed brothels (Huang 2011: 87–90). As the sex industry expanded rapidly in the 1960s in response to an enlarged U.S. military presence on the island, police intensified their surveillance of all forms of nonmarital sexuality and pornography (Ding 2000; Huang 2011: 92–100). A new sexual order gradually emerged in which a normative model of "respectable" heterosexual femininity and marital sexuality coexisted uneasily with a persistent sexual double standard for men and women (Chang 1999; Ding and Liu 1999; Ho 2007; Huang 2011: 104–111).

As residents of these three societies experienced the evolving legal, economic, and cultural environments of the 1980s, they did not share identical expectations of acceptable sexual behavior. PRC residents, in cities and villages, had little premarital sexual experience unless with their affianced, prostitution was criminalized and relatively rare, concubinage was illegal, and long-term cohabitation outside of marriage was invisible if not nonexistent. In Hong Kong, by contrast, heterosexual liaisons were only lightly policed, and men had considerable freedom to pursue sexual intimacy outside of marriage through purchasing sexual services from prostitutes or cultivating longer-term extramarital relationships. Martial law Taiwan was characterized by a more contradictory sexual climate in which, although monogamy was prescribed in law, prostitution flourished in both legal and illicit forms and police responded alternatively by cracking down on nonmarital sexual liaisons and turning a blind eye to men's heterosexual prerogatives.

In the past two decades, however, sexual norms and the state's regulatory roles have partially converged across the three societies. Courtship now routinely involves sexual intimacy for women as well as men (Chang 1996; Chang et al. 1997; Chow and Lum 2008; Farrer 2002; Ho 2007; Yan 2011; Zhang 2011), and even in rural China premarital sex is no longer stigmatized (Friedman 2006; Yan 2003). Yet the place of sexual fidelity within marriage remains contested. Although the courts and public opinion across the region uphold the ideal of marital monogamy, sexual intimacy is now far less exclusively confined to marriage. During divorce hearings, Taiwanese courts can use evidence of extramarital relationships to establish fault, and courts in all three jurisdictions can assign compensation to the nonblameworthy spouse, but marital infidelity for ordinary citizens rarely generates consequences in other domains of social and economic life, such as advancement in the workplace.

At the same time, there are some significant gender disparities in how societal anxieties about sexual fidelity are expressed. Men espouse greater approval of extramarital sex (Parish, Laumann, and Mojola 2007), and a wife's infidelity is generally perceived as more threatening to a marriage than a husband's (Chang 1999; Ho Chapter 7; Shen Chapter 11). In practice, however, an increasing number of women do engage in extramarital and nonmarital sexual relationships. For instance, Farrer and Pei found that Shanghai women were as capable as their male counterparts of finding extramarital partners, making time for and legitimating their affairs, and managing deception in their relationships (Farrer and Sun 2003; Pei 2011). This is likely true for Hong Kong and Taiwan women as well. Yet the stakes in pursuing extramarital relationships and the likelihood of doing so may vary between men and women and among them by class, ethnicity, residence, and educational level. As we discuss later in the chapter, these distinctions become more salient with enhanced cross-border mobility across the region and the greater sexual opportunities such movement provides for some groups of men and women.

INCREASED ACCEPTANCE OF SAME-SEX INTIMACY

In all three jurisdictions, the state has reduced its surveillance and regulation of sexual relationships between consenting men and women. However, to what extent have there been comparable shifts in recognizing forms of intimacy that do not align with heterosexual desires? For some observers, the years since 1980 map onto a linear shift from "sex for reproduction" to "sex for pleasure" (Pan 2006: 28). And, indeed, when one observes the greater tolerance for premarital and extramarital sexual relationships between consenting men and women and the legal position that emotionally unsatisfying marriages provide sufficient grounds for granting divorce, it appears that the logic of "sex for pleasure" has gained legitimacy in all three societies. However, perhaps an even stronger indicator of reduced state oversight of sexual relationships is to be found in changing legal attitudes toward homosexuality and the increased social visibility and acceptance of same-sex relationships.

In imperial China, the social and erotic expression of same-sex intimacy was generally confined to a continuum of behaviors that coexisted with heterosexual marriage, so long as such behaviors did not challenge existing social hierarchies (Chou 2000; Hinsch 1990; Sang 2003; Wu 2002).[17] The Ming and Qing legal statutes did penalize certain sexual acts, specifically anal sex between men, whether forced or consensual (Kang 2012; Somer 2000), but overall the law did not criminalize nonheterosexual relationships (Balzano 2007; Chou 2000; Hinsch 1990; Ruskola 1994). The concept of homosexuality as a specific sexual orientation, even identity, was introduced in the early twentieth century through Western sexology discourses but did not enjoy widespread societal or legal recognition (Sang 2003). Following the precedent set by the revised 1907 Qing legal code, Republican laws did not explicitly criminalize same-sex sexual behaviors, including sodomy.

After 1949, sustained campaigns against prostitution, concubinage, and nonmarital intimacy in the PRC created a more restrained and repressed sexual climate. Yet the government took no steps to alter legal statutes so as to criminalize sodomy or other homosexual acts (Balzano 2007; Kang 2012: 234–236; Li 2006). In practice, however, those who engaged in consensual same-sex relations were often sanctioned outside of the legal system: Party membership could be revoked, jobs lost, and the individuals detained without trial or even sent to labor camps (Balzano 2007; Kang 2012: 236). But, without explicit statutes, the PRC courts could not criminalize homosexuality; they could only condemn homosexual acts as harmful to society.[18]

In an ironic about-face, the post-1978 effort to build a rule of law in the PRC explicitly criminalized sex between men by identifying male anal sex with hooliganism in the new criminal law. Despite this criminal association, punishment typically followed only when such behavior was coerced or violent (Balzano 2007; Kang 2012). Thus it was not homosexuality (同性恋) as a category that came under legal sanction but a specifically male sexual behavior. By contrast, sexual relations between women have never been identified as a legal problem in the PRC (Kang 2012). Reinforcing this process of legally codifying criminal sexual behavior was the 1989 pathologization of homosexuality in the second edition of the *Chinese Classification and Diagnostic Criteria of Mental Disorders* (Kang 2012).

In the second decade of PRC economic and legal reforms, however, the trend to criminalize homosexual intimacy was reversed. The Revised Criminal Law of 1997 deleted any specific reference to the crime of hooliganism that previously had been used to punish male anal sex (Jeffreys 2006; Kang 2012; Li 2006; Rofel 2007).[19] In 2000, the Ministry of Public Security announced that "members of the Chinese public have the right to choose their own sexuality"; in 2001, homosexuality was no longer explicitly pathologized as a mental illness (Jeffreys 2006: 10; Kang 2012). Transgender individuals were granted the right to marry in 2003, and recent years have witnessed a spate of public wedding ceremonies for gay and lesbian couples, although such marriages to date are not sanctioned by the state.[20]

Currently there are over 300 LGBT organizations throughout China that work to advance the rights and the public visibility of gay men and women through magazines, hotlines, support groups, and even an Internet television station dedicated to gay viewers (Rofel 2013). Nevertheless, legal reforms and the growth of grassroots nongovernmental organizations (NGOs) and media do not, by any means, indicate a wholesale acceptance of gay sexuality or the end of repressive actions on the part of police, the medical establishment, or PRC society more generally. To this day, administrative policies that criminalize behaviors deemed to "disrupt the public order" are used by police to detain men found engaging in consensual sex and to disperse openly gay gatherings and events.[21] Although the very existence of these events points to a more open societal attitude toward homosexuality and its presence in the PRC public sphere, it would be rash to suggest that homosexual relationships have acquired the same kind of normativity attributed to heterosexual intimacies or that legal recognition of same-sex marriage is an imminent possibility in the PRC.

In Hong Kong, British law and legal precedents have generally shaped the overall direction of both local ordinances and the application of legal statutes. In the treatment of homosexual and transgender relationships, however, Hong Kong law has often lagged behind legal reforms not only in the United Kingdom but even in the PRC. Only in 1991 did the Hong Kong Legislative Council decriminalize private, adult, noncommercial, and consensual homosexual relations, and only in 2005 did the High Court strike down laws that created a different age of consent for same-sex as opposed to opposite-sex sexual acts. Gays and lesbians still confront discrimination in their daily lives and lack legal recognition of their relationships and family forms (Erni Chapter 8).

Public bias in Hong Kong extends to transgender individuals and couples as well. Only in May 2013 did the high court reverse two lower court decisions prohibiting Miss W, a transgender woman, from marrying her boyfriend (Erni Chapter 8). Reaffirming a procreative heterosexual bias in legal definitions of marriage, the judge ruling against Miss W argued that "it is difficult and unrealistic to consider marriage to be entirely unconnected with procreation" (Voigt 2013), an association that the United Kingdom had rejected as early as 1947 (Liu 2011). Despite growing public support in Hong Kong for new laws to penalize discrimination on the basis of sexual orientation and greater acceptance of same-sex marriage,[22] the narrow legal victory in the Miss W case, as John Erni contends in Chapter 8, was secured in large part by claiming that hers was not a same-sex marriage. Although the final ruling acknowledged new bases for defining gender and sexual intimacy, it nonetheless reaffirmed that legal marriage in Hong Kong remained a union of one man and one woman.

Taiwan legal codes followed the precedent set by the Republican government on the mainland prior to 1949 by not explicitly criminalizing sodomy or homosexuality. Nevertheless, both under martial law and after 1987, sexual and gender deviancy were punished under statutes that banned behavior deemed "deleterious to virtuous customs" (妨害風化罪 or 妨害善良風俗).[23] Because homosexuality was never explicitly named or prohibited in law, its threat was simultaneously nebulous and yet far reaching. As Fran Martin argues, nonnormative sexualities have acquired public intelligibility in Taiwan through "a set of laws that remains anxiously preoccupied with protecting the moral and cultural integrity of the Chinese nation" (Martin 2003: 14; Huang 2011). In this regard, Taiwan resembles the PRC, where police crackdowns on businesses and events associated with homosexuality are justified to this day in the name of "public morality" (Rofel 2007: 96).

That said, societal acceptance of gays and lesbians in Taiwan has expanded rapidly over the past two decades, and, although openly declaring a nonheterosexual identity or preference is not without consequence, more women and men have found ways to maintain same-sex relationships throughout adulthood. Taipei now hosts the largest annual gay pride parade in all of Asia, and same-sex sexuality and identity have become recognizable and at times sensationalized topics discussed avidly in the media and public discourse. Declining marriage rates across Taiwanese society provide some support as gays and lesbians seek to deflect familial pressure to marry and bear children (Hu 2011). A 2013 poll commissioned by the Taiwan Alliance to Promote Civil Partnership Rights found that 53 percent of those surveyed favored legalizing same-sex marriage (Lee 2013).

The current absence of explicit legal protections for gays and lesbians, however, creates a climate of vulnerability with regard to the right to share property, make medical decisions, and bear or adopt children. These vulnerabilities have sparked ongoing activist efforts in Taiwan to recognize civil unions as well as same-sex marriage, both goals as yet unrealized (Kuo Chapter 9; Lee 2013; "Support for Same-Sex Marriage" 2013). When a transgender marriage case came to public attention in 2013, Taiwanese officials followed the precedent set by the Hong Kong courts in the Miss W case, upholding the couple's right to remain married but explicitly rejecting any framing of the case that would endorse same-sex marriage rights (Hsu 2013; Lin 2013).

If we look broadly across each of the three jurisdictions over the past twenty years, we see that the letter of the laws and their enforcement have reduced sanctions against heterosexual and homosexual relationships outside marriage. Paralleling these legal changes have been tectonic shifts in public attitudes toward previously stigmatized sexualities (Kong 2010).[24] Nevertheless, despite these significant shifts in legal and community norms, at present all three jurisdictions still restrict marriage to one man and one woman, effectively eliminating the right to marry for gays and lesbians. Thus, although the overarching conclusion about a sexual revolution across these Chinese societies holds true, legal rules and logics remain tethered to heterosexual moorings.

MARRIAGE, PARENTHOOD, AND SUBREPLACEMENT FERTILITY

Throughout the world, marriage historically has preceded parenthood, and children born to unmarried parents or fathered by someone other than their mother's husband were often stigmatized. In the wealthy countries of the West these conventions held through most of the twentieth century, but attitudes shifted after 1970; by 2009, more than a third of births in the OECD (Organisation for Economic Co-operation and Development) countries were to unmarried women or women not in a legal relationship with the father. In countries as economically and culturally diverse as Mexico, France, Sweden, and Slovenia, fewer than half of children were born to married mothers by 2009.[25] This pattern of nonmarital childbearing has been coupled with dramatic declines in overall fertility (Lesthaeghe 2010). In many parts of the world, therefore, the new millennium has simultaneously witnessed very low rates of childbearing and the "delinking" of procreation from marriage.

In Chinese societies, attitudes toward ideal family size are also changing, but attitudes that link (and sequence) marriage and parenthood have not moved in the same directions as in OECD countries. Despite soaring divorce rates, increased tolerance for nonmarital sexuality, and below-replacement fertility in all three of our locales, childbearing continues to take place largely within the context of marriage.[26] In other words, conditions and value orientations that delink procreation from marriage must be differentiated from those that shape decisions about the number of children a woman will bear and the timing of childbearing.

During the 1960s and 1970s, governments in all three jurisdictions introduced family planning and modern contraception to reduce birth rates; and, in response, the total fertility rate (TFR) fell dramatically in Hong Kong, Taiwan, and China.[27] However, the actions of the PRC government were more deliberate and ultimately more interventionist than those in the other two locales. As Yong Cai and Wang Feng (Chapter 4) explain, the PRC government's initial effort to reduce births combined policies to enforce a higher age at first marriage with improved access to contraception and incentives to delay second births and prohibit third or higher-order pregnancies. However, with the introduction of the one-child policy in 1979, the controls and penalties escalated: Not only did the new policy dictate specific birth quotas, but it also imposed heavy penalties on those who failed to comply with the policy.[28] The PRC, therefore, was the only state of the three to directly dictate marital fertility. In Hong Kong and Taiwan, by contrast, governments never proscribed the number of births either inside or outside of marriage, and the radical decline in fertility was the decision of individual couples responding to their own calculations of the value of becoming pregnant, enlarging the size of their family, and supporting their children throughout their educational years.

Recent responses to subreplacement birth rates also vary among our three settings. By 2005 the TFRs in Hong Kong, Taiwan, and urban China all hovered at the subreplacement rate of 1.0, but only in Hong Kong and Taiwan have governments expressed growing anxiety about plummeting birth rates.[29] Taiwan President Ma Ying-jeou recently described the country's shrinking number of births as "a serious national security threat" (Branigan 2012). Hong Kong officials have discussed tax incentives to encourage couples to have a third child, and the Taiwan government has offered subsidies for child care, and in some locales, even a monetary bonus for each birth (Branigan 2012; Hogg 2005). Nevertheless, neither government has engaged in systematic efforts to destigmatize childbearing outside of marriage, and both Taiwan's Artificial Reproduction Act and Hong Kong's Human Reproductive Technology Ordinance restrict access to reproductive technologies to married couples. Thus, even when these governments consider incentives to increase births, they do not waiver in their disapproval of nonmarital childbearing.

Because none of our contributors directly compares an individual's desire to be married with the desire to have a child, we cannot analyze whether these extremely low fertility rates indicate a deliberate rejection of parenthood or whether the desire to have children differs between men and women. Were we to have such information, we could better evaluate the extent to which contemporary patterns of marriage and childbearing represent a radical break with traditional norms of family formation and the high value placed on becoming a parent. If we had these data we also could follow Lesthaeghe's (2010) analytic trajectory and estimate whether current low levels of fertility will persist or whether these societies will experience a fertility rebound as women bear children later in life regardless of marital status. Although none of our authors directly explored this question, recent demographic research on declining birth rates across Asia provides a useful framework for comparison. In general, this literature confirms our argument that changes in marriage must be understood alongside both transformations and continuities in the norms for family formation.

In his analysis of Western Europe's second demographic transition (SDT), Lesthhaeghe argued that the SDT was driven by a fundamental "disconnection" (2010: 211) between marriage and procreation supported by a cultural shift that endorsed "individual autonomy and self-actualization" (2010: 245). Lesthhaeghe supported his theory of diffused SDT trends by adding data on East Asia to suggest that postmaterialist and expressive value orientations were emerging in Asia as well, especially in Japan, where he found greater evidence of premarital cohabitation, conception, and what he termed "shotgun marriages" (2010: 237–238). In concluding his assessment of whether Japan was, in fact, experiencing a second demographic transition similar to that in the West, however, Lesthaeghe argued that "the only missing ingredient so far is parenthood among cohabiting couples" (2010: 239). Needless to say, this "missing ingredient" is not trivial, especially when one considers decisions about becoming a parent in relation to marriage and family formation.

Looking across East and Southeast Asia, demographers Gavin Jones and Bina Gubhaju (2009) find that, despite more than a decade of subreplacement fertility rates, marriage and parenthood remain tightly linked. Even with educational parity among women and men and an increase in the age at marriage across the nine countries surveyed by the authors, they conclude that "marriage can rarely be separated from its expected outcome in Pacific Asia, the bearing and raising of children" (2009: 258). Similarly, in Hong Kong, Taiwan, and China the linkage between marriage and parenthood and the nearly universal expectation that childbearing should occur only within marriage continue to define the parameters of marital deinstitutionalization. Ultimately, then, we disagree with Lesthaeghe's argument that similar value orientations have spurred reduced fertility rates in Europe and Asia (see also Jones 2007). Although we document similar declines in childbearing within marriage, we do not find a concomitant trend of childbearing outside of marriage that would support the conclusion that marriage and parenthood have become definitively "delinked" in these Chinese societies.[30]

CROSS-BORDER INTIMACIES AND MARRIAGES

For centuries, even millennia, China has been a civilization where ideas, objects, and people moved along trade routes and across lines of conquest that stretched far from the metropole. Sojourning men, hundreds or even thousands of miles away from their natal home, returned periodically to marry and faithfully sent remittances to build homes for children and grandchildren whom they might never know. Parents contracted marriages for their children by moving strategically within the same nested hierarchy of markets that allowed for the extensive flow of crops, goods, and services (Duara 1988; Skinner 1964–1965). Moreover, because the norms of succession and inheritance were more uniform and obligatory in China than in societies that used wills and testaments to cement family fortunes, marriage provided a valuable opportunity for both individuals and families to forge societal alliances and allocate resources (Watson 1991).

By the mid-twentieth century, however, the consequences of civil war and British colonial policies constrained the geographic reach of such marital strategies. Taiwan became a de facto independent state after 1949, and both Beijing and Taipei blocked family reunification of spouses or parents and children separated by the Taiwan Strait. Crossing the border between Hong Kong and Guangdong became more difficult after 1960, and families that for generations had arranged marriages effortlessly across the border restricted them to local marriage markets. Beijing turned its back on the economic resources of the coastal areas, blocked Hong Kong radio and television, and stigmatized citizens with kin in Taiwan. Family connections that had stretched across these borders and been reproduced through adoption, fictive kin, and betrothals were severely attenuated if not completely severed.

After the PRC's opening to world markets and global trade in 1979 and the resumption of cross-Strait ties in 1987, these barriers to cross-border intimacy and marriage quickly began to erode. With Hong Kong's subsequent reintegration into China's national orbit in 1997 and the expansion of Taiwanese investment in China throughout the 1990s and 2000s, opportunities multiplied for men and women to meet and form intimate bonds across borders. The gendered impact of these cross-border intimacies has not been uniform, however, and such differences have fostered growing gender disparities in marital and sexual experiences in all three locales. For instance, because Hong Kong men in their twenties and thirties are far more likely either to be transferred by their companies or to seek new entrepreneurial opportunities in China than Hong Kong women, men have more opportunities to find a spouse or lover in China than their female counterparts. Moreover, because the Pearl River Delta has attracted millions of young unmarried women from across China to work in factories and offices, the sex ratio is often in the man's favor. As a result, by 2006, 42.7 percent of marriages in Hong Kong involved a spouse from the mainland, 84 percent of whom were female (Hong Kong Census and Statistic Department 2009a).

Among married couples, long-term separations as a result of cross-border migration provide different kinds of opportunities for husbands and wives. Shen (Chapter 11) finds that, among Taiwanese couples where the husband works in China and the wife resides in Taiwan with their children, both spouses adopt gender-specific strategies for living as temporary singles. Like Chinese women who reside apart from their husbands (Liu-Farrer 2010), Taiwanese wives may take pleasure in decreased housework pressures and greater opportunities to enjoy leisure activities with peers. Unlike their Chinese counterparts, however, Taiwanese women may be less likely than their husbands to engage in extramarital sexual relationships (Shen Chapter 11; Freeman 2011: 211–218; Liu-Farrer 2010). Despite these differences, in both cases migration and the marital separations that ensue often reinforce traditional gender role expectations of husbands as economic providers and wives as domestic housekeepers and caretakers. Certainly, wives actively create meaningful lives for themselves when separated from their husbands, but these marital separations do not necessarily transform dominant gender role expectations within marriage.

When marriages join spouses of different nationalities, gender asymmetries may combine with other forms of inequality and marginalization. Since 1987, unions between Taiwanese and PRC citizens have created hundreds of thousands of new families, but only a tiny fraction of these have included a Taiwanese woman. Moreover, because the national origin of noncitizen spouses matters more in Taiwan than in Hong Kong due to the different sovereign statuses of the two jurisdictions, Chinese wives in Taiwan face heightened state scrutiny of their marriage motives in a context where cross-Strait marriages stand in for broader political contestation between China and Taiwan. Although political and social concerns about Chinese wives are not altogether absent in Hong Kong, such concerns do not translate into policy responses such as those in Taiwan that create unequal trajectories toward citizenship and national incorporation for spouses of "Mainland" as compared to "foreign" origin (Friedman Chapter 12).[31]

A NEW ERA OF FAMILY, MARRIAGE, AND SEXUALITY?

Across the centuries, states and markets have regulated marriage and family formation in Chinese societies. In accordance with Confucian orthodoxy, state regulation was indirect, and markets functioned primarily at the microlevel. The emperor exercised authority over men in their official roles, and men in turn ruled their families as a microcosm of the imperial state. These parallels extended to sexual and marital relations: Just as the emperor's preference for a consort trumped that of all other men, so fathers chose wives for their sons and husbands dictated the needs and desires of their wives. Within this Confucian, patriarchal universe, marriage strategies were family strategies designed to maximize the assets—human and material—of the patrilineal family.

In the early twentieth century, reformers of many political persuasions attacked Confucian orthodoxy and identified reform of the family with reform of the state (Glosser 2003). In the stronger, modern China they envisioned, parents would not control their children's choice of a spouse and marriage would be based on love between a young man and woman. Within these new modern marriages, men and women would have equal rights to divorce and to own property. However, even as reformers criticized the hierarchical and mercenary strategies of the existing status quo, they did not reject the core set of family roles and responsibilities anchored in principles of collective and intergenerational reciprocity that limited the degree to which the institution of marriage could be viewed as the "personal property" of two spouses (Ocko 1991: 320).

That both the Nationalists and Communists conflated reform of the family and the fate of the nation is well established. What is less obvious, and yet essential to understand when we assess more recent changes in marriage, is the enduring respect for the value of intergenerational reciprocity and lifelong commitments to family ties that extend beyond those between a husband and wife. Thus, for example, when Jun Zhang and Peidong Sun document Shanghai parents' deep engagement in their children's marriages (Chapter 5), when Hsiu-hua Shen explains the family commitments that allow Taiwan couples to remain married despite long separations and repeated sexual infidelity (Chapter 11), or when married men in Hong Kong with multiple sexual partners identify themselves as better husbands and fathers than their own fathers (Ho Chapter 7), we see quite clearly how marriage remains inextricably linked to the institution of family in contemporary Chinese societies. In short, while we clearly observe the deinstitutionalization of marriage in these three Chinese societies over the past thirty years, we simultaneously identify strong continuities in the "rules of the game" for family formation, especially in the insistence that marriage precede childbearing and in broad support for the norm of lifelong reciprocity between generations. As a result, the institution of family appears more robust and far less deinstitutionalized across the region than that of marriage.

One confirmation of this conclusion can be found by briefly comparing the different family strategies of gay men and lesbians.[32] Across all three societies, gay men consistently report feeling more pressure to marry than their lesbian counterparts precisely because they recognize a filial obligation as sons to produce children who will continue the patriline; as a result, gay men are more likely to marry heterosexually to fulfill this obligation (Chou 2000; Hu 2011; Kong 2010; Rofel 2007). Lesbians, on the other hand, may be better positioned to withstand familial and societal marital expectations precisely because their procreative capacities are not deemed essential to natal family reproduction, although as daughters they, too, are socialized to view marriage as part of the normative transition to adulthood (Engebretsen 2009; Hu 2011). In the absence of same-sex marriage as a legal option, gay men and lesbians face different pressures with regard to marriage and childbearing, and these very differences confirm the continued relevance of filial obligations and intergenerational reciprocity to the institution of marriage in these three Chinese societies.

As anthropologist Lisa Rofel writes about the PRC: "Family is the metonym for belonging, not simply to the nation-state but to Chinese culture writ large" (2007: 100). Given this familial model of cultural and national belonging, how might we reassess the relationship between family and nation and the legal privileges states create for married persons across these Chinese societies? Both Erni and Kuo (Chapters 8 and 9) adopt a logic similar to that advocated by American political philosopher Jean Cohen, who argues that "it is no longer justifiable to construe a single model of intimate association as intrinsic to . . . national identity nor to assume that there is only one morally right way to conduct intimate relationships" (2002: 14).[33] Building from this position, Erni and Kuo argue that in Hong Kong and Taiwan marriage need not be tied to procreation, childbearing need not necessarily follow marriage, and marriage need not be limited to heterosexual unions. However, courts in both of these jurisdictions continue to reject arguments that depart from traditional understandings of marriage as a heterosexual, procreative union. More flexibility is evident in responses to cross-border heterosexual intimacies, although as the chapters by Ho, Shen, and Friedman underscore, state regulation of cross-border unions also reflects the contested status of families formed across China, Taiwan, and Hong Kong. The gendered role expectations of these new intimacies, the presumed class affiliations of those who pursue cross-border relationships, and fears in Hong Kong and Taiwan about the various threats posed by Mainland Chinese women confirm that the relative weighting of private and public ordering remains very much a matter of debate in these societies, especially when sexual intimacies and family formation stretch across increasingly porous political boundaries.

At the beginning of this introduction, we emphasized that marriage is a multifaceted relationship, simultaneously an intimate, private bond and a social, public institution. The chapters to follow document the diverse negotiations currently taking place across Taiwan, Hong Kong, and urban China as a result of this complex interface of private and public needs and desires. Given the broad structural changes in the context and content of marriage today, it is not surprising that the authors characterize the contemporary marital landscape as highly contested and contradictory. Only through their detailed assessments can we grasp the diverse trajectories of change and the potential futures for marriage, sexuality, and family that they portend.

NOTES

1. "Taiwanese Woman to Marry Herself" 2010; "The Woman Who Married Herself" 2010.

2. AA制婚姻; retrieved on December 13, 2013, from http://v.youku.com/v_show/id_XMzc1MjIxODIo.html.

3. BBC News Asia, "Hong Kong Tycoon Recruits Husband for Lesbian Daughter"; retrieved on September 9, 2012, from http//m.bbc.co.uk/news/world-asia-19733003.

4. The percentage of nonmarital births in the PRC is difficult to confirm due to the politicized nature of such statistics with implementation of the one-child policy. We found estimates of 5.6 percent for 1993 (http://en.wikipedia.org/wiki/Legitimacy_(law)) but no recent figures. Reports of local governments fining women who bear children outside of marriage suggest that the practice is ongoing despite its illegality under national population policies (Zhou and Wang 2013). In Taiwan, nonmarital births grew from approximately 1.7 percent in 1981 to 4.51 percent of all births in 2010 (Taiwan Department of Household Registration, Ministry of the Interior, "Number and Rates of Birth, Death, Marriage and Divorce, 1981–2012"). Hong Kong rates of nonmarital childbearing are the highest of the three, rising from 5.8 percent of all births in 1981 to 13.9 percent by 2010 (The Hong Kong Council of Social Service, 2013; available at www.socialindicators.org.hk/en/indicators/family_solidarity/27.4). None of these figures, however, comes close to percentages for the United States and the

European Union. By 2011, U.S. rates of nonmarital childbearing were just shy of 40 percent, and in the European Union as a whole, 40 percent of births took place outside of marriage. Moreover, countries as diverse as Belgium, Bulgaria, Estonia, France, Iceland, Slovenia, Norway, and Sweden showed rates of 50 percent or higher (Carl Haub, "Rising Trend of Births outside Marriage," Population Reference Bureau; retrieved on September 2, 2013, from www.prb.org/Publications/Articles/2013/nonmarital-births .aspx).

5. One exception to this norm of universal marriage for women was the practice of sworn spinsterhood among a small community of women in the early twentieth-century Pearl River Delta region (Sankar 1978; Siu 1990; Stockard 1989).

6. For example, by 1982 among those between age forty and forty-four, 94.3 percent of men and 99.8 percent of women had married at least once (1982 Census, table 71; available at http://chinadataonline.org/member/census1982/ybListDetail .asp?ID=1).

7. In those areas of the Mainland and Taiwan where young girls were brought in as adopted daughters-in-law (童養媳) when a son was still a child, brides could be several years older than their future husbands. As Wolf and Huang argued, these arrangements were motivated less by poverty and more by the desire to cultivate harmonious mother-in-law and daughter-in-law relations. Because couples were raised together as children, however, these marriages often were less "successful" in producing offspring, and a significant number ended in divorce (Wolf and Huang 1980).

8. Ideally we would want median rather than mean ages because means are distorted upward by the small number of individuals who marry at unusually old or young ages. However, data limitations require that we use mean age at first marriage.

9. Because of different census years in the three jurisdictions, we will not have data for every year.

10. A woman's family could pursue divorce only under a highly limited set of conditions: for instance, spousal abandonment of more than three years, severe physical abuse (by the husband or his parents or grandparents), or the husband selling his wife to another man (Bernhardt 1994: 189).

11. The Nationalist 1931 Civil Code specified ten conditions for divorce that applied equally to men and women; the Communists' Jiangxi Soviet code permitted unconditional divorce in principle.

12. Article 17, 1950 Marriage Law. On the face of it, the law guaranteed no-fault ex parte divorce because it did not specify any conditions under which divorce would be granted. But the procedural requirement of mediation undermined the law's promise of divorce on demand, creating a tool that could be applied loosely or strictly according to Party agendas and societal responses (Huang 2005).

13. Family law reforms in 1996 and 1998 gave mothers and fathers equal parental rights and eliminated the provision automatically granting child custody to the father on divorce (Lee 1998–99). Changes to the law in 2002 aimed to redress women's

weaker property claims in marriage and recognize the contributions made by a non–wage-earning spouse to the marital estate. These and later reforms throughout the 2000s were initiated under pressure from a growing women's movement that fought to eliminate traditional social norms and cultural principles enshrined in family law that discriminated against women as daughters, wives, and mothers (Chen 1999; Kuo 2007; Lee 1998–99).

14. The CDR in Hong Kong rose from 0.3 in 1978, to 0.91 in 1991, to 2.01 in 1998, to 2.55 in 2008. For China as a whole the rate rose for these years from 0.18 to 0.6 to 0.96 to 1.7, but the Shanghai CDR rose from 0.27 in 1978 to 1.32 in 1991, to 2.26 in 1998 to 3.3 in 2008. In Taiwan, the shift for these years was from 0.63 to 1.26 to 2.0 to 2.43 by 2008 (Sources: for Hong Kong, Hong Kong Census and Statistics Department 2007a, 2007b, 2009a, 2009b; for China, Zhongguo Minzheng Tongji Nianjian 2012, Zhongguo Tongji Nianjian 2012; for Shanghai, Shanghai Tongji Nianjian 2008; for Taiwan, Taiwan Department of Household Registration, Ministry of the Interior, "Number and Rates of Birth, Death, Marriage and Divorce, 1981–2012."

15. Based on an interview on June 19, 2009, with a lawyer at the Hong Kong law firm that claimed to handle the highest number of divorce cases.

16. In her research in rural China, Ke Li found that relatives and friends may be deeply involved in the process of mobilizing for a court appearance and may be asked to testify in court (see Li and Friedman forthcoming). Legally, however, the court may address the grievances of only the two principles.

17. For instance, in some late imperial portrayals of "utopian polygamy," female same-sex intimacy was portrayed as compatible with and even supportive of polygamous marriages (Sang 2003: 49–52; Wu 2002).

18. For example, in the famous 1957 Heilongjiang case of consensual sex between two male labor camp inmates, the court could not penalize their behavior as criminal due to the absence of explicit legal prohibitions (Balzano 2007; Kang 2012).

19. Kang (2012) builds on existing legal scholarship within China to argue that the decriminalization of male anal sex after 1997 was an unintended consequence of efforts to regularize China's legal codes and strengthen the rule of law. He contends that the PRC legal system has never included homosexuality under its purview but only specific sexual behaviors. After 1997, sex between men could also be criminalized as a form of prostitution.

20. Two recent instances of public wedding ceremonies involving same-sex couples, one in Beijing in 2009 and one in Fuzhou in 2012, suggest that public acceptance may be growing ("Gay Wedding Reflects Growing Tolerance in China" 2012; Zhang 2011). For the rights of transgender individuals to marry in the PRC, see "Hong Kong Court Allows Transgender Woman to Marry a Man" 2013.

21. For instance, in its twelve-year history, the Beijing Queer Film Festival has experienced repeated harassment from public security officials intent on forcing the

organizers to cancel the festival. In response, festival organizers have shifted to a guerrilla style of film screenings and discussions, moving from site to site to avoid police detection. The most recent festival held in June 2013 was the first to take place without government interference (Beijing Queer Film Festival; retrieved on August 15, 2013, from www.bjqff.com).

22. In a 2005 survey, only 28.7 percent of respondents supported a law barring discrimination, but in a November 2012 survey support rose to 76 percent. In 2005, 38.9 percent of respondents thought homosexuality conflicted with community morals, but by 2012, 71.5 percent said they had absolutely no prejudice against homosexuals and roughly similar proportions (32.7 percent and 39 percent) either explicitly supported or explicitly rejected same-sex marriage (Lau 2011: 7730; Chung et al. 2012; "Sexual Minorities Need Legal Shield" 2012).

23. See Criminal Law (刑法), Book 2, Chapter 16-1 (available at http://law.moj .gov.tw/LawClass/LawParaDeatil.aspx?Pcode=C0000001&LCNOS=%20230%20% 20%20&LCC=2) and the Social Order Maintenance Act (社會秩序維護法), Book 3, Chapter 2, Articles 80–84 (available at http://law.moj.gov.tw/LawClass/LawAll.aspx? PCode=D0080067).

24. See also Human Rights Watch report of 2012 of an incident on July 5, 2011, where a CCTV host in the PRC urged greater respect for gays and lesbians in response to a homophobic slur by a celebrity guest (2012: 322).

25. "Share of Births Out of Wedlock and Teenage Births." Social Policy Division, Directorate for Employment, Labour and Social Affairs, OECD. Last updated February 24, 2012. Retrieved on December 16, 2013, from www.oecd.org/dataoecd/ 38/6/40278615.pdf.

26. See note 4 above.

27. In 1970 the TFR was 3.42 in Hong Kong, 4.0 in Taiwan, 3.2 in urban China, and 6.3 in rural China. By 1990 the TFRs were respectively 1.28 in Hong Kong, 1.81 in Taiwan, 1.3 in urban China, and 2.4 in rural China (Chen et al. 2011; Tu 2000: 23; World Bank 2012).

28. There are exceptions to the one-child limit for women with urban residence. In early years, women whose healthy child had died or who had given birth to a disabled child were permitted a second birth as long as they could prove that the next pregnancy would not result in a second disabled child. In marriages where both spouses were only children, they were permitted a second birth five years after the first, and after 1990 several provinces began to allow a second child in cases where only one partner was an only child. In addition, most provinces allow second births to women who have remarried, regardless of whether they or their new husband had a child in their first marriage (Gu et al. 2007).

29. In 2005 the TFR in Hong Kong was 0.97, in Taiwan 1.12, in urban China 1.0, and in rural China 1.7 (Chen et al. 2011; World Bank 2012).

30. Lesthaeghe also admits that his model is unable to account for the impact of state-driven population policies such as China's one-child policy, which he argues would have to be lifted before one could assess whether China was experiencing a second demographic transition (2010: 248, n8). Unlike this volume, therefore, his analysis gives little attention to legal reforms or state policy consequences.

31. The term *foreign spouse* in Taiwan typically refers to wives from Southeast Asia, especially Vietnam, Indonesia, Thailand, Cambodia, and the Philippines.

32. One could also see the centrality of intergenerational ties in the emphasis on family in Hong Kong's gay pride parade. In 2005, the Hong Kong parade emphasized "the primacy of family life in Chinese culture," and participants marched behind such banners as "Hate is not a family value" and "Don't be prejudiced against your children" (Lau 2011: 793).

33. Sociologist Judith Stacey makes a similar argument but ties it specifically to democratic forms of governance: "A democratic state has no business dictating or even favoring any particular brand of intimacy or family life. It should value the quality and substance of relationships over their form" (2011: 202).

REFERENCES

Balzano, John. 2007. "Toward a Gay Friendly China?" *Law and Sexuality* 16: 2–43.

Becker, Gary. 1991. *A Treatise on the Family*, enlarged edition. Cambridge, MA: Harvard University Press.

Bernhardt, Kathryn. 1994. "Women and the Law: Divorce in the Republican Period." In *Civil Law in Qing and Republican China*, Kathryn Bernhardt and Philip C. C. Huang, eds., pp. 187–214. Palo Alto, CA: Stanford University Press.

Branigan, Tania. 2012. "Taiwan Offers Baby Bonus to Fix Plummeting Birth Rate." *The Guardian*, January 23. Retrieved on January 25, 2012, from www.guardian.co.uk/world/2012/jan/23/taiwan-low-birth-rate.

Chang, Jui-shan. 1996. "Negotiating Sexual Permissiveness in a Contemporary Chinese Setting: Young People in Taipei." *International Journal of Sociology of the Family* 26(1): 13–35.

———. 1999. "Scripting Extra-Marital Affairs: Marital Mores, Gender Politics and Infidelity in Taiwan," *Modern China* 25(1): 69–99.

Chang, Jui-shan, Adolf K. T. Tsang, Ruey-Hsing Lin, and Ping-Keung Lui. 1997. "Premarital Sexual Mores in Taiwan and Hong Kong: Two Pathways to Permissiveness." *Journal of Asian and African Studies* 32(3/4): 265–285.

Chen Chao-ju (陳昭如). 1999. "權利, 法律改革與本土婦運: 以台灣離婚權的發展為例" (Rights, Legal Reform and the Native Women's Movement: The Development of the Right to Divorce in Taiwan). 政大法學評論 (*Chengchi Law Review*) 62: 25–74.

Chen, Jiajian, Robert D. Retherford, Minja Kim Choe, Xiru Li, and Hongyan Cui. 2011. "Rural–Urban Differentials in Later Marriage, Longer Birth Interval, and Fewer Births in China, 1975–2005." Paper presented at the 25th Population Census Conference, Seoul. Available at http://ancsdaap.org/cencon2011/Papers/EWC/EWC_slides_2011_Chen.pdf.

Cherlin, Andrew J. 1978. "Remarriage as an Incomplete Institution." *American Journal of Sociology* 84: 634–650.

———. 2004. "The Deinstitutionalization of American Marriage." *Journal of Marriage and Family* 66 (November): 848–861.

Chou, Wah-shan. 2000. *Tongzhi: Politics of Same-Sex Eroticism in Chinese Societies.* New York: The Haworth Press.

Chow, Wing Sun, and Terry Lum. 2008. "Trends in Family Attitudes and Values in Hong Kong." Final Report submitted to Central Policy Unit Hong Kong SAR Government, Department of Social Work and Social Administration, The University of Hong Kong.

Chung Ting Yiu (鍾庭耀) et al. 2012. "香港市民對不同性傾向認識之權利意見調查" (Opinion Survey of Hong Kong Residents' Views of Homosexuals' Personal Rights). Hong Kong: Hong Kong University Public Opinion Center.

Cohen, Jean. 2002. *Regulating Intimacy: A New Legal Paradigm.* Princeton, NJ: Princeton: University Press.

Cott, Nancy F. 2000. *Public Vows: A History of Marriage and the Nation.* Cambridge, MA: Harvard University Press.

Davis, Deborah, and Stevan Harrell, eds. 1993. *Chinese Families in the Post-Mao Era.* Berkeley: University of California Press.

Diamant, Neil. 2000. *Revolutionizing the Family: Politics, Love, and Divorce in Urban and Rural China, 1949–1968.* Berkeley: University of California Press.

Ding, Naifei. 2000. "Prostitutes, Parasites, and the House of State Feminism." *Inter-Asia Cultural Studies* 1(2): 305–318.

Ding Naifei (丁乃非), and Liu Jen-peng (劉人鵬). 1999. "新台灣人是不習於淫行的女人?" (New Taiwanese Are [Good] Women "Unaccustomed to Immoral Sexual Behavior?"). 性/別研究 (*Working Papers in Gender/Sexuality Studies*) 5 & 6: 438–443.

Duara, Prasenjit. 1988. *Culture, Power, and the State: Rural North China, 1900–1942.* Palo Alto, CA: Stanford University Press.

Engebretsen, Elisabeth Lund. 2009. "Intimate Practices, Conjugal Ideals: Affective Ties and Relationship Strategies among Lala (lesbian) Women in Contemporary Beijing." *Sexuality, Research, and Social Policy* 6(3): 3–14.

Evans, Harriet. 1997. *Women and Sexuality in China: Female Sexuality and Gender since 1949.* New York: Continuum.

Farrer, James. 2002. *Opening Up: Youth Sex Culture and Market Reform in Shanghai*. Chicago: The University of Chicago Press.

Farrer, James, and Zhongxin Sun. 2003. "Extramarital Love in Shanghai," *The China Journal* 50 (July): 1–36.

Freeman, Caren. 2011. *Making and Faking Kinship: Marriage and Labor Migration between China and South Korea*. Ithaca, NY: Cornell University Press.

Friedman, Sara. L. 2006. *Intimate Politics: Marriage, the Market, and State Power in Southeastern China*. Cambridge, MA: Harvard University Asia Center, Harvard University Press.

"Gay Wedding Reflects Growing Tolerance in China." *China Daily*, Oct. 20, 2012. Retrieved on November 1, 2012, from www.chinadaily.com.cn/china/2012-10/20/content_15833812.htm.

Glosser, Susan L. 2003. *Chinese Visions of Family and State, 1915–1953*. Berkeley: University of California Press.

Gu, Baocheng, Wang Feng, Guo Zhigang, and Zhang Erli. 2007. "China's Local and National Fertility Polices at the End of the Twentieth Century." *Population and Development Review* 33(1): 129–147.

Hajnal, John. 1953. "Age at Marriage and Proportions Marrying." *Population Studies* 7: 111–136.

———. 1982. "Two Kinds of Preindustrial Household Formation System." *Population and Development Review* 8(3): 449–494.

Hershatter, Gail. 1997. *Dangerous Pleasures: Prostitution and Modernity in 20th-Century Shanghai*. Berkeley: University of California Press.

Hinsch, Brett. 1990. *Passions of the Cut Sleeve: The Male Homosexual Tradition in China*. Berkeley: University of California Press.

Ho, Josephine Chuen-juei. 2007. "Sex Revolution and Sex Rights Movement in Taiwan." In *Taiwanese Identity from Domestic, Regional, and Global Perspectives*, Jens Damm and Gunter Schubert, eds., pp. 123–139. Munster: LIT.

Hogg, Chris. 2005. "HK Promotes 'Three Child Policy.'" *BBC News*, February 22. Retrieved on March 30, 2012, from http://news.bbc.co.uk/2/hi/asia-pacific/4286723.stm.

Hong Kong Census and Statistics Department. 2007a. "Marriage and Divorce Trends 1981–2006." *Monthly Digest of Statistics*, November.

———. 2007b. *Demographic Trends in Hong Kong: 1981–2006*. Hong Kong: Government Printer.

———. 2009a. *Women and Men in Hong Kong: Key Statistics*. General Household Survey, Hong Kong: Government Printer.

———. 2009b. "Press Release November 11." Retrieved on November 21, 2011, from www.info.gov.hk/gia/general/200911/11/P200911110152.htm.

"Hong Kong Court Allows Transgender Woman to Marry a Man." 2013. Retrieved on August 27, 2013, from www.theguardian.com/world/2013/may/13/hong-kong-court-transgender-marriage.

Hsu, Jenny W. 2013. "Taiwan Reinstates Transgender Couple's Marriage." *The Wall Street Journal*, August 9. Retrieved on August 15, 2013, from http://blogs.wsj.com/chinarealtime/2013/08/09/taiwan-reinstates-transgender-couples-marriage/tab/print/.

Hu, Yu-Ying. 2011. *Gender, Transnational Culture, and New Media: Enacting Female Queer Sexuality in Taiwan*. PhD dissertation, Department of Gender Studies, Indiana University, Bloomington.

Huang, Hans Tao-Ming. 2011. *Queer Politics and Sexual Modernity in Taiwan*. Hong Kong: Hong Kong University Press.

Huang, Philip C. C. 2005. "Divorce Law Practices and the Origins, Myths, and Realities of Judicial 'Mediation' in China." *Modern China* 31(2): 151–203.

Human Rights Watch. 2012. World Report 2012. Retrieved on August 21, 2013, from www.hrw.org/sites/default/files/reports/wr2012.pdf.

Jeffreys, Elaine. 2006. "Introduction: Talking Sex and Sexuality in China." In *Sex and Sexuality in China*, Elaine Jeffreys, ed., pp. 1–20. London and New York: Routledge.

Jones, Gavin. 2007. "Delayed Marriage and Very Low Fertility in Pacific Asia." *Population and Development Review* 33(3): 453–478.

Jones, Gavin, and Bina Gubhaju. 2009. "Factors Influencing Changes in Mean Age at First Marriage and Proportions Never Marrying in the Low-Fertility Countries of East and South East Asia." *Asian Population Studies* 5(3): 237–265.

Kang, Wenqing. 2012. "The Decriminalization and Depathologization of Homosexuality in China." In *China In and Beyond the Headlines*, Timothy B. Weston and Lionel M. Jensen, eds., pp. 231–248. Lanham, MD: Rowman and Littlefield.

Kong, Travis S. K. 2010. *Chinese Male Homosexualities: Memba, Tongzhi and Golden Boy*. New York: Routledge.

Kuo, Shu-chin Grace. 2007. "A Cultural Legal Study on the Transformation of Family Law in Taiwan." *Southern California Interdisciplinary Law Journal* 16: 379–396.

Lau, Holning. 2011. "Grounding Conversations on Sexuality and Asian Law." *University of California Davis, Law Review* 44: 772–792.

Lee, James, and Wang Feng. 1999. *One Quarter of Humanity: Malthusian Mythology and Chinese Realities, 1700–2000*. Cambridge, MA: Harvard University Press.

Lee, Joy. 2013. "Support for Same-Sex Marriage Skyrockets to over 50%: Survey." *The China Post*, August 7. Retrieved on August 15, 2013, from www.chinapost.com.tw/taiwan/national/national-news/2013/08/07/385785/Support-for.htm.

Lee, Li-ju. 1998–99. "Law and Social Norms in a Changing Society: A Case Study of Taiwanese Family Law." *Southern California Review of Law and Women's Studies* 8: 413–444.

Lesthaeghe, Ronald. 2010. "The Unfolding Story of the Second Demographic Transition." *Population and Development Review* 36(2): 211–251.

Li, Ke, and Sara L. Friedman. Forthcoming. "The Wedding of Marriage, Nation, and State in Modern China: Legal Consequences for Divorce, Property, and Women's Rights." In *Domestic Tensions, National Anxieties: Global Perspectives on Modern Marriage Crises*, Kristin Celello and Hanan Kholoussy, eds. New York: Oxford University Press.

Li, Yinhe. 2006. "Regulating Male Same-Sex Relationships in the People's Republic of China." In *Sex and Sexuality in China*, Elaine Jeffreys, ed., pp. 82–101. London and New York: Routledge.

Lin, Enru. 2013. "Genderqueer and Proud." *Taipei Times*, July 22, p. 12.

Liu, Athena. 2011. "Exacerbating Corbett: *W v Registrar of Marriages*." *Hong Kong Law Journal* 41(3): 759–783.

Liu-Farrer, Gracia. 2010. "The Absent Spouses: Gender, Sex, Race and the Extramarital Sexuality among Chinese Migrants in Japan." *Sexualities* 13(1): 97–121.

Martin, Fran. 2003. *Situating Sexualities: Queer Representation in Taiwanese Fiction, Film and Public Culture*. Hong Kong: Hong Kong University Press.

Ocko, Jonathan. 1991. "Women, Property, and Law in the People's Republic of China." In *Marriage and Inequality in Chinese Society*, Rubie S. Watson and Patricia Buckley Ebrey, eds., pp. 313–346. Berkeley: University of California Press.

Pan Suiming. 2006. "Transformation in the Primary Life Cycle: The Origins and Nature of China's Sexual Revolution." In *Sex and Sexuality in China*, Elaine Jeffreys, ed., pp. 21–42. London and New York: Routledge.

Parish, William L., Edward O. Laumann, and Sanyu Mojola. 2007. "Sexual Behavior in China." *Population and Development Review* 33(4): 729–756.

Pei, Yuxin. 2011. "Multiple Sexual Relationship as a New Life Style: Young Women's Sexuality in Contemporary Shanghai." *Women's Studies International Forum* 34: 401–410.

Platte, Erica. 1988. "Divorce Trends and Patterns in China." *Pacific Affairs* 61(3): 432–456.

Rofel, Lisa. 2007. *Desiring China: Experiments in Neoliberalism, Sexuality, and Public Culture*. Durham, NC: Duke University Press.

———. 2013. "Grassroots Activism: Non-Normative Sexual Politics in Post-Socialist China." In *Unequal China: Political Economy and Cultural Politics of Inequality*, Wanning Sun and Yangjie Guo, eds., pp. 154–167. New York: Routledge.

Ruskola, Teemu. 1994. "Law, Sexual Morality and Gender Equality in Qing and Communist China." *Yale Law Journal*. 103: 2531–2565.

Sang, Tze-lan D. 2003. *The Emerging Lesbian: Female Same-Sex Desire in Modern China*. Chicago: The University of Chicago Press.

Sankar, Andrea. 1978. *The Evolution of the Sisterhood in Traditional Chinese Society: From Village Girls' Houses to Chai T'angs in Hong Kong.* PhD dissertation. University of Michigan, Ann Arbor.

"Sexual Minorities Need Legal Shield," Editorial. 2012. *South China Morning Post,* November 18: 16.

Shanghai Tongji Nianjian (上海统计年鉴, Shanghai Statistical Yearbook). 2008. Retrieved on May 1, 2011, from www.stats-sh.gov.cn.

Shanley, Mary Lyndon. 2002. "Public Values and Private Lives." *Law and Social Inquiry* 27(4): 923–940.

Singer, Jana B. 1992. "The Privatization of Family Law." *Wisconsin Law Review* 1443–1567.

Siu, Helen F. 1990. "Where Were the Women? Rethinking Marriage Resistance and Regional Culture History." *Late Imperial China* 11(2): 32–62.

Skinner, G. William. 1964–1965. "Marketing and Social Structure in Rural China, 3 parts." *Journal of Asian Studies* 24: 4–43; 195–228; 363–399.

Somer, Matthew. 2000. *Sex, Law, and Society in Late Imperial China.* Palo Alto, CA: Stanford University Press.

Stacey, Judith. 2011. *Unhitched: Love, Marriage, and Family Values from West Hollywood to Western China.* New York: New York University Press.

Stockard, Janice E. 1989. *Daughters of the Canton Delta: Marriage Patterns and Economic Strategies in South China, 1860–1930.* Palo Alto, CA: Stanford University Press.

Sunstein, Cass, and Richard Thaler. 2008. "Privatizing Marriage." *The Monist* 91 (3 and 4): 377–387.

"Support for Same-Sex Marriage on the Increase: Poll." 2013. *Taipei Times,* August 8. Retrieved on August 15, 2013, from www.taipeitimes.com/News/taiwan/archives/2013/08/08/2003569217.

Taiwan Department of Household Registration, Ministry of the Interior. "Number and Rates of Birth, Death, Marriage and Divorce, 1981–2012"; retrieved on February 13, 2013, from http://sowf.moi.gov.tw/stat/month/m1-02.xls.

"Taiwanese Woman to Marry Herself." 2010. *The Telegraph,* October 22. Retrieved on March 30, 2012, from www.telegraph.co.uk/news/worldnews/asia/taiwan/8080685/Taiwanese-woman-to-marry-herself.html.

Tran, Lisa. 2011. "The ABCs of Monogamy in Republican China: Adultery, Bigamy, and Conjugal Fidelity." *Twentieth-Century China* 36(2): 99–118.

Tu, Ping. 2000. "Trends and Regional Differentials in Fertility Transition." In *The Changing Population of China,* Xizhe Peng and Zhigang Guo, eds., pp. 22–33. Oxford, UK: Oxford University Press.

Voigt, Kevin. 2013. "Transsexual Wins Right to Marry in Landmark Hong Kong Case."
May 13. Retrieved on August 27, 2013, from www.cnn.com/2013/05/13/world/
asia/hong-kong-transsexual.

Wang Feng and Quanhe Zhang. 1996. "Age at Marriage and the First Birth Interval:
The Emerging Change in Sexual Behavior among Young Couples in China." *Population and Development Review* 22(2): 299–320.

Watson, Rubie S. 1991. "Afterword: Marriage and Gender Inequality." In *Marriage and
Inequality in Chinese Society*, Rubie S. Watson and Patricia Buckley Ebrey, eds.,
pp. 347–368. Berkeley: University of California Press.

Wolf, Arthur, and Chieh-shan Huang. 1980. *Marriage and Adoption in China,
1845–1945*. Palo Alto, CA: Stanford University Press.

"The Woman Who Married Herself." 2010. BBC News, November 9. Retrieved on
March 30, 2012, from www.bbc.co.uk/news/world-asia-pacific-11722248.

World Bank. 2012. World Development Indicators (data base). Available from http://
data.worldbank.org/data-catalog/world-development-indicators.

Wu, H. Laura. 2002. "Through the Prism of Male Writing: Representation of Lesbian
Love in Ming-Qing Literature." *Nan Nü* 4(1): 1–34.

Yan, Yunxiang. 2003. *Private Life under Socialism: Love, Intimacy, and Family Change
in a Chinese Village, 1949–1999*. Palo Alto, CA: Stanford University Press.

———. 2011. "The Changing Moral Landscape." In *Deep China: The Moral Life of the
Person*, Arthur Kleinman, Yunxiang Yan, Jing Jun, Sing Lee, Everett Zhang, Pan
Tianshu Wu Fei, and Guo Jinhua, eds., pp. 36–77. Berkeley: University of Califor-
nia Press.

Zhang, Everett Yuehong. 2011. "China's Sexual Revolution." In *Deep China: The Moral
Life of the Person*, Arthur Kleinman, Yunxiang Yan, Jing Jun, Sing Lee, Everett
Zhang, Pan Tianshu Wu Fei, and Guo Jinhua, eds., pp. 106–151. Berkeley: Univer-
sity of California Press.

Zhongguo Minzheng Tongji Nianjian (中国民政统计年鉴, Chinese Statistical Yearbook of Civil Affairs). 2012. Retrieved on October 2, 2012, from www.infobank.cn.

Zhongguo Tongji Nianjian (中国统计年鉴, Statistical Yearbook of China). 2012. Retrieved on February 27, 2013, from www.infobank.cn.

Zhou, Lihua, and Wang Xiaodong. 2013. "New Law Would Fine Unmarried Mothers."
China Daily USA, June 3. Retrieved on September 2, 2013, from http://usa.china
daily.com.cn/china/2013-06/03/content_16557604.htm.

MARRIAGE AND SEXUALITY IN
THE PEOPLE'S REPUBLIC OF CHINA

Part I

2 ON THE LIMITS OF PERSONAL AUTONOMY

PRC Law and the Institution of Marriage

Deborah S. Davis

THE LITERATURE ON MARITAL DEINSTITUTIONALIZATION primarily addresses how individual men and women change their marital and sexual behaviors (Cherlin 2004). Thus, to track the nature and speed of deinstitutionalization researchers observe when people decide to marry, whether they have children inside or outside of marriage, or whether they accept same-sex marriage. But deinstitutionalization also applies to state actions and in particular to legislation that establishes the formal laws and procedures through which marriages are publicly recognized and conjugal rights protected. As discussed in Chapter 1, the party-state in the PRC has repeatedly taken the initiative to rewrite the rules under which couples marry, divorce, or bear children. Moreover, in contrast to the process through which the Hong Kong and Taiwan governments have altered marriage ordinances or civil codes, the PRC government has often acted unilaterally with little role for citizen input. Using the vocabulary of Jana Singer (1992) or Jean Cohen (2002), one would say that, in the PRC more than in the other two societies, public priorities of the national elite have consistently trumped the preferences of local communities and the personal wishes of individual men and women.[1]

However, the trajectory of state efforts to regulate sexuality, fertility, and marital behavior has been uneven. Consequently, close reading of statute and court interpretations not only identifies significant changes in the legal constraints within which individuals understand and experience their marriages but also reveals how the party-state has repositioned itself with respect to the institution of marriage, alternating among the roles of social engineer, administrative regulator, and legal referee as it recalibrated the degree of direct control over citizens' personal lives. In this chapter I focus on the shifts in statute and legal interpretations since the CCP abandoned socialism as an economic blueprint and embraced the legitimacy—even superiority—of the market-based logic of voluntary contract. A major, but less deliberate, consequence of this shift has been the increased legitimacy and autonomy of the private sphere and a more general tendency for courts to protect individual civil rights rather than collective interests. At the same time, as individual civil rights have come to the fore in the judicial domain, however, the party-state has not terminated the one-child policy nor abandoned its long-standing position of equating the health of family life with the health of the nation. Instead, the party-state has assumed a contradictory position whereby, on one hand, it generally acts as referee when upholding the logic of private contract and the right to privacy but retains its earlier role of social engineer when it exercises the right to control the reproduction of the nation's population and aligns family policies with goals for national development. But before addressing the current contradictions within the stance of the party-state, I first summarize the government's earlier initiatives to change individual behavior and redefine the state's relationship to the institution of marriage.

FULFILLING A REVOLUTIONARY GOAL:
THE MARRIAGE LAW OF 1950

During the 1920s and 1930s, CCP reformers attacked all elements of marriages that they considered feudal and drafted regulations to promote free choice and ideally love-based marriages, communal property arrangements, and mutual consent divorce. Significantly, the first piece of legislation after the establishment of the People's Republic was the 1950 Marriage Law that prohibited concubinage, child betrothals, and restrictions on remarriage of widows and allowed divorce when both parties petitioned to dissolve the marriage or when mediation failed (Marriage Law of the PRC 1950). In its entirety, the 1950 law increased the autonomy of the married pair and contravened traditions that had made women "daughters-in-law before wives" (Watson and Ebrey 1991: 351) or treated children as the property of their father's patriline (Ocko 1991: 314, 319). Yet several other provisions served to strengthen state regulation over the institution of marriage.

First, the 1950 Law narrowed the definition of what constituted marriage. The earlier regulations in the revolutionary base areas had treated long-term cohabitation as de facto marriage. By contrast, the 1950 Marriage Law recognized as legally married only those who registered with the state (Palmer 1995). Second, the law replaced the earlier promise of unilateral divorce with vague language that suggested no-fault divorce but in practice required mediation and thereby gave local state agents ultimate control over whether to grant a divorce (Alford and Shen 2004; Diamant 2000; Huang 2005; Li and Friedman forthcoming). Moreover, in the case of divorce, concern with the collective "needs of production" (Article 23) could trump the individual interests of either spouse. Finally, as Palmer (1995) has emphasized, even as the law protected children born outside marriage, it simultaneously limited procreation to marriage more absolutely than had either pre-1949 law or custom. Through such provisions, the Communist party-state placed marital fertility and reproduction firmly within the state's purview and conflated the interests of the state with those of the conjugal pair. Or, as Jender Lee has observed, the 1950 law supported an ideal of marriage that "entrust[ed] the conjugal family with the goal of forming a new society" (Lee 2006: 289).

In the first three years after passage of the 1950 Marriage Law, millions availed themselves of the new freedom to divorce, and the state supported these plaintiffs (Diamant 2000). However, not surprisingly, local magistrates and community leaders who perceived a link between a rapid upsurge in the number of divorces and social instability soon responded by more vigorously exercising their administrative power to rule on the success or failure of mediation. Divorce became increasingly hard to obtain, and by 1978 only the most extreme cases of abuse or political stigmatization justified marital dissolution (Diamant 2000; Huang 2005; Ocko 1991; Palmer 1995).

DEPARTING FROM THE HIGH-SOCIALIST BLUEPRINT: THE 1980 MARRIAGE LAW

The 1980 Marriage Law, like its 1950 predecessor, reflected major realignments of political power and priorities in Beijing (Marriage Law of the PRC 1980). In 1980, the new leadership under Deng Xiaoping abandoned the CCP's past antipathy to markets and private ownership; simultaneously it stepped back from the party's historical role of social engineer. Because of the high barriers to divorce in the 1960s and 1970s, there was broad-based support inside and outside the party for allowing those who had been trapped for decades in dysfunctional or abusive marriages to divorce. Although previous guidelines from the Supreme People's Court in 1951 had instructed lower courts to grant divorce when affection had broken down (Li and Friedman forthcoming), it was the Marriage Law of 1980 that for the first time explicitly identified the complete breakdown of affection (感情确已破裂) as legitimate grounds for divorce even when only one spouse petitioned the court (Marriage Law of the PRC 1980: Article 25).

Other elements of the new statute, however, continued to subordinate conjugal life to state aspirations. Most dramatically, unlike the 1950 law, the 1980 law explicitly required couples to practice family planning (Articles 2 and 12). As a result, the party-state simultaneously increased a couple's control over the duration of their marriage and division of their property and decreased their control of marital fertility and reproduction.

Beyond specific revisions to the Marriage Law, broader economic and demographic changes also encouraged the courts to interpret statute under societal conditions that had begun to diverge dramatically from those of the Mao era. In the two decades after 1980, the Chinese economy grew faster and became more deeply enmeshed in the global economy than even the most optimistic members of the Politburo could have predicted. At the same time, the long-standing barriers to migration out of the countryside fell, and between 1980 and 2000 China experienced the largest peacetime migrations in history. And, as recently as 2011, this trend showed no sign of decelerating (Yeh et al. 2011).[2]

To accommodate long-distance migration, many couples endure long separations, and millions of children are left behind to be cared for by relatives in a parent's home village (Liang, Lin, and Duan 2008). As the economic, administrative, and social conditions that had stabilized rural households during the Mao years disappeared, marital norms also changed. Young migrants might return to their village to marry, but they rarely lived in the new home built for them by their parents. Divorce now involves addressing a migrant daughter-in-law's claim to family assets to which she may have made little direct contribution. And elderly parents and their children must create new norms and strategies to deal with disputes over family property and obligations across ever-greater geographic distances (Yan 2003, 2009).

The growth of private firms, many owned by families, has further complicated the division of conjugal assets, and rising expectations for elaborate engagement gifts and dowries have created new conflicts when engagements are broken or marriages dissolved. But perhaps most challenging has been the increased value of village real estate and the explosive growth of home ownership in cities and towns following the rapid privatization of urban housing (Davis 2002, 2010). In 1988, while almost all rural families lived in a home they had built and owned, less than 15 percent of urban households had any ownership claim to their primary residence; by 2007, ownership rates among families with urban household registration (户口) had risen to 82 percent (Gao 2010: 5). When combined with even higher rates of ownership in rural China, Chinese families now enjoy the highest level of home ownership in the world (Khan and Riskin 2005; Wang 2013: Wang 2003). Moreover, between 2001 and 2010 the average value of homes grew so much faster than wages that banks began issuing intergenerational mortgages (Cai 2010), and after divorce very few men or women could acquire new homes of equivalent size or location (Davis 2010).

Rapidly increasing geographic mobility, affluence, marketization, and privatization of conjugal assets were not the only macrolevel shifts that altered the experience of marriage. China's integration into the global economy also exposed citizens to new sexual norms. Whether through mass media or direct contact with sojourners from Hong Kong and Taiwan, both men and women became increasingly tolerant of premarital and extramarital sexual relationships (Farrer 2002; Pei 2011; Yan 2003).

Given the new statutory emphasis on prioritizing emotional satisfaction in adjudicating divorce and the CCP's more general abandonment of the puritanical rhetoric of the Cultural Revolution, divorce rates rose quickly, and between 1980 and 2000 it was rare for a judge to reject a divorce petition through adjudication (Li and Friedman forthcoming). However, as divorce rates continued to climb (see Figure 1.1) and fewer people made any effort to hide premarital or extramarital affairs, both ordinary citizens and officials became dissatisfied with the 1980 law and advocated stricter regulation of marriage.[3] The national leadership responded to this unease with an unusual invitation for the public to voice their opinions as to how the Marriage Law should be revised.

NEW LAW FOR NEW CHINA:
THE REVISED MARRIAGE LAW OF 2001

In the years prior to passage of the 2001 Revised Marriage Law, a wide range of views emerged (Alford and Shen 2004; Palmer 2007). On one side were those who argued that greater freedom to dissolve marriages had not translated into greater happiness. On the contrary, they cited a greater incidence of battering, abandonment, and divorce and argued for a new law that would restore traditional morality, criminalize adultery, introduce a concept of marital rape, and punish those who had bought property for mistresses (Alford and Shen 2004). On the other side were liberals like Qiu Renzhou, who argued that the first obligation of the law was to protect individual rights not to promote social stability, and Li Yinhe of the Chinese Academy of Social Sciences, who equated further restrictions with a return to the politicized policing of private life rampant during the Cultural Revolution (Alford and Shen 2004). In the same vein, Shanghai sociologist Xu Anqi (2000) opposed those who wanted to add additional prohibitions and punishment by emphasizing that the new freedoms were signs of a more advanced culture and civilization.

After five years of deliberation, the National People's Congress finally approved a significantly revised Marriage Law in April 2001 that represented a defeat for those who wanted to impose greater public oversight and punishment (Marriage Law of the PRC 2001). The Revised Law supported marriage as a voluntary commitment and reinforced the ideal of marriage as a private agreement in which the state intervened only at the request of either party. Or, as summarized by Margaret Woo (2003), the 2001 revisions not only highlighted the language of individual rights, but they also represented a more general shift in civil law jurisprudence whereby courts entered into citizens' personal disputes only when one or both parties requested adjudication.

However, the revisions did not totally ignore those who wanted the law to punish sexual infidelity. For the very first time the Marriage Law explicitly distinguished between the spouse who was at fault (过错方) and the spouse who was innocent (无过错方)[4] and noticeably increased the number of behaviors that legally established fault. For example, the number of articles dealing with bigamy increased from one to six, and those on cohabitation where one party was married increased from zero to four.[5]

In addition, the revised law further inserted the language of private ownership and individualization of property rights into the marital relationship. Not only was all property that had been acquired before marriage deemed to be personal property in the absence of a formal agreement to the contrary, but so too were all items that one spouse identified for his or her personal use. Article 19 explained the use of prenuptial agreements and introduced new vocabulary such as "to each their own" (各自所有) that stressed individual possession before and after marriage. In these provisions the Revised Law of 2001 consistently tilted away from privileging both communal property and conjugal claims and strengthened individual ownership of private property. After entry to the World Trade Organization (WTO) in 2001, the Chinese leadership routinely urged increased protection of contracts, private property rights, and individual choice in articulating the blueprint for national advancement; not surprisingly, the revised Marriage Law incorporated this very same rhetoric and logic.

As we saw in Figure 1.1, the divorce rate rose steadily between 1980 and 2000 but then spiked upward after 2003. To what can we attribute the sudden upsurge after 2003? Without a systematic comparison of characteristics of divorcing couples as well as the grounds by which courts granted or rejected petitions for divorce, we cannot distinguish the impact of legal and administrative reforms from the underlying demographic shifts among those divorcing. That is, even in the absence of new statutes or court instructions, cultural and economic changes shaping individual and community norms with regard to marriage might have independently driven up the divorce rate. For example, perhaps as a result of the warp speed of economic growth, high rates of migration, and intensive exposure to the popular cultures of Taiwan and Hong Kong, men and women who married after 1980 increasingly saw less stigma in divorce when spouses no longer shared the same lifestyles or when one party was unfaithful or intimidated the other. However, because we do know that in September 2003 the Ministry of Civil Affairs issued a regulation (Minfa 2003) that radically reduced community supervision of marriage and divorce and thereby increased the ability of individuals to enter or leave their marriages entirely on their own volition, we can be reasonably confident that this 2003 government decision was particularly decisive and thereby marks an additional, and substantial, retreat from direct state regulation of the institution of marriage.

Prior to fall 2003, the regulations on registering marriages required those wishing to marry or divorce to present written permission from their village head or their employer.[6] Article 49 of these 2003 regulations eliminated all such requirements, thereby intensifying the privacy of marital decisions and further reducing barriers to divorce. Henceforth, clerks at marriage registries could grant a divorce when neither party objected and the two parties appeared together with their original marriage certificate, their household registration, valid identity cards, two photos, and a written agreement (协议) that explicated conditions for child custody and division of property (Minfa 2003). The total cost was under 50 yuan, and the process could take less than two hours.[7] By contrast, if one party contested the divorce, and the one seeking divorce needed to petition the court, a case could take many months and cost several thousand yuan for even the least complex dispute (Li and Friedman forthcoming).[8]

INTERPRETATIONS OF THE SUPREME PEOPLE'S COURT

Chinese law is terse and often leaves provisions vague. For example, when Article 17 of the 2001 revised law defined conjugal property, it simply stated that conjugal property was all other property that should (应当) belong to jointly owned property (共同所有的财产). Article 18 defined personal property in a similarly circular fashion: "Other property that must belong to one spouse will be considered personal." To deal with such statutory vagueness, officials in lower courts seek guidance from the Supreme People's Court (SPC), which then clarifies or elaborates the statutory provisions through a variety of written responses, of which judicial interpretations (司法解释) are generally considered most definitive (Finder 1993). In fact, in the view of some legal scholars, because the NPC Standing Committee in 1981 authorized the SPC to interpret all national laws on its own when dealing with civil disputes, the SPC (and not the National People's Congress) has had a "near monopoly of the law making power . . . in matters relating to civil justice" (Fu and Cullen 2011: 27).

In regard to the Marriage Law of 1980, the SPC has issued many guidelines, but six stand out: 1984 and 1989 opinions that, although insisting on the requirement to register marriages, gave protection to de facto marriages when couples had not violated other legal restriction;[9] a 1989 opinion on defining what constituted complete loss of affection; a 1993 opinion on child support after divorce; a 1993 opinion on how to divide property at divorce; and a 1996 interpretation on how to handle the allocation of apartments after divorce when the apartment had been rented or purchased from an enterprise or municipal real estate office (Supreme People's Court 1989, 1993a, 1993b, 1996). Taken together, these opinions supported the argument that the state must recognize the paramount place of personal satisfaction in marriage but must also protect the rights of children to parental support, the rights of both parties to equal claims to conjugal property, and the right to financial support if either spouse is unable to be self-supporting.

Since adoption of the revised law in 2001, the SPC has issued interpretations of the Marriage Law in 2001, 2003, and 2011, each of which can be read as further articulating the priorities of the party-state in regard to marriage as an institution and in terms of the preferred limits on state oversight of conjugal relationships. In addition, because in 2009 and 2010 detailed drafts of the third interpretation circulated on the Internet, one can identify which issues were most problematic when lower courts needed to apply the revised statute to adjudicating marital disputes. I first summarize the broadest shifts among the three interpretations and then look more closely at provisions related to marital sexuality that were addressed in the two drafts but were absent in the final 2011 interpretation. In this way, examples of judicial silence illustrate the party-state's retreat from the role of strong regulator to the less interventionist position as a legal referee who adjudicates disputes over marital fidelity or property only when one party asks for court intervention.

THE FIRST, SECOND, AND THIRD INTERPRETATIONS
OF THE 2001 REVISED MARRIAGE LAW

The SPC issued its first interpretation of the revised law in December 2001 (Supreme People's Court 2001). In that interpretation, the court focused first on definitional problems that had arisen in regard to phrases that had been absent in the earlier version of the statute. After the 2001 revisions, these terms—such as family violence, invalid marriage, cohabitation, and intimidation—could establish grounds on which to require financial compensation in cases of divorce. Of even greater importance than clarification of terms, however, was the statement that courts could not withhold divorce from the party at fault if he or she had met the criteria for divorce as specified in Article 22 of the revised law. In this way the SPC instructed lower courts to differentiate criteria for granting a divorce from those for awarding compensation. In cases of divorce where one party could prove to the court that the other had been bigamous, cohabitated with lovers, abused children, or abandoned the family, the court would award compensation, but the court could not deny either party the freedom to divorce and remarry. In this way the interpretation of December 2001 simultaneously authorized compensation to the spouse who had suffered abuse at the hand of the other and supported the right of the abusive or adulterous spouse to end the marriage. A third significant shift toward decreased state intervention into conjugal life was the eighth provision, which increased protections for common law or de facto marriages recognized by local communities that the 1994 Marriage Registration Regulations had severely restricted. In fact, some scholars have concluded that the 2001 interpretation went so far as to "conditionally" acknowledge these technically illegal households (Wang 2007).

The second SPC interpretation issued on December 24, 2003 (Supreme People's Court 2003), further strengthened the court's increased deference to plaintiff initiative and to defense of personal rights (人身权). For example, the first provision of this second interpretation explicitly explained that the law did not outlaw cohabitation and that cohabitation became a legal issue only when justifying divorce or assigning compensation at divorce. Also noteworthy were the detailed instructions in the twenty-second provision supporting property rights of parents-in-law as well as the individual spouses in regard to wedding gifts or the new conjugal home. The law and the courts may have wanted to deal with marriage as a contract between two individuals, but the rapid increase in the market value of housing now required substantial financial investments by others beyond the conjugal pair. By reaffirming judicial protection of the property rights of any persons who had invested in a marital home, this 2003 interpretation weakened earlier protection of conjugal claims and in particular put wives at a disadvantage because of the traditional expectation that a man and his family provide a residence for the new couple, while the woman and her family furnish the new home. In this way, the SPC's principled support of the logic of voluntary contract and property rights served in practice to disadvantage women (Li and Friedman forthcoming).

In August 2011, the SPC issued the third interpretation of the marriage law (Supreme People's Court 2011). In several ways, this interpretation further privileged individual property rights and weakened communal claims to conjugal property. The revised law had gone to some length to specify and support individual property rights within a marriage but had left protection of conjugal communal property, including the marital home, only vaguely defined.[10] Thus, as the value of residential real estate escalated, lower courts increasingly requested guidance. Three provisions of the 2011 interpretation illustrate how provisions to protect individual property rights weakened earlier assumptions about a couple's shared rights to a marital home.

Like the second interpretation of 2003, the 2011 interpretation privileged parental investments in a married child's residence if the parents had invested and registered the residence in their child's name before the marriage (provision 7). The tenth provision privileged the ownership claims of the spouse who made the down payment even if, after the marriage, both parties paid the mortgage, and the eleventh provision protected the rights of third parties when one spouse sold the marital home without consulting the other. More-over, in contrast to the 2009 draft circulated on the Internet that had restricted the third party's right of ownership if the spouse who had not been consulted had no other residence, the final version privileged the rights of the new owner over the spouse by declaring that the third party retained ownership even if the property was the sole residence of the uninformed spouse.

The most glaring tension between competing individual rights, however, did not concern distinguishing first-order claims to property but rather the contradictions between the state's support for arguments rooted in claims to privacy and its continued insistence that, ultimately, marital fertility was a state matter. Here in its ninth provision the interpretation explained why lower courts must refuse to hear a husband's suit for compensation when a wife refuses to become pregnant on the grounds that a woman has the free-dom to choose not to become pregnant. Significantly, the lack of freedom to become pregnant after the first birth is not addressed in this provision. De-fending an individual woman's right to control the decision to become preg-nant does not reduce the state's more general control over marital fertility and the reproduction of the population. With regard to this contradiction, the third interpretation, like the two earlier ones and the drafts that circulated in 2009 and 2010, remains notably silent.

Finally, the third interpretation departs from the 2009 and 2010 drafts by remaining silent on the issue of sexual fidelity in marriage. A closer look at this silence highlights those areas where the party-state and the larger society are renegotiating the conditions under which the state should be allowed to regulate intimate relationships and the terms under which citizens may turn to the courts to resolve marital disputes.

THE PARTY-STATE AND SEXUAL FIDELITY

As the party-state has reduced direct control of the economy and extended legal protection of private contracts and ownership of personal property, it has also steadily withdrawn from policing citizens' sexual relationships. However, when citizens ask the court to intervene in cases of sexual infidelity using the logic of contract, we observe uncertainty about how to respond from within the court and among its officers.

Both the 2009 and 2010 drafts of the third interpretation included guid-ance in regard to rulings on issues of sexual fidelity where the final interpre-tation of August 2011 remained silent. The first issue that was subsequently ignored involved a question about the legality of loyalty compacts (忠诚协议) between married spouses. The question and the proposed response appeared only in the 2009 draft, when the SPC declared that such compacts were enforceable as civil contracts as specified in Article 55 of the Civil Procedure Law.[11] The second concern that appeared in these earlier drafts but was subsequently ignored in the final interpretation was the legality of compensation payments to lovers on termination of cohabitation.[12] Here the 2009 and 2010 drafts stated that the courts would not accept petitions for compensation because Article 54 of the Civil Procedure Law protected only legal behavior and such relationships were illicit. By contrast, in the final draft of the third interpretation, the court made no comment on compensation payments and thus appeared to have removed itself entirely from ruling on issues of sexual fidelity or the financial arrangements of extramarital relationships.

The silence of the August 2011 interpretation on the loyalty compacts and compensation to former lovers suggests that the current leadership finds it less necessary for the state to regulate sexual intimacy or marital fidelity than either conjugal property or marital fertility. Or it could simply mean that the court officers were divided on where they stood and decided to issue an interpretation that clarified only the most pressing issues surrounding disputed claims to property. A brief discussion of the phenomenon of loyalty compacts that the 2009 draft interpretation found legally enforceable but that subsequent drafts ignored illustrates the reluctance of the state to return to the active policing of private life and sexuality that it had quite willingly assumed during the Mao years.

I do not yet know when a court first heard a dispute over a loyalty compact, but from legal handbooks and publications, the model case appears to have involved an agreement drawn up in June 2000 by a couple in Shanghai, both of whom had previously been divorced. In May 2002 the wife discovered the husband was having an affair, and the husband then sued for divorce. The wife then countersued for the 300,000 yuan compensation specified in their loyalty compact. The husband appeared in court, the Minhang district court ordered mediation, and the wife settled for 250,000 yuan (Jia 2008: 80–81). However, in 2004, on the husband's appeal, the Shanghai City Court voided the lower court award on grounds that infidelity was an emotional not legal issue, that Article 4 of the Marriage Law that mandates loyalty is aspirational, that the loyalty compact violates personal freedom and the right to privacy, and that one cannot specify damages prior to an offence (Li 2009).

Based on materials from law firm websites, legal journals, and court cases published since the Shanghai City Court decision in 2004, I can identify two opposing viewpoints. Arguments in support of loyalty compacts emphasize that individuals sign these compacts voluntarily and that no provisions violate the law or harm other persons or society. Moreover, the marriage law gives spouses the right to make agreements about division of conjugal property at any time in a marriage, and Article 46 of the Marriage Law gives the innocent party the right to compensation. (Fan 2010; Jia 2008; Li 2009; Zhao 2010).

Arguments against legal recognition of loyalty compacts like that of the Shanghai City Court, emphasize that infidelity is an emotional or moral issue, not a legal one. In addition, they note that such compacts violate constitutional protection of personal freedom (人身自由的权利) and that, according to civil law, one cannot allocate damages via a contract in advance of an offence. Finally, they note that Article 46 of the Marriage Law already allows the innocent party to sue for compensation in cases of adultery, abuse, or cohabitation. Therefore, they see no need for additional legally binding agreements (Fan 2010; Guo 2010; Jia 2008: 31; Xu 2010).

The August 2011 interpretation avoided dealing with these competing views on the legality of loyalty compacts; more important, it ignored all questions relating to marital or extramarital sexuality and thus confirmed the party-state's steady retreat from the Maoist role of social engineer and moral arbiter of the private sphere and intimate relationships. In addition, the interpretation underlines the more specific secular trend whereby the party-state increasingly delinks marriage and sexuality but preserves the connection between marriage and fertility.

CONCLUSION

Reviewing the progression of the party-state's logic in statute and SPC guidance, legal scholar Margaret Woo observes a shift to a "more individualized concept of citizenship" that stands in contrast to the earlier "corporatist view" where "citizens [were] defined by class and belong[ed] to collectivist social groups encouraged and promoted by the state" (Woo 2003: 10, 127). But when one compares the state's retreat from regulating divorce or the decisions that have enlarged individual rights to property acquired during a marriage with the state's unwavering stance on its right to dictate marital fertility and reproduction of the population, one observes how the older role of the party-state as social engineer not only lingers but on occasion trumps the newer one of legal referee, who enters family disputes only when a crime has been committed or when asked to uphold an individual's statutory civil rights.

The one-child-per-couple policy began as party policy, not as law, and from its initial implementation terms varied across provinces. It was also envisioned to expire twenty years after the Central Party Document was first issued in September 1980 (Greenhalgh 2008). However, not only did the policy persist beyond 2000, but it was ultimately written into law, despite the proliferation of multiple exceptions at local levels (Gu et al. 2007). The 2001 Revised Marriage Law (Articles 2 and 16) required spouses to practice birth planning, and the 2001 Law on Populations and Family Planning grew directly from the 2000 Central Committee and State Council Decision on Strengthening Population and Birth Planning (Palmer 2007: 686). However, it is also the case that Article 18 of the Population and Family Planning Law "advocated" rather than specified a single child and that "specific measures" with regard to a second child could be formulated at the levels of "province, autonomous region, or municipality under the Central Government" (Population and Family Planning Law 2001). Moreover, the state has done little to prevent wealthier families or those who travel easily outside China from having second or even third births.[13] Thus, overall it appears that the state has reduced the ferocity with which it once enforced the one-child policy. Nevertheless, a contradiction remains: Legally, the party-state has greatly enlarged individual freedom to handle decisions about one's property and sexuality by limiting itself to the role of legal referee, but, simultaneously, the party-state has retained the roles of social engineer and regulator with the right—even obligation—to monitor and control marital fertility.[14]

In 1995 Michael Palmer concluded that the 1980 Marriage Law essentially offered women "greater freedom to divorce in exchange for the requirement that they surrender control of their reproduction" (Palmer 1995: 132). By 2007, Palmer no longer argued for tit-for-tat exchange but rather stressed how the Chinese state treats marital fertility as a "demographic problem to be dealt with by bureaucratic regulation, rather than an issue of reproductive rights" (Palmer 2007: 686), a position clearly articulated in the 2001 Population and Family Planning Law (Chapters 1, 3, and 4).

Legal scholar and former head of the Hong Kong University Law Faculty Fu Hualing makes an even broader claim. In the contradiction between greatly increased freedom to divorce and no freedom to control one's own fertility, Fu identifies the more general "paradox" of legal reform in China as "severe repression in core policy and the lack of restrictions in peripheral areas" (Fu 2007: 697). I would not assign the expanded protection of personal property rights and the greater freedom to create or dissolve marriages to the periphery of law and policy. Rather, I would argue that, even in core areas, the party-state may hold contradictory positions. Thus, when we review the legal-administrative framework for marriages we find statutes and court interpretations becoming ever more supportive of marriage as a voluntary contract in which the state intervenes only when a specific law has been broken or when at least one party asks for adjudication. Moreover, this greater deference to personal choice goes beyond a simple retreat from the government's earlier role as social engineer to a position that deliberately privileges certain individual preferences. Thus, in terms of the state's overall position toward the institution of marriage, we see the PRC tilting toward a preference for private ordering parallel to what Cohen (2002) and Singer (1992) observed in North American and European courts and to what Erni (Chapter 8) and Kuo (Chapter 9) describe in recent court decisions in Hong Kong and Taiwan.

However, because the Chinese party-state continues to enforce the one-child policy, it does not consistently privilege the personal. On the contrary, while the Chinese party-state since 2003 has increasingly deferred to individual preferences when regulating marital sexuality and conjugal property, it continues to directly regulate marital fertility as a state prerogative. Thus, deinstitutionalization of marriage in the PRC follows a similar trajectory to that in Taiwan or Hong Kong with respect to reduced state interference in conflicts over private property and sexual intimacy but not in regard to public policy preferences concerning marital fertility. The consequences of this contradictory stance are limited personal autonomy for PRC citizens and a historically unique recalibration of state sanctions to regularize the institution of marriage.

NOTES

1. However, it would be a mistake to view the current Chinese situation as uniquely contradictory or politicized. Courts in many jurisdictions struggle to apply laws that are not internally consistent, and statutes may lag behind or jump ahead of social norms and practice (Cohen 2002; Franck 2009; Shanley 2002). For example, in the American experience, it was only in 1965 that the U.S. Supreme Court ruled in *Griswold v. Connecticut* that a 1879 state law criminalizing the use of contraception was unconstitutional on the grounds that it violated the right to marital privacy. And

only in 1967 did the U.S. Supreme Court in *Loving v. Virginia* strike down Virginia's Racial Integrity Act of 1924 and thereby end race-based legal restrictions on marriage. U.S. laws permitting no-fault divorce on the basis of irreconcilable differences first passed in California in 1969 but only became a reality in the state of New York four decades later, in 2010.

2. In 2011, the population of Chinese workers who had left their rural homes to work in cities reached 252,000,000, up by 4.4 percent from 2010. *Xinhua*, April 28, 2012; available at http://news.xinhuanet.com/local/2012-04/28/c_123050775.htm.

3. Thus, for example, an editorial in *People's Daily* identified the reappearance of concubinage, bigamy, and mistresses as a source of social instability and justification for drafting a more restrictive statute ("Quanguo renda" 2000).

4. Articles 12, 33, and 46.

5. See Articles 3, 10, 12, 32, 45 and 46 for treatment of bigamy and Articles 3, 12, 32, and 46 for treatment of cohabitation.

6. To marry, couples also needed to provide a certificate that they had passed a premarital health exam.

7. In a visit on October 31, 2011, to the Pudong district registry, I was told that they currently imposed no fees to register an uncontested, no-fault divorce.

8. In May 2010 interviews with Guangzhou lawyers currently handling divorce cases, they reported that in their experience mutually agreed-upon divorces handled by the marriage registrar took less than a week to process, while cases that went to court took a minimum of six months, and those that involved disputes over division of property as long as three years.

9. The 1994 Regulations on Control of Marriage Registration overrode these opinions by effectively abolishing de facto marriage, a policy that the 2001 and 2003 SPC interpretations subsequently reversed, thus again further decreasing state regulation of sexual relationships (Wang 2007).

10. Thus Article 17 of the 2001 revised law states that both parties have equal right to management of conjugal property, but in the two articles (39 and 40) that deal with division of property at divorce the law is extremely vague. The law states that, in cases of divorce where the parties agree how to split conjugal property, the court should protect the interests of women and children, and in case of divorce the richer party must compensate the lower-income party if the latter had cared for children and the elderly during the marriage.

11. See Provision number 6 (Supreme People's Court 2009).

12. See Provision number 8 (Supreme People's Court 2009) and Provision number 2 (Supreme People's Court 2010).

13. In 2002 18 percent of all births in Hong Kong were to PRC mothers; in 2006 it had risen to 40 percent and by 2009 to 44 percent. Hong Kong Census and Statistics Department, 2009. Interviews and personal observations in Beijing, Chengdu, and

Shanghai between 2004 and 2011 confirm the freedom of wealthy families to flout the rules but also the persistent problem of local household registration (户口), which becomes an issue when an over-quota child, even one born outside China, wishes to enroll in a public senior high school.

14. Here I am stressing the shift in the language and logic of the law. When one looks at actual cases, and in particular when one looks at the many restrictions rural residents face in selling their homes or gaining compensation for sale of the use rights of their property, it is clear that the state does not uniformly protect individual property rights and that for villagers state control is direct and restrictive. For example, villagers can sell their village homes only to fellow villagers, and contracted farm land belongs to the collective. I am indebted to Karen Ke Li for highlighting this caveat, specified in Article 62 of the Land Administration Law amended in 2004, which places greater restriction on sale of rural as compared to urban residences.

REFERENCES

Alford, William P., and Yuanyuan Shen. 2004. "Have You Eaten? Have You Divorced?" In *Realms of Freedom in Modern China*, William Kirby, ed., pp. 234–263. Palo Alto, CA: Stanford University Press.

Cai, Peter Yuan. 2010. "China's Housing Crisis." *East Asia Forum*, January 18; retrieved on December 10, 2011, from www.eastasiaforum.org/2010/01/18/chinas-housing-crisis-2/.

Cherlin, Andrew J. 2004. "The Deinstitutionalization of American Marriage." *Journal of Marriage and Family* 66: 848–861.

Cohen, Jean. 2002. *Regulating Intimacy: A New Legal Paradigm*. Princeton: Princeton University Press.

Davis, Deborah. 2002. "When a House Becomes His Home." In *Popular China*, Perry Link, Richard Madsen, and Paul Pickowicz, eds., pp. 231–250. Lanham, MD: Rowman and Littlefield.

——. 2010. "Who Gets the House? Re-Negotiating Property Rights in Post-Socialist Urban China." *Modern China* 36(5): 463–492.

Diamant, Neil. 2000. *Revolutionizing the Family: Politics, Love, and Divorce in Urban and Rural China, 1949–1968*. Berkeley: University of California Press.

Fan Shuwei (范书伟) 2010. "夫妻忠诚协议的效力判断" (Judgment of the Efficacy of Conjugal Loyalty Compacts); retrieved on March 31, 2011, from Henan Province Court Website at http://hnfy.chinacourt.org/public.detail.php?id=108440.

Farrer, James. 2002. *Opening Up: Youth Sex Culture and Market Reform in Shanghai*. Chicago: The University of Chicago Press.

Finder, Susan. 1993. "The Supreme People's Court of the People's Republic of China." *Journal of Chinese Law* 7(2): 144–243.

Franck, Jens-Uwe. 2009. "'So Hedge Therefore, Who Join Forever': Understanding the Interactions of No-Fault Divorce and Premarital Contracts." *International Journal of Law, Policy, and the Family* 23: 235–276.

Fu, Hualing. 2007. "Commentary on 'Transforming Family Law in Post-Deng China.'" *The China Quarterly* 191 (September): 697–698.

Fu, Hualing, and Richard Cullen. 2011. "From Mediatory to Adjudicator Justice: The Limits of Civil Justice Reform in China." In *Chinese Justice: Civil Dispute Resolution*, Margaret Y. K. Woo and Mary Gallagher, eds., pp. 25–57. Cambridge, UK: Cambridge University Press.

Gao, Lu. 2010. "Achievements and Challenges: 30 Years of Housing Reforms in the People's Republic of China." *Asia Development Bank Economics Working Paper*, No. 198, April.

Greenhalgh, Susan. 2008. *Just One Child: Science and Policy in Deng's China*. Berkeley: University of California Press.

Gu Baochang, Wang Feng, Guo Zhiggang, and Zhang Erli. 2007. "China's Local and National Fertility Policies at the End of the Twentieth Century." *Population and Development Review* 33(1): 129–147.

Guo Zhanhong (郭站红). 2010. "夫妻忠诚协议的法学思考" (Judicial Reflections on Husband and Wife Signing Loyalty Agreement) 宁波大学学报 (*Ningbo University Journal*) 23(2): 2008–2011.

Hong Kong Census and Statistic Department. 2009. "Press Release November 11"; retrieved on November 21, 2011, from www.info.gov.hk/gia/general/200911/11/P200911110152. Htm.

Huang, Philip C. C. 2005. "Divorce Law Practices and the Origins, Myths, and Realities of Judicial 'Mediation' in China." *Modern China* 31(2): 151–203.

Jia Mingjun (贾明军). 2008. 现代婚姻家庭经典案例 (*Contemporary Marriage and Family Representative Cases*). Shanghai: Shanghai Jiaotong daxue chubanshe.

Khan, Aziz, and Carl Riskin. 2005. " China's Household Income Distribution, 1995 and 2002." *The China Quarterly* 182: 356–384.

Lee, Jender. 2006. Review of *Chinese Visions of Family and State* by Susan Glosser. *Gender and Society* 20(2): 289.

Li Naizhong (黎乃忠). 2009. 从婚姻的契约性本质论夫妻忠诚契约的效力 (On the Legally Binding Force of Marital Loyalty Contracts from the Perspective of the Fundamental Character of the Marriage Contract). Unpublished MA thesis, Southwest University of Political Science and Law, China.

Li, Ke, and Sara L. Friedman (forthcoming). "The Wedding of Marriage, Nation, and State in Modern China: Legal Consequences for Divorce, Property, and Women's Rights." In *Domestic Tensions, National Anxieties: Global Perspectives on Modern Marriage Crises*, Kristin Celello and Hanan Kholoussy, eds. New York: Oxford University Press.

Liang, Zai, Lin Guo, and Charles Chengrong Duan. 2008. "Migration and the Well Being of Children." *Yale China Health Journal* 5: 25–46.

Marriage Law of the PRC. [1950] 1975. Beijing: Foreign Language Press. Chinese original. Retrieved on August 30, 2005, from www.chengdu.gov.cn/govenrment/policydetail.jsp?

Marriage Law of the PRC. 1980. Chinese original retrieved on November 12, 1999, from www.chinalawinfo.com/cyfl/l/LAW_1.029. English version retrieved on May 19, 2005, from www.unescap.org/esid/psis/population/database/poplaws/pop.

Marriage Law of the PRC, Revised. 2001. Chinese original retrieved on October 3, 2004, from www.hun-yin.com; English translation retrieved on May 15, 2005, from www.nyconsulate.prchina.org.

Minfa (民法). 2003. 婚姻登记工作暂行规范 (Temporary Regulations on Work for Registering Marriages), September 24. 民政法律法规 (*Civil Laws and Regulations*) (November): 421–443.

Ocko, Jonathan. 1991. "Women, Property, and Law in the People's Republic of China." In *Marriage and Inequality in Chinese Society*, Rubie S. Watson and Patricia Buckley Ebrey, eds., pp. 313–346. Berkeley: University of California Press.

Palmer, Michael. 1995. "The Re-Emergence of Family Law in Post-Mao China." *The China Quarterly* 141: 110–135.

———. 2007. "Transforming Family Law in Post-Deng China: Marriage, Divorce, and Reproduction." *The China Quarterly* 191: 675–698.

Pei, Yuxin. 2011. "Multiple Sexual Relationship as a New Life Style: Young Women's Sexuality in Contemporary Shanghai." *Women's Studies International Forum* 34: 401–410.

Population and Family Planning Law of the People's Republic of China. 2001. Order of the President No. 63, December 29. Retrieved on February 11, 2013, from http://english.gov.cn/lawshttp://english.gov.cn/laws/2005-10/11/content_75954.htm.

"Quanguo renda changhui jvxing lianzu huiyi." 全国人大常委会举行联组会议 (The Standing Committee of the National People's Congress Opens a Joint Group Session). 2000. People's Daily (人民日报), December 26: 1.

Shanley, Mary Lyndon. 2002. "Public Values and Private Lives." *Law and Social Inquiry* 27(4): 923–940.

Singer, Jana B. 1992. "The Privatization of Family." *Wisconsin Law Review* 1443–1567.

Supreme People's Court (最高人民法院). 1989. "关于人民法院审理离婚案件如何认定夫妻感情确已破裂的若干具体意见　来源 38号" (Several Concrete Opinions on How to Deal with Establishing the Complete Breakdown of Spousal Affection during a Divorce Case, No. 38). Available at http://china.findlaw.cn/lawyers/article/d228430.html.

———. 1993a. "关于人民法院审理离婚案件处理子女抚养问题的若干具体意见30号" (Several Concrete Opinions on How to Deal with Child Support during a Divorce Case, No. 30). Available at http://china.findlaw.cn/fagui/p_1/26237.html.

———. 1993b. "关于人民法院审理离婚案件处理财产分割问题的若干具体意见32号" (Several Concrete Opinions on How to Deal with Division of Property during a Divorce Case, No. 32). Available at www.arq.gov.cn/Article/flfg/msf/hyjt/200701/8551.html.

———. 1996. "关于审理离婚案件中公房使用、承租若干问题的解答" (Explanation of Several Questions about How to Handle Use and Rental of Public Housing during a Divorce Case). Retrieved on July 29, 2009, from hun-yin.com.

———. 2001. "关于适用《中华人民共和国婚姻法》若干问题的解释 （一）" (First SPC Interpretation of Several Questions in Regard to Marriage Law of the PRC). Available at www.law-lib.com/law/law_view.asp?id=16795.

———. 2003. "最高人民法院关于适用《中华人民共和国婚姻法》若干问题的解释 （二）" (Second SPC Interpretation of Several Questions in Regard to Marriage Law of the PRC). Available at www.court.gov.cn/qwfb/sfjs/201108/t20110815_159794.htm.

———. 2009. 关于适用《中华人民共和国婚姻法》若干问题的解释 （三）(征求意见稿) (Draft in Regard to Several Questions Involving the Third Interpretation of the Marriage Law of the PRC). Retrieved on January 26, 2010, from http://qsz.fyfz.cn/blog/qsz/index.aspx?blogid=453324.

———. 2010. "关于适用《中华人民共和国婚姻法》若干问题的解释 (三) (征求意见稿)" (Draft in Regard to Several Questions Involving the Third Interpretation of the Marriage Law of the PRC). Retrieved on December 13, 2010, from www.cnr.cn/gundong/201011/t20101116_507327072.html.

———.2011. "关于适用婚姻法若干问题解释(三)" (Third SPC Interpretation of Several Questions in Regard to Marriage Law of PRC). Available at www.court.gov.cn/qwfb/sfjs/201108/t20110815_159794.htm.

Wang , Annie Y. 2007. "Unmarried Cohabitation: What Can We Learn from a Comparison between the United States and China?" *Family Law Quarterly* 47(1): 197–217.

Wang Baoan (王保安). 2013. "走中国特色住房保障道路" (Following China's Particular Road to Housing Security). 人民日报 (*People's Daily*), April 10; available at www.mof.gov.cn/buzhangzhichuang/bzzcwba/bzzcwbazywg/201304/t20130410_816045.html.

Wang, Feng. 2003. "Housing Improvements and Distribution in Urban China." *The China Review* 3(2): 121–143.

Watson, Rubie S., and Patricia Buckley Ebrey, eds. 1991. *Marriage and Inequality in Chinese Society*. Berkeley: University of California Press.

Woo, Margaret.2003. "Shaping Citizenship: Chinese Family Law and Women." *Yale Journal of Law and Feminism* 15: 99–134.

Xu Anqi (徐安琪). 2000. "限制离婚不应是修改婚姻法的主要目标" (Restricting Divorce Is Not the Main Objective of Restructuring the Marriage Law), November 12. Retrieved on July 10, 2013, from www.people.com.cn.

Xu Hua (徐华) 2010. "第三插足侵害配有全的民事救济" (Civil Recompense when a Third Party Damages Spousal Rights) 南方论刊 (*Nanfang Lunkan*) 10; retrieved on November 12, 2010, from http://china.eastview.com/kns50/detail.aspx?QueryID+60&CurRec=1.

Yan Yunxiang. 2003. *Private Life Under Socialism*. Palo Alto: Stanford University Press.

———. 2009. "Conclusion." In *The Individualization of Chinese Society*, pp. 273–294. Oxford, UK: Berg.

Yeh, Anthony G. O., Xu Xu, and Kaizhi Liu. 2011. *China's Post-Reform Urbanization*. International Institute for Environment and Development (IIED) and United Nations Population Fund (UNFPA). Retrieved on January 13, 2014, from http://pubs.iied.org/10593IIED.html.

Zhao Min (赵 敏). 2010. "忠诚协议效力问题的法律分析" (Legal Analysis of Question about Efficacy of Loyalty Compacts). 广西政法管理干部学院报 (*Journal of Guangxi Administrative Institute of Politics and Law*) 25(3): 64–68.

3 LOVE, SEX, AND COMMITMENT

Delinking Premarital Intimacy from
Marriage in Urban China

James Farrer

*Hong: When I first got to know this guy, oh, my heart would
jump. My face would redden; I was so excited. It didn't matter
what I was doing; whenever I saw him, it put me in a good mood;
it was a good feeling. I think that is the first phase of being in love.
Only with that kind of feeling can you say you are in love.*

Interviewer: Do you now think of love and marriage as separate?

*Hong: Not at all; even with my first love when I was eighteen, I
thought love was about getting married. My attitude scared that
guy away!*

—(female, twenty-five, shop owner, migrated to Shanghai from
Anhui as a student)[1]

HONG'S DESCRIPTION OF LOVE as a passionate emotional experience and her interpretation of love as leading to marriage might have sounded familiar even
to Chinese in the 1980s (see Jankowiak 1993). Love marriages have been the
ideal in urban China for decades, and, as described by Zhang and Sun in
Chapter 5, marriage remains an overwhelming goal (and pressure) for both
young Chinese and their families. Much of the rest of Hong's story, however,
would have shocked Chinese of a previous generation. First of all, a few days
after meeting this young man, a salesman who was four years her senior, Hong
moved in with him. As she described it:

It's normal. Nowadays a lot of young people are not living in their hometown but are on their own. I moved to Shanghai when I was sixteen. I came
to Shanghai to study and work. I felt I was one of those people floating on
the edge of things. So, if you are able to find someone who matches you, and
the guy and the girl have an attraction, then having sex is normal. It's like a
piece of paper; it's going to tear sometime. It's just a matter of time. Look, the
divorce rate is so high. . . . If you live together, try out married life, have sex,
then you will know everything about each other. If you break up, you won't

have a problem with marital property; you won't have children. If you are not satisfied, you can just leave; there's no burden. . . . I mean, premarital sex and cohabitation are both for the purpose of getting to know each other, right? In any case it sounds better than "divorce."

In Hong's case, she had in fact just broken up with this boyfriend after one year. Despite the romantic beginning, he had turned out to be "too chauvinistic," she said: violent tempered, jealous, and controlling. Breaking up wasn't the result she had hoped for, but neither was it tragic. After all, she had already had "five or six" boyfriends, the longest lasting four years. She also had experienced at least one "one-night love," a night of passion with no hint of commitment.

Her story illustrates a dramatic change in the rules of the game for love and sex among young urban Chinese, particularly regarding the meanings of premarital sexual intimacy for women. In the 1980s, a woman who had lost her virginity before marriage faced social stigma and even legal punishment (Zhou 1989). Now we see a decoupling of premarital intimacy from the institution, if not the goal, of marriage as well as childbearing. Young people still profess to want marriage, but they also espouse an acceptance of premarital sex (Jankowiak and Moore 2012; Pan and Huang 2011; Zhang 2011) according to an individualistic ethos that values personal fulfillment over social conformity (Yan 2011). One consequence of these new value orientations is a notable increase in the turnover in premarital partners (Li and Xu 2004). As we see in Ho's and Shen's discussions of extramarital relationships in Hong Kong and Taiwan (Chapters 7 and 11), marriage itself is not disappearing as a central social institution in any of these Chinese societies, but sexual intimacy may be detached from marriage in a variety of ways that weaken the previously well-institutionalized links between sexual intimacy and marriage (Cherlin 2004).

This delinking of love relationships from marriage can be thought of as part of the broader trend toward favoring personal and private desires over the preferences of local communities or the Party-state as described in Chapter 1. Unlike the legal institution of marriage, dating relationships are governed by informal social conventions, or "rules of the game," that because they are not encoded in laws change more readily in response to cultural and social pressures. In the West, similar changes in youth culture have been described as "a formalization of informalization" through which young people created more flexible and permissive scripts to govern their intimate relations (Wouters

1987). For example, in a study of courtship conventions in the United States, Beth Bailey describes the transition from domestically oriented "courting" to a system of "dating" that emphasized youth independence but also self-regulation according to a complex set of informal rules, including a gendered expectation that women would limit sexual intimacy (Bailey 1988; also Waller 1937). Later in the twentieth century the culture of "dating" itself was supplanted by new conventions of "hooking up," in which women were expected to be sexually active (but not "slutty") (Hamilton and Armstrong 2009). Such relationship conventions serve as shared cultural frameworks within which couples engage in the "emotion management" central to relationship maintenance (Wouters 1992).

Looking at related changes in China, we also can observe a development from a domestically focused and closely monitored courtship system in the 1980s to a more individualistic culture of dating in the late 1990s and 2000s (Jankowiak and Moore 2012). Free choice of marriage partners predates these shifts in dating culture, with some urban Chinese choosing their own spouse as early as the Republican period. In a survey of marriages in Chengdu, 17 percent of respondents married between 1933 and 1948 described their marriage as based on "individual choice," increasing to 40 percent for those married between 1949 and 1957 (Xu and Whyte 1990: 715). Under the influence of the 1950 Marriage Law, by the 1960s and 1970s young people even in small towns and villages were able to arrange their own marriages with a far greater degree of autonomy than before (Yan 2003).

Still, no culture of casual dating, or premarital sexual experimentation, seems to have emerged in rural or urban areas during the high socialist period (Chan, Madsen, and Unger 2009; Xu and Whyte 1990; Yan 2003). Rather, family involvement and community surveillance limited intimacy between youth even in urban areas. Premarital sex remained taboo through the 1980s. Women who were known to have lost their virginity could be shamed within a work unit, denied an administrative position, or treated as second-rate marriage partners (Zhang 2011; Zhou 1989). Consequently, women were very careful about their sexual choices, and couples who became intimate usually married. In a survey conducted in 1997, less than 10 percent of urban couples married prior to 1987 reported having sex before marriage (Xu 1997). Most tellingly, the average number of premarital dating partners reported by urban couples marrying in the 1980s was roughly one, meaning that most people married their first partner (Li and Xu 2004: 84).

A true culture of dating emerged in major cities such as Shanghai in the 1990s (Farrer 2002). Couples entered and exited relationships much more easily and frequently. Xu and Whyte found that less than 30 percent of Chengdu couples marrying from 1977 to 1987 reported more than one dating relationship before marriage (1990: 715). In contrast, in their 2001 survey, Li and Xu found an average of 3.3 relationships among youth in Shanghai and Chengdu; a mere 18 percent had dated only one person, while 11 percent had dated six or more partners (2004: 84). Most found partners through social interactions at school and work.

Perhaps the most significant changes involved increasingly free sexual relations before marriage (Parish, Laumann, and Mojola 2007). By 2000, 32.6 percent of respondents in a national survey of unmarried people aged twenty-five through twenty-nine admitted having had premarital sex, with this proportion increasing to 61.7 percent in 2006. While the mean age of marriage was increasing (see Cai and Wang Chapter 4), the mean age of first sexual intercourse for people aged twenty through twenty-nine actually declined from 22.33 in 2000 to 21.88 in 2006 (Pan 2007; Pan and Huang 2011). Contraception was increasingly accessible in urban areas, but premarital pregnancy was common. A review of various local studies of urban women undergoing mandated premarital examinations showed that between 11 and 32 percent had experienced premarital pregnancy, with 86 to 96 percent ending in induced abortion. In one of these studies conducted in central Xuhui district in Shanghai in 1999, 79 percent of women reported premarital sex, 32 percent had experienced premarital pregnancy, and 27 percent had experienced abortion (Qian, Tang, and Garner 2004). Given these patterns, access to abortion was clearly as important as the availability of contraception in allowing women to delink sexual activity from marriage and childbearing.

Despite these changes, premarital chastity remained among the thorniest issues in Chinese courtship culture (Farrer et al. 2012). When ranking the important criteria for choosing a potential dating partner, respondents in a 2001 survey of Shanghai and Chengdu residents split into extremes: Roughly 40 percent considered chastity as very important, although roughly one-third considered it not important at all (Li and Xu 2004: 53, 170–178). Numerous surveys of university students conducted since 2000 still found substantial minorities who disapproved of premarital sex under any circumstances (Gao 2004; Liao 2005; Ma and Shi 2003; Sun and Sun 2006), though they also found a shrinking "permissiveness" gap between males and females, as well as a decrease in the sexual double standard (Pan and Yang 2004; Pan 2007; Pan and Huang 2011).

Though marriage has remained an important goal for most urban Chinese young people, "love relationships" (恋爱关系) in practice have become increasingly independent of marriage. Some relationships have lasted years, and, given the increasing turnover in dating partners, most relationships would not end in marriage. As marriage in urban China has been delayed, especially for educated men and women (see Chapter 4), the period of life spent in (or pursuing) such informal love relationships has expanded. Except for the minority who still believe that marriage is the only appropriate context for sex, most young urban Chinese have found a new normative context for sexual intimacy in the dating/love relationship. In sum, by the first decade of the millennium, the "love relationship" had become a new legitimate cultural scenario for sexual intimacy.

RELATIONSHIP SCRIPTS AS FEELING RULES

This cultural scenario had normative dimensions, especially regarding the expression of love itself. Previous research on Chinese youth points to the centrality of passionate feelings and emotional expression in courtship relationships (Farrer 2002; Jankowiak 1993; Jankowiak and Moore 2012; Yan 2003; Zhang 2011). Surveys of university students from 1991 to 2006 found that one of the most consistently held beliefs was that sexual behavior should be based on love (Pan and Huang 2011). Everett Zhang's research also points to "love" as the key ideology of China's sexual revolution (Zhang 2011). Love could be described as the new sacred value in the field of sexual behavior, and either premarital or extramarital sexual behavior could be justified as an expression of romantic feelings (感情) or love (爱情) (Farrer 2002, 2006; Farrer and Sun 2003).

But what is a "love" relationship, and what does it entail? Love may have a universal psychological and physiological basis, but it also is expressed and represented in specific cultural practices (Jankowiak 1993). Moreover, as love and sex become partly detached from marriage and childbearing, we can expect these cultural codes to become elaborate and explicit, in a sense making up for the lack of certainty that institutions provide (Swidler 2001). Sexual/dating conventions, such as the "date" and the "hookup" or the "love relationship," can be thought of as scripts for intimate behavior (Gagnon and Simon 1973; Laner and Ventrone 2000). Scripts for sex also may become detached from expectations of love, as in the "hookup" script in the United States. So we might also ask if there are now sexual scripts in urban China that do not entail the expression of love.

Using data from qualitative interviews, I provide a general description of the common scripts, or the cultural scenarios for relationships, that urban youth follow in premarital intimate relationships. Drawing on ethnographic fieldwork among Shanghai youth begun in the mid-1990s (see Farrer 2002, 2006; Farrer et al. 2012), for this chapter I use transcribed interviews conducted in Shanghai between 2003 and 2007 by ten trained graduate interviewers. The interview sample consisted of thirty-three males and thirty-five females, aged twenty to twenty-eight, all Shanghai residents, recruited by the interviewers from their personal networks.[2] Of course, no such qualitative sample can represent the voices of all urban Chinese, but a qualitative analysis such as this can give us some idea of cultural currents among educated urbanites, a group particularly prone to delaying marriage (see Chapters 1 and 4).[3] To balance the limitations of this qualitative sample, throughout the chapter I make relevant comparisons with probability sample survey data from other studies.

Shanghai, of course, is not a typical Chinese city, nor can college graduates represent all members of their generation. However, as already noted, larger trends in number of partners and premarital sex in Shanghai do not dramatically deviate from those in other metropolitan cities (see Qian et al. 2004). Within Shanghai, of course, this is not a random sample. Because many respondents were recruited from the personal networks of Shanghai-based graduate student researchers, as a whole, they might have been more sexually "conservative," or conventional, than young people more active in Shanghai's cosmopolitan nightlife scenes, gay and lesbian scenes, or the flourishing international dating scenes in the city (Farrer 2011, 2013). Still, the multiple erotic worlds of the big city supported varied or alternative sexual scripts that also are referenced in the accounts of some of the informants quoted in the following pages.

A central focus of relationship scripts is the expression and management of emotions. The Chinese relationship ideal of "*tan lian'ai*" (谈恋爱), or literally "talking love," can be thought of as a linked set of "feeling rules" or norms for expressing various elements of "love" within a developing relationship. As implicit "feeling rules," relationship scripts define what we should feel, shouldn't feel, and would like to feel, involving the performance of various forms of "emotion work" to make the relationship realize these normative ideals (Hochschild 1979, 2003).

One tool for analyzing the social construction of love is looking at the relational script in terms of its primary normative demands. In his triangular theory of love, Sternberg describes romantic love in terms of three main normative components: commitment, intimacy, and passion (1986, 1988). Put simply, commitment involves a wish for exclusivity and continuity, passion involves expressing sexual desire, and intimacy involves communication and a feeling of togetherness. In a sociological analysis of romantic love, these normative components can be thought of as interrelated but analytically separable "feeling rules," things one "should do" within a relationship as part of the "emotional management" of being in love and showing we are in love (Wouters 1992). Ethnographically, we can analyze cultural variations in the culture of love by investigating how these three components are expressed in a particular relationship script (Farrer, Tsuchiya, and Bagrowicz 2008).

The reason I suggest this approach is that it allows us to ask how the culturally scripted expressions of love relate to the larger institutional changes described in the previous section: the delinking of romantic relationships from the institution of marriage. That is, as romantic relationships become increasingly separate from marriage in actual experience—though not always separate from the goal of marriage—how do young people signal commitment, passion, and intimacy? What do they emphasize and why?

Although informants used a variety of terms to speak about their romantic relationships, they have a clear shared sense of what it means to be in a "love relationship."[4] According to informants, a love relationship has three broad stages: (1) the initial stage of being attracted and expressing passion and (2) the second stage of getting to know each other (increasing intimacy), which may lead to a breakup or to (3) the third stage of the relationship, based on deeper emotional ties instead of mere feelings of infatuation. In this third stage, many couples begin to plan seriously for marriage, and they may even cohabit, especially if they are both living away from their parents. Given the continuing assumption that a successful romance is a prelude to marriage rather than to another romance, it is not surprising that these three general stages of increasing commitment and intimacy broadly resemble those that Jankowiak (1993) identified in his study of romantic love in urban China in the early 1980s. However, thirty years later, changes in this script—particularly the acceptability of having sex and breaking up—have greatly altered the expectations of love relationships, contributing to the separation of sexuality and intimacy from marriage.

The discussion that follows is an exposition of the feeling rules implicit in the scripts for intimate relationships. First is a discussion of the standard script for love relationships organized in terms of the three components of love: commitment, passion, and intimacy. The next, much shorter, section looks at emergent relationship scripts that violate the norms of love relationships and are not oriented toward marriage or seen as commitments. The conclusion discusses how these scripts relate to the larger changes described in this volume, especially the partial deinstitutionalization of marriage as a framework for understanding new norms for intimate relationships.

LOVE AS COMMITMENT: AIMING FOR A COMMON
FUTURE (BUT KEEPING OPTIONS OPEN)

The conventional script of love relationships is defined largely in terms of increasing levels and signs of commitment with an implied goal of marriage. Informants' discussions focused on differing ways of expressing and registering commitments within this script.

Encounters with Destiny

Relationships obviously begin with a meeting; however, by 2000 in urban Shanghai there was no longer a conventional way of meeting a partner. Meetings between the sexes generally were unorganized, occasional, and inconsistently monitored by outsiders. As found in a sample survey in Chengdu and Shanghai by Li and Xu, social proximity at work or school was the most important factor in relationship formation. Although most people dated people from the same city, geographical proximity within the city played a less important role in dating, with neighborhood and family ties now less important than institutional settings (Li and Xu 2004: 88). For six informants in my study, the first meeting happened on the Internet.

Given that young people typically met in prosaic and familiar settings or through groups of relatively familiar people, they struggled to explain why one would choose a particular individual as one's most important and only life partner. Out of all the possible attractive partners, why is this one extraordinarily or uniquely attractive? One conventional way of managing this dilemma among interview informants was the frequent evocation of the concept of *yuanfen* (缘分), usually translated as destiny or fate. According to the survey of young people in Shanghai and Chengdu, 79.1 percent of respondents believed in this idea of destiny (Li and Xu 2004: 81). Although not explicitly about feelings, talking about destiny functioned also as a feeling rule or an indirect way of emphasizing the emotional content of a relationship over other more pragmatic, rational, or impersonal considerations:

> Yes, I believe in it [destiny]. If it wasn't for that meeting, if I hadn't by chance met her, then how could we have started a relationship? We hadn't made a plan to meet up before, so, yeah, that is destiny. (male, twenty-four, a clerk in a joint venture company, Shanghai native)

Informants had various interpretations or associations with the concept of destiny: (1) the traditional notion of destiny, which codes the encounter of two people in relationships as something predestined; (2) the feeling of being attracted at the first encounter; (3) an unusual coincidence that occasioned a meeting; (4) an inexplicable power to overcome obstacles and meet again, which would not happen in normal circumstances; (5) meeting an especially desirable person; or (6) a cherished romantic opportunity. All of these definitions emphasize the singularity of the meeting, the uniqueness of the partner, and the mysterious emergence of an emotional attachment at a particular moment. Far from dying out, the traditional discourse of destiny seems particularly useful for describing meetings through the twenty-first century medium of the Internet:

> I believe this was destiny, because I met her on the Internet. It was the first time I had used Skype, the chat program, and I was on the Internet looking for someone to chat with, and I found her. She was the very first person I chatted with. I think with that kind of chat program there are hundreds of thousands of people on line on any day. So how is it that out of all those people, I found her? That is really destiny. (male, twenty-five, engineer, Shanghai native)

Informants emphasized that, even though destiny may have brought them together, it still required two people to make an active effort to seize the chance and to develop the relationship. The Chinese concept of destiny was thus like the "mythic code of love" described by Anne Swidler (2001) in Americans' conversations about love. In Swidler's analysis, this metaphysical notion of love expressed the unique and absolute qualities attributed to love (for example, "love conquers all," "till death do us part," "star-crossed lovers," and so on). At the same time, this mythic code exists side by side with a more

pragmatic or prosaic code that emphasizes the efforts people make in organizing and sustaining a relationship ("working on a relationship," "making
compromises," and the like).

Similarly, in talking about destiny, Chinese young people found a mythic
or metaphysical code of attraction that emphasized the unique, magical, and
enduring qualities of attraction while also embracing a prosaic code of the
pragmatic choices and practical efforts necessary for making a relationship
work with an attractive partner. As Swidler points out, however, these codes
are not mutually exclusive in everyday life. They simply have different uses
in different relationship contexts. The discourse of destiny was used to express and explain the profound emotional commitments—or leap of faith—
involved in establishing a romantic relationship. The conventional use of this
language was thus a feeling rule tied to the central expectation of love relationships—commitment and exclusivity—while accounting for the fact that
a relationship began with an ephemeral moment of intersubjective attraction
as well as being subject to any number of ongoing pragmatic and materialistic
considerations. Talking about destiny was thus a feeling rule for expressing
commitment in a context in which commitments remained uncertain.

Declaring Feelings

After meeting a partner, someone must act to overtly establish the relationship as a dating/love relationship. Conventionally this is the man. Verbal declaration was the most often used way of declaring love. But not all informants
chose to declare love in a face-to-face context. Some informants reported
writing a letter; some informants reported declaring through text messages or
e-mail; and still others made a phone call to declare love (表白). Some expressions were: "Do you want to be my girlfriend/boyfriend?", "Let's be together,"
"I like you," "You are a good girl," and "I want to take care of you."

Although verbal means were more socially accepted, sexual behaviors such
as holding hands, kissing, hugging, and engaging in sexual intercourse were
occasionally used by informants to declare love. Five informants reported
having sex as a way of establishing a relationship. Though men were expected
to take the first step, sometimes a woman created a situation in which a man
would know he should declare his love through words or gesture:

> On that day, I asked her out to the City God Temple. Suddenly there was a
> downpour, and neither of us had an umbrella. So we were completely soaked,
> and we went under an eave to get out of the rain. She told me that she had dust

in her eye and asked me to blow it out. After that, her eyes were closed, and she wouldn't open them. So, of course, I got her meaning, and then I kissed her. After that, I asked her if she would be my girlfriend, and she agreed. So that's how it was, and we began to be officially boyfriend and girlfriend. (male, twenty-four, graduate student looking for a job, migrated to Shanghai from Anhui as student)

Verbally declaring a relationship was an important sign that one had entered into a formal "love relationship" as opposed to one of the more "ambiguous relationships" described in the following pages. Declaring love is an expression of commitment focused on the norm of exclusivity.

Signaling Loyalty and Trust: Managing Jealousy and Temptation

The "emotional management" of premarital relationships requires balancing two conflicting principles, exclusivity and individual choice. Loyalty is a primary expectation of being in a love relationship. Trust is based on an expectation of loyalty. Signaling both loyalty and trust is a way of expressing emotional commitment in a fluid social and sexual context not always conducive to either. Sexual fidelity is one common expectation of loyalty, but the acceptable boundaries were open to interpretation. Because youth are not married, do not live together, and are not always certain of their relationships, they may maintain dating relationships while also pursuing other opportunities for social, emotional, or sexual involvement with the opposite sex. Trust thus involves learning to manage feelings of jealousy, as the following interview quotation shows:

As long as I know he loves me, then it is okay. If I know he is going out by himself (with another woman), then it's as if I've got something on him, and I will say, "How can you do that? It's insulting to me. You should be better to me." I might say that kind of thing, but in my heart, even though I make a big deal out of it, it is not such a big deal because he actually really loves me, and he doesn't love anyone else. He has told me very clearly that he has a very good female friend. That girl likes him very much and even asked him to have sex with her. And he has been out with her many times. At first I was really angry, but later I didn't say anything because I know that if I show I am upset, he will say, "You know, I don't love her." I really believe him. (female, twenty, university student, Shanghai native)

As this example shows, expressions and expectations of loyalty and trust are thus negotiated relative to one's own behavior and past experiences with a partner. In the context of youth dating, some sexual interest in others is assumed to be normal for both men and women.

Loyalty and trust are norms, but some young people allow themselves involvements outside of the primary relationship, which they describe as "ambiguous" relationships (see the following) or more blatantly as "cheating." A residual interest in other sexual possibilities is also described as being "flower hearted" (花心). Many informants see being "flower hearted" as different from cheating or disloyalty and less serious in its impact on the relationship. To be "flower hearted" means being emotionally open to the opposite sex, but it doesn't necessarily imply any physical or emotional cheating. For example, one young woman described how she continued seeing two former lovers while dating her current serious boyfriend:

> Actually, I know in my heart that those two guys still really care about me. I haven't told them I have a boyfriend. Still, I don't date with them very often, and our relationship is not as intimate as before. But I still keep up a connection. I don't know if that crosses a line, but I don't want to hurt them or make them lose hope. (female, twenty-five, graduate student, migrated to Shanghai from Hubei as student)

Cheating, including sexual involvement, was not uncommon among the informants, with roughly one out of six men and women describing an experience of cheating on a partner and roughly the same number having been cheated on by a partner. Males showed a greater tendency toward cheating, but some female informants also cheated.[5] Some informants maintained that sexual exclusivity mattered only in marriage, not in a dating relationship. Moreover, two male informants held a gendered double standard; sexual exclusivity as a rule applies only to women, not to men. Still, most informants recognized that opportunities for cheating existed both for men and women.

Although the rule of romantic exclusivity seemed clear, it was open to flexible interpretation in its actual practice. This sort of delicate and duplicitous emotional management was also seen in marriages (as described in Chapters 7 and 11 by Ho and Shen), but for some unmarried urban couples the ambiguous nature of commitments could make this management even more complex. Dealing with jealousy and one's own desire for involvement with others was a skill of "emotional management" that both women and men mustered to signal loyalty and trust, but one that also kept their own options open.

Acting Responsibly: Signaling Concern

As with signals of loyalty and trust, displaying a sense of responsibility is an expression of being in a true love relationship, as opposed to more casual or ambiguous relationships. Responsibility was expressed in various ways by informants. In past years, when premarital sex was less socially accepted, the idea of "responsibility" was strongly associated with a man's promise to marry a woman he was intimately involved with, especially if she had "given" her virginity to him. Today, the linkages of love, sex, and marriage are flexible, and the idea of responsibility revolves around protecting a partner's feelings and providing practical help, along with concern for his or her future welfare. Some male informants echoed sentiments expressed by their Hong Kong contemporaries (as discussed by Ho in Chapter 7), defining responsibility as taking care of and protecting their girlfriends materially. This gendered sense of responsibility is expressed in the following quotation:

> A boyfriend, first of all, should have a sense of responsibility. Even more so, he has to protect his partner; I believe that, in society, boys are in a stronger position, so they should protect girls. This kind of protection is not only in terms of their actions but also in terms of emotional and material support. If you decide on a relationship, then you should keep to it. As for girls, they also have a responsibility, but this responsibility has more the meaning that even though you are dependent on a boy and are making him deal with many things, that your reliance on him has a limit. But I believe that responsibility is the most important thing between boyfriends and girlfriends. (male, twenty-four, company employee, migrated to Shanghai from Hunan as a student)

Whereas the rule of exclusivity expresses commitment to the present dating relationship, the rule of responsibility expresses a commitment to the future as well as concern for the present well-being of the partner. Most informants saw marriage as the ultimate goal of relationships, with the relationship serving as a process of testing and proving commitment. Informants were more likely to aim their dating relationships at marriage as they grew older and more experienced in relationships:

> I think people at different ages have different understandings. At my age, a dating relationship should have a goal of marriage. It shouldn't just be about

wanting someone's attention and care when you are lonely or just dating for the sake of dating and just seeing how things turn out. I believe only this kind of relationship [aimed at marriage] is a real love relationship. (female, twenty-four, IT engineer, migrated to Shanghai as student [province of origin not noted])

For those who did not want to get married, had not yet thought of this seriously, or couldn't see a future with a particular partner, this ideal of acting responsibility or showing expectations for a common future could be perceived as a burden:

I believe that the feeling in this moment is more important than what happens after. By being seriously emotionally involved in the relationship at this moment, then that moment will be a happy one. If you have to put some kind of expectations or time limit on it, then I think you are shackling yourself, or something like a shackle. (male, twenty, university student, migrated to Shanghai from Changsha as a student)

Although the symbolic burden of an imagined common future remains a central theme in Chinese courtship culture, this type of occasional complaint shows that acting "responsibly" toward a partner can be undesirable, especially for youth whose emotional state does not match with the script for a love relationship leading to marriage.

Meeting Parents: Sealing the Deal
Introducing a partner to one's parents was a major stage marker in the love relationship script. Most informants identified the importance of meeting parents whether they had already done it or not. Generally speaking, it was not necessary, and often not desirable, to meet parents until the relationship had developed to the point of considering marriage, as the following discussion conveys:

I believe that talking to parents about a relationship, this is something you do when you have decided that both of you want to . . . , have already gotten to the point of talking about marriage. When thinking about your parents, you certainly don't want to take just every boyfriend to see them—every time you have a boyfriend, just taking him over. Your parents would be exhausted by that. And when you start talking to your parents, it becomes something for the whole family to discuss. And so, if you had a problem, it would be a lot of trouble. So I am not too willing to do that, talking about my relationship with my parents.

Interviewer: So it means that you would want to be decided on marriage before bringing it up?

Interviewee: Yes, 80 percent decided. (female, twenty-three, company employee, Shanghai native)

Informants perceived telling parents about plans for marriage as satisfying parental expectations. As described by Zhang and Sun in Chapter 5, parental concerns about finding marriage partners could begin when a child is in his or her early twenties, so introducing a partner to the parents could relieve parents' worry about a child's marriage prospects. At the same time, parents' recognition could further solidify the commitment. For some informants, meeting the parents served as a form of functional engagement:

I feel that you have to meet the parents. Even if you have already told your parents about him, you have to have a formal meeting. One reason is to let your parents know: We are together, and we are quite serious. If you don't meet the parents, then they will probably think that you are just playing around. After meeting, then the parents will recognize the relationship. Back then, I felt that before we met his parents, they really didn't think we were really together. Only after we met face to face did they recognize that we were really together. That was the New Year break after we started our relationship. He said we have to get our parents' approval before we can continue our relationship. He felt that, even if we were good together, but the parents were against it, it wouldn't work out. I agreed with his view. (female, twenty-four, company employee, Shanghai native)

In talking about parents, the gendered nature of the love relationship script becomes most apparent. Chinese parents were notoriously pragmatic about their daughter's partner choices, but women sometimes borrowed their parents' voice to express pragmatic concerns they would not voice themselves. In general, women have more "conditions" for a partner (Li and Xu 2004: 58), putting emphasis not only on the quality of the relationship but also on the career and economic prospects of the young man. According to informants, women's parents usually voiced explicit requirements for the men, including personal virtues, family background, financial conditions, working ability, stable job, house, height, and so on. Some Shanghainese parents emphasized that the man must be from Shanghai. Attributing some of these concerns to parental pressure could be a way for women to avoid appearing too demanding or materialistic in their own partner choices. Some informants reported that meeting the woman's parents was more important than meeting the man's, and they dared not take this step until they were quite sure of their plans. Several female informants asked to meet their boyfriends' parents but refused to take the man to meet their parents unless all conditions were ripe for marriage.

Finally, asking parents on both sides to have dinner together was seen as a more formal and serious way to solidify the relationship than meeting parents on one side only. In an increasingly informal courtship culture, this meeting often represented, or substituted for, a formal engagement ceremony. In the contemporary love script, parental approval represented a seal on the relationship and also a final chance to negotiate the conditions of a marriage or argue for a breakup.

Breaking Up: The Escape Clause of Relationship Commitment

The most radical change in the love relationship script since the 1980s was the normalization of breaking up as the end point rather than marriage. Before the more liberal sexual climate of the 1990s there was an aura of inevitability about most serious love relationships that made a breakup seem like humiliation or moral failure. This was especially true if the couple had crossed the line into sexual intercourse (Jankowiak 1993; Zhou 1989). In the first two decades of the reform era, however, the average number of premarital dating partners of Shanghai couples increased from roughly one to more than three (Li and Xu 2004: 84). Accordingly, breaking up has become a widely accepted outcome in the script for love relationships.

Breakups had several conventional causes. The availability of alternative sexual and romantic partners framed some informants' narratives of breaking up. This was especially true for the younger male informants who were interested in sexual experimentation. The following example comes from a young man who has had many girlfriends:

> Of course I am a bit bored. Maybe if a girl is prettier, then the boredom comes on a bit later, but if a girl is not as pretty or lacks charm, then you will get bored more quickly. Like in a half a month, or a month, you will be bored. With her

I was bored after about two or three months. But with her, she is really easygoing, so I have a really stable and easy life. I play around outside as much as I want, and she doesn't try to stop me. That's a pretty good situation, so I am lazy about doing anything about it. So I am not interested in changing one now. Unless I meet one I really like, I won't change. She is very loyal to me. . . . But, yes, I have definitely thought of breaking up with her and even think about it almost every moment of the day. But the question I am thinking about is whether it is worthwhile to destroy this settled lifestyle. Maybe the most likely possibility is that I will meet a very nice girlfriend whom I like very much; then I will break up with her. (male, twenty-two, university student, Shanghai native)

The perceived increase in sexual and romantic alternatives also was associated with the pluralization of sexual possibilities in urban Chinese society. This included scenarios for casual heterosexual sex described in the following paragraphs, as well as relationships with married people (see Farrer and Sun 2003; Ho and Shen, Chapters 7 and 11) and same-sex partners (see Chapter 1). As young people "entered society" they encountered new challenges to their own established couplings. The following example, of a man whose girlfriend left him for a relationship with a more affluent woman, illustrates this expansion of possibilities:

She became very close to another girl in our class. But that girl is homosexual. She has more money, and she bought many things for my girlfriend. And because from the third year we weren't living nearby, we obviously grew apart. And at that time, that girl was really taking care of my girlfriend, and my girlfriend started relying on her more and more. . . . At the time, I realized that that girl could satisfy her demands, like buying her expensive perfume, buying expensive cosmetics, classy jewelry, but I couldn't supply these things. And that girl's attentiveness to her far, far exceeded my attentiveness to her. So she easily made her final decision and went to be with that girl. I think that is the main reason she didn't want to see me. Finally, on New Year's Eve, she called me and told me not to go see her anymore and just to take care of myself. (male, twenty-two, various freelance work, Shanghai native)

Most typically, breakups were described as a way of responding to a lack of or decline in intimacy and passion. One young woman described how she started thinking about breaking up with her boyfriend:

At first I started going out with him because we had feelings for each other, but toward the end, well, at that time at school, he would take me to play computer games. We started out by playing games together. In the beginning we would play one game together, but later we would just each play our own games. Sometimes when we would go out, we would just go to an Internet café, and he would do his thing and I would do mine, and we wouldn't even talk until late in the evening, when I would say, "I want to go home." And he would say, "Okay, you go on home," just like that. Maybe it just crept up slowly. Maybe he just felt we were already established, so we didn't need to show it to each other, but I felt that we should be more like we were before. (female, twenty-five, company employee, Shanghai native)

This story is about the loss of intimacy as well as passion. Whereas the attraction of other sexual possibilities seemed to play a greater role in young men's narratives of breaking up, women's narratives tended to emphasize diminishing intimacy. In both men's and women's narratives, however, both elements of fading passion and diminished intimacy were often present in varying degree.

Some relationships ended because partners had already moved on to another relationship, or were "cheating." As the following example shows, a breakup might be preceded by a long period of both suspicion and self-doubt:

I just didn't want to bring it up. I knew a few things about her behavior, and I knew she had some ideas, and that she had a guy outside. So after two months, after our relationship had developed through mid-July, I felt that we were in a crisis, and I was always trying to keep my balance. Actually, I really wanted to find an opportunity to bring it all out in the open, or communicate with her, and let her tell me what was going on, but she didn't. We couldn't find a way. So I just moved out, and she understood why. (male, twenty-five, company clerk, migrated to Shanghai from Fujian as a student)

In addition to the motivational components of the relationship, external pressures figure in narratives of breaking up. Both geographic and career mobility were common causes of estrangement. Moving apart could be part of a narrative of growing apart emotionally, as in the following story by a young woman:

The reason we split up is that we did not go to university in the same city. After I got to university, I was one of those girls who had to try out everything, really proactive. But boys usually grow up more slowly than girls, and he just lived more or less like in high school, such as playing computer games, such as going out to play. And so when we called on the phone, we would both talk about what we had done every day, and our topics just didn't match up. The things he talked about, I had no interest in them, and the things I talked about, he had no interest in them. So pretty quickly I felt we didn't have the intimacy that we had when we were together. (female, twenty-four, company employee, Shanghai native)

As this excerpt shows, sometimes geographic mobility could be used as an excuse for ending a relationship that was already failing.

Other practical concerns also figured into breakup stories, such as one partner failing to pass the university entrance exam, parental opposition to a match, different attitudes toward money, or a sense that a partner had poor career prospects. Greater mobility in other areas of life created both risks and opportunities for breaking up. Nonetheless, even discussions of these more practical issues had a strong emotional component, including a sense that distance or income differences would lead to a loss of mutual feeling. These discussions suggest that an increased cultural emphasis on emotional intimacy and sexual passion may encourage more frequent thoughts of breaking up when such intimacy and passion were lacking or when more attractive partnerships are available. Breaking up is now an accepted and sometimes preferred end to a relationship. Expressing commitment might be the central focus of the love relationship script, but commitments were limited by an uncertain, competitive, and tempting sexual and social environment.

EXPRESSING PASSION: NORMATIVE SEX

Other than the normalization of breakups, the other significant change in the love relationship script since the 1980s has been the normalization of sexual intercourse as an expression of romantic love. As previously described, sex is a relatively new and controversial convention of youth dating culture. However, most youth do recognize it as a convention—that is, something other people "normally" do and are expected to do. Still, many youth interviewed for this study said that they would not do it themselves, an ambivalent attitude also found in recent survey data research on attitudes toward premarital sex among educated youth in China (Pan and Yang 2004; Yang and Yao 2002). Still, among the interviewees for this study, forty (58.8 percent) had sexual intercourse experience with their partner, and twenty-eight (41.2 percent) hadn't. Although this is a convenience sample, the numbers are very close to the results of national survey samples already described (see Pan 2007, 2008). Based on such surveys, we can say that premarital sex is now an acknowledged and widely accepted practice in urban Chinese youth culture, although it remains a contested practice. A substantial minority of youth still value chastity, especially for women (Li and Xu 2004).

The "feeling rules" for expressing passion in a love relationship emphasize the unique and unplanned nature of sexual desire. Informants often employed a discourse of "nature" or "occurring naturally" to describe the timing of sex within a relationship. Sex is conventionally described as an unplanned spontaneous act between the two people with overwhelming attraction. Many informants used colloquial terms conveying a natural course of events—"an effortless conclusion" (顺理成章), "going with the flow" (水到渠成), "following nature's way" (顺其自然), or "natural" (自然)—to highlight both the spontaneity of sexual activity or the influence of external contexts such as staying together for the first time at home or in a hotel while traveling.

The usefulness of the rhetoric of "naturalness," especially for young women, seemed to be in deflecting responsibility for the decision to have sex. While sex was permitted within the youth culture, it was still frequently condemned in the larger adult society, and planning for it made youth, particularly women, feel morally culpable. A man who planned sex, for example by purchasing condoms, also might appear cunning or manipulative. The notion of sex happening "naturally" was therefore a way of explaining sexual activity as an effect of a vaguely defined emotional/spatial/social context rather than as an outcome of calculation or planning. The following story shows this pattern:

> It was two months [after we met]. At the time I didn't say anything. I just got a hotel room with her, but it wasn't like we necessarily were planning to do that thing [have sex]. It was just petting each other, and I hadn't thought we would make love, but, without thinking about it, I just entered her. Afterwards we both were really surprised. It was such a simple thing. We hadn't foreseen it. It was just an effortless conclusion. (male, twenty, university student, migrated to Shanghai from Changsha as a student)

This ideal of romantic naturalism had, however, the unintended consequence of decreasing planning for contraception and increasing the likelihood of pregnancy and abortion (see Jankowiak and Moore 2012). It might contribute to the relatively high rates of premarital pregnancy already described and the high incidence of abortion among unmarried women despite the easy accessibility of condoms and other contraceptive methods (Qian et al. 2004).

Although the timing of first sex might be left to "nature," informants also emphasized the larger context of the relationship itself. The context of the love relationship—of commitment and intimacy—had become the most important legitimation for expressing passion through sexual intercourse. In this context, first sex happened as a natural result of increased intimacy and commitment. Informants highlighted markers of intimacy, such as mutual understanding, and markers of a committed relationship, such as declared feelings, as the prerequisite for having sex the first time.

Female informants, however, often described the motives for sex as meeting the expectations of their boyfriend. Some female informants said that they had sex for the first time before they were mentally ready because their boyfriends repeatedly urged them to do so; they agreed to do it only to please their boyfriends and to foster intimacy. Some of them saw sex as a sacrifice women made for the sake of love (that is, an expression of their commitment to him rather than of their own desire). In most cases boyfriends played the dominant role in initiating first sex, and women sometimes described themselves as half-willing, uncertain participants, as the following story illustrates:

At the time it was winter vacation, and I bought tickets to go home. So that day we had gone out for a walk in the city, and it was really late, and he still didn't go back. We just sat out on one of those long benches holding onto each other, because I was going back in just two days. And it would be more than a month, so he just didn't want to let go. So we were sitting there hugging each other the whole time, and we realized it was eleven o'clock and my dorm would close. So I told him he should go back. Suddenly, he asked me to go back with him to his place, so that before I left we could have more time together. At first I strictly refused, because I thought our relationship had not developed to that step. But he kept explaining to me that nothing would happen. He just wanted to talk, that was all. After all, we would be separated for a long time. After he worked to persuade me for a long time, the dorm was already closed, and I agreed to go back with him. At the time, I had no idea how things were going to turn out; I just felt that he was really sad, and I had a responsibility to stay with him. After we went back, oh well, it all just happened. Even though before going I had made up my mind not to let anything happen, but once two people are

together on the same bed it is impossible for something not to happen. When
he made that request [to have sex], I was a little afraid at the time, because I
felt reluctant to have sex with a guy I really didn't understand all that well. But
he pleaded pitifully, and I thought that refusing him would hurt his feelings,
so half willing, half going along, that's how I had sex the first time. (female,
twenty-five, graduate student, migrated to Shanghai from Hubei as a student)

As this retrospective account illustrates, some women reported being pushed,
persuaded, and cajoled into their first sexual experiences with a boyfriend. In
contrast, more sexually experienced women were generally more proactive in
pursuing sex. Two male informants also reported that their first sexual experience was actually initiated by their girlfriends, though they themselves were
not yet mentally prepared.

The reluctance of many women to have sex often was associated with the
idea of female chastity. Breaking up after having sex is perceived as a "loss"
or "harm" for women (see Farrer at al. 2012). Some male informants also described sex as a particularly heavy responsibility because of a woman's loss of
chastity. Consequently, they associated the act of having sex with a promise
of marriage. More than one-quarter of informants (seven males, thirteen females) said that sex was permissible only when both of them had met parents
and marriage was only a matter of time. Other informants had a more casual
attitude toward sexual intercourse. For many informants, simply being in a
relationship was a sufficient condition for having sex. More than twenty informants (almost equally divided between the two sexes) agreed that sex was
permissible if the two people had affection for each other and the relationship had developed to a certain stage. For these informants, sex based on love
was "responsible," although sex out of basic physical needs was interpreted
as irresponsible. A minority of informants (ten male and one female) did not
interpret sex as an expression of commitment at all. In this (more commonly
male) view, if a person felt like having sex, he or she should be allowed to do it.

With ongoing or multiple sexual experiences, young people often described a development toward a more tolerant or permissive perspective. Permissiveness, however, might still retain the conventional meanings of sex as a
means of expressing emotions:

In the past I probably put more emphasis on romantic feelings. Now I don't see
it so idealistically. Not as the past, when I thought that when two people have
sex, it means they are going to stay together afterwards. Now I don't have that

way of thinking. Of course, now the aspect of romantic feeling is still there, but there are many other ways of looking at it, like the happiness of physically enjoying that side of life. And I think that if two people's relationship has developed to a certain stage, then it is just a natural thing to do. You shouldn't think of it in such a pragmatic fashion. For some people, making love is a very goal-oriented thing. I take a more aesthetic view. I can't think about it that way. (female, twenty-three, sales in a joint venture, migrated to Shanghai from Sichuan as a student)

Regardless of the moral orientations of young people toward this still-controversial practice, the general easing of the ban on premarital sexual intercourse has allowed for a more uninhibited expression of passion within relationships. This finding is in keeping with Li and Xu's survey results showing that more recent dating couples were far more likely to describe their relationships as passionate and emotionally intense than were respondents from previous dating cohorts (Li and Xu 2004: 102). The freer expression of sexual passion is an important factor in the emotional intensification of premarital love relationships. Conversely, it has also become an expectation of relationships, and a decline in passionate feelings could become a reason for breaking up.

DEVELOPING INTIMACY: CONSTANT COMMUNICATION

In addition to commitment and passion, increasing intimacy—a growing sense of togetherness and frequent communication—is a further normative feature of the love relationship script. As previously described, a decline in intimate conversation could be perceived as grounds for breaking up. Couples expressed intimacy primarily through spending time together on dates and maintaining a near constant communication through digital media. Unlike couples in the 1980s whose courtship centered on noncommercial activities, dating in the 2000s was more likely to involve socializing and consuming in commercial venues. However, despite media emphasis on the increased materialism of youth (particularly young women; see Bergman 2010), most informants did not seem to strive for luxurious dates or a level of high consumption, emphasizing the desire to spend time together on dates and express intimacy verbally and physically.

For many people already in a long-term relationship, spending time together, even at home, was more important than what they actually did on a date, and as they planned for marriage they began to express reservations about the expenses of dates. Rather than consumption, most informants emphasized the companionship on a date:

> As for expectations of his behavior, I just feel that I have that feeling, and I am thinking about him, then he should just be there to give me a hug, and that's enough. I just want him to be by my side, only being together; even if we are not doing anything, it's comforting. (female, twenty-five, flower shop owner, migrated to Shanghai from Anhui as a student)

In addition to face-to-face meetings, dating couples engaged in frequent electronic communication when they didn't see each other. Although the technologies were changing rapidly, the most frequently used electronic means mentioned by informants were cell phone, cell phone text messages, e-mail, and online chatting via MSN, QQ, or Skype. Many informants reported that they sent text messages or called each other on a daily basis. Some informants met their partners through the Internet, and some even declared their love the first time through text messages. Some chatted online when not in the same city, and others wrote love letters through e-mail. In general, the expectation was one of constant, usually daily, communication, as the following example illustrates:

> Usually I write him text messages. When I was studying, my cell phone bill was usually 100 *yuan*. When I was dating him, it was 200 *yuan*. Almost all of it was communicating with him. From morning till night the phone was busy, especially when I was in school; we were far apart from each other. (female, twenty-one, university student, Shanghai native)

In sum, the conventions of love relationships in urban China emphasize all three components of Sternberg's component theory of love: passion, intimacy, and commitment. In particular, the increased acceptance of premarital sex over the past two decades provides a culturally legitimate means of expressing passion for young people. Similarly, the increased access to digital media provides the means for constant communication in relationships, an important means of maintaining intimacy. As the previous discussion shows, many of the conventions of Chinese dating relationships focus on the expression of commitment, including the ideal of destiny, clear verbal declarations of love, the norms of loyalty and responsibility, a focus on marriage, and expectations of sexual conduct focused on committed relationships. Not all young people are comfortable with this heavy emphasis on commitment, however, and alternative cultural scenarios of premarital sexual intimacy have also emerged.

EMERGENT SCRIPTS AND AMBIGUOUS RELATIONSHIPS

Up until now the discussion has focused on the script of the formal romantic love relationship. From the interviews, however, it is clear that other types of relationship scripts are proliferating. Outside of these formal love relationships, many informants talked about types of relationships that might involve romantic feelings or sexual acts but did not fit the going definition of "love relationship." These may involve new relationship forms that clearly flout the ideals of exclusivity and responsibility, or these relationships might be described as "ambiguous" or not fitting clearly into any conventional definition (Zi 2006).

Short-Term Sexual Relationships

Since the 1990s, multiple sexual relationships have become more common, and Shanghai men and women are beginning to develop their own sexual scripts outside the "love relationship" scenario. Such alternative sexual scenarios seem more likely to be supported in the varied sexual scenes of heterogeneous cities such as Shanghai and may even be a reason some people are attracted to the city (Pei 2011). In some contexts, such as nightlife scenes, relationships that are not accepted by mainstream society may be recognized as conventional subcultural practices and associated with explicit scripts. For example, the term "one-night love" (一夜情) was popularized in print media in the 1990s and associated with nightclubs. Later the term "multiple-night love" (多夜情) was coined to describe sexual relationships that are not one-night stands but are not recognized as "love relationships." Clearly gay and lesbian sexual scripts found more support in the sexual scenes of cities such as Shanghai, as did international dating scripts in the "contact zones" of the city's cosmopolitan nightlife (Farrer 2002, 2011).

The rise of the Internet also led to a proliferation of new sexual scripts. For example, the coded term "4-1-9" ("for one night") refers to a short-term sexual encounter, and "3p" indicates a sexual encounter among "three people," a ménage à trois. The slang term "doing splits" (劈腿), imported from Taiwan, refers to simultaneously maintaining multiple long-term sexual relationships (Baidu Baike 2011). The popularization of these alternative sexual scripts—often through online media—means that the love relationship scenario described earlier in the chapter could be seen as only one among many conventionalized sexual scripts. But in a society still oriented to the goal of marriage, the commitment-oriented love relationship remains the dominant sexual scenario or master narrative toward which even unconventional scripts refer as a point of contrast (Farrer et al. 2012).

"Ambiguous Relationships"

Some relationships fail to fit within any script. Or it may be that the participants involved tactically refuse to acknowledge that they are following a particular script. These may be called an "ambiguous relationship" (暧昧关系) (Suo 2006; Zi 2006). Most ambiguous relationships incorporated a sense of emotional intimacy, and some involved sexual behavior, but not all. Although some ambiguous relationships might develop into serious love relationships, they can be distinguished from love relationships in two important ways that also help illustrate the nature of the latter. First, and most important, is the lack of explicit commitment to a common future. Marriage is generally not considered a possibility, and the notion of "responsibility" to the relationship is not invoked. Second, because there is no acknowledged commitment or responsibility, the two people involved do not have to observe the rule of exclusivity. Some informants even reported four or five ambiguous partners at the same time. In practice, informants used the term *ambiguous* to label several types of relationship situations:

1. An evolving relationship without firm commitment. At this stage, partners might date, hold hands, or kiss. This may simply be a way of talking about a love relationship that is not yet formalized.
2. An intimate physical or emotional relationship with a person other than one's own partner. There may be close emotional ties and even a short-term commitment between the two, but one of them may still be involved deeply with another partner, including marriage, as the following story illustrates:

   > I feel that I have had two love relationships, but some people don't agree. With my first guy, when I met him he already had a girlfriend, and I knew his girlfriend, it was like that "boyfriend of a friend" type of thing. At the point that I got involved in an ambiguous relationship with him, those two had already married. Actually, I don't feel like talking about it that much, but to summarize it, with us two, sometimes, I couldn't control myself and would go to see him, and sometimes he

couldn't control himself and would come to see me, but we were always really repressed, and we stayed in that ambiguous relationship a long time. (female, twenty-four, consultant, Shanghai native)

The informant's reluctance to talk about her "ambiguous relationship" might be taken as evidence for the degree to which these relationships do not conform to the standards of the conventional "love relationship" scenario.

3. A sexual relationship with no future commitment between two single people. Sometimes these relationships may be purely sexual, but they are different from a one-night stand in that the relationship sometimes lasts for several months or longer, but one or more of the partners has a reason for denying that this is a serious "love relationship," as the following example illustrates:

> I know that we can't think about having a common future together because we are the kind of relationship that began with sex before we even really got to know each other. I think that relationships that begin that way don't have a future. I think I could always date him, but we could never be marriage partners. (female, twenty-four, company employee, Shanghai native)

These relationships may involve varying degrees of intimacy and passion but generally little in the way of commitment. Rather than "boyfriend" or "girlfriend," people involved in ambiguous relationships may call each other "brother" (大哥), "little sister" (小妹), "intimate opposite-sex friend" (异性密友), "*aimei* partner" (暧昧对象), "soul mate" (知己), or "boudoir friend" (闺蜜). Other terms sometimes used simultaneously with ambiguous relationships were "the third affection" (第三种感情), "the third type of relationship" (第三种关系), "informal relationship" (非正式关系), or "unusual relationship" (非常关系). The proliferation of terms for relationship partners and the types of relationship partners indicates the popular interest in these types of uncommitted romantic relationship scripts. The chief characteristic they share is an even greater distance from the institution of marriage than we see in the new love relationship script.

RELATIONSHIP SCRIPTS AND NEW NORMS OF INTIMACY

Throughout several chapters in this volume, we witness a move from a public to a private ordering of intimate life. In marriage, as in other matters, people have begun to place their individualized desires and plans above those of the collectivity (Yan 2011). Among my Shanghai respondents, we repeatedly heard them explain their intimate lives in terms of individuated decisions both about when to marry (as seen in Cai and Wang Chapter 4) as well as when or if to initiate a sexual relationship. Such logics do not originate solely within personal and private calculation. Rather they are pervasive throughout the market-oriented economic policies that positively promote individual consumer choices and further valorize a proliferation of sexual as well as other types of personal desires (Farquhar 2002; Farrer 2002; Rofel 2007). Exposed to transnational flows of sexual images and ideas, China has experienced a "sexualization" of public culture (Pan 2007) and a "revolution" in sexual behavior (Pan 2007, 2008; Zhang 2011). As this chapter has described, this sexualization of culture includes a redefinition of normative relationship scripts to include sexual intercourse.

This chapter and the research in this volume as a whole also point to a delinking of sexual intimacy from marriage, or even a deinstitutionalization of marriage more generally (Cherlin 2004). Still, the concepts of individualization and deinstitutionalization are not enough to account for the changes described in this chapter. What we are witnessing is not simply the weakening of institutional structures and their replacement by individual strategies but the production of new cultural scripts for intimacy. As in other complex modern societies, these scripts form a cultural tool kit or cultural repertoire rather than a system of strict rules or laws, but they do have an organizing and orienting function in explaining and justifying sexual behavior (Swidler 2001).

In particular, unmarried Chinese men and women orient themselves to one dominant scenario, the idea of the *lian'ai guanxi* or "love relationship," that develops through several conventional stages of increased intimacy and commitment leading ultimately to marriage. Thus, in contrast to societies such as the United States where the idea of "hooking up" without a relationship has strong currency among university women and men (Hamilton and Armstrong 2009), the educated urban youth interviewed for this study remained culturally oriented toward marriage, even though all around them marriage is delayed, divorce rates are increasing, and various scripts for nonmarital sex are proliferating.

The reasons for a continued focus on the marriage-oriented love relationship script are complex but clearly include both state influences on public sexual politics and a resilient Chinese family culture with a strong marriage orientation (see Zhang and Sun Chapter 5). The Party-state still pressures print and broadcast media producers to promote "healthy" (that is, conservative) attitudes toward sexuality, and the public school system and parents similarly emphasize sexual self-control and premarital chastity (Farrer 2006).

Women also describe less of a subjective sense of sexual agency than men. Even the new love script remains highly gendered. Men are expected to express affection and care, and women are expected to react to their advances and make prudent romantic choices. With regard to sexual intercourse, women clearly remain the sexual gatekeepers, but now they also are expected to be sexually available. Men are expected to create a romantic sexual scene, and women to "go with the flow." In some ways this situation resembles the "going steady" culture of mid-twentieth-century America, in which women were expected to be both sexual and virginal (Bailey 1988).

Still, the new script I have described is much more permissive of female sexual expression than previous relationship scripts in China. It is delinked from childrearing and also much less tied to an explicit promise to marry a partner. Important factors in the greater number of premarital dating partners seem to be ready access to contraception and abortion and the diminished stigma associated with "losing virginity" for women, making exiting a relationship less costly. This change is expressed as a new discursive ethics of sexuality based on "feelings" rather than on chastity. Although these sexual norms still are widely contested among youth, the standard script that has emerged defines sex as permissible in a "love relationship" regardless of future commitments (Farrer 2002, 2006; Farrer et al. 2012).

The sexual options that have become available are actually more varied than a focus on love relationships would imply. The love script legitimates sex only within a committed relationship. However, some sexually experienced informants evoked another set of sexual scripts, many involving little or no focus on commitment. These included a variety of possible scenarios from "one-night love" to "doing splits" between multiple relationships. These scripts represented a near complete delinking of sexuality from marriage or from any type of intimacy or commitment.

The delinking of relationships from marriage, young people's increased mobility between relationships, and a greater choice among sexual scripts have important social and psychological consequences, introducing a much higher degree of uncertainty, in terms of both relationship goals and possible outcomes, into the intimate lives of young people. Young people have more chances to enter and exit relationships and more variations in the models of relationships available to them. This increase in sexual choice and uncertainty may be one reason why—ironically, perhaps—Chinese youth invest so much in the arts of displaying commitment in dating relationships, as we have seen in this chapter. As Swidler argues in the U.S. case, people tend to develop the most elaborate cultural discourses when dealing with difficult choices and dilemmas rather than the taken-for-granted features of social life (Swidler 2001). Managing uncertainty in commitments has become a common dilemma for Chinese youth.

If we look at the expression of romantic love in terms of Sternberg's (1986, 1988) triangular model of three components—intimacy, passion, and commitment—it is clear that Chinese youth have developed social conventions for the expression of all three components within the dominant script of "love relationship." However, it is the search for commitment that most deeply engages the rhetorical efforts of urban Chinese youth. This is partly a result of the marriage focus of youth, and the Confucian legacy of a duty to marry, influenced by parents. This is partly the result of anxieties about the social consequences of premarital sexual intercourse. However, at least in part, the emphasis on expressing commitment in relationships—through talk of destiny, loyalty, responsibility, and promises to marry—seems to be a way to regain some ground of certainty in an emotional terrain of increasing ambiguity, risk, and fluidity in intimate relationships. Young people are well aware that both they and their partners are free to make other choices and that the partners they choose may turn out not to be the "right choice" after all. The relationship conventions described in this chapter provide reassurance on both grounds—the certainty about the appropriateness of the choice and the reliability of the partner as a partner—both of which require some cultural support when they are being challenged by a larger choice-oriented society. In sum, in conversations around love relationships we see a heightened concern about solidifying and redefining relational commitments in an environment of increased individual autonomy.

At the same time, another type of reaction to these uncertainties and choices can be seen in a proliferation of relationship scripts that separate rather than combine these three components of commitment, intimacy, and passion. As we have discussed, these alternative scripts are supported by the multiple sexual subcultures and the anonymous social backdrop of urban life in Shanghai. Small-town youth might find less social support for such scripts. Some scripts for relationships—such as a brief passionate 4-1-9 (for one night) affair—may involve no commitment and only the shallowest expression of intimacy. Some types of ambiguous relationships (for example, soulmate) involve deep intimacy but no sexual involvement. Other relationships, such as affairs with married people, may involve both intimacy and passion but no commitment to a common future. And as we see in Chapters 7 and 11 by Ho and Shen, other types of relationships, including marriages, may involve both commitment and intimacy but no sexual passion. In urban China we thus may be on the verge of social changes in which not only is sexual intimacy delinked from marriage and childbearing, but the various components of love may be separable from one another, with some partnerships focused on commitment and others on passion or intimacy, depending on the desires and needs of individuals. The fragmentation of romantic love into diverse relationship scripts does not mean an end to love relationships and marriage but increased alternatives that coexist alongside these relationship models.

NOTES

1. The names of informants in this chapter are pseudonyms. Informant quotes in this chapter are from interviews with thirty-three males and thirty-five females, aged twenty to twenty-eight, all Shanghai residents, though twenty-six were born outside Shanghai. Only two had ever lived abroad, each for two years. Interviews typically lasted ninety minutes and were conducted between 2003 and 2007 by trained Chinese graduate assistants in private locations in Shanghai and transcribed in Chinese. The English translations are by the author. More details on the process of collecting and coding data are provided below.

2. Analysis of the data followed the procedures for issue-based grounded theory described by Robert Weiss (1995). Interviewers and the author worked together to generate broad coding categories that were further refined during the process of coding. All interviews were read, and alternative points of view on a topic were carefully noted and separately coded. Nonetheless, this is strictly qualitative research. There are no scientific procedures for assuring coder reliability. The findings represent one reading of several hundred transcript pages, so that other valid theoretical readings of the data are possible.

3. All were either two-year college or university graduates or current students. We should not assume they were more sexually active than less-educated youth. As Pan finds, educated youth have had lower rates of premarital sexual activity than same-age counterparts without higher education, though this gap decreased in the 2000s (Pan and Yang 2004; Pan and Huang 2011).

4. Other expressions for being in an established love relationship include "talking friends" (谈朋友) or "talking love" (谈恋爱). Young people use a variety of terms

to describe romantic feelings, including the verbs "like" (喜欢) and "love" (爱) or the noun "romantic feelings" (感情).

5. Three times as many male informants (nine) reported cheating on a partner as did females (three). However, twice as many males (six) reported a partner cheating on them as did female informants (three). These inconsistencies could indicate greater male sensitivity to cheating, but it also might indicate an interviewer selection bias toward male informants with richer sexual biographies.

REFERENCES

Baidu Baike. 2011. 劈腿 (Doing Splits). Retrieved on November 25, 2011, from http://baike.baidu.com/view/113.htm.

Bailey, Beth. 1988. *From Front Porch to Back Seat: Courtship in Twentieth Century America*. Baltimore, MD: Johns Hopkins University Press.

Bergman, Justin. 2010. "China's TV Dating Shows: For Love or Money?" *Time World*. June 30, 2010. Retrieved on November 11, 2011, from www.time.com/time/world/article/0,8599,2000558,00.html#ixzz1dN6nsLtq.

Chan, Anita, Richard Madsen, and Jonathan Unger. 2009. *Chen Village: Revolution to Globalization*. Berkeley: University of California Press.

Cherlin, Andrew J. 2004. "The Deinstitutionalization of American Marriage," *Journal of Marriage and Family* 66 (November): 848–861.

Farquhar, Judith. 2002. *Appetites: Food and Sex in Post-Socialist China*. Durham, NC: Duke University Press.

Farrer, James. 2002. *Opening Up: Youth Sex Culture and Market Reform in Shanghai*, Chicago: The University of Chicago Press.

———. 2006. "Sexual Citizenship and the Politics of Sexual Storytelling among Chinese Youth." In *Sex and Sexuality China*, Elaine Jeffries, ed., pp. 102–123. London: Routledge.

———. 2011. "Global Nightscapes in Shanghai as Ethnosexual Contact Zones." *The Journal of Ethnic and Migration Studies*. 37(5): 747–764.

———. 2013. "Good Stories: Chinese Women's International Love Stories as Collective Sexual Story Making." *Sexualities* 16(1): 12–29.

Farrer, James, Gefei Suo, Haruka Tsuchiya, and Zhongxin Sun. 2012. "Re-Embedding Sexual Meanings: A Qualitative Comparison of the Premarital Sexual Scripts of Chinese and Japanese Young Adults." *Sexuality & Culture* 16(3): 263–286.

Farrer, James, and Zhongxin Sun. 2003. "Extramarital Love in Shanghai." *The China Journal* 50: 1–36.

Farrer, James, Haruka Tsuchiya, and Bart Bagrowicz. 2008. "Emotional Expression in *tsukiau* Dating Relationships in Japan." *Journal of Social and Personal Relationships* 25(1): 169–188.

Gao Heping (高和平). 2004. "大学生性态度现状调查研究" (A Survey Study of the Sexual Attitudes and Real Circumstances of University Students). 四川心理科学 (*Sichuan Psychological Science*) 4:44–47.

Gagnon, John H., and William Simon. 1973. *Sexual Conduct: The Social Sources of Human Sexuality*. Chicago: Aldine.

Hamilton, Jennifer, and Elizabeth Armstrong. 2009. "Gendered Sexuality in Young Adulthood: Double Binds and Flawed Options." *Gender & Society* 23(5): 589–616.

Hochschild, Arlie. 1979. "Emotion Work, Feeling Rules, and Social Structure" *American Journal of Sociology* 85(3): 551–575.

———. 2003. *The Commercialization of Intimate Life: Notes from Home and Work*. Berkeley: University of California Press.

Jankowiak, William R. 1993. *Sex, Death, and Hierarchy in a Chinese City: An Anthropological Account*. New York: Columbia University Press.

Jankowiak, William, and Robert L. Moore. 2012. "China's Emergent Adults: Gender, Work, Dating, and Life-Orientation." In *Inner Worlds of the Adolescence Identity: Evolutionary, Developmental and Cultural Perspectives*, Bonnie Hewlett, ed., pp. 277–300. New York: Routledge.

Laner, Mary Riege, and Nicole A. Ventrone. 2000. "Dating Scripts Revisited." *Journal of Family Issues* 21(4): 488–500.

Li Yu (李煜) and Xu Anqi (徐安琪). 2004. 婚姻市场中的青年择偶 (*Youth Spousal Choice in the Marriage Market*). Shanghai: Shanghai Academy of Social Sciences Press.

Liao Haihua (廖海华). 2005. "大学生恋爱观的分析及正确引导" (Analyzing and Correctly Guiding the Love Attitudes of University Students). 衡阳师范学院学报 (*Hengyang Normal University Bulletin*) 26(2): 115–117.

Ma Jingbo (马静波) and Shi Shaoming (施晓明). 2003. "对大学生性观念的调查与思考" (A Survey and Analysis of University Students' Sexual Attitudes). 上海理工大学学报 社会科学版 (*Shanghai Science and Engineering University Bulletin*, Sociology edition) 25(3): 28–30.

Pan Suiming. 2007. *The Accomplishment of Sexuality Revolution in China: Preliminary Reports on a Compared Study between 2000 and 2006*. Beijing: Institute for Research on Sexuality and Gender, Renmin University of China.

———. 2008. 中国性革命的实证 (*The Accomplishments of the Sexual Revolution in China*). Kaohsiung: Manyu Press.

Pan Suiming (潘绥铭) and Huang Yingying (黄盈盈). 2011. "青少年心中的性与爱之关系" (The Relationship between Love and Sex in the Minds of Youth) 百科知识 (*100 Kinds of Knowledge*). May. Available at www.sex-study.org/news.php?isweb=2&sort=1&id=502.

Pan Suiming (潘绥铭) and Yang Xin (杨蕊). 2004. 性爱十年：全国大学生性行为的追踪调查 (*Love and Sex Ten Years: An In-Depth Nationwide Study of the Sexual Lives of University Students*). Beijing: Academy of Social Sciences.

Parish, William L., Edward O. Laumann, and Sanyu A. Mojola. 2007. "Sexual Behavior in China: Trends and Comparisons." *Population and Development Review* 33(4): 729–756.

Pei, Yuxin. 2011. "Multiple Sexual Relationships as a New Lifestyle: Young Women's Sexuality in Contemporary Shanghai." *Women's Studies International Forum* 34(5): 401–410.

Qian, Xu, Shenglan Tang, and Paul Garner. 2004. "Unintended Pregnancy and Induced Abortion among Unmarried Women in China: A Systematic Review." *BMC Health Services Research* 4(1). Available at www.biomedcentral.com/1472-6963/4/1.

Rofel, Lisa. 2007. *Desiring China: Experiments in Neoliberalism, Sexuality, and Public Culture*. Durham, NC: Duke University Press.

Sternberg, R. L. 1986. "A Triangular Theory of Love." *Psychological Review* 93(2): 119–135.

———. 1988. "Triangulating Love." In *The Psychology of Love*, R. L. Sternberg and M. L. Barnes, eds., pp. 119–138. New Haven, CT: Yale University Press.

Suo, Gefei. 2006. "A Tentative Comparison of Conceptions of Love and Relationship between Chinese and Americans." Unpublished MA thesis, Shanghai International Studies University, Shanghai.

Sun Jianping (孙建萍) and Sun Jianhong (孙建红). 2006. "大学生性观念性健康调查及健康教育对策" (A Survey of University Students' Sexual Attitudes and Behaviors and Corresponding Policies) 中国公共卫生 (*Chinese Public Health*) 22(6): 645–646.

Swidler, Anne. 2001. *Talk of Love: How Culture Matters*. Chicago: The University of Chicago Press.

Waller, Willard. 1937. "The Rating and Dating Complex." *American Sociological Review* 2: 727–734.

Weiss, Robert. 1994. *Learning from Strangers: The Art and Method of Qualitative Interview Studies*. New York: The Free Press.

Wouters, Cas. 1987. "Developments in the Behavioural Codes between the Sexes: The Formalization of Informalization in the Netherlands 1930–85." *Theory, Culture and Society* 4(23): 405–428.

———. 1992. "On Status Competition and Emotion Management: the Study of Emotions as a New Field." *Theory, Culture and Society* 9(1): 229–252.

Xu Anqi (徐安琪). 1997. 中国婚姻质量研究 (*Research on Chinese Marital Quality*). Shanghai: Shanghai Academy of Social Sciences.

Xu, Xiaohe and Martin King Whyte. 1990. "Love Matches and Arranged Matches: A Chinese Replication." *Journal of Marriage and the Family* 52(3): 709–722.

Yan, Yunxiang, 2003. *Private Life under Socialism: Love, Intimacy, and Family Change in a Chinese Village 1949–1999*. Palo Alto, CA: Stanford University Press.

———. 2011. "The Changing Moral Landscape." In *Deep China: The Moral Life of the Person*, Arthur Kleinman, Yunxiang Yan, Jing Jun, Sing Lee, Everett Zhang, Pan Tianshu, Wu Fei, and Guo Jinhua, eds., pp. 36–77. Berkeley: University of California Press.

Yang Xiong (杨雄) and Yao Peikuan (姚佩宽). 2002. 青春与性 1989–1999: 中国城市青少年的性意识和性行为 (*Youth and Sex 1989–1999: A Survey of Sexual Attitudes and Behavior of Chinese Urban Youth*). Shanghai: Shanghai People's Press.

Zhang, Everett. 2011. "China's Sexual Revolution" In *Deep China: The Moral Life of the Person*, Arthur Kleinman, Yunxiang Yan, Jing Jun, Sing Lee, Everett Zhang, Pan Tianshu, Wu Fei, and Guo Jinhua, eds., pp.106–151. Berkeley: University of California Press.

Zhou, Xiao. 1989. Virginity and Premarital Sex in Contemporary China. *Feminist Studies* 15(2): 279–288.

Zi Xuan (梓轩). 2006. "男女暧昧关系大检阅" (An Overview of Male–Female Ambiguous Relationships). 文苑 (*The Literary World*) 1B: 52–53.

4 (RE)EMERGENCE OF LATE MARRIAGE IN SHANGHAI

From Collective Synchronization to Individual Choice

Yong Cai and Wang Feng

SINCE 1950, AGE AT FIRST MARRIAGE HAS RISEN noticeably in both affluent OECD nations and in emergent economies throughout the world. Driving this trend are such structural changes as increasing enrollment of women in postsecondary education and expansion of white-collar jobs. By remaining in school into their early twenties, women delay entry to the marriage market; in aspiring to a career, men delay marriage until they are professionally established. These delays not only reduce parental control over a child's marriage and give young adults greater latitude in choice of spouse and timing of marriage (Jones 2007; Mason, Tsuya, and Choe 1998; Oppenheimer 1988, 1994; Sweeney 2002; Tsuya and Bumpass 2004), but they also partly explain the emergence of below-replacement birth rates as couples delay childbearing as well (Lesthaeghe 2010).

China's experience with marriage and family formation in the past several decades parallels that found elsewhere, but in China the trajectory has been more volatile and the sources of change have been unique to its social and political setup. In China, age at first marriage rose steadily between 1950 and 1979 but then fell after 1980 and only swung upward again after 1990.[1] To explain China's distinctive path to late marriage, this chapter identifies two underlying forces, which sometimes operated in concert and at other times appeared to be in opposition: state intervention and individual choice. During the first phase, between 1950 and 1979, marriage age rose in response more to state intervention than to individual desire. The initial shift to later age of marriage was an integral part of a CCP campaign to create a new form of modern marriage that would liberate young men and women from the control of older family members, but at the same time it was part of a systematic effort to reinstitutionalize marriage around state rules and priorities. By contrast, the shift upward after 1990 followed from a new state orientation that granted individuals more latitude in deciding their personal life, including when and whether to marry. Rising marriage age in recent decades therefore is more directly linked to individual volition and choice than to explicit state policies.

But changes in marriage age, like those in frequency of divorce, signaled a break from traditional Chinese marriage practices. Historically, and unlike European societies where marriage and mate choice ideally rested with two individuals (Schofield 1985; Macfarlane 1986), in China norms as to when and whom to marry had long been outside the confines of individual decision making and preferences. Marriage was not based on romantic love and individual choice but on a family's collective goal to continue the family line and build economic, social, and political alliances (Lee, Wang, and Ruan 2001; Yang 1959). Early and universal female marriage was therefore a defining feature of Chinese society that had both demographic consequences and far-reaching social and economic effects (Hajnal 1953, 1982; Lee and Wang 1999; Malthus 1798; Wolf and Huang 1980).

Suppression of individual desires and marital decision making was a major source of social discontent among the young, and China's marriage and family traditions were consequently among the main targets of China's twentieth-century social revolutions. Both Nationalist reformers and Communist revolutionaries prioritized changes to marriage practices in their striving for modernity. Footbinding, arranged marriage, gender inequality, and many other "feudal" family institutions were deemed obstacles to China's rejuvenation. Women's emancipation, freedom of marriage, and liberation from patriarchal control were among the important tenets of the reformist May 4th movement in 1919.

However, it was only after the founding of the People's Republic of China in 1949 that the traditional marriage system and women's role in the Chinese family came under wholesale attack. Among the very first legislative actions of the communist regime was passage of a new marriage law that prohibited arranged and forced marriage; abolished polygamy, concubinage, and "little daughter-in-law" marriage; and stipulated that marriage should be a free decision between an adult man and an adult woman. However, even with lofty ideals and sometimes drastic actions, changes on the ground were probably more evolutionary than revolutionary, particularly in rural villages where the vaguely worded law with no clear punishment for noncompliance had limited impact on deeply rooted patriarchal power and tradition.

In overthrowing the old marriage regime, where family and kin elders controlled marital decision making, the communist government strengthened the autonomy of the couple. At the same time the state reinstitutionalized marriage, it also liberated individuals from the old cultural institutions, thereby encouraging new "rules of the game" for modern socialist marriages. Individuals' new marital independence, however, was limited (Croll 1981). Lack of private space, both at home and in public, further facilitated the omnipresent interference in individual choice. Even as the decision to marry increasingly became the choice of the young couple (Davis and Harrell 1993; Whyte 1990, 1993), the Chinese state retained an active role by requiring registration, dictating minimum marriage ages, and confining all births to monogamous married couples (see Davis Chapter 2). In this way, the new Marriage Law expanded the scope and nature of biopolitical state power by managing individuals and their marriages in the name of promoting a stronger nation and improved population quality (Foucault 1998).

Over the first two decades after the initial implementation of the 1950 Marriage Law, age at first marriage rose only gradually. However, when the government sought new ways to slow population growth via the 1970s policy of late marriage, longer birth interval, and fewer births (晚、稀、少), state policy systematically raised marriage age well above the statutory minimums of eighteen for women and twenty for men and marked one of the most direct government interventions to reshape marriage and marital fertility of any modern society (Coale 1989; Wang and Tuma 1993). Such a forceful intervention not only ran counter to the communists' early promises of individual choice in marital decisions but also invited strong resistance and complaints. Nevertheless, the subsequent decision in 1979 to go beyond the exhortations and rewards of the "later, longer, fewer" campaign and dictate one birth each for all women represented an even more radical state intervention in population control (Greenhalgh 2008; Wang, Cai, and Gu 2012).

Implementation of the one-child policy coincided with a new marriage law in 1980 that raised the minimum ages of marriage to twenty for women and twenty-two for men. These minimum ages, however, were actually lower than de facto ones enforced by local governments during the "later, longer, fewer" campaign. Thus, the 1980 law unexpectedly reversed the earlier trends of an ever-higher age at first marriage. The consequence of this convergence,

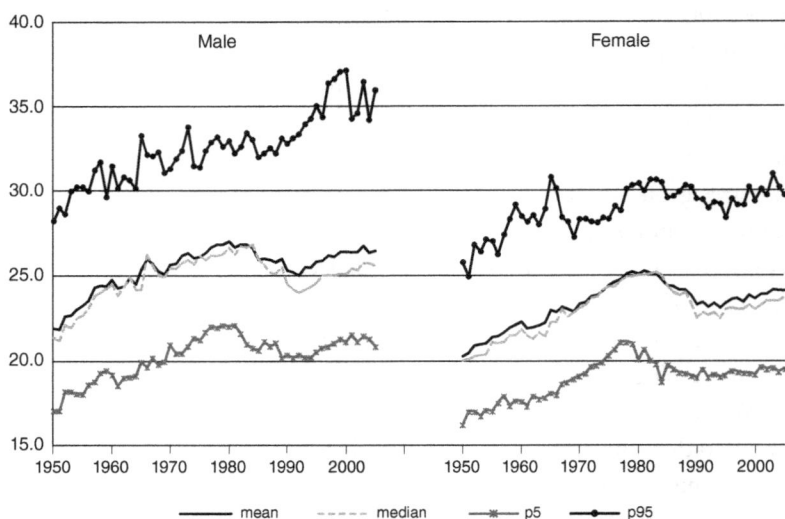

Figure 4.1. The rise of age at first marriage, Shanghai, 1950–2005.
SOURCE: Calculated using 2005 1% Population Change Survey.

ironically, was a short-lived baby boom between 1980 and 1983 that canceled out the initial impact of the one-child policy (Coale 1989; Feeney et al. 1989).

Within a few years, however, as the one-child policy became routinized and urban couples lost control over procreation, individuals regained some control over the timing of dating and mating. Thus, as the government retreated from policing the timing and dissolution of marriage to focus on the number of births, marriage choices were returned to individuals and their families, and the average age at first marriage after 1990 again trended upward and soon exceeded the statutory minimums. Such trends are seen throughout China but are most prominent in urban China, especially in cities such as Shanghai (see Table 1.1 and Figure 4.1).

In the remainder of this chapter, we use urban Shanghai as a location to examine this uneven trajectory toward late marriage in contemporary China. We summarize broad shifts and then analyze different dimensions of change. We focus on the differences between females and males and give particular attention to variation by time and across different levels of education. Beyond tracing the change in marriage ages in Shanghai over a half century, our analysis also explains how different underlying forces drove these shifts.

SHANGHAI: SETTING AND DATA SOURCE

The history of Shanghai captures several of the most critical economic and social transformations in China over the last two centuries. As one of the original five ports opened to Western commerce under the Treaty of Nanjing of
1842, Shanghai like Guangzhou quickly incorporated many elements of Western culture as it emerged as a cradle of China's modernization. By the early
twentieth century, Shanghai had already grown from a small coastal town
into an economic center of the Far East and the world.[2] After 1949, Shanghai again became a national leader of fundamental economic and political
change. Although Shanghai was no longer a free port once the Communist
Party assumed control, it remained one of few windows that China kept open
to the outside world. Shanghai's new state-owned economy dominated Chinese industry. After market reforms reopened Shanghai to the world in the
early 1980s, the city not only retained its domestic leadership position but
also became one of the world's major economic and financial centers. Today,
Shanghai is China's largest and wealthiest city with a population of over 23
million and a per capita GDP in excess of US$10,000.

Shanghai has also led the nation in promoting and enforcing government
policies to delay marriage and childbearing. As early as 1958, city leaders advocated population control and late marriage (Guo 1996), and shortly after the
end of the Great Leap Forward famine, they further intensified their efforts. In
1963, the city was the first to implement local rules to raise the marriage age
beyond the statutory minimum, and in 1971 the leaders exhorted residents
to delay both marriage and childbearing. By 1974, Shanghai was effectively
enforcing a minimum marriage age of twenty-five for males and twenty-three
for females; in August 1978, the city government pushed for an even higher
minimum of twenty-seven for urban men and twenty-five for urban women.[3]

In the absence of new national legislation, municipal policies could only
advocate late marriage as "advanced behavior" and offer financial and welfare
rewards to those who met the government's definition of late marriage. In reality, however, the "late marriage age criterion" was implemented as a compul-
sory rule. Those who did not answer the call could be denied their application
for marriage registration. Moreover, because the city government controlled
such necessities as job assignment and housing provision, compliance could
be relatively easily enforced. Subsequently, Shanghai's approach of using late
marriage in combination with exhortation to lengthen birth intervals and

bear fewer children was adopted as a national policy, although few places enforced an age of marriage as high as Shanghai's.

China's revision of the Marriage Law in 1980 signaled a new era in the state's intervention in the institution of marriage. Although the 1980 revision of the Marriage Law designated minimum marriage ages (twenty for women and twenty-two for men) that were two years higher than those stipulated in the 1950 law, these minimums fell well below those set by the birth planning policies of the 1970s. Moreover, the 1980 law also marked a turning point in the state's attitude toward governing society based on voluntary participation and rule of law rather than administrative fiat. In these ways, changes in the 1980 marriage law were consistent with the larger blueprint for other economic and social reforms that revitalized and rejuvenated a society still emerging from the turmoil of the Cultural Revolution.

The revision of the Marriage Law in 1980, however, did not mean that the Chinese government had totally abandoned the policy of late marriage as a method of population control. Rather, the enforcement of "late marriage" continued and was further incorporated into local birth control regulations. Thus, for example, in Shanghai's Birth Planning Regulations of 1981, late marriage ages were still five years above the legal minimums, and only in 1990 were they lowered to three years above the legal minimums. According to the 1990 revision of Shanghai's Birth Planning Regulation, couples who met "late marriage age" criteria could have one week of vacation time for their honeymoon and more time for parental leaves. Nevertheless, as we saw in Table 1.1 and Figure 4.1, average age at first marriage for men and women in 1990 was below those of both 1970 and 1980.

Although there were no further revisions to government regulations on marriage age following the 1990 publication of the Birth Planning Regulations, in other demographic dimensions Shanghai experienced profound transformations after 1980. In 2010, Shanghai boasted China's lowest fertility and mortality, with total fertility lower than 1.0 and life expectancy higher than eighty years. Yet, because of massive in-migration from other parts of China, the population has expanded from 13 million to 23 million in just two decades. By the early twenty-first century, over a quarter of Shanghai's population were migrants from other provinces, two out of five workers were migrants, and a third of all marriages involved a nonnative partner. Among babies delivered in Shanghai in 2007, over 40 percent were born to parents who were not native Shanghainese (Ruan 2009). Shanghai, in other words, is now a new Shanghai.

To explore how the institution of marriage has changed in this new Shanghai, we use data from China's Inter-Census Survey of 2005 conducted by the National Bureau of Statistics. In China, a full population census takes place every ten years at years ending with a zero, and an inter-census population survey, also referred to as a 1 percent population sample survey or mini-census, is conducted in years ending with a five. A mini-census is very similar to a full census except in its probabilistic design. The mini-census uses a Probability Proportionate to Estimated Size (PPES) sampling method to ensure representation at the provincial level, with resident groups in rural areas and neighborhood committees in urban areas as primary sampling units (called enumeration districts). Target populations are all current residents in the selected enumeration districts, with or without a local household registration, and include those who maintain local household registration but were away at the time of enumeration. The 1 percent survey questionnaire in 2005 was very similar to the census questionnaires of 2000 and 2010, with thirty-five items at the individual level and twenty items at the household level. The data used in this analysis are a 15 percent subsample of the mini-census for Shanghai.

Using the mini-census data we can track changes in marriage age between 1950 and 2005.[4] To generate data needed to estimate variation between ages of spouses, we used a computer algorithm to match marriage partners within a household according to their relationship with the household head. Due to a selective effect on or through mortality, age at marriage for early years calculated from the survey could present some biases.[5] However, further examination indicates such a bias is minimal in Shanghai and does not change the trend of marriage age, as we shall describe in the following pages.[6]

FROM COLLECTIVE SYNCHRONIZATION TO INDIVIDUAL CHOICE

As illustrated in Figure 4.1, Shanghai has experienced two distinct episodes of rising age at first marriage. By comparing summary statistics that capture both central tendencies and variability in changes in marriage age, we can identify three distinct phases: 1949 to 1979, 1980 to 1990, and post-1990.

During the first phase, the trend toward later marriage for both men and women in Shanghai was more gradual and linear than in the nation as a whole

(Coale 1989; Wang and Yang 1996). However, one does observe some minor interruptions during the period of the Great Leap Forward around 1960 and a slightly faster pace of change for men in the 1950s and for females after 1970. These interruptions in the pattern reflect in part the government's drive to integrate birth control targets within the push for late marriage.

Then, quite unexpectedly and dramatically, the upward trend in age at first marriage was reversed after 1980; by 1990, mean age at first marriage had dropped to 25.3 for males and 23.3 for females. In the subsequent fifteen years, one observes a steady rise for both men and women similar to that found across all of China (Zhang and Gu 2007).

A comparison of mean and median ages also identifies increasing variation within marriage cohorts. Generally, median ages at first marriage do not depart greatly from mean ages. However, as the mean is sensitive to those marrying at the oldest age, the mean values are usually higher than the medians. But in Shanghai means and medians for both men and women were almost identical during the years of forced synchronization, illustrating the compressed range of ages at marriage during this time period. Only when the government loosened its control over marriage age do we see the reemergence of a positively skewed marriage age distribution, especially on the male side (see Figure 4.1). Individuals began to marry at different ages, with more at the higher ages, instead of concentrating at or near the age stipulated by the government.

Another interesting shift since 1990 is the greater differences between the men and women who are the last to marry and all others. For example, in Figure 4.1 we observe how, in the decades of state intervention, the rising age at first marriage among the last 5 percent to marry (the ninety-fifth percentile) had some distinctive spikes while their slopes paralleled those of the mean, particularly for men. After 1990, however, the ninety-fifth percentile age for the last marrying men spikes up while mean and median only creep higher. By contrast, among women, the reduced role of state intervention initially pushed mean age down among the last 5 percent to marry, but then in the late 1990s the trend reversed and settled at around age thirty. Unlike the mean and median ages, which have yet to reach the historical highs of the early 1980s, among those in the ninety-fifth percentile, or the last 5 percent to marry, age at first marriage has now reached a historical high. A new era of delaying marriage has begun, starting with a group of pioneers.

Trends in Figure 4.1 on the first 5 percent to marry tell a different but equally interesting story. Here one sees a pattern that has no distinctive shift after 1990. In fact, the story among these men and women who marry first is a persistent incidence of underage marriage. Thus, even in Shanghai, where the social and cultural environment makes the population more receptive to the idea of late marriage and where the government has had more effective control over its population than in other regions, there was still a nontrivial proportion of people marrying before reaching the legal minimum age. Prior to 1980, when the legal minimum age at marriage was still twenty for males and eighteen for females, there were marriages formed under these ages.[7] Similarly, there were also marriages taking place, as shown by the fifth percentile curves in Figure 4.1, under the legal age of twenty-two for males and twenty for females after 1980, as reported for other, less urban locales in China (Davis and Harrell 1993). However, the relaxation of marriage age control in the 1980s had a smaller effect on the first 5 percent to marry than on the last 5 percent, suggesting that there is likely a new culturally defined minimum age at marriage.

Another distinction between the changes in the first and second upturn in marriage age is that, whereas the marriage age range remained constant or even shrunk after 1990, variability as captured by changes in the standard deviation from mean age of marriage has increased. As shown in Figure 4.2,

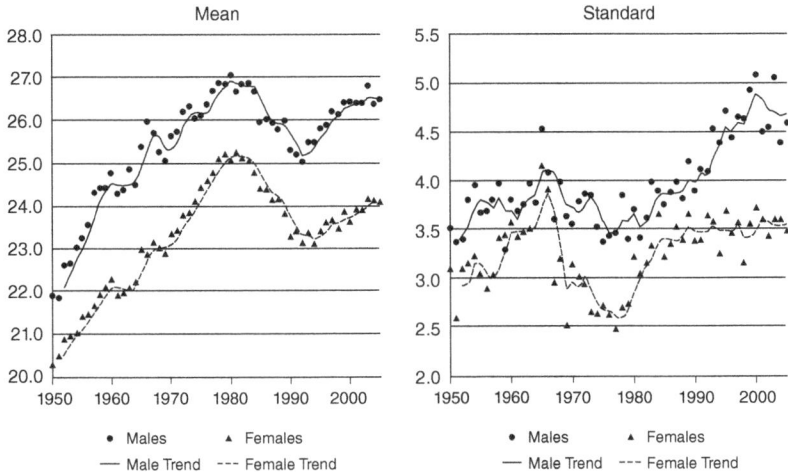

Figure 4.2. Mean and standard deviation of age at first marriage, Shanghai, 1950–2005.

SOURCE: Calculated using 2005 1% Population Change Survey.

parallel to the rise in marriage age up through the late 1970s was a decline in the variability of marriage age, especially for women (right panel). The variability for women declined from 3.5 years to below 2.5 years before it started to reverse in 1980, most likely due to the loosening of age at marriage controls and the start of individual liberalization in marriage timing. By the 1990s, the standard deviation for women's age at first marriage had returned to the level of the pre–"late marriage" era. For men, although the decline in the 1970s was not as steep, the increase since 1980 was much stronger, reflecting changes in marriage norms and marriage market conditions. Such a contrast in standard deviation suggests that between 1970 and 1980 a forceful government policy effectively synchronized marriage age across regions and social strata, while the diverse economic, cultural, and social forces empowering individual choice as part of market reforms have promoted more variability in the decades since 1990.

A similar shift away from state-forced synchronization to greater individual freedom can also be observed in a comparison of the age differences between husbands and wives. While the new marriage law of 1950 broke many traditions of the Chinese marriage system, it nevertheless enforced female age hypergamy by stipulating a two-year age difference between the male and female minimum age at marriage. The institutionalization of age hypergamy combined with the push for later age of marriage virtually eliminated the practice found in some parts of China where parents preferred daughters-in-law to be older than grooms. Such an effect can be seen in Figure 4.3, where we see that the proportion of females marrying a younger husband plunged in the 1950s and then stabilized at about 20 percent. It can be argued that this pattern is a result of legally institutionalized age hypergamy.

The forced synchronization of marriage age not only routinized a two-year age difference between males and females but also reduced the variation in age differences between spouses. As shown in the right panel of Figure 4.3, by the late 1970s variability in the age difference between spouses reached its lowest point. The factors shaping age difference, however, vary over time. Prior to 1970, change was driven partly by the declining percentage of women marrying younger men (as shown in the left panel of Figure 4.3), whereas more recently the age gap is widening as many men marry younger women. Shanghai residents not only marry later but also to spouses of a wider age range.

The changing age at first marriage in Shanghai reflects both cultural resilience and cultural transformation. The recent changes in the marriage insti-

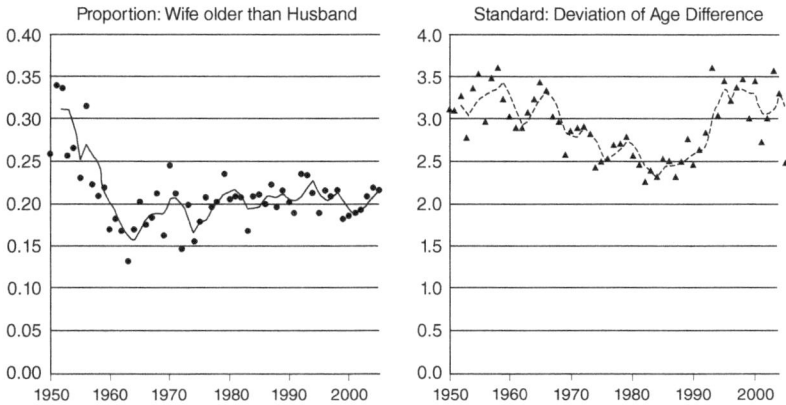

Figure 4.3. Age difference within married couples by marriage year, Shanghai, 1950–2005.

SOURCE: Calculated using 2005 1% Population Change Survey.

tution, however, seem to be more evolutionary than revolutionary. As shown by the experiences of Shanghai couples, even the forceful push toward "late marriage" by government fiat only had a temporary effect. Looking from a long-term perspective, therefore, age at first marriage in urban Shanghai has been rising steadily and gradually, but looked at with a finer temporal metric the intensity and sometimes even the direction of change varied by period and institutional conditions.

CHANGING PATTERNS OF INDIVIDUAL BEHAVIOR

As of 2005, we observe both a higher mean age at first marriage and greater variation around that higher mean (Figure 4.2). What, however, have been the effects of these changes on individuals' expectations for and experiences of marriage itself? In particular, to what extent can we interpret a higher marriage age and greater variation as a choice to never marry? And can we now identify those who are both most likely to delay marriage and those who will never marry? The connection between late marriage and the rising marriage age is obvious, but to equate the delay with a retreat from or rejection of marriage is not.

Overall, even in Shanghai, delayed marriage has not yet translated into large numbers of men and women never marrying. Rather, as we see in Table 4.1, at age thirty-five through thirty-nine, only 6 percent of males and

Table 4.1. Current marital status by age, Shanghai, 2005.

Sex	Age Group	N	Never married	First marriage	Remarried	Divorced	Widowed
			Percentage				
Male	25–29	3,437	38.6	60.8	0.2	0.4	0.0
	30–34	3,393	12.0	85.6	0.7	1.7	0.1
	35–39	3,258	6.1	89.8	1.9	2.1	0.1
	40–44	3,490	5.4	87.9	2.8	3.8	0.2
	Total	13,578	15.6	80.9	1.4	2.0	0.1
Female	25–29	3,597	23.6	75.3	0.5	0.6	0.1
	30–34	3,328	5.7	91.0	1.5	1.7	0.1
	35–39	3,071	2.0	91.6	3.3	2.8	0.3
	40–44	3,262	0.8	91.1	3.7	3.7	0.8
	Total	13,258	8.5	86.9	2.2	2.2	0.3

SOURCE: Calculated using 2005 1% Population Change Survey.

2 percent of females had never married in 2005. Among those age forty to forty-four, virtually all females were married and only 5 percent of men were still single.[8]

However, these percentages should be read with caution in predicting changes in the future. The marriage profiles in Table 4.1 reflect experiences of different age cohorts and young people aged twenty-five to twenty-nine in the year 2005 may not follow in the footsteps of those born ten or fifteen years earlier. It is possible, therefore, that in the future the trend of late marriage we see in Shanghai and in China as a whole may result in a higher percentage of both women and men never marrying. Using published Chinese statistics, we calculated that, for urban China as a whole, a very significant change took place between 1995 and 2008. In 1995, only 10 percent of women aged twenty-five to twenty-nine had never married. By 2008, the share increased to 27 percent. Even among those aged thirty to thirty-four, the share of never-married women increased from 2 to 6 percent. These numbers of never-married women for urban China as a whole are very close to the numbers in Shanghai as of 2005.

Should the trend we observe between 1995 and 2008 continue, it is highly likely that changing sociocultural norms and demographic conditions will increase the future likelihood of less marriage among China's urban residents. However, the factors are gender distinct and therefore require a gender-specific hypothesis about the impact of delayed marriage on the probability of never marrying. The first sociocultural factor affecting women's likelihood of never marrying is the currently socially prescribed belief that a woman over the age of thirty is an undesirable bride (see Zhang and Sun Chapter 5, for analysis of the discourse on surplus women [剩女]). The other demographic factor is the unbalanced sex ratio at birth that has persisted since the early 1980s in China, and that has created a significantly larger number of men than women in every cohort coming of age since the late 1990s (Cai and Lavely 2007). As these excess men reach their marriage age, they will experience greater difficulty finding a bride.

Social patterns of late marriage in Shanghai provide further insight into the future trajectory of changes in the marriage institution in China. A large body of literature on marriage timing in other settings has already established a clear link between marriage timing and an individual's social and economic characteristics such as gender, educational attainment, employment, earnings, place of residence, and race (Jones 2007; Mason et al. 1998; Oppenheimer 1988, 1994, 1997; Sweeney 2002; Thornton and Lin 2004; Tsuya and Bumpass 2004). These studies are based on populations not only in the United States but also in a number of Asian settings. In Shanghai, among women aged twenty-five to thirty-four in 2005, higher levels of educational attainment are associated with a high likelihood of never marrying. Whereas only 6 percent and 18 percent of women in this age cohort with junior and senior high school education respectively were single, nearly 40 percent of the college educated had never married. Similarly, at age thirty-five to forty-four, when marriage was indeed universal among women with junior high school or lower educational attainment, more than 4 percent of college-educated women in Shanghai had still never unmarried, suggesting that this is the group of women most likely to forego marriage altogether.

Moreover, over time, we observe an increased degree of variation by levels of education. To illustrate such a change over time, we calculate the likelihood (or risk) of getting married by gender at each age for two ten-year time periods: 1971–1980 versus 1996–2005. The period-based risks are then interpreted for a syndicated cohort (that is, a cohort assumed to live through its life with the currently observed age pattern of marriage to illustrate the cumulative risk of marriage). The results are presented in Figure 4.4. During the period of forced collective synchronization in the 1970s, we find little variation in marriage timing by education. The only exception was women with only primary education, whose age of marriage was significantly younger than that

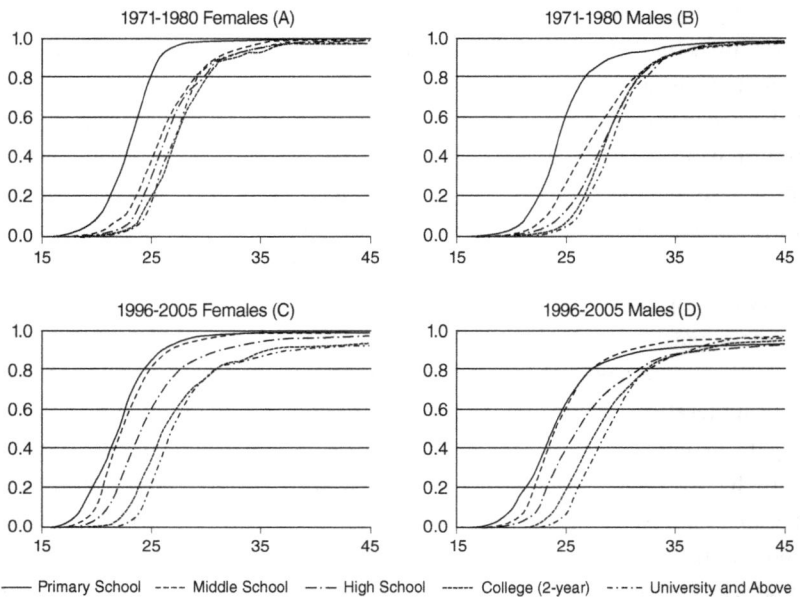

Figure 4.4. Marriage patterns in Shanghai by age, gender, and education, 1971–1980 versus 1996–2005 (Kaplan-Meier estimates of cumulative risk of getting married).

SOURCE: Calculated using 2005 1% Population Change Survey.

of women in other educational groups (Panel A of Figure 4.4). As a result of forced synchronization, we observe virtually no difference among women with other levels of education. Another notable feature of this earlier period is that, by age thirty-five, virtually all women, regardless of educational attainment, had married. A similar pattern of convergence is seen for males where only the least educated group deviates from the median age.[9]

As levels of educational attainment rose after 1980, we also see greater differentiation in marriage timing by level of education. For example, over the decade from 1971 to 1980, females, regardless of educational attainment, eventually converged at universal marriage (Figure 4.4 top panels), whereas if the marriage risk of the 1996 to 2005 decade holds, about 2 percent of all women will stay single at the age of forty-five, and among those with the highest education level, the percentage of singles could reach 7 percent. Thus, by 2005, we see a pattern among women with the highest levels of education that departs from similarly educated women in earlier decades as well as from their less-educated age peers.

For men, the story for the 1996 to 2005 decade is different but equally interesting. Given an imbalanced sex ratio both historically and in recent decades (Cai and Lavely 2007; Coale and Banister 1994) and the strong emphasis in Chinese culture on continuing the family patriline, many have worried about the consequence of a distorted sex balance: a large number of so-called surplus men who cannot find a suitable marriage partner. However, because marriage is a symbol of social success and status (Lee and Wang 1999; Wang and Tuma 1993), it is unlikely that all men will be affected equally by the demographic deficit. Indeed, our data from Shanghai documents not only the ability of high-status men to marry but increasingly their greater likelihood of marrying as compared to their high-status female age peers. Although men with a primary school education start to marry at earlier ages and at a faster pace than other men, by their late twenties they are less likely to marry than those with a middle school education (see Figure 4.4, Panel D). In fact, if men with the lowest level of education do not marry before the age of thirty, their chances of ever marrying are significantly diminished, a predicament they share with the most educated women. At the same time, males with higher levels of education who generally delay marriage quickly catch up. By age thirty-five, the cumulative risk of getting married across three levels of education—high school, two-year college, and four-year university—converges (see Figure 4.4, panel D). Most importantly, whereas there are more "late marriages" among men with university-level education, these men eventually become, by age forty-five, the group most likely to have ever been married.

The divergence in marriage patterns between males and females with the highest levels of education (two-year college and university degrees) confirms our earlier observation that both individual choice and strong cultural preferences determine age of marriage. Because women face cultural norms of educational hypergamy and age hypergamy, better-educated women often must make a choice between marrying a man with less education or not marrying at all. By contrast, the best-educated men are able to delay marriage even until age forty and still translate their status advantage into marital opportunities (see Figure 4.4, Panels C and D).

CONCLUSION AND DISCUSSION

In a time span of half a century, the institution of marriage, a traditional social pillar of Chinese society, has witnessed profound changes as showcased by the marriage patterns documented for residents of Shanghai, China's most cosmopolitan city. The first socialist marriage law of 1950 liberated individuals from the rules of their family elders and led to a gradual increase in age at marriage but did not weaken the marriage institution itself. The state's enforcement of late marriage in the 1970s pushed age at marriage to a historical high, reducing individual differences and creating a collective synchronization. When such intervention weakened, marriage age first fell and then slowly began to rise again. However, the most recent upturn in age at first marriage is accompanied by greater age variation among newly married couples. And, unlike the first era of late marriage that was reversed when state intervention was withdrawn, the current trend carries its own momentum and appears to show no signs of reversal or even of having reached a plateau.

Simultaneous with the reemergence of late marriage, we also find a move away from the traditional model of universal marriage. Such a trend resembles what has taken place in societies elsewhere, including those in East Asia, and departs from the patterns seen only two decades ago in urban China, where delay of marriage was associated with a "stalled wall," after which almost all young people eventually married (Whyte 1993). As of 2005 and based on data from the 2005 population sample survey, however, 22 percent of college-educated men and 16 percent of college-educated women had yet to marry by age thirty-five. With the rapid expansion of higher education in China, especially women's education, we predict that China may face a marriage revolution characterized by more and more young people choosing to stay out of the marriage institution altogether, a revolution that has already occurred in neighboring societies such as Japan and South Korea.

The reemergence of late marriage in Shanghai takes place in the broad context of rapid socioeconomic liberalization, marketization, and globalization. Romantic relationships and self-fulfillment have replaced family obligation and patrilineal reproduction as the primary rationale for marriage (see Farrer Chapter 3). At the same time, a highly competitive environment that puts a price tag on virtually everything has turned mate choice and marriage decisions into a rational calculation weighing costs and benefits. Although we were not able to directly analyze connections between socioeconomic factors and marriage decisions, our analysis demonstrates that there is a very strong relationship between education and marriage. Education has direct effects on the timing of marriage, but it also influences the relative position of men and women in the marriage market.

Rising age at marriage is just one aspect of multifaceted changes in China's marriage institution. Increasing rates of premarital sex, cohabitation, divorce, and extramarital sex also pose challenges to an institution that for a thousand years was deeply embedded in a kinship system that subordinated the individual desires of men and women to advancement and reproduction of patrilineal, patrilocal, and patriarchal families. Further analysis should examine marriage not only as an outcome but also as an agent of social change that has profound effects on many other aspects of Chinese society.

There is a clear parallel between changing marriage patterns in China and what Cherlin (2004) has labeled the "deinstitutionalization" of marriage in the United States and other Western societies. As we have documented in this chapter, entrance into marriage and family formation has begun to deviate dramatically from the traditional expectations of Confucian familism. Yet, unlike the deinstitutionalization of marriage in the United States, alternative forms of family and household formation have not emerged as quickly as changes in the age of first marriage or proportions delaying marriage past age thirty-five. Marriage in China remains a strong social institution, and, unlike in the West, it is still the exclusive gateway to parenthood (Lesthaeghe 2010; Whyte 1995). Moreover, whereas changing patterns of marriage and household formation in the West are rooted deeply in a strong culture of individualism, in China both in 1950 and over the past several decades changes in the rules of the game for marriage have often been promoted by an active state with its own social and political agendas. Unlike in the United States, where individuals on the margins seek the state's protection for nontraditional preferences and behaviors, in China the state leads the way to change and replace social norms based on Confucian tradition with laws and rules that not only directly promote its socioeconomic and political agendas but also indirectly legitimate and encourage individual choices in private life. It would not be an exaggeration to say that the major changes to the marriage institution in China over the last half century have derived from negotiations between social traditions and an active government with its own social and demographic goals.

It is still too early to appreciate fully the implications of reemergence of late marriage in Shanghai for the institution of marriage in China. Whyte (1995) concludes his analysis of marriage change in China as follows: "Only if the social structure in the PRC were altered in ways that gave young people (and others) more personal autonomy and weakened the links between premarital behavior and chances for desirable futures would we expect them to feel free to act on these new ideas." It appears that these structural changes have now arrived, as personal choices and self-fulfillment are increasingly the driving motivation behind changes in marriage in China. This trend will likely continue for decades to come. Will China become more like the United States, where cohabitation has become a de facto competitor of marriage, or more like Japan, where marriage stays largely intact as a social institution but many choose to stay away? In the absence of clear indicators, we hesitate to make such a prediction, at least for now.

NOTES

1. Thus, for example in Shanghai, China's largest and most cosmopolitan urban center, mean age at first marriage first rose from twenty for females and twenty-two for males in the early 1950s to twenty-five for females and twenty-seven for males by the late 1970s, the highest among any Chinese cities. Yet mean marriage age dropped precipitously after 1980, by two years both for females and males, only to be followed by a gradual rise again, approaching the level of the previous peaks by the early twenty-first century (see Table 1.1).

2. Shanghai's population totaled 1.3 million in 1910 and doubled to 2.6 by 1927. By 1932, Shanghai had become the world's fifth largest city and home to 70,000 foreigners.

3. In rural counties of Shanghai, the minimum age then was twenty-five for men and twenty-three for women.

4. We are able to do so because the survey contains information on not only the current marital status of the population in 2005 but also the year and month of the first marriage.

5. If healthier individuals marry later and also live longer, an estimate of marriage age based on survivors' information could produce an average age higher than what was truly the case.

6. Nationally, estimated ages at first marriage based on the 2005 mini-census for women married between 1940 and 1970 were about 0.5 to 1.0 year higher than those estimated from the 1988 Fertility Survey. The difference is in the opposite direction but smaller for men. The exact reasons for such a gap and for the gender difference require further investigation. One main suspect is the large rural/urban gap in mortality and marriage in China. No major difference is found for Shanghai, for either males or females.

7. It is possible that many of those "underage marriages" were to migrants who married elsewhere before moving to Shanghai. Due to limitation in our data, we cannot check this hypothesis.

8. This age pattern is rather similar to what was observed in Taiwan only decades earlier, where the share of never-married women aged twenty-five to twenty-nine increased substantially from 9 to 32 percent between 1970 and 1990, but the number at age forty through forty-four increased only from 1 to 5 percent, showing still a prevalent marriage regime (Thornton and Lin 2004: 204).

9. The convergence for males among different educational groups also occurred by age thirty-five, but the level of convergence is below one, or 100 percent marriage, as was the case for females (top right panel of Figure 4.4).

REFERENCES

Cai, Yong, and William Lavely. 2007. "Child Sex Ratios and Their Regional Variation." In *Transition and Challenge—China's Population at the Beginning of the 21st Century*, Zhongwei Zhao and Fei Guo, eds., pp. 108–123. Oxford, UK: Oxford University Press.

Cherlin, Andrew J. 2004. "The Deinstitutionalization of American Marriage." *Journal of Marriage and Family* 66: 848–861.

Coale, Ansley J. 1989. "Marriage and Childbearing in China since 1940." *Social Forces* 67(June): 833–850.

Coale, Ansley J., and Judith Banister. 1994. "Five Decades of Missing Females in China." *Demography* 31(3): 459–479.

Croll, Elizabeth. 1981. *The Politics of Marriage in Contemporary China*. Cambridge, UK: Cambridge University Press.

Davis, Deborah, and Stevan Harrell, eds. 1993. *Chinese Families in the Post-Mao Era*. Berkeley: University of California Press.

Feeney, Griffith, Wang Feng, Zhou Mingkun, and Xiao Baoyu. 1989. "Recent Fertility Dynamics in China: Results from the 1987 One Percent Population Survey." *Population and Development Review* 15(2): 297–322.

Foucault, Michel. [1976] 1998. *The History of Sexuality* Vol. 1: The Will to Knowledge. London: Penguin.

Greenhalgh, Susan. 2008. *Just One Child: Science and Policy in Deng's China*. Berkeley: University of California Press.

Guo, Shenyang. 1996. "Determinants of Fertility Decline in Shanghai: Development or Policy?" In *China: the Many Facets of Demographic Change*, Alice Goldstein and Wang Feng, eds., pp. 81–96. Boulder, CO: Westview Press.

Hajnal, John. 1953. "Age at Marriage and Proportions Marrying." *Population Studies* 7: 111–136.

———. 1982. 'Two Kinds of Preindustrial Household Formation System." *Population and Development Review* 8(3): 449–494.

Jones, Gavin. 2007. "Delayed Marriage and Very Low Fertility in Pacific Asia." *Population and Development Review* 33(3): 453–478.

Lee, James, and Wang Feng. 1999. *One Quarter of Humanity: Malthusian Mythology and Chinese Realities, 1700-2000*. Cambridge, MA: Harvard University Press.

Lee, James, Wang Feng, and Danching Ruan. 2001. "Nuptiality among the Qing Nobility: 1640–1900." In *Asian Population History*, Tsui-jung Liu et al., eds., pp. 353–373. Oxford, UK: Oxford University Press.

Lesthaeghe, Ronald. 2010. "The Unfolding Story of the Second Demographic Transition." *Population and Development Review* 36(2): 211–251

Macfarlane, Alan. 1986. *Marriage and Love in England, Modes of Reproduction 1300–1840*. Oxford, UK: Basil Blackwell.

Malthus, Thomas. 1798 (reprint 1998). "An Essay on the Principle of Population." Amherst, NY: Prometheus Books.

Mason, Karen O., Noriko O. Tsuya, and Minja K. Choe. 1998. *The Changing Family in Comparative Perspective: Asia and the United States*. Honolulu: The East-West Center.

Oppenheimer, Valerie K. 1988. "A Theory of Marriage Timing." *American Journal of Sociology* 94: 563–591.

———. 1994. "Women's Rising Employment and the Future of the Family in Industrial Societies." *Population and Development Review* 20: 293–342. .

———. 1997. "Women's Employment and the Gains to Marriage: The Specialization and Trading Model of Marriage." *Annual Review of Sociology* 23: 431–53.

Ruan, Danching (阮丹青), ed. 2009. 重塑上海人: 上海新老居民一体化研究 (*Remaking Shanghainess: A Study of Integration of New and Old Residents in Shanghai*). Shanghai: Xuelin chubanshe.

Schofield, Roger. 1985. "English Marriage Patterns Revisited." *Journal of Family History* 10(1): 2–20.

Sweeney, Megan M. 2002. "Two Decades of Family Change: The Shifting Economic Foundations of Marriage." *American Sociological Review* 67(1): 132–147.

Thornton, Arland, and Hui-sheng Lin. 2004. *Social Change and the Family in Taiwan*. Chicago: The University of Chicago Press.

Tsuya, Noriko O., and Larry L. Bumpass. 2004. *Marriage, Work, and Family Life in Comparative Perspective: Japan, South Korea, and the United States*. Honolulu: University of Hawaii Press.

Wang, Feng, and Nancy Tuma. 1993. "Changes in Chinese Marriage Patterns during the Twentieth Century." In *Proceedings of the IUSSP International Population Conference*, pp. 337–352. Montreal: IUSSP.

Wang, Feng, and Yang Quanhe. 1996. "Age at Marriage and the First Birth Interval: The Emerging Change in Sexual Behavior among Young Couples in China." *Population Development Review* 22(2): 299–320.

Wang, Feng, Yong Cai, and Baochang Gu. 2012. "Population, Policy, and Politics: How Will History Judge China's One-Child Policy?" *Population and Development Review* 38 (supplement): 115–129.

Whyte, Martin King. 1990. "Changes in Mate Choice in Chengdu." In *Chinese Society on the Eve of Tiananmen*, Deborah Davis and Ezra F. Vogel, eds., pp. 181–214. Cambridge, MA: Harvard University Press.

———. 1993. "Wedding Behavior and Family Strategies in Chengdu." In *Chinese Families in the Post-Mao Era*, Deborah Davis and Stevan Harrell, eds., pp. 189–218. Berkeley: University of California Press.

———. 1995. "From Arranged Marriages to Love Matches in Urban China." In *Family Formation and Dissolution: Perspectives from East and West*, Chin-Chun Yi, ed., pp. 33–83. Sun Yat-Sen Institute for Social Sciences and Philosophy, Book Series (36). Taipei, Taiwan: Academia Sinica.

Wolf, Arthur, and Chieh-shan Huang. 1980. *Marriage and Adoption in China, 1845–1945*. Palo Alto, CA: Stanford University Press.

Yang, C. K. 1959. *Chinese Communist Society: The Family and the Village*. Cambridge, MA: Harvard University Press.

Zhang Guangyu and Gu Baochang. 2007. "Recent Changes in Marriage Patterns." In *Transition and Challenge: China's Population at the Turn of the Twenty-First Century*, Zhongwei Zhao and Fei Guo, eds., pp. 124–139. Oxford, UK: Oxford University Press.

5 WHEN ARE YOU GOING TO GET MARRIED?

Parental Matchmaking and Middle-Class Women
in Contemporary Urban China

Jun Zhang and Peidong Sun

> *There are only a limited number of good young men. For my
> daughter's marriage, I struggled over whether I should come [to
> the Shanghai matchmaking corner] and seek my luck. As for
> young Shanghai men, the older good ones are difficult to find, and
> the rest is a mingling of good and bad who might actually trap
> you. Personally, I really don't want to come. But if I don't come,
> my daughter's marriage problem still has not been solved by now!*
>
> —Ms. Ho, a mother with a thirty-one-year-old graphic designer
> single daughter[1]

> *I am really touched that parents came [to the Shanghai
> matchmaking corner] so early in the morning to interact with
> strangers on their children's behalf. . . . Even without a boyfriend,
> you can still enjoy life on the weekends. You can spend time with
> your parents, try good food, do some shopping, meet with friends,
> or do some reading. There are all sorts of things to do. Why would
> you put matchmaking in the first place, prioritized in your life?
> Totally unnecessary!*
>
> —Jessica, a twenty-eight-year-old single career woman

THREE DECADES AFTER THE LAUNCH OF MARKET REFORMS, Shanghai is a leading
exemplar of China's embrace of globalization and modernization. Yet every
weekend since 2005 in the center of metropolitan Shanghai, middle-aged parents have gathered in People's Park to find mates for their college-educated
children. This "matchmaking corner" (相亲角) seems a jarring revival of "tradition" in China's most cosmopolitan city. Moreover, it is a practice that some
college-educated daughters with good jobs, like Jessica quoted above, find totally unnecessary. However, when one listens to parents such as Mrs. Ho, their
matchmaking efforts seem to be a rational response to the many uncertainties
faced by parents in late middle age. Not only have market reforms created

new uncertainties about this generation's own economic and social position, but they also have created new anxieties about the future happiness and security of their children, especially college-educated daughters who have delayed marriage beyond their late twenties and thus have fallen into the stigmatized category of surplus women or *shengnü* (剩女). Nor are these parental matchmaking corners, driven by high levels of anxiety among middle-aged and elderly urbanites about the futures of their children and themselves, limited to fast-paced, competitive Shanghai. They also exist in other big cities, such as Beijing and Shenzhen, and thus provide more general insights into how radical economic and social transformations have broadly affected expectations of marriage across different generations.

This chapter explores new expectations of marriage from the parents' perspectives, revealing parental concerns, anxieties, and frustrations about the marriage market in a changing urban environment.[2] Some of our evidence comes from secondary sources and census figures, but most comes from hundreds of hours of fieldwork in the matchmaking corner of Shanghai's People's Park from September 2007 through June 2008, with follow-up interviews conducted in 2009. Through extended and sometimes repeated conversations, we built trust with parents and directly witnessed the dynamic process of matchmaking.

Some scholars have seen intense parental investment in their children's marriage as a revival of traditional practices. However, our fieldwork reveals that parental matchmaking is less a residue or revival of traditional practices and more a response to contemporary demographic and economic pressures and to the parents' strong connections to the socialist past, albeit rearticulated through the language of market. To assume continuity of traditional marriage practices distorts our understanding of contemporary urban China in several ways. First, it discounts the experiences of a generation whose life courses have been defined by decades of socialist revolution. Second, it neglects the connection between social structure and cultural practices. Scholars have demonstrated that marriage practices and internal dynamics within the couple and the family are shaped by both specific social contexts and larger historical processes in China (see, for example, Davis and Harrell 1993; Friedman 2006; Whyte 2005; Whyte and Parish 1984; Yan 2003). A focus on parental matchmaking therefore enables us to explore how marriage practices have been influenced by such forces as the intense intergenerational ties created by the one-child policy, the uncertainties of market-oriented economic reforms, ongoing contestation over gender paradigms, and the ideological legacies of a socialist and revolutionary past.

We begin by examining the crucial socioeconomic and demographic contexts for the marriage pressures confronted by urban daughters (see also Chapters 1 and 4). Specifically, we highlight how norms of hypergamy for brides create tensions for single daughters that are exacerbated by high expectations of educational and professional success. We then contextualize the marriage pressure on urban daughters in relation to the discursive field of "surplus women" that emerged out of contestations over gender roles shaped by the diverse political movements and economic forces of China's tumultuous twentieth and early twenty-first centuries. After exploring the institutional, social, and cultural contexts of parental matchmaking, we use our ethnography to illustrate how different life experiences have influenced parental perceptions of the matchmaking corner and have fashioned their choices and expectations regarding marriage and family.

UNMARRIED URBAN DAUGHTERS AND THE EMERGING MIDDLE CLASS

People's Park is a central landmark in metropolitan Shanghai, but since June 2005 a corner of the Park has also become a market-like place, serving as a venue for parental matchmaking on weekends and national holidays.[3] Matchmaking is not unusual in contemporary societies, but rarely do parents take as much initiative as those in the matchmaking corners of Chinese cities. Nor is there often such a clearly defined and lively location as in Shanghai.

The "matchmaking corner" in People's Park is divided into two sections. The first is the "free zone." Here one observes some seniors looking for partners for themselves, but the majority of participants are parents seeking the best match for their only son or daughter. Parents write down their children's basic information such as age, height, and monthly salary on pieces of paper and then clip them to pieces of string tied between the trees, place them on bushes, or lay them on the ground. They sit patiently, waiting for other parents to make inquiries about their children. They also walk around, jotting down the information of those whom they consider candidates for their children. The second section is the "amateur matchmaker zone" (业余红娘区) where the professional or voluntary matchmakers gather. These matchmakers usually have their own rosters of single youngsters for parents to screen. We did interviews and observations in both sections, but most of our attention focuses on parents in the first zone who sought a spouse for their own child.

Besides parental presence, another distinctive feature in the matchmaking scene is that to-be-matched people are predominantly female. The matchmaking agents in the corner distinguish the male candidates from their female counterparts in terms of the handling fee. One of their advertisements made the distinction explicitly: "Amateur Matchmaker: Hundreds of excellent men and women are waiting for you. Free application and recommendation for men. No over-aged women." Parents of single men can have their sons listed in the rosters for free, while parents of single women had to pay 90 Chinese yuan (roughly US$13 in 2008). A recurring comment we heard from the parents was that "there are so many excellent girls here, while excellent boys are just scarce." One of our interviewees estimated that the gender ratio here was one man for every ten women, and another even mentioned one for every twenty.

The urban daughters in the matchmaking corner share many characteristics. Usually aged between twenty-five and thirty-five, these young women hold at least a bachelor's degree. They either grew up in Shanghai or moved to Shanghai for work after their college education. They are company employees, civil servants, or professionals such as accountants, lawyers, and research fellows. Thus, by virtue of their occupational position and good education, they represent secure members of China's new middle class (Li 2004). However, for parents of single women, a daughter's entry into the middle class can create new anxieties.[4]

During the Maoist period, status and income differentials between different jobs and between men and women were relatively small, and although marriage did involve "matching gates" (门当户对), the expectations of an urban woman's parents were not that different from those of a man (Davis 2000). Moreover, the ideological emphasis on the leading role of the urban proletariat suppressed preferences for professionals and made employment in state-owned enterprises (SOEs) a distinct advantage for men (Whyte and Parish 1984). In addition, because most urban work units provided relatively comprehensive and reliable social benefits to all employees regardless of occupation, the material consequences of marrying a man of any particular job status were muted.

Over the successive waves of economic reforms since 1980, the occupational hierarchy has shifted dramatically in both ideological and structural terms (Davis and Wang 2009; Naughton 2007). Many intellectuals and state officials "plunged into the sea" (下海) and became entrepreneurs in the private sector. While many state-owned enterprises confronted with hardship and bankruptcy laid off large number of employees, privately owned factories actively recruited rural migrants and turned China into the "world's factory." The status of workers, who were associated with either SOE layoffs or rural migrants, plunged vis-à-vis white-collar employees and professionals. Simultaneously, the revival of commerce and trade and the arrival of transnational companies created job opportunities for lawyers, accountants, and managers that required higher education (Hoffman 2010). Reform did not mean that no state jobs were desirable. In fact, with the government reforms promoted by the late leader Deng Xiaoping (Shambaugh 2000), civil servant posts became highly prized among college graduates because of their stability and social benefits.

Not required to fight for resources with brothers as a result of the one-child policy implemented since the late 1970s, urban daughters have become the center of family investment (Fong 2002); as the number of spots in college grew rapidly, women's rates of enrollment rose faster than those of their male peers.[5] Furthermore, because the expanded educational opportunities among urban daughters coincided with the expansion of white-collar and professional jobs, the generation born after 1980 has had relatively easy access to China's new middle class. But contemporary norms of hypergamy still require that women marry men who are older than they and who boast equal or superior educational and occupational status.[6] As a result, the increased gap between blue-collar and white-collar wages and the success of women in both university exams and the professional job market have created a situation in which college-educated women who have not married by their late twenties are perceived as having limited opportunity to marry. These women are called "surplus women" in the media. And for parents of only daughters, the educational and professional success they so intently advocated for their daughters now has become a source of great anxiety.

Despite the norm of hypergamy, women should have a demographic advantage in the marriage market. Nationwide, the sex ratio of boys to girls at birth has increased steadily from the "natural" rate of 106:100 in the late 1970s to 120:100 in 2004. Although census data is not irrefutable (Zhai and Yang 2009), it is widely accepted that by 2009 men outnumbered women in every cohort under the age of thirty. Even in Shanghai, where sex ratios are not as

Table 5.1. The never-married population with college education and above, divided by age group according to the 2000 Shanghai Census.

Age group	Total number		Never-married men		Never-married women	
	Men	Women	Number	As percentage of the total number of men	Number	As percentage of the total number of women
25–29	7136	4883	4310	60%	1898	39%
30–34	5656	3600	1113	20%	412	11%
35–39	5117	2401	357	7%	103	4%
40–44	2764	1033	112	4%	28	3%
45–49	2590	1095	49	2%	34	3%
50 and over	5526	5889	152	1%	138	2%

SOURCE: Shanghai Population Census Office (上海人口普查办公室). "Shanghai 2000 Population Census Assembly" (上海市2000人口普查统计资料汇编), Retrieved on April 28, 2010, from http://chinadataonline.org/member/census2000/ybtableview_c.asp?ID=3885.

distorted as in rural areas, it is men, not women, who are more likely never to marry in every age group, including among those with a college degree (see Table 5.1).

To summarize, census data depict a reality that differs both from the "surplus women" discourse and from parents' perceptions that there are more excellent women than men. The question, therefore, is not whether these parents are correct that there are surplus women, but *why* parents feel so anxious and what their anxiety reveals about broader concerns regarding the institution of marriage in China's major cities. Research repeatedly has shown that urbanization and industrialization raise the average age at first marriage, but as Cai and Wang explained in Chapter 4, in Shanghai it is only very recently that these macrosocietal changes rather than explicit state interventions have driven marriage ages upward in the same direction as other societies (Goode 1963; Raymo 1998; Retherford, Ogawa and Matsukura 2001; United Nations 2008). In addition, in China men and women from both the generation of the parents in the marriage corner and that of their unmarried children have been deeply affected by China's unique one-child policy. In most cases, the parents represent the first generation of urban residents limited to a single child and their children the first generation of singletons.

In response to the one-child policy, the parents of daughters and sons have channeled substantial energy into providing unprecedented opportunities for their only child to develop careers and lifestyles that are compatible with their educational and economic status. Part of this parental strategy includes encouraging daughters to delay finding a boyfriend until they are at least securely established in university. Thus, although as Farrer observed (Chapter 3), there is an emerging culture among urban, educated youth in which extensive dating relationships are separated from marriage, many daughters in our study did not have much dating experience when they were in school. Meanwhile, in an era when monogamy and heterosexuality confront multiple challenges, finding "Mr. Right" and establishing a stable marriage require more than a simple match of age, education, and occupation. It is in this social context that the discourse of "surplus women" and parental anxieties about their daughter's marriage prospects flourish in Chinese cities.

SHENGNÜ: CHANGING GENDER PARADIGMS

"*Shengnü*" (剩女) means literally "surplus women" in Chinese. It is a play on the homonym "*shengnü*" (圣女), or "saintly women." To understand the discourse of "surplus women," we trace the changing ideological and practical relationships among women's roles, family, and the state. These relationships have created the context in which marriage and parental matchmaking practices take on new meaning and significance in the reform era.[7]

We do not know exactly when *shengnü* first entered popular discourse, but by 2007 the term had appeared among the 171 new words highlighted in "The Chinese Language Life Report" published jointly by the Ministry of Education and the National Language Committee (ZYSZBK 2007). Pervasive as the term has become, *shengnü* is by no means clearly defined. But one widely circulating definition found on the search engine *Baidu* matches the understandings of those we met at the Shanghai matchmaking corner: *shengnü* are "young women born in the 1970s, who are also known as the '3S'—Single, Seventies, and Stuck." "Seventies" refers to the decade of their birth, meaning that they were between the ages of 30 and 40 in 2010. In many newspaper discussions, however, the age threshold drops to 27 or 28 (Liang 2006; Liu 2008). An often-quoted online chart, entitled the "Ranking of Surplus Men and Women" (剩男剩女等级表), distinguishes four different levels of surplus women by age: twenty-five to twenty-seven, twenty-eight to thirty-one, thirty-two to thirty-six, and thirty-seven and older. By inference, we conclude that the late twenties represent the threshold of becoming a *shengnü*.[8]

Although the issue of age is ambiguous, the marital status and socioeconomic status of surplus women are relatively clear cut. Newspapers and online discussions often describe them as "well-educated, well-paid, smart women." In general the defining features are single, urban, young, well-educated women with stable jobs that bring in a decent income, all of which are common features among the daughters of those looking for suitors in Shanghai's matchmaking corner.

Clearly the term *surplus women* is not a neutral description of a demographic phenomenon. Although the term *surplus men* coexists with *surplus women*, the latter appears much more frequently in everyday usage. In the already-mentioned "2006 Chinese Language Life Report," there was not even an entry for "surplus men." Most important, in the marriage market urban single men are identified positively as "golden bachelors" (黄金单身汉) or "diamond single men" (钻石王老五). Derogatory terms for single men do exist, but as in Hong Kong they are explicitly class coded and clearly distinguish desirable urban, middle-class, single men from their counterparts with lower socioeconomic status (see Ho's discussion of the derogatory term *lou* in Chapter 7). By contrast, terms for single women, such as *old maid* (老姑娘), are used across the social strata, and the terms *surplus women* and *failed dog* (败犬) are reserved for urban, middle-class, single women.[9] The derogatory nature of these distinctively gendered terms does not derive from concerns that uncompromising single women are exacerbating the marriage squeeze faced by men. Instead, the terms underscore how single women threaten conventional assumptions that success as a wife trumps success in the workplace and that remaining single is abnormal and represents failure as a woman (Jin 2009).

A reporter from the *Chinese Women's Post*, the newspaper published by the All-China Women's Federation, openly critiques these normative gender expectations regarding marriage:

> The word *surplus* indicates anxiety with respect to heterosexual marriage: Regardless of whether one is male or female, one should marry someone of the opposite sex by the publicly acknowledged age, or her or his personal life is questionable. Furthermore, the existence of these people and their growth in number also constitute a social problem. . . . The derogatory term *surplus women* is necessary to show them that, no matter how successful they are in educational and career accomplishments, they are nothing if they do not obtain the favor of men. (Lü 2009)

Lü's critique highlights a significant shift in prevailing gender ideology in the aftermath of the widespread rejection of the socialist blueprint and the rapid commodification of contemporary urban life. As they enthusiastically embrace markets and career success, young urban women also espouse new definitions of femininity that reject both traditional visions of unequal gender difference and the homogenizing models of the socialist era that collapsed distinctions between men and women (Evans 1997; Honig and Hershatter 1988; Wu 2009). As Lü's critique makes abundantly clear, however, finding a middle path between these two extremes is by no means an easy task for educated urban women today.

In contrast to the socialist model of a masculinized woman, the image of women in reform-era China has become softer and gentler in terms of both the female body and womanly virtues. One also observes a return of the discourse of "virtuous wives and good mothers" (贤妻良母), whose duties are to "take care of the husband and teach the children" at home (相夫教子), discourses that were largely rejected during the Maoist era. Such an attitude is illustrated by the 2008 article "On Family Harmony" in the leading official newspaper *The People's Daily*:

> Wives should learn to shift the focus of life from the self to the family, actively and consciously overcoming the weakness in their personalities. Look after and be considerate of the husband, and respect elders. Take more care of the family and manage the family. Continuously increase the solidarity and attractiveness of the family so that the husband could release his work pressure in the thoughtful and caring familial love, and enjoy the company of the family in a relaxing family environment. (Yongchun, November 21, 2008)

Unlike during the Maoist decades when women's care of the family was considered a means to serve the country (Evans 2002), reform-era gender discourses herald women's concern for home and family as an end in itself. Mass media often explicitly endorse an elite ideal of "men leading the outer domain and women leading the inner domain (男主外女主内)," explicitly invoking a return to separate gendered spheres in presocialist Chinese society (Bray 1997; Ko 2005; Mann 1997, 2002). An elitist paradigm clearly unavailable to working-class and poor women, the vision of women's "preferred" sphere as an inner domain has now achieved broad ideological purchase in reform-era urban China.

This gender ideology finds expression in the recurring "women return home" (妇女回家) debates since the launch of market reforms (Jiang 2001; Ouyang 2003; Yang 2007).[10] Arguing that encouraging women to work outside the home was a state imposition, high-profile scholars such as Sun Liping have suggested that it is better for women to stay home where they belong (Sun 1994). Focusing on whether women should quit their jobs and return home, these debates have reemerged during each economic downturn, as if "women returning home" provides a cure for economic crises encountered during critical moments in the process of market reform. Most recently, this line of argument resurfaced during national debates in 2001 focused on how economically independent urban women with good educations had intensified competition for the best professional and white-collar jobs, creating more pressure on men seeking those positions.

Women's commitment to work is also seen as a major cause of family conflict, while men's full engagement in paid employment is rarely questioned (Evans and Li 2007; Zhang 2006; see also Ting Chapter 6). Independent and successful career women, often labeled "strong women" (女强人), become seen as a "failing social gender" (失败的社会性别) (Yang 2007) because their outstanding performance in the workplace overshadows that at home. This tension between success at home and success in the workplace is thus particularly prominent among middle-class urban women and drives many of the challenges they are perceived to face in the marriage market.

As marriage itself is being redefined in the reform era and marital unions become increasingly fragile, unmarried women receive greater attention and even blame as a potential "source" of the problem. They often are criticized as "self-indulgent" and "picky," their selectiveness about a marriage partner portrayed as a threat to the social order. Such an attitude is well represented in the argument by two established scholars, Ye Wenzhen and Lin Qingguo:

> Family relations formed through marriage can reinforce the married ones' sense of social responsibilities, on the one hand, and increase the social cost when they go off the rails, on the other hand. Hence, an increasing number of people staying out of marriage is not good for the stability of the social order. . . . Because the over-aged single women have high quality (高素质), they are very likely to be picked by married men as collaborators in extramarital emotional activities, which pose potential threats and challenges to existing marriage relations. (Ye and Lin 1998: 18)

It is in this contested field surrounding the gendered division of labor, women's entry into desirable white-collar professions, and efforts to redefine marriage as a tool of social control that the surplus women discourse emerged.

The active participation of the market-driven media seeking apolitical and entertaining content further popularized this sensational and provocative debate. Amplifying the logic and imagery of this discourse are the single successful young women featured in online blogging, television soap operas such as *My Queen*, novels such as *Shengnü's Golden Age*, and comic strips such as "Mr. Right Must Be Found." Local television channels used the opportunity to produce a series of matchmaking reality shows, such as *Take Me Out*, *Let's Date*, and *Go Forward for Love*, attracting a diverse audience across the boundaries of class and age.[11] Matchmaking agents using *shengnü* as an eye-catching phrase for marketing purpose have flourished online and offline. A matchmaking economy has thrived with great momentum from the discourse of *shengnü*, which in turn sustains the discourse in everyday life, creating a discursive field that reinforces the centrality of marriage, heightens the tensions among different social roles particularly for urban middle-class women, and exacerbates parental anxieties about their daughter's marital future.

In short, the proliferation of the *shengnü* discourse attests to the influence of a gender paradigm that privileges career accomplishment for men and marriage and homemaking for women. Urban middle-class women in China today, therefore, are caught between the revival of a selective, elitist gender ideology of the past; their parents' investments in their well-being; the nation-state's development agenda; intense job competition; and the media's market interests. The message that consistently emerges from these contradictory forces is that marriage is more essential for the female than the male life course, providing fertile ground for urban matchmaking corners to flourish.

PARENTAL MATCHMAKING CORNER: A PERSONAL BUSINESS THAT HAS BECOME PUBLIC

In the Shanghai matchmaking corner, parents come from diverse backgrounds and social strata, with ages ranging from fifty to seventy. Some are civil servants, high school teachers, or faculty members; some are managers and small business owners; and some are workers. More than half of our interviewees had already retired. In terms of education, most had been to high school; occasionally they had college degrees.[12] Long-term local residents sat side-by-side with newcomers, most of whom had accompanied their children and, in some cases, their spouse to Shanghai. From what we observed, mothers slightly outnumbered fathers. With only a few exceptions, these parents had their own apartments in Shanghai, whether purchased from their work units or obtained from the commercial real estate market. In sum, parents seemed secure and well established in Shanghai. However, when we listened to them explain what they wanted for their children and what drew them to the matchmaking corner, we identified several different strands of anxiety.

Many of these parents had been sent down to the countryside for reeducation in their teens during the Maoist years. They consciously chose not to marry in the countryside because they feared it would prevent them from returning to the city if marriage in a village assigned them a permanent rural household registration. As a result, many remained single in their early thirties and returned to their home cities as "over-aged youth" (大龄青年) whose own marriage problems were seen by some as a socially destabilizing force. The official state newspaper, *The People's Daily*, published a series of reports addressing this issue, and state organizations such as the Women's Federation, the Youth League, and the Union were called on to organize parties and summer camps, providing channels and services to solve the marriage problems of this particular birth cohort.[13]

State intervention in the dating scene, however, was not unique to the post-Cultural Revolution era. One key feature of the CCP's plan for modernization was to free individuals from the authority of the family yet simultaneously subject them to that of the state. In line with these ambitions, before the Cultural Revolution stigmatized dancing and dating as "bourgeois" and "corrupt" (Whyte and Parish 1984), employers organized parties to provide occasions for singles to meet. In the early 1980s, dance parties and other matchmaking activities were again promoted via local Unions and the Youth Leagues. To those who were born and raised after 1949, such state interventions seemed unsurprising in the "cradle-to-grave" institutional background of the planned economy that was naturalized by decades of political mobilization.

The mass dating culture of the past left such a strong imprint on parents' own lives that many parents we interviewed called for government intervention to solve the problems of their children. On one Sunday, a woman handed us a note that read, "Government shall provide the platform to share our concerns for our children's marriage. Parents also do matchmaking for the children in the matchmaking corner in People's Park. By doing so we can expedite important business of marriage (婚姻大事)." She insisted that we convey their concern to the government. The mother whom we were interviewing concurred: "Only if the government, the Women's Federation would come to the stage—hold some activities for them, set a time, and [hold the activities] several times a month. Once per week? Once a week is impossible. Then twice a month. Let the young people themselves find [their suitors in the activities]."

Another such person was Dong Chao, a shareholder and chief financial officer in a large company, who as a father questioned the absence of the government in the dating scene:

> The government is taking care of the labor issue, but not marriage. What are you doing, Head of the Civil Affair Bureau? The Labor Bureau pays attention. At least each street committee has an office to handle job recommendations. But how about matchmaking? The train of thought of the government is problematic, including that of the central government. They deal with the employment issue at the level of social stability, but not the matchmaking issue. . . . People are the top priority (以人为本), [but] what is there without a family? . . . Why can't the government do something? 50,000 yuan is enough. It doesn't matter where the office is. At least you can have it in the street committee. The street committee is enough. Why don't they just do that? (Interview S31)

The alternative to government intervention was the market, and although almost all parents distrusted commercial matchmaking services, they themselves used the language of the market to describe the matchmaking corner as a venue that provided opportunities to meet with suitors outside their conventional social circles. Nevertheless, despite their constant references to "the market," parents expressed ambiguous attitudes toward the market. While markets offer choices, they also turn people into objects to be selected and imply the loss of dignity and social status. Li Yuan was a mother who felt embarrassed about her presence in the matchmaking corner. She had been a doctor before retirement, and her husband was a retired senior engineer who enjoyed a special allowance from the State Council. They had two apartments in downtown Shanghai. Their daughter had graduated from a prestigious university in Shanghai with a master's degree and was currently a faculty member:

> Now I worry about nothing except my child's marriage. Look at my child: elementary school, junior high, senior high, all the way to Tongji University. After Tongji, she got a job. What is left is her marriage. Suddenly, she *fell into the free market* (掉到自由市场来了). Everybody said that this [the matchmaking corner] is a free market. How can anyone come to a park to find a suitor? This is somehow like grabbing some pedestrian and getting married. You can't bring it to the table! Every time I am so afraid to be recognized. Other people

would say, "Isn't your child excellent? How come she needs to come to the free market?" (Emphasis added; Interview S27)

Ironically, it is the parents who infuse the matchmaking corner with references to a labor market. Parents hung flyers that listed both their daughter's accomplishments and requirements for an acceptable son-in-law. He must be at least a certain height, with a certain educational and income level. Some parents had a strong preference for those with Shanghai household registration, while others did not consider it crucial as long as the young ones were "excellent" in terms of education, occupation, and income. Hypergamy is explicit: The young men are expected to be equivalent or better off than the women, although some parents could accept men younger than their daughter.

In terms of housing, it was common to see explicit expectations for the male suitor to provide the apartment for marriage (also see Zhang 2010). For many parents, providing an apartment for marriage is an obligation of the young man and his family. The parents' requirements for suitors reveal acceptance of the norms of hypergamy, yet such norms weave together male privileges and men's larger economic and social responsibilities in marriage. The housing requirement rarely derived from parents' inability to afford an apartment for their daughter but rather from their expectation that the man or his family needed to meet this basic standard of wealth. As the previously mentioned Dong Chao put it:

> You parents of boys, don't you know that boys are going to grow up? . . . Parents of boys have the responsibility [to provide the apartment for marriage]. . . . He must have an apartment at this age . . . As for the requirements of the apartment, if they have to live with the parents, it has to have one living room and three bedrooms. At least they would have a child. If not with the parents, it shall still have two bedrooms. In fact, I have two apartments. But the man would not live in our place. (Interview S31)

Dong Chao's situation was not an exception. In fact, many of our interviewees had two apartments. For the parents of urban daughters, the ability of the young man to provide an apartment for the married couple was first a demonstration of his family's financial standing. Second, an apartment for the new nuclear family also meant that their daughter would not have to deal with the stressful in-law relationship under the same roof. Meanwhile, this expectation was tempered by parents' recognition of soaring real estate prices in Shanghai in recent years. Many parents of daughters indicated that they would provide financial aid for the young couple to purchase an apartment before marriage because they considered it unlikely that the young couple could cope with the down payment and installments by themselves.

When asked about the need to meet certain physical and material conditions, some parents justified their requirements by pointing out that matchmaking naturally started with the match of tangible conditions in an environment full of strangers. As a mother said, "Look, in the park, I don't know you, and you don't know me. If we don't talk about conditions, what can we talk about? There is obviously no emotional base to begin with" (Interview S6). Not to deny emotions or romantic feelings, parents frankly admitted that they were simply more practical than their daughters in mating choices.

Interestingly, on the one hand, parents put down the explicit terms for the potential suitors and justified such practices to themselves; on the other hand, they still lamented that a proper suitor now was defined only by physical and material conditions. In our interviews, parents sometimes contrasted the current practices to those of the past. Many parents stated that when they married they had no requirements other than compatible personalities and class composition (阶级成分). Dong Chao's wife described to us how she met and ended up marrying him: "I didn't tell him that he felt like a father figure after we first met. Later I dated him, but he didn't have an apartment. I still wanted him. I thought he was a nice person" (Interview S31).

A chief officer in a police station, Ruan Xiang spoke in even greater detail when asked about his own courtship:

> At that time, dating often did not start with two people meeting each other but rather by being introduced to each other by someone in between. In our day, we paid attention to the person's character (人品) and whether the person was honest or not. We didn't ask the person where she or he worked and how much the salary was, because we all knew about the income. The salary was usually 36 yuan or 45 yuan. One would not have much more than the other. We paid close attention to character and family education (家教). Some families were relatively poor, but as long as the person had a real job, it was all the same. Women would like to find men who were relatively honest, good natured, and content with what they had. For men, the kind of women they were looking for were virtuous (贤惠), who could be a good wife and mother, take care of the family, be the housewife (主妇) as well as aid the husband and teach the child

(相夫教子) . . . Because of the notions formed during the long Cultural Revolution, we tried not to find those with bad class backgrounds. (Interview S28)

Yet careful examination reveals that parents did have material expectations and requirements besides good personalities and class background when they were young. For example, they wanted to know if the person had an urban rather than rural household registration and if he or she worked in a famous state-owned unit in Shanghai. If the answer was yes, then a person and his or her family knew that after marriage the couple would have a desirable working-class social status as well as stable income, a pension, and access to housing, medical care, and child care. In sum, couples and their parents did not use the same metric of material success as that of parents today, but marriage was still seen as a means to secure an advantageous societal position (Lü and Perry 1997; Yan 2003).

That said, the materialism implicit in parents' discussion of mate choice does not mean that all parental concerns can be reduced to rational economic calculation. Rather, their focus on material success is intertwined with a strong sense of the parents' responsibility to establish a good life for their daughters. Ms. Han's words best illustrated this feeling on the part of parents: "This is something fundamental about being a human, to finish our historical mission (历史使命). Do you understand? This is my duty. As a mother, I assume this [finding a suitor for the daughter] is my duty" (Interview S30).

Because of this sense of responsibility, parents intervene in their daughter's dating life when they see their daughter does not have time or social circles in which to find the right person. Thus, although Shanghai offers a rich nightlife (Farrer 2002, 2010), the young women in our interviews did not seem to share that lifestyle. Some mentioned that they often slept a lot on the weekend to make up for missed sleep during the busy and stressful work week. They spent their free time reading books, surfing the Internet, and chatting with friends. Their workplaces did not seem to provide many opportunities for these young women to meet potential suitors. Dong Chao attributed his daughter's marriage problem to the corporate structure in contemporary Shanghai. He said,

In the past, a textile factory could have more than 10,000 people. It was very easy to find someone. Nowadays there are some companies with fewer than one hundred people. The actual social circle thus is much smaller. In our society . . . people who don't know each other will not socialize together. (Interview S31)

Many young women also worked in gender-segregated environments, as one mother described her daughter's situation:

> When she goes to work, she sits in front of the computer all day. Her depart-
> ment does not have many young men. There are other departments too. But
> how can you go from one department to another at work? . . . She is very busy
> at work and under tremendous pressure. She does not have time to be exposed
> to the outside world. Her social circle is so limited! (Interview S34)

Seeing that their daughters lacked dating opportunities, some determined parents have been to the matchmaking corner for five years, whether rain or shine. Meanwhile, they are well aware of the low success rate here. Parents described their own endeavors in the matchmaking corner as hard work.

Uncle Yan's case is a nice illustration. When we approached Uncle Yan, he sat quietly near the lake, with a visibly anxious look on his face. Next to him was his daughter's information and academic certificates: born in 1978, 164 cm, and working in the R&D department of an American company with a monthly income between 5,000 and 6,000 yuan (roughly US$714 and $857 in 2008). There were also the requirements for the suitor: 175 cm in height, a stable job. In many people's eyes, Uncle Yan had a decent Shanghai-based family. He and his wife worked at the same research institute in Shanghai. They had two apartments in the city, one to live in and one to rent out. Besides the information about his daughter he displayed, his daughter had been to the United States and France respectively for two years for advanced training. Worried about his daughter's unmarried status, Uncle Yan became a frequenter of the matchmaking corner on the weekends. His endeavors were not without any return. Once he got the information of a young man who allegedly gradu-ated from Fudan, one of the most esteemed institutions of higher learning in China, from another parent in the park. His daughter went to meet the young man but came back disappointed. As it turned out, the young man's educa-tional experience was not quite as described. Uncle Yan and his daughter felt that the boy's parents had deceived them, and there was no follow-up after the first meeting. On another occasion, Uncle Yan found a possible suitor online. His daughter chatted several times with him, but, again, she was disappointed and told her father that she sensed the young man was arrogant and thought too highly of himself. Nevertheless, Uncle Yan was not discouraged:

> Although the majority will not succeed, we can do nothing but come here to
> try our luck. Maybe there is an opportunity, right? Maybe we will meet the

suitable one. But it doesn't mean we would find someone once we come here (也不是说一定来了就要有什么收获). (Interview S23)

Uncle Yan admitted that the process was exhausting. "I think it is really tiring. . . . It is not easy for the parents, [but] . . . I don't think I have a choice; I have to take full responsibility for her."

In some cases, parents' sense of responsibility seemed to be a consequence of feelings of guilt and regret. Parents, like teachers, often told students, and girls in particular, that while in school they should focus on studying and not date. Uncle Yan told us that his daughter had never dated anyone during her school time. He said, "When she was at school, she spent all her time studying. . . . As parents, we also thought that our child should focus on studying when she was at school, and focus on work when she was working. Parents are traditional."

Without identifying the people involved, Mr. Xiao criticized a person he knew who had imposed a "no dating during school time" policy, but now the mother had become frantic about finding her daughter a husband:

> He isolated his daughter. If his daughter was dating a classmate, he immediately scolded her, "We parents raised you with great effort. You should not see anyone but focus on getting into college and finding a good job." They wanted their daughter to excel. Some classmate at school was interested in the daughter, but they were so protective that they did not allow her to stay in contact. Such a case is pretty common. Later, when the daughter reached the age of thirty, the mother began to feel regret: She should have let her go out dating. Now it is too late. All the good guys are married. (Interview S5)

Xia Feng was the kind of father Mr. Xiao described. Xia Feng became a sales representative after he retired from a factory as a worker. He has a son and a daughter, both of whom graduated with master's degrees from Fudan University. While his son easily found a wife, his daughter remained single, and he was deeply worried. He told us that his daughter used to be very popular at school:

> In fact, one guy was very serious about her. But I didn't give my permission. . . . I said, "You are at school, and you should study. Being at school means ignoring what happens outside and focusing on your schoolwork. This is an absolute principle. . . . If you find someone who really likes you, you can date him after you graduate [from college]. If you date him now, you need to look

for jobs when you graduate, and you will be away from each other, right?" . . .
I really didn't know the dating reality nowadays in Shanghai. . . . I will regret
my behavior until my death. (Interview S9)

While the previous state-orchestrated mass dating culture conditioned
this generation of parents to see marriage as something other than a personal
or individual decision, parents also see themselves as shouldering an embar-
rassing task by seeking proper suitors in public venues. Parental matchmaking
therefore is considered less as a form of interference or imposition of parental
authority and more as a buffer zone that protects their daughter's dignity. The
previously mentioned Uncle Yan said, "They [daughters] have self-esteem. The
corner here is a low-class, aberrant place (档次很低的野路子); they would not
like to be seen in such a place."

An old man who joined our conversation during our interview in the park
echoed this parental concern:

> You [young women] can't really go out to find a suitor. In the end, parents
> would ask other parents or friends, among the adults, to introduce you to
> suitors. You young girls won't look for a suitor yourself. You still want your
> face, right? It is impossible to do something like that, it is really embarrassing,
> right? . . . It is all for our children. If it were not for our children, who would
> come to places like this? Parents really have no other options. They actually
> don't like to talk about their children in public. [Daughters] are so busy at
> work. Time goes fast, and they are getting old. Really, it is a serious problem.
> We don't have options. Do you think we like to come to this place? We don't
> either. (Interview S35)

Hours of conversation with parents reveal a complicated picture of parental matchmaking practices in contemporary urban China that differ substantially from those of the late imperial era (Ebrey 1990, 1993; Mann 1997, 2002).
First, parents are not imposing their decisions on their children. As parents
emphasized, their role was just to screen the candidates and to seek choices
that could be presented to their children who would decide to take the chance
or not. Second, parents today do not primarily use a daughter's marriage to
build a family network or maintain a household's social status. Instead, they
are driven by their emotional, affectionate ties to their daughters and a deep
sense of responsibility for their daughters' lives. Even among daughters we
interviewed who resisted seeing "marriage" as a must, all acknowledged the
sincere care offered by their parents.

Meanwhile, the legacy of the socialist period does directly impinge on the parental generation. For most of their lives, state or workplace authorities were involved in every stage of their intimate relationship, from matchmaking to applying to get married, and from mediating familial disputes to applying for divorce (Whyte and Parish 1984; also see Davis Chapter 2). Urban dwelling in the same period was notoriously crowded and lacked basic amenities (Lu 2006). Hallways used as cooking spaces and shared bathrooms were common features in state-sponsored housing. Vivid street life, now often viewed nostalgically as emblematic of a cozy neighborhood environment, was often a result of the lack of space at home. The spatial divide between the public-outer and the private-inner was quite blurred, and one lived under the constant gaze and scrutiny of neighbors, colleagues, work units, the Party, and the government. For this generation of parents, marriage was personal yet never private. The internalization of the gaze of the other seems to persist among this generation who grew up and lived through this period; through their views we can observe the continuing significance of public recognition in family and marriage practices in the postsocialist setting. It is because of such life experiences that parents accepted without pleasure the seemingly awkward matchmaking corner as a site to look for marital prospects for their beloved children.

But there are also clear differences from the norms of the socialist past, and all the parents we interviewed acknowledged that their children lived in a very different work environment from theirs. Their daughters had much more pressure and competition at work, with the constant threat of layoffs. Skyrocketing living and educational expenses make it far harder to maintain a household than in the 1980s when they were raising their children. For the younger generation, who do not have the benefit of state-sponsored housing, urban real estate prices have gone far beyond what many individuals can afford, and only by relying heavily on one or both sets of parents can a young couple buy an apartment (Davis 2010). Financial pressure, the lack of a well-orchestrated and implemented social welfare system, and the emotional bond among generations due to the one-child policy thus create ever-closer interdependence among family members of different generations.

The parents' sense of the volatility and insecurity of the outside world then shaped their requirements for their children's suitors and motivated parents to find a man who would be able to provide at least as good a life as her parents had. Many parents stated that they had tried to take good care of their beloved daughters in the first part of their lives, and they wished that a similar or even better family environment could continue after marriage. Being responsible parents, therefore, meant choosing the proper person who could provide their daughter with shelter from the outside volatile world. Unlike filial piety that emphasizes children's moral obligations to their parents, in contemporary urban China, principles of enduring family obligation often highlight the parents' undying devotion to their children.

CONCLUSION

As key social institutions, marriage and family are now confronted with a variety of challenges in urban China, from strict limits on marital fertility (Davis Chapter 2), a dating culture among urban youth that displays an increasingly open attitude toward premarital sex (Farrer Chapter 3), and voluntary delays in marriage (Cai and Wang Chapter 4), to broader shifts in the courts and workplaces that have destigmatized divorce and even extramarital affairs (Davis and Friedman Chapter 1; Davis Chapter 2). These challenges bear similarities to forces that led to the "deinstitutionalization" of marriage in Western societies, as seen in the weakening of social norms as well as the diminished practical importance of marriage (Cherlin 2004). But whereas in North America and Europe broad cultural shifts prioritizing companionship and individual choice drove marital changes, in China the party-state's deliberate decision to introduce market reforms and to reduce control over and intervention in citizens' intimate lives has often been decisive. As a result, individuals of different generational, gender, and class backgrounds now have greater freedom to renegotiate the meanings of marriage but within the new pressures of a highly competitive market economy and the state's rigid limitations of the one-child policy.

The existence of parental matchmaking corners indicates, however, the enduring significance of marriage in urban China and the powerful effects of a selective rendering of traditional gender ideology—"men leading the outer domain and women the inner domain"—on contemporary matchmaking expectations and strategies. Despite the elitist roots of this gender paradigm, it has been rearticulated as an ostensibly universal ideal precisely at a time when educational opportunities and new middle-class jobs have made educated women more competitive with their male counterparts in the "outer domain." Although the parents who frequent Shanghai's matchmaking corner rarely if ever contest the surplus women discourse and remain committed to finding the right match for their daughters, some young women have begun to reappropriate the *shengnü* discourse to assert their own "refusal to compromise"

(不能将就) when it comes to marriage and pursuing an individually desirable lifestyle.

Given the intense, intergenerational bonds created by the one-child policy and solidified by the economic insecurities of the reform era, it is not surprising either that parents remain anxious about their daughter's marital future or that daughters are generally unwilling to openly rebuff their parents' matchmaking efforts. Not only has this generation of parents focused all their resources on the health and success of their only child, but their own support in old age is tied to their single child's success and happiness. Moreover, parents' endeavors cannot be interpreted simply as the imposition of patriarchal authority. Their anxiety and expectations are heartfelt, often out of genuine concern for their daughter's marital status. Such mutual understanding across the generations further supports the existence of matchmaking corners.

The practices of parental matchmaking also reveal the everlasting presence of a public gaze in marriage practices, despite the increasing turn to private preferences in cases involving marital dissolution. As shown in the cases we describe in the preceding pages, parental anxieties are often framed through the real or imagined gaze of others: how others might view their presence in the matchmaking corner and what these others might say about their daughters. Parents' experiences of such a public gaze derive from earlier participation in group dating and from histories of close monitoring of their intimate lives by work units and supervisors. Even though the political and social settings in which the public gaze was embedded have been removed, the internalization of that gaze has made it possible for parents to enter the matchmaking corner, albeit unpleasantly, and to transform their daughter's personal business into a public event. Carefully unpacking the diverse motivations behind parental matchmaking practices thus allows us to understand the complex political, economic, and cultural crosscurrents that shape the meanings of marriage and family in urban China today.

NOTES

This paper is partly based on research conducted for the project "Parental Matchmaking and Marketization of Mating Choice: On the Matchmaking Corner in People's Park in Shanghai" in East China University of Political Sciences and Law, 2010 (Project Number: 10H2K032).

1. All the direct interview quotations in this chapter were excerpts from interviews conducted in the matchmaking corner of Shanghai's People's Park from September 2007 through June 2008, with follow-up interviews conducted in 2009. Interviews were originally in Mandarin, translated into English by the authors.

2. Our research was designed to focus more on the parents than the daughters, and our interviews with the daughters were designed to study what they thought about their parents' actions. Although we have interviews that indicate the daughters' perceptions of love and marriage, our findings generally support Farrer's insights into urban youth dating culture (Chapter 3).

3. Having heard about Beijing's matchmaking corner, six parents organized a similar one in Shanghai's People's Park in June 2005. They distributed leaflets to passersby, encouraging the parents to become involved in finding marriage prospects for their children. The first meeting attracted more than 100 people, and over 500 showed up for subsequent meetings. The corner became well known after a local Shanghai TV channel featured a special report on the corner in August 2005 (Zhu and Hu 2006).

4. We acknowledge that the term *class* (阶级) is ideologically loaded, especially in China, and terms such as *middle stratum* (中产阶级) are often preferred in everyday language. However, because the focus of the article is not the formation of class, we use the term *class* loosely to refer to the midrange social group in society, a group that distinguishes itself by often office-based, white-collar jobs that typically require a college education.

5. In the four-year colleges, the number of female students as a percentage of the total number of students rose from 23.4 percent in 1980 to 39.2 percent in 2000 (Song 2006).

6. Studies point out that, since the initiation of market reforms, married couples increasingly have resembled each other in education and class background (Zhang 2003). Li Yu's study shows that fewer mate choices cross class boundaries, and educational homogamy has increased dramatically in the past decade (2008). In line with Li, Yi and Zhao argue that higher education is a watershed point in the marriage market. Regardless of gender, people with college education tend to look for partners who also have a college education (2007). For age hypergamy, see Chapter 4.

7. Our discussion focuses mostly on women and assumes a gender paradigm of binary sexes. Without denying diversity in gender and sexual practices, we note that the binary gender model and heterosexuality still represent the cultural and legal mainstream in contemporary China. Meanwhile, due to space constraints, we do not discuss the changing social role of men and masculinity.

8. We have not found evidence that the age of thirty is a transitional moment concerning women's marriage status. Instead, analysis of online discussion and our interviews show that stress is built up substantially in the mid- and late twenties for urban single women, which to some degree coincides with the mean marriage age nationwide (Cai and Wang Chapter 4).

9. The term *failing dog* means the dog that fails in dog competitions. It originally came from Japan and gained popularity in China due to the Taiwanese soap opera *My Queen*, in which the leading character is a successful single career woman aged thirty-three.

10. The "women-return-home" debate was mostly among scholars, including some prominent scholars such as Sun Liping and Li Yinhe, in the mid-1990s. The debate was divided along gender lines, with male scholars advocating that women return home and female scholars arguing the opposite. For their arguments, see the 1994 and 1995 issues of the leading social science journal in China, *Shehuixue Yanjiu* (*Journal of Sociological Studies*).

11. The Chinese title of the TV soap opera *My Queen* is *Baiquan Nüwang* (败犬女王); *My Queen* is its original English title. The novel *Shengnü's Golden Age* is named *Shengnü de Quansheng Shidai* (剩女的全盛时代), by Liu Su (Guilin: Guangxi Shifan Daxue Chubanshe, 2010). The author of the novel *Shengnü's Golden Age* claimed that she wove the stories of her friends together into the novel. The comic strip "Must Be Found the Mr. Right" (original English title) has as its Chinese title "一定可以嫁出去," by Yun Qin and Shuyi Zeng (Guilin: Guangxi Shifan Daxue Chubanshe, 2010). These two authors were single women born in the 1980s. They were published first online and then in paperback. These print media are complemented by reality TV shows such as *Take Me Out* (非诚勿扰), *Let's Date* (让我们约会吧), and *Go Forward for Love* (为爱向前冲).

12. Such an educational distribution coincides with the educational pattern of their peers, as the Cultural Revolution and the "sent down youth" movement deprived many members of this generation of their educational opportunities during the 1960s and 1970s.

13. See *People's Daily*'s reports on days such as June 20, July 3, September 8, and December 27, 1984; and January 2, March 1, and May 8, 1985.

REFERENCES

Bray, Francesca. 1997. *Technology and Gender: Fabrics of Power in Late Imperial China.* Berkeley: University of California Press.

Cherlin, Andrew J. 2004. "The Deinstitutionalization of American Marriage." *Journal of Marriage and Family* 66 (November): 848–861.

Davis, Deborah, ed. 2000. *The Consumer Revolution in Urban China*. Berkeley: University of California Press.

———. 2010. "Who Gets the House? Renegotiating Property Rights in Post-Socialist Urban China." *Modern China* 36(5): 463–492.

Davis, Deborah, and Stevan Harrell, eds. 1993. *Chinese Families in the Post-Mao Era.* Berkeley: University of California Press.

Davis, Deborah, and Wang Feng, eds. 2009. *Creating Wealth and Poverty in Postsocialist China*. Palo Alto, CA: Stanford University Press.

Ebrey, Patricia Buckley. 1990. "Women, Marriage, and the Family in Chinese History." In *Heritage of China: Contemporary Perspectives on Chinese Civilization*, Paul S. Ropp, ed., pp. 197–223. Berkeley: University of California Press.

———. 1993. *The Inner Quarters: Marriage and the Lives of Chinese Women in the Sung Period*. Berkeley: University of California Press.

Evans, Harriet. 1997. *Women and Sexuality in China: Female Sexuality and Gender since 1949*. New York: Continuum.

———. 2002. "Past, Perfect or Imperfect: Changing Images of the Ideal Wife." In *Chinese Femininities, Chinese Masculinities: A Reader*, Susan Brownell and Jeffrey N. Wasserstrom, eds., pp. 335–360. Berkeley: University of California Press.

Evans, Harriet, and Yinhe Li (李银河). 2007. "关于女性主义的对话" (Conversation over Feminism). 社会学研究 (*Sociological Research*) 4: 118–125.

Farrer, James. 2002. *Opening Up: Youth Sex Culture and Market Reform in Shanghai*. Chicago: The University of Chicago Press.

———. 2010. "A Foreign Adventurer's Paradise? Interracial Sexuality and Alien Sexual Capital in Reform Era Shanghai." *Sexualities* 13(1): 69–95.

Fong, Vanessa L. 2002. "China's One-Child Policy and the Empowerment of Urban Daughters." *American Anthropologist* 104(4): 1098–1109.

Friedman, Sara. 2006. *Intimate Politics: Marriage, The Market, and State Power in Southeastern China*. Cambridge: Harvard University Asia Center; distributed by Harvard University Press.

Goode, William Josiah. 1963. *World Revolution and Family Patterns*. New York: Free Press of Glencoe.

Hoffman, Lisa M. 2010. *Patriotic Professionalism in Urban China: Fostering Talent*. Philadelphia: Temple University Press.

Honig, Emily, and Gail Hershatter. 1988. *Personal Voices: Chinese Women in the 1980's*. Palo Alto, CA: Stanford University Press.

Jiang Yongping (蒋永萍). 2001. "世纪之交关于阶段就业, 妇女回家的大讨论" (The Trans-Century's Debate about "Staged Employment" and "Women Going Back Home"). 妇女研究论从 (*Women's Research Monographs*) 39(2): 23–28.

Jin Yihong (金一虹). 2009. "我们能否告别 '剩女' 时代" (Can We Say Farewell to an Era of "Surplus Women"?). 中国妇女报 (*Chinese Women's Post*) December 8: A03.

Ko, Dorothy. 2005. *Cinderella's Sisters: A Revisionist History of Footbinding*. Berkeley: University of California Press.

Li Qiang (李强). 2004. 转型的时期: 中国社会分层 (*An Era of Transformation: Social Stratification in China*). Shenyang: Liaoning Jiaoyu Chubanshe.

Li Yu (李煜). 2008. "婚姻的教育匹配: 50年来的变迁" (Trends in Educational Assortative Marriage: 1949–2000). 中国人口科学 (*Chinese Demography*) 3: 73–79.

Liang Guosheng (梁国胜). 2006. "剩男剩女多为中层成功人士" (Most Surplus Men and Surplus Women Are Successful Middle-Class People). 中国青年报 (*China's Youth Newspaper*), November 13: 2.

Liu Sen (柳森). 2008. "剩男剩女是个什么问题?" (What Is It about the "Leftover Men and Women"?). 解放日报 (*Liberation News*), January 19: 5.

Liu Su (苏鋈). 2010. 剩女的全盛时代 (*Shengnü's Golden Age*). Guilin: Guangxi Shifan Daxue Chubanshe.

Lu, Duanfang. 2006. *Remaking Chinese Urban Form: Modernity, Scarcity, and Space, 1949–2005*. London and New York: Routledge.

Lü Pin (吕频). 2009. "'剩男' '剩女' 不一样" ("Surplus Women" Are Different from "Surplus Men"). 中国妇女报 (*Chinese Women's Post*). December 24: A3.

Lü, Xiaobo, and Elizabeth J. Perry, eds. 1997. *Danwei: The Changing Chinese Workplace in Historical and Comparative Perspective*. Armonk, NY: M. E. Sharpe.

Mann, Susan. 1997. *Precious Records: Women in China's Long Eighteenth Century*. Stanford, CA: Stanford University Press.

———. 2002. "Grooming a Daughter for Marriage: Brides and Wives in the Mid-Qing Period." In *Chinese Femininities, Chinese Masculinities: A Reader*, Susan Brownell and Jeffrey N. Wasserstrom, eds., pp. 93–119. Berkeley: University of California Press.

Naughton, Barry. 2007. *The Chinese Economy: Transitions and Growth*. Cambridge, MA: MIT Press.

Ouyang Hexia (欧阳和霞). 2003. "回顾中国现代历史上 '妇女回家 '的四次争论", (The Four Debates on "Women Returning Home" in Modern Chinese History) 中华女子学院学报 (*University Journal of China's Women's University*) 15(3): 6–9.

Qin Yun (秦赟) and Zeng Shuyi (曾书仪). 2010. 一定可以嫁出去 (*Must Be Found the Mr. Right*) (original English title). Guilin: Guangxi Shifan Daxue Chubanshe.

Raymo, James M. 1998. "Later Marriages or Fewer? Changes in the Marital Behavior of Japanese Women." *Journal of Marriage and Family* 60(4): 1023–1034.

Retherford, Robert D., Naohiro Ogawa, and Rikiya Matsukura. 2001. "Late Marriage and Less Marriage in Japan." *Matrimonios tardíos y menores matrimonios en Japón* 27(1): 65–102.

Shambaugh, David L. 2000. *The Modern Chinese State*. New York: Cambridge University Press.

Shanghai Population Census Office (上海人口普查办公室). *Shanghai 2000 Population Census Assembly* (上海市2000人口普查统计资料汇编), Retrieved on April 28, 2010, from http://chinadataonline.org/member/census2000/ybtableview_c.asp?ID=3885.

Song Tao (宋韬). 2006. "我国高等教育入学机会性别差异现状评述" (The Gender Differences in Accessing Higher Education in China.) 中国青年研究 (*Research on Chinese Youth*) 8: 57–61.

Sun, Liping (孙立平). 1994. "建性别角色关系" (Reconstructing Gender Roles and Relations) 社会学研究 (*Sociological Research*), 65–68.

United Nations, Department of Economic and Social Affairs, Population Division. 2008. "World Marriage Data 2008." Retrieved on January 20, 2014, from http://www.un.org/esa/population/publications/WMD2008/WP_WMD_2008/Data.html.

Whyte, Martin King. 2005. "Continuity and Change in Urban Chinese Family Life." *The China Journal* 53: 9–33.

Whyte, Martin King, and William L. Parish. 1984. *Urban Life in Contemporary China*. Chicago: The University of Chicago Press.

Wu, Juanjuan. 2009. *Chinese Fashion: From Mao to Now*. New York: Berg.

Yan, Yunxiang. 2003. *Private Life under Socialism: Love, Intimacy, and Family Change in a Chinese Village, 1949–1999*. Palo Alto, CA: Stanford University Press.

Yang, Feng (杨凤). 2007. 当代中国女性发展研究 (*Studies on Women's Development in Contemporary China*). Beijing: Renmin Chubanshe.

Ye Wenzhen (叶文振) and Qingguo Lin (林擎国). 1998. "中国大龄未婚人口现象存在的原因及对策分析" (Why There Is a Population of Over-aged Singles and How to Handle It). 中国人口科学 (*Chinese Demography*), 16–22.

Yi Cuizhi (易翠枝), and Xiaoshi Zhao (赵小仕). 2007. "婚姻市场的教育匹配与分成极其经济影响" (Educational Match and Stratification in the Marriage Market and Their Economic Impact). 商业时代 (*Business Times*) 11: 12–13, 73.

Yongchun (永春). 2008. "家庭和谐初探" (Discussion on Family Harmony). 人民日报 (*People's Daily*), November 21: 6.

Zhai Zhenwu (翟振武), and Yang Fan (杨凡). 2009. "中国出生性别比水平与数据质量研究" (Study on the Level and Data Quality of Sex Ratio at Birth in China). 人口学刊 (*Population Periodical*) 176(4): 3–10.

Zhang Li. 2010. *In Search of Paradise: Middle-Class Living in a Chinese Metropolis*. Ithaca, NY: Cornell University Press.

Zhang Lixi (张李玺). 2006. 角色期望的错位: 婚姻冲突与两性关系 (*The Misplaced Expectations of Gender Roles: Marriage Conflicts and Gender Relations*). Beijing: Zhongguo Shehui Kexue Chubanshe.

Zhang Yi (张翼). 2003. "中国阶层内婚制的延续" (The Continuation of the Intra-Class Marriage in China). 中国人口科学 (*Chinese Demography*) 4: 39–47.

Zhongguo Yuyan Shenghuo Zhuangkuang Baogao Ketizu (ZYSZBK; 中国语言生活状况报告课题组). 2007. 中国语言生活状况报告 2006 (*2006 Chinese Language Life Report*). Beijing: Shangwu Yinshuguan.

Zhu, Ling (祝玲), and Xiaoling Hu (胡小玲). 2006. 婚介婚托黄牛纷来抢市场, 组建人叹息相亲角 "变味" (Marriage Brokers Came to Snatch Market Shares, Organizers Sighed, the Matchmaking Corner Has Changed). 新闻晚报 (*Evening News*), December 28.

6 CONTINUITIES AND CHANGES

Five Decades of Marital Experiences in Hong Kong

Kwok-fai Ting

OVER THE LAST FIFTY YEARS, both the expectations and the realities of marriage have changed substantially for Hong Kong residents. Dating has become disconnected from seeking a mate, and couples increasingly cohabit before marriage.[1] Divorce rates have risen quickly and, as noted in Chapter 1, fertility rates have stabilized far below replacement levels. Married households have also shifted away from the male-breadwinner model as most women remain in the labor force after marriage and dual career families prevail, particularly among those with the highest levels of education.[2] Not surprisingly, many view these changes with alarm. A recent report issued by the Hong Kong Council of Social Services went so far as to argue that there had been a tenfold decline in family solidarity over the previous decade because fewer people had chosen to marry, more couples had broken up, and a greater number of families had reported domestic violence.[3] In a public statement issued in 2012, the Catholic Diocese of Hong Kong also expressed explicit concern that the trends of increasing divorce, single parenthood, liberal attitudes toward sex, and dual working parents damaged not only the quality of family life but even the well-being of society as a whole (Catholic Diocese of Hong Kong 2012).

Although many of these recent trends mark departures from the traditional Chinese ideals of marriage and family, it is not as obvious that the quality of marriage has deteriorated. Moreover, scholarship in other affluent societies suggests that it is premature to conclude that these changes indicate a threat to social stability. Rather, what we observe in Hong Kong may more accurately parallel what scholars have observed in Europe and North America, where marriage remains a highly desirable social status even as many couples adopt new forms of intimacy and commitment (Amato 2004; Cherlin 2004; Glenn 1993; Skolnick 1991; Thornton and Young-DeMarco 2001; Wilson 2002).

To place the Hong Kong experience within this broad scholarly discussion of new patterns of sexual intimacy and marital arrangements, this chapter first provides an overview of societal-level shifts since the 1960s and then uses recent household survey data to explore variation by class, gender, and birth cohort. Through this two-step process, the chapter not only provides an empirical overview of changing behavior but also speaks more generally about the future prospects of marriage as a core social institution in contemporary Hong Kong.

MARRIAGE IN CONTEMPORARY HONG KONG

Historically, Hong Kong was a society that embraced the ideal of universal marriage for men and women. However, because of its status as an entrepot and seaport and the frequent population movement in and out of Mainland China, marriage and family formation have varied significantly from decade to decade. In some decades, Hong Kong was primarily a destination for male sojourners whose families would remain in a home village in China, the Philippines, or elsewhere in Southeast Asia. In other decades, entire families migrated as refugees with no desire to return to the communities they left behind. In still other decades, the borders were highly porous and tens of thousands arrived to start new lives in Hong Kong. In other years, migration was reduced to a trickle. As a result, there have been stark fluctuations in the percentage of the populace who never married.

To reflect on the trend of singlehood for the last five decades, we track the percentage of men and women who had never married by their late forties (age forty-five to forty-nine), an age at which in traditional Chinese society almost all women and most men would have married at least once. Closer examination reveals dramatic variations by time and gender. In 1961, women in their late forties were considerably more likely than men to have never married, but ten years later the pattern had reversed and it was men who were less likely to have married than women. By 1981, the gender gap had increased to the point that 9.2 percent of men but only 2.3 percent of women had never married by their late forties (Hong Kong Census and Statistics Department 1982). Never-married men continued to be more common in 1991, but by 2001 the percentage converged at around 8 percent for both men and women, and by 2011

14.2 percent of men and 13.6 percent of women had never married by their late forties, a trend that may signal a fundamental shift in the desirability of marriage (Hong Kong Census and Statistics Department 1993, 2012a).

Recent shifts in migration policy in Hong Kong partly account for these fluctuating marriage rates over the past fifty years. Prior to October 1980, the Hong Kong government allowed those who passed Boundary Street in Kowloon to remain in Hong Kong. After October 23, 1980, the government replaced this "touch base policy" with a policy of immediate repatriation that dramatically curbed decades of immigrant influx from the Mainland. Because most of those who had benefited from the "touch base policy" were young men, the ratio of men per 1,000 women among people aged twenty-five through forty-four rose from 1,160 to 1,223 between 1961 and 1981 (Hong Kong Census and Statistics Department 1982), thereby creating a favorable marriage market for women that partly explains the greater likelihood of women having married in 1971 and 1981 than in 1961.

The marriage trends since 1981 tell yet another story. Restrictions on immigration remain in place, but in response to the rapid integration of the Hong Kong and Chinese economies there is now frequent contact between Hong Kong and Mainland citizens, and nearly half of all new marriages now include a spouse from outside Hong Kong.[4] However, because it is primarily Hong Kong men who leave Hong Kong to work in China, and because the standard of living in Hong Kong remains higher than in most parts of China, relatively few of these cross-border marriages involve Hong Kong women marrying a man from the Mainland.[5] A large influx of Mainland wives since 1980 has also affected the gender ratios in Hong Kong. By 2011, the previous "excess" of men had been eliminated, and there were only 861 men per 1,000 women among Hong Kong residents aged twenty-five through forty-four (excluding foreign domestic helpers) (Hong Kong Census and Statistics Department 2012a).

In addition to migration policy, another factor affecting marriage rates was the major post-1980 expansion of tertiary education that led to the current situation in which a higher percentage of both men and women complete postsecondary studies. As noted in the discussion of marriage rates presented in Table 1.1, higher education is associated with lower rates of marriage, and in Hong Kong the effect has been particularly dramatic for women. When we compare the 2011 marriage rates in Hong Kong by educational level, as shown in Table 6.1, among those aged forty-five through forty-nine we observe little variation among men, but among women there is a progressive relationship

Table 6.1. Percentage of never-married persons aged forty-five through forty-nine, 2011.

Highest education completed	Male	Female
Primary school	11.4	7.4
Secondary school	14.0	12.8
Matriculation and associate degree	14.3	18.9
College	14.6	25.0
Total	13.9	13.9

SOURCE: Ting. 2013a.Figures were compiled by the author based on the 5 percent sample data of the 2011 census.

between higher levels of education and a lower likelihood of marrying. Among women with only primary education, 7.4 percent had never married by their late forties; for those with some secondary schooling, the percentage jumps to 12.8 percent, and among college graduates it soars to 25.0 percent (as opposed to only 14.6 percent of college-educated men who had never married). Most starkly, it appears that college-educated women in Hong Kong have fewer suitable choices than college-educated men as their rates of never marrying exceed those of their male peers.[6]

CHANGE AND CONTINUITY IN THE EXPERIENCE OF MARRIAGE

While most Hong Kong people still marry, the experience of marriage and the degree of satisfaction with the quality of marriage have changed. To examine the parameters and drivers of these changes, we first summarize the overall trends of change and continuity. The first marker of change relates to young people's control over spousal choice. Figure 6.1, based on Mitchell's (1972) survey of married couples in 1967, shows a dramatic and steady decline in arranged marriages for each cohort of Hong Kong residents born after 1915.

As the norm of arranged marriage disappeared in Hong Kong, courtship practices also changed, and dating became a routine practice for young adults seeking their own mates. Yet, as Farrer (Chapter 3) documents for Shanghai, dating conventions evolve from one generation to the next or even from one birth cohort to another. Thus, using the 1996 Social Change and Economic Life Survey, Ting (2002) found that the average age at which people had their first date dropped from 24.6 for men and 20.4 for women in the cohort born between 1940 and 1945 to 18.8 for men and 18.7 for women who were born twenty-five years later. In addition, almost half of women and men in the

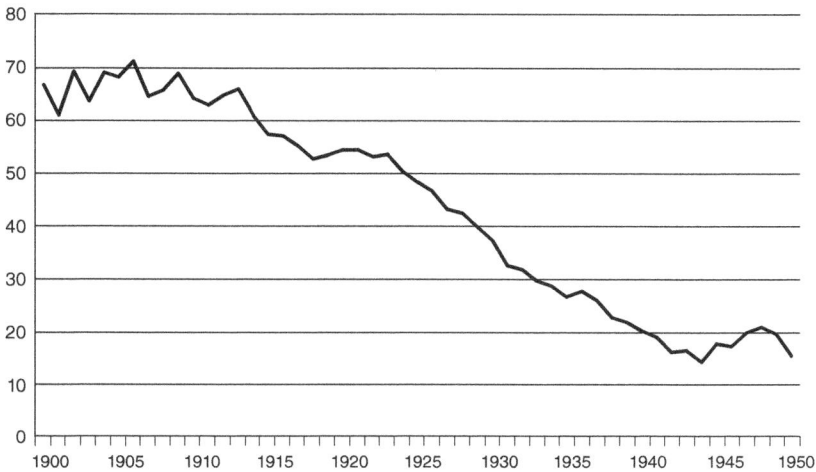

Figure 6.1. Percentage of marriages arranged by parents or other relatives.

SOURCE: Figures are computed by the author based on data from the Urban Family Life Survey conducted in 1967. The data file was generously provided by the investigator. See Mitchell 1972 for a description of the survey.

youngest birth cohorts, those born between 1965 and 1969, had had their first date while still in secondary school.[7] However, based on a 2009 survey, Ting (2012) has also found that at the same time that Hong Kong youth were beginning to date at younger ages, they were also spending more years dating before they married. Thus, for those born in the early 1950s, the average length of courtship with their current spouse was twenty-seven months, whereas for those born in the late 1970s it had increased to forty-four months.

Historically, Chinese families sought to match the social status of the bride and groom (門當戶對) but usually with a preference that the man's background should be slightly superior or hypergamous to that of the bride. However, in contemporary Hong Kong, as in other affluent societies (Kalmijn 1998; Mare 1991), such gender-distinct hypergamy with respect to education has been slightly reduced. Ting (2012) compares the relative levels of education between spouses across twenty-five years and shows a steady rise in the percentage of couples with equal levels of education, from 69 percent among those who married in 1981 to 88 percent among those who married in 2006. Accordingly, the percentage of husbands with more education than wives declines, from 22 percent to 10 percent during the same period.

One of the most dramatic changes in marital experience in the past few decades has been the rise in age at first marriage. As summarized in Table 1.1, we observe a steady increase in the mean age at first marriage for women in Hong Kong. However, this chapter uses the median to probe more deeply into the causes of the shifts among Hong Kong women and men.[8] In 1971, the median age at first marriage was 27.8 for men and 22.9 for women; by 1991 it had risen to 29.1 for men and 26.2 for women, and by 2011 to 31.2 for men and 28.9 for women (Hong Kong Census and Statistics Department 2008, 2012b). While higher age at first marriage signals less direct control by parents and perhaps longer periods of dating to find the most compatible mate, empirically it is difficult to equate later age of marriage with greater or lesser marital satisfaction or satisfaction with the institution of marriage (Goldstein and Kenney 2001). Thus, while some scholars (Popenoe 1993) have interpreted higher age at first marriage as evidence of a retreat from marriage or a less satisfying marital life, other evidence suggests the opposite. Bumpass, Martin, and Sweet (1991) and Heaton (2002), for example, showed that marrying at an older age actually enhanced marital stability, probably due to greater maturity and more resources to deal with marital problems.

To address in more detail how variations in birth cohort, gender, social class, and other characteristics of individuals and their households affect the experience of marriage, we draw on the responses of 726 married men and women from the 2009 Hong Kong Family Life Survey to conduct a fine-grained multivariate analysis of the correlates of marital satisfaction in contemporary Hong Kong. The Hong Kong Family Life Survey was conducted in 2009 by face-to-face interviews with ever-married persons who were under sixty years old. Subjects were drawn from a random sampling of household addresses provided by the Census and Statistics Department, Hong Kong SAR Government. The purpose of the survey was to collect information on family life in Hong Kong, and marital relationship was one of the key study areas. Due to the nature of this analysis, we confined our sample to respondents who lived with their partners at the time of the survey.[9]

DETERMINANTS OF MARITAL QUALITY

To assess the quality of marriage in Hong Kong, our 2009 survey asked respondents from three birth cohorts about several dimensions of their marriage, from a global question about marital satisfaction to more specific questions that captured the degree of sharing, joint activities, intimacy, and

trust.[10] From the viewpoint of a traditional family, none of these marital qualities is important for achieving collective goals, but as marriage has become a
more individual decision, personal feelings about one's marriage are crucial
to maintaining the relationship. These measures give us some indication as to
whether marriage today tends to be fragile and contentious, as many scholars
have observed (Beck and Beck-Gernsheim 1995; Bellah et al. 1985; Popenoe
1993).

Debates about whether the institution of marriage is in decline often ignore variations in marital experience between generations, between men and
women, or among different social classes. Without longitudinal data we cannot directly address the question about change over time; however, by comparing birth cohort differences in marital satisfaction, it may be possible to
identify patterns of variation across generations.[11] From Table 6.2, we can observe that older men report less satisfaction than younger men, that men are
more satisfied than women on all five dimensions, and that those in the lowest social rank, accounting for 21 percent of the sample, consistently report

Table 6.2. Level of marital quality by birth cohort, sex, and social class.

By groups	N	Satisfaction	Sharing	Activity	Intimacy	Trust
By birth cohort/age group						
1960 and before	306	5.8	5.3	4.6	4.4	5.3
1961–1970	269	5.8	5.4	4.8	4.8	5.4
1971 and after	151	5.9	5.7	5.3	5.5	5.7
F		1.2	6.2	15.4	25.7	4.5
p <		0.300	0.002	0.001	0.001	0.012
By sex						
Female	431	5.7	5.3	4.7	4.6	5.3
Male	295	6.0	5.7	5.0	5.0	5.6
F		25.2	19.1	8.3	10.5	13.3
p <		0.001	0.001	0.003	0.001	0.001
By social class						
Lowest	149	5.5	5.1	4.4	4.2	5.1
Lower middle	264	5.9	5.6	5.0	4.9	5.5
Middle and above	313	6.0	5.6	5.0	5.1	5.6
F		7.9	10.9	8.8	14.8	8.6
p <		0.001	0.001	0.001	0.001	0.001
Total	726	5.8	5.5	4.9	4.8	5.5

SOURCE: Hong Kong Family Life Survey, 2009.

the lowest levels of satisfaction. Nevertheless, as the highest possible score was 7 and the average satisfaction scores varied from 5.5 to 6.0 for all groups, whether defined by birth cohort, gender, or class, it seems that individuals from all sociodemographic backgrounds were relatively satisfied with their marriages.

In most societies, men and women have different expectations for their marriages. Ho (Chapter 7) vividly shows how in Hong Kong men construct an identity as a "good guy" in their marriages and see themselves as having different marriage ideals from their partners. Shen (Chapter 11) illustrates how in Taiwan husbands and wives in transnational families craft their own ways of dealing with long-term marital separation. The survey results summarized in Table 6.2 also confirm gender differences in marital experiences, as Hong Kong men reported statistically higher levels of satisfaction than women on all five dimensions of marital quality. These results also accord with earlier studies in Hong Kong that found lower levels of satisfaction among married women than married men (Family Planning Association of Hong Kong 2004; Shek 1995, 1996), although it remains unclear the extent to which traditional Chinese culture, which emphasizes gender role differentiation, explains the lower satisfaction of wives.

In the multivariate analysis we assess how birth cohort, class, and gender, together with a range of other variables, affect marital quality. Because the gender difference in marital experiences is well documented, we run our models separately for men and women to reveal which aspects of their lives are most important in determining the perceived level of marital quality. In the analysis, we consider three sets of factors in separate steps. The first set of factors includes sociodemographic variables such as class and birth cohort, which differentiate marital experiences by respondents' social locations. We divide our respondents into three birth cohorts born before 1961, between 1961 and 1970, and after 1970, with the oldest cohort used as the reference group in the model. The second set comprises premarital experiences, including age of first date, years dating spouse, income homogamy, and education homogamy. In terms of income homogamy, we asked our respondents to compare who had a higher income just before their marriage. Their responses were coded into a dichotomous variable, coded 1 if the wife had a higher income and 0 otherwise. Education homogamy was constructed by comparing the couple's years of education. Again, a dichotomous variable was created, coded 1 if the wife had a higher education and 0 otherwise. It was not possible to include age of first marriage in the analysis because this variable is perfectly collinear with birth cohort and length of marriage. The third set of variables measures the conditions of married life, comprising the wife's employment status (1 = employed, 0 = not employed), whether living with parents (1 = yes, 0 = no), number of children, and whether living with a domestic helper (1 = yes, 0 = no). In Table 6.3, we present these three sets of variables as nested models for the purpose of comparison.

In model 1, we can observe a significant gender effect, which confirms our earlier finding that men tend to report a higher level of marital quality than women. Such a gender difference persists when we introduce premarital experiences in model 2 and marital factors in model 3. Because the gender effect remains largely unchanged after controlling for premarital and marital experiences, the gender difference in perceived marital quality cannot be explained by these control variables. Social class also has significant and positive effects on marital quality in all three models, indicating that people of higher socioeconomic status generally feel that they enjoy higher marital quality than do those of inferior status. Also of note is that the class advantage is approximately the same for women and men, and the effects remain largely unchanged as we introduce additional factors in models 2 and 3.

We capture social change through a comparison of three birth cohorts: those born before 1961 (the reference group), between 1961 and 1970, and after 1970.[12] The results in model 1 reveal that those born after 1970 report a significantly higher level of marital quality than those born before 1961, but there is no significant difference between those born between 1961 and 1970 and those born before 1961. After adding premarital experiences to model 2, the cohort effects remain unchanged. However, when we control for length of marriage, wife's employment, living situation, number of children, and presence of a domestic helper in model 3, the cohort effects attenuate, and only men born in 1971 and after report more positive marital quality than the oldest birth cohort.

In terms of the premarital experiences considered in model 2, only the number of years dating one's spouse exhibits a significant effect on the full sample. Interestingly, when analyzed by gender, length of dating has a positive effect on women but not on men. That is, dating for longer enhances women's marital quality but does not improve men's marriages. This relationship

Table 6.3. Regression analysis of marital quality.

Predictors	All (N = 726)	Female (N = 431)	Male (N = 295)
	Model 1		
Intercept	−0.784***	−0.945***	−0.232
Male	0.395***		
Cohort: 1961–1970[a]	0.108	0.218	0.019
Cohort: 1971 and after[a]	0.456***	0.569***	0.338**
Social class	0.213***	0.248***	0.171***
R^2	0.112	0.096	0.070
	Model 2		
Intercept	−1.034***	−1.288***	−0.464
Male	0.377***		
Birth cohort: 1961–1970[a]	0.098	0.208	0.029
Birth cohort: 1971 and after[a]	0.458***	0.550***	0.375**
Social class	0.202***	0.224***	0.170**
Age of first dating	0.012	0.018	0.008
Years dating spouse	0.038**	0.077***	0.000
Wife higher education	−0.092	−0.233*	0.032
Wife higher income	−0.031	−0.162	0.080
R^2	0.125	0.140	0.075
	Model 3		
Intercept	−0.648*	−0.212	−0.440
Male	0.345***		
Birth cohort: 1961–1970[a]	0.063	−0.016	0.136
Birth cohort: 1971 and after[a]	0.357*	0.078	0.531**
Social class	0.198***	0.214***	0.140*
Age of first dating	0.009	0.007	0.008
Years dating spouse	0.037**	0.061**	0.006
Wife higher education	−0.078	−0.220*	0.075
Wife higher income	−0.010	−0.163	0.080
Length of marriage	0.001	−0.018	0.017*
Wife's employment	−0.224**	−0.178	−0.239**
Live with parents	0.117	0.242	0.022
Number of children	−0.123**	−0.096	−0.148**
Has domestic helper	0.123	0.042	0.216
R^2	0.148	0.165	0.125

NOTE: * $p < 0.05$; ** $p < 0.01$; *** $p < 0.001$

[a] 1960 and before is the reference category for comparison.

SOURCE: Hong Kong Family Life Survey, 2009.

continues in model 3 when marital experiences are controlled for. Although dating at a younger age has generally been considered unfavorable to a good marriage, it has no effect among Chinese in Hong Kong. In model 2, we introduce two measures of deviation from the homogamy norm on marriage matching. We find that educational matching is consequential although income matching is not. Consistent with the popular belief that it is difficult for a professionally successful woman to have a happy marriage, we find that women with more education than their husbands report lower levels of marital quality. However, violating the homogamy norm does not hurt men's marital experiences. Model 3 further replicates this gender difference even when the marital factors are controlled for.

In model 3, when we add the marital conditions, we find that length of marriage has different consequences for women and men.[13] For women, length of marriage has no effect on perceived marital quality, but for men it contributes to better marital quality. In the case of men, the cohort effect remains significant after controlling for the length of marriage. In other words, the cohort effects for men, reported in the preceding paragraphs, cannot be attributed to life-cycle development; thus it seems reasonable to interpret the cohort effect as indicative of social changes.

Between 1981 and 2011, labor force participation rates among married women of all ages rose only from 43.1 to 51.7 percent. However, in the case of married women aged twenty-five through thirty-four, labor force participation rates increased substantially from 45.4 to 73.4 percent. For those who consider the family to be in decline, employment by married women indicates an individualistic orientation that weakens familism and lowers the quality of marital life. It has been argued that wives' employment creates competing demands between family and work roles that damage the quality of family life and that the negative effect is greater for women than men (Amato et al. 2003). Others, such as Schoen and associates (2002), cautioned that the negative effects of women's employment might appear only in unhappy marriages.

Turning to our results, we find that a working wife does have a negative effect on marital quality in the full sample, and it remains in the male subsample. Thus, while the trend toward a higher rate of labor force participation among married women could be a key negative influence on marital quality, it is particularly decisive for men's assessment of their marital life. This gender difference is remarkable, as women do not see their own employment as a factor hampering the quality of marriage, whereas men report lower marital quality when their wives' commitment is divided between family and work.

The three measures of family composition have different effects. Coresiding with parents or living with domestic helpers does not change perceived marital quality. Thus, marital quality in the nuclear family is not necessarily any better than that in the extended family. It is particularly interesting to note that living with parents, often in-laws, has no effect on marital quality for the female subsample, which is contrary to the conventional wisdom that in-laws are difficult to get along with. While live-in domestic helpers may disturb spousal privacy, they do not affect marital quality. Lastly, we find that the number of children has an effect on the full sample, suggesting that each additional child lowers marital quality, and in the subsample analysis the negative effect appears to be greater for men than women.

CONCLUSION

Rapid social and economic transformation present challenges for the institution of marriage in the modern world, and Hong Kong is no exception to this global trend. The public perception of changes in marriage practices often takes a pessimistic view, as many people make reference to the past or an imaginary past (Coontz 1992). To assess the prospect of marriage in the future, this chapter focuses on how satisfied Hong Kong adults are with their marriages and how perceived marital quality varies both with individual characteristics such as gender, birth cohort, and socioeconomic status, and with the conditions of their marriages and current household arrangements. Overall, we find that, although both the men and women in our sample are satisfied with their marriages, men report higher levels of marital quality than do women across various dimensions. The findings further reveal that those with a higher social status enjoy greater satisfaction in marital quality. For men, it is clear that those in the youngest birth cohort are more satisfied with their marriages than those in the older cohorts, indicating social change across generations. In contrast, although there is no evidence that perceived marital quality deteriorates among women across birth cohorts, neither do we observe the higher levels of satisfaction among younger women that we do among younger men. These cohort trends provide important clues suggesting that marriage is still a robust institution in Hong Kong, although longitudinal evidence is needed for a more conclusive judgment.

The analysis of our 2009 survey reveals important gender differences in terms of marital quality, although we do not directly explore the underlying causes for this split. However, when these results are considered together with the rising number of college-educated women who never marry, it appears that the institution of marriage is less appealing to the most economically successful women than it is to their male peers. This split also appears in the multivariate analysis for wives with more education than their husbands.

Without longitudinal data we cannot address questions about the degree or the drivers of change in the institution of marriage in Hong Kong. Hence, we cannot directly dispute or confirm arguments by scholars such as Lesthaeghe and Surkyn (2004), who identify a shift to postmaterialist values of self-actualization as the key driver of change. Nor can we adjudicate between scholars such as Ulrich Beck and Elizabeth Beck-Gernsheim (1995), who argue that intimate relationships must be chaotic in modern times, and those such as David Popenoe (1993), who see current trends as direct, negative, but reversible.

Our results, however, can respond to those who find the institution of marriage in decline in Hong Kong. A large majority of Hong Kong adults marry and have children, women and men both look to spouses for trust and emotional support (Ting 2013b), and most married people are happy with their relationship, according to recent survey data (Hong Kong Census and Statistics Department 2010). Overall, therefore, the micro- and macrolevel data support those who find marriage to be an evolving, yet still highly cherished, social institution for Chinese in Hong Kong. Marriage as a social institution continues to be an attractive social arrangement, as demonstrated by Erni (Chapter 8) in the case of transsexuals who fight fiercely for the right to marry in Hong Kong and in the narratives of nonmonogamous men interviewed by Ho (Chapter 7), many of whom have tried very hard to establish themselves as "good guys" within a family framework. Nor is Hong Kong an exception among other Chinese societies, as Shen (Chapter 11) documents in her work on Taiwanese transnational families, who work out their own terms for keeping a marriage intact despite geographical separation and sexual infidelity. While the experiences of marriage may differ among people of different cohorts, social class, and gender, marriage remains central to social life in Hong Kong.

NOTES

1. According to Koo and Wong (2009), approximately 15 percent of married persons had cohabited with their current spouse before marriage; for the younger cohort born between 1966 and 1975, the proportion of cohabitation increased to 28 percent.

2. Between 1981 and 2011, the proportion of female workers in the labor force increased from 34.5 to 48.3 percent (or 44.6 percent, excluding foreign domestic workers). The latest population census indicates that although 51.7 percent of married women were in the labor force in 2011, among younger married women aged twenty-five to thirty-four the rate increased to 73.4 percent.

3. The Hong Kong Council of Social Services, the largest NGO in the territory, launched the Social Development Index, which traces Hong Kong's social development. This index consists of a "family solidarity" domain together with fifteen others. In the 2010 report, the family solidarity index had dropped from –93 to –906 between 1998 and 2008 (last retrieved on April 2, 2014, from www.socialindicators.org.hk/sites/default/files/shares/files/publication/SDI2010%20report%20%2825%20Oct%2011%29.pdf).

4. By 2011, there were 26,032 such marriages, compared to 58,369 marriages registered in Hong Kong (figures from Hong Kong Census and Statistics Department 2012b: 71, 74).

5. According to the government's estimates, 15,776 men versus 675 women found their mates across the border in 1986. By 2011, the gender imbalance in cross-border marriages had changed significantly, but men were still more likely to find a spouse across the border than women. The respective totals were 20,167 men and 5,865 women (figures from Hong Kong Census and Statistics Department 2012b: 74).

6. A recent survey of unmarried women by the Hong Kong Young Women's Christian Association (2004) reported that 76.9 percent of the respondents thought that the absence of a suitable partner was the primary reason for not marrying. The other relevant factors were enjoyment of personal space (57.0 percent), fate (47.6 percent), busy with work (24.3 percent), and no faith in marriage (24.1 percent).

7. Forty percent of women and 49 percent of men in the 1965–1969 birth cohort, compared to 13 percent of women and 15 percent of men in the 1940–1944 birth cohort, had begun dating in school (Ting 2002: 60).

8. The median age is the age by which 50 percent of the relevant population has married; the mean is the arithmetic average and will be higher than the median if a minority marries at a very late age.

9. Kwok-fai Ting and Vivian Lou were the principal investigators of the survey, which was funded by The Chinese University of Hong Kong under the research scheme Chinese Studies Major Area.

10. Marital satisfaction was measured by the level of agreement with the item: "You are satisfied with your relationship with your spouse." Sharing was measured by two items: "You can reveal your mind to your partner" and "Your partner shares your feelings when you are not happy." Activity together was indicated by two items: "You and your spouse take part in leisure activities together" and "You and your spouse have common hobbies." Intimacy was measured by the item: "You and your spouse

often hold hands together and touch each other." Finally, trust was measured by two items: "Your spouse gives you a strong sense of security" and "You trust your spouse's decision." Each question was measured on a scale of agreement from 1 to 7, with higher scores indicating higher levels of agreement and thus greater satisfaction. Further analysis of all eight marital quality items indicated a very high Cronbach's alpha, $\alpha = 0.88$, suggesting a high level of internal consistency. Common factor analysis with oblique rotation also revealed a single factor structure; thus we computed an overall Marital Quality Scale based on the factor scores.

11. A technical issue in cohort analysis is that year of birth is perfectly associated with age in cross-sectional data, making it impossible to distinguish between cohort effects and age effects (Mason and Fienberg 1985). For social scientists, biological age per se is not of any substantive interest; rather, age is often used to index life-course characteristics. In the present analysis, length of marriage, although closely related to age, is a more relevant life-course determinant of marital satisfaction (Bradbury, Fincham, and Beach 2000; Van Laningham, Johnson, and Amato 2000) and is a better substitute for age. It also lessens the problem of a perfect association, although a high correlation between year of birth and length of marriage is to be expected. In our sample, the correlation between year of birth and length of marriage was −0.81, meaning that each variable explains 64 percent of the variation in the other variable. Given the relatively high correlation, both variables should be included in the model to avoid misleading interpretations. For instance, a significant effect found for the length of marriage could actually reflect cohort differences if the latter were not properly controlled for.

12. Including year of birth and length of marriage in the model entails a collinearity issue because of their high correlation. While collinearity will not bias the estimation, it reduces the chance of revealing a statistically significant effect because of the larger standard error for the estimate. In the full sample, the variance inflation factor is 2.85 for year of birth due to the presence of length of marriage in the model, which is not particularly high when compared to models with quadratic terms for capturing nonlinear effects.

13. We did not detect any nonlinear effects when a squared term was added to the model, and we subsequently removed it from the model to avoid the collinearity issue.

REFERENCES

Amato, Paul R. 2004. "Tension between Institutional and Individual Views of Marriage." *Journal of Marriage and Family* 66: 959–965.

Amato, Paul R., David R. Johnson, Alan Booth, and Stacy Rogers. 2003. "Continuity and Change in Marital Quality between 1980 and 2000." *Journal of Marriage and Family* 65: 1–22.

Beck, Ulrich, and Elizabeth Beck-Gernsheim. 1995. *The Normal Chaos of Love*. Cambridge, UK: Polity Press.

Bellah, Robert N., Richard Madsen, William M. Sullivan, Anne Swidler, and Steven M. Tipton. 1985. *Habits of the Heart: Individualism and Commitment in American Life*. Berkeley: University of California Press.

Bradbury, Thomas N., Frank Fincham, and Steven Beach. 2000. "Research on the Nature and Determinants of Marital Satisfaction: A Decade in Review." *Journal of Marriage and the Family* 62: 964–980.

Bumpass, Larry, Teresa C. Martin, and James A. Sweet. 1991. "The Impact of Family Background and Early Marital Factors on Marital Disruption." *Journal of Family Issues* 12: 22–42.

Catholic Diocese of Hong Kong. 2012. "Some Proposals for the New Government of HKSAR from the Catholic Church in Hong Kong." [On-line]. Available at www .catholic.org.hk/v2/en/pressrelease/family_E.pdf.

Cherlin, Andrew J. 2004. "The Deinstitutionalization of American Marriage." *Journal of Marriage and Family* 66: 848–861.

Coontz, Stephanie. 1992. *The Way We Never Were*. New York: Basic Books.

Family Planning Association of Hong Kong. 2004. *Family Planning Knowledge, Attitude and Practice in Hong Kong Survey 2002*. Hong Kong: The Family Planning Association of Hong Kong.

Glenn, Norbert D. 1993. "A Plea for Objective Assessment of the Notion of Family Decline." *Journal of Marriage and Family* 55: 542–544.

Goldstein, Joshua R., and Catherin T. Kenney. 2001. "Marriage Delayed or Marriage Forgone? New Cohort Forecasts of First Marriage for U.S. Women." *American Sociological Review* 66: 506–519.

Heaton, Tim B. 2002. "Factors Contributing to Increasing Marital Stability in the United States." *Journal of Family Issues* 23: 392–409.

Hong Kong Census and Statistics Department. 1982. *Hong Kong 1981 Census: Main Report*. Hong Kong: The Government Printer.

———. 1993. *Hong Kong 1991 Population Census: Main Report*. Hong Kong: The Government Printer.

———. 2008. *A Graphic Guide on Hong Kong's Development (1967–2007)*. Hong Kong: The Government Printer.

———. 2010. *Thematic Household Survey Report No. 44: Relationships among Family Members*. Hong Kong: The Government Printer.

———. 2012a. *2011 Population Census: Main Report*, vol 1. Hong Kong: The Government Printer.

———. 2012b. *Demographic Trends in Hong Kong, 1981–2011*. Hong Kong: The Government Printer.

Hong Kong Young Women's Christian Association (with Centre on Behavioral Health, University of Hong Kong) (香港基督教女青年會、香港大學行為健康教研中心). 2004. 單身女性狀況及需要問卷調查研究 (*Survey on Single Women's Conditions and Their Needs*). Hong Kong: Hong Kong Young Women's Christian Association.

Kalmijn, Mathew. 1998. "Intermarriage and Homogamy: Causes, Patterns, Trends." *Annual Review of Sociology* 24: 395–421.

Koo, Anita C., and Thomas W. P. Wong. 2009. "Family in Flux: Benchmarking Family Changes in Hong Kong Society." *Social Transformations in Chinese Societies* 4: 17–56.

Lesthaeghe, Ron J., and Johan Surkyn. 2004. "Value Orientations and the Second Demographic Transition (SDT) in Northern, Western and Southern Europe: An Update." *Demographic Research* 3: 45–86.

Mare, Robert D. 1991. "Five Decades of Educational Assortative Mating." *American Sociological Review* 56: 15–32.

Mason, William M., and Stephen Fienberg, eds. 1985. *Cohort Analysis in Social Research*. New York: Springer-Verlag.

Mitchell, Robert E. 1972. *Family Life in Urban Hong Kong*. Taipei: Orient Cultural Service.

Popenoe, David. 1993. "American Family Decline, 1960–1990: A Review and Appraisal." *Journal of Marriage and Family* 55: 527–543.

Schoen, Robert, Nan M. Astone, Kendra Rothert, Nicole J. Standish, and Young J. Kim. 2002. "Women's Employment, Marital Happiness, and Divorce." *Social Forces* 81: 643–662.

Shek, Daniel. 1995. "Gender Differences in Marital Quality and Well-Being in Chinese Married Adults." *Sex Roles* 32: 699–715.

———. 1996. "Marital Quality and Psychological Well-Being of Married Adults in a Chinese Context." *Journal of Genetic Psychology* 156: 45–56.

Skolnick, Arlene. 1991. *Embattled Paradise: The American Family in an Age of Uncertainty*. New York: Basic Books.

Thornton, Arland, and Linda Young-Demarco. 2001. "Four Decades of Trends in Attitudes toward Family Issues in the United States: The 1960s through the 1990s." *Journal of Marriage and Family* 63: 1009–1037.

Ting, Kwok-fai. 2002. "Timing of a First Date and Changing Pre-Marital Experiences." *Journal of Youth Studies* 5(1): 55–63.

——— (丁國輝). 2012. "從婚前行為看近年婚姻意義的變遷" (Premarital Behavior and the Changing Meanings of Marriage in Hong Kong). In 從社經指標看香港社會變遷 (*Hong Kong in Transition: Economic and Social Indicators of Development*), Chack-kie Wong (王卓祺), Po-san Wan (尹寶珊), and Chi-kin Law (羅智健), eds., pp. 21–40. Hong Kong: Hong Kong Institute of Asia-Pacific Studies, The Chinese University of Hong Kong.

———. 2013a. "香港婚姻制度的前景" (The Future Prospect of the Marriage Institution in Hong Kong). 紫荊論壇 (*Bauhinia Tribune*) 8: 2–11.

———. 2013b. "香港夫妻的性別觀念與感情關係" (Sex-Role Traditionalism and Emotional Intimacy between Marital Partners in Hong Kong). In 面對挑戰: 台灣與香港之比較 (*Facing Challenges: A Comparison of Taiwan and Hong Kong*), Wenshan Yang (楊文山), and Po-san Wan (尹寶珊), eds., pp. 163–177. Taipei: Institute of Sociology, Academia Sinica.

VanLaningham, Jody, David R. Johnson, and Paul R. Amato. 2000. "Marital Happiness, Marital Duration, and the U-Shape Curve: Evidence from a Five-Wave Panel Study." *Social Forces* 78: 1313–1341.

Wilson, James Q. 2002. *The Marriage Problem: How Our Culture Has Weakened Families*. New York: Harper Collins.

7 AN EMBARRASSMENT OF RICHES

Good Men Behaving Badly in Hong Kong

Petula Sik Ying Ho

HONG KONG TODAY IS A SOCIETY where cosmopolitan values of individuality and personal fulfillment intermingle with changing norms of Chinese family life to create new intimate life possibilities for both men and women. The transition from a British colony to a Chinese SAR is often understood primarily in terms of Hong Kong's political reintegration into the Chinese nation and economy, but in fact it has also precipitated multiple social and cultural transformations with far-reaching consequences for gender, sexuality, and family. In this chapter I focus on how the expansion of the Hong Kong economy into its Guangdong hinterland has profoundly reconfigured Hong Kong men's sense of themselves as family members and as romantic and sexual partners. To date, studies of men's intimate lives have focused on those who have taken "second wives" or mistresses in China (Lang and Smart 2002; Lin and Ma 2008; So 2003). But the experiences of these men also speak to a much broader set of questions about the centrality of border crossings to new configurations of male–female relationships in Hong Kong and across the border. Of particular interest to this chapter is how potential border crossings validate men's rustic yearnings for traditional and obedient women who seem less demanding than materialistic and pragmatic Hong Kong women.

Literal and figurative border crossings create new sexual and gender geographies for Hong Kong men. The border between Hong Kong and the Mainland is not just a physical site; it is also defined by legal constraints on mobility and social relationships. It is reflected in a set of cultural assumptions Hong Kong men hold about women in the Mainland, which shape their performance of masculinity in an era when border crossing is both possible and common. The narratives of these Hong Kong men show how their intimate life choices are not just about sexual desires but also about the fulfillment of material needs, affective desires, and social recognition in the face of rapid social changes in Hong Kong and new roles for and expectations of Hong Kong women.

The eroticization of difference and distance in cross-border intimacies is one element of these men's desires. However, Hong Kong men also often explain their romantic involvement with Mainland women through an indirect critique of Hong Kong women, who are portrayed as too materialistic and pragmatic. Even for men who have not entered into cross-border intimacies, the border may still represent economic and sexual possibilities that have subtly affected how they define their manhood and position themselves in the dating and marriage markets in both Hong Kong and China. Some Hong Kong men may also take pride in the fact that they can still find Hong Kong women as partners, while recognizing the large reserve of women across the border.

The research on which this chapter is based elucidates the life circumstances and familial and sexual strategies used by Hong Kong men who might be seen as "nice guys" or good "husband material" by Hong Kong women due to their educational backgrounds, professional status, and gender role performances. It addresses how these men define and negotiate their masculinity by questioning conventional standards of being a good man to create a space for sexual freedom in the context of colonial history, the "one country, two system" arrangement of the SAR citizenship regime, and Hong Kong's greater economic integration with China. Although the sample of twelve is primarily one of convenience, it includes men of different ages and marital statuses.[1] All were ethnic Chinese, born and raised in Hong Kong, who considered themselves local residents ("Hong Kong people"). All except one had received at least a university education; two had studied overseas. All identified themselves as straight. Four were unmarried. One was divorcing his second wife for another married woman, who was divorcing her husband. None claimed to be totally open with his partners about his sexual relationships. Two said their partners knew about their extramarital relationships. Ten had engaged in commercial sex at least once in their lives.

Recent empirical studies of Hong Kong men have suggested that changing social conditions have increased gender-role stress. Some of the key sources of strain are the reduction of financial contributions from men to their families due to salary cuts, high rates of unemployment, and a more general sense of heightened competition from the proliferation of economic ties between Hong Kong and the Mainland (Lang and Smart 2002; Newendorp 2008). But some of the pressure is more specifically tied to women's recent gains in education and the job market. Hong Kong women now are as likely to complete a postsecondary degree as their male peers, and almost three-quarters of young married women are now in the labor force (Ting Chapter 6). As a result, women in Hong Kong have not only become more economically and socially independent, but they also are more willing to express demands for sexual loyalty and to expect men to put more effort into meeting women's needs. In response, we witness the growing popularity of the derogatory label "Hong Kong girls" (港女), which implies demanding and materialistic women who require high maintenance (Huang 2010; Yip 2008).

To understand how Hong Kong men's sexual choices and their emerging sense of masculinity are related to the pressure on "Hong Kong guys" (港男) to meet the expectations of Hong Kong women, this chapter offers a new way of mapping Hong Kong men's desire that highlights "intra"-national border-crossing relationships and how they affect sexual and marriage practices in Hong Kong. Specifically, we explore (1) how the new marital and sexual practices of these Hong Kong men are being reframed by easy access to Mainland women with the opening of the border; (2) how Hong Kong men articulate new discourses about being responsible and worthy in the context of the now dominant and reconfigured relationship with China; and (3) how the new configurations of masculinity allow new discourses of self-awareness and humility to emerge.

CHANGING SEXUAL AND MARITAL PRACTICES

Similar to the situation of Taiwanese men who leave their families behind when they move to work in China (Shen Chapter 11), Hong Kong men who cross the border into China enjoy economic opportunity and material benefits (or compensation for poor job prospects in Hong Kong), as well as a means of enhancing masculinity and satisfying their affective and sexual needs. These opportunities, however, also challenge dominant sexual and marital practices in Hong Kong and may heighten the gap between social and personal expectations regarding sex, love, and marriage. In the process, popular and individual concepts of masculinity may be reconfigured as the men who search for intimacy across the border develop new perceptions of themselves as a "good catch" in the dating and marriage market and of Mainland women as targets of rescue and protection. Eager to feel respected, even heroic, they also have created new ethics of what constitutes being a responsible and worthy husband in situations where they cannot live up to social expectations that they act as good men who are monogamous and sexually loyal to their wives.

I Am a Good Catch! New Model of Ideal Husbands

Responses to the interview question "Are you a good guy?" shed light on the changing sexual and marriage expectations of Hong Kong men given their new access to cross-border romance and intimacy. Many interviewees felt that, if a man is willing to marry his girlfriend, he is a good guy. The men knew they were causing some women great distress by their multiple sexual relationships but argued that if a man wants to get married and does not give up a stable relationship or marriage too easily, he deserves a "20 percent discount" (to be forgiven) from his partner for extramarital relationships or for sometimes failing to meet her expectations. In general, the men view a "good guy" as someone who is willing to be committed through marriage, financial or asset management, or simply to "come home." Interviewees seemed very aware that they were seen as "nice guys" and good husbands because of their income, educational background, social status, and above-average gender performances, and they were often critical of Hong Kong women, describing them as pragmatic, materialistic, and hard to please. At the same time, however, they took pride in being able to manage these high-maintenance women by giving them the financial security and social status that they wanted in marriage. Chang, a thirty-three-year-old physiotherapist, and Lee, age thirty, a fireman, made these observations:

> One of the most important defining features of a "good guy" is whether you would marry your girlfriend in the end. If you say yes, then you are no doubt a "good guy." (Chang)

At the first interview, Chang was about to marry his long-time girlfriend and was proud to show us his wedding photos. He said he was not sure whether he could cut off his relationship with his female colleague, a long-time secret lover, but he would try because he was keen to be a good husband. When we interviewed him again after two years, he had had a daughter with his wife and was more determined than ever to terminate his relationship with his lover because of the competition posed by his lover's other boyfriend. Chang was serious about his marriage and was eager to be a good father:

I want to be a good father to my daughter. I haven't given my daughter the time and attention that I imagined I would give her before she was born. I thought I would spend a lot of time with her, but I just do not have the time and energy to do this. I am not proud of this. (Chang)

Lee was single and had been cohabiting with his longtime girlfriend, an overseas-educated local Chinese woman, for more than three years. He was not sure how long he could resist marriage, but he argued that, because he was willing to perform, as far as possible, the general role of a husband, this indicated that he qualified as a good guy:

> If you go down to Causeway Bay and interview 100 women, I bet ninety of them would agree that being willing to get married is a sufficient criteria for defining whether you are good or not. I am one out of the ten who have made it clear to my girlfriend that I will not marry her, but I can offer her the kind of lifestyle that most Hong Kong women want—no prostitution, no gambling, and coming home on time. For her mother's birthday, I have a gift prepared, and she has no need to worry. I look clean and tidy and presentable. Isn't that enough? (Lee)

In a second interview, Lee explained that he had injured his leg in a soccer game a year previously and had had an operation and six months of leave. He was grateful that his girlfriend had taken good care of him when he needed her most and was determined to continue to live with her. Lee felt that his religion was also an important factor:

> Many women in Hong Kong have fantasies about firemen, and so I and my colleagues are always attracting women's gazes from breakfast till dinner. But this is not what I want anymore. If not for my Christian background, I would be more ruthless in my work and in my relationships. When I ask myself why I am who I am, I cannot but admit that it is because I have those Christian values implanted in me! (Lee)

Recently, Lee planned to move to a new flat with his girlfriend. He argued that holding joint property with one's partner was an important expression of love and commitment:

> In fact, we are not buying the property together. She doesn't have much. I paid for everything, but I have decided to have her name on the contract. If you go around the whole of Hong Kong to talk to women, I am sure that most of them

would prefer to have their name on the flat rather than on a marriage certificate. Isn't this an important act of commitment? (Lee)

Lee added that giving up one's financial autonomy is crucial to give a woman the sense of security that she needs. He said,

> I give her every cent of my salary every month. She gives me $150 Hong Kong dollars (US$20) every day for my daily expenses. If I need to go out and eat with my friend, I will let her know, and she will leave a $500 note in my pocket early in the morning. All my colleagues in the Fire Services hate me for doing this and have said that I should never brag about this in front of their wives. (Lee)

When asked whether Chang and Lee would consider having Mainland women as their girlfriends and partners, they said that they were open to the possibility and knew they could win such women if they wanted to, but they simultaneously expressed a sense of pride that they do not have to go for "Mainland girls" (大陸妹) as their partners. Like the Taiwanese men described by Shen (Chapter 11), they attributed different roles and qualities to Mainland and Hong Kong women and felt the latter were more suitable as long-term girlfriends or wives.

I Want to Be a Hero for Once in My Life!
New Targets of Rescue

Other men, however, claimed that they would marry or at least date Mainland women, raising the question of what marriage means to Hong Kong men in this new, cross-border context. The case of Cheung helps us understand men's needs and desires—not just sexual desires, but other needs, including self-esteem and social recognition. Going across the border also enhances their masculinity through their purchasing power and cosmopolitan qualities and expands access to more diverse sexual experiences.

Cheung, forty, a businessman who travels to China, often described this urge to "save" as man's "natural instinct":

> Like the sparrows, the males go in search of food. If you like a woman, you will want to improve her life and protect her. I have noticed how this is a strong desire in most of these guys, and they derive a lot of satisfaction from providing a more comfortable life for their women, if they can afford to do so. (Cheung)

Chow, a thirty-eight-year-old designer, also spoke about offering financial help and/or repaying someone's debts when asked about relationships with

Mainland women. Chow was in love with Tina, a sex worker from Mongolia, whom he had met on the Internet. He knew that he would be seen as a stupid guy who allowed himself to be ripped off by a prostitute, but he really felt sorry for Tina and wanted her to stay in Hong Kong. He claimed that he would never have a live-in girlfriend, and he would never allow a woman to take charge of his life, but it is clear that he had given up these ideals in his relationship with Tina. "The Immigration Department is questioning her, and I don't want to see her travel in and out of Hong Kong like this. I will consult an immigration lawyer to find out more." He hoped to encourage her to go back to studying by offering financial help and repaying her debts:

> I come from a good family. The money I have is not really mine. Her family is poor. I don't mind helping her out, even as a friend. I know that this money may not really be for repaying her parents' debts. I also hope that, one day, she will trust me enough to tell me what this is all about. (Chow)

Knowing that he might be cheated thus did not make Chow want to leave the relationship. He found it a big challenge to relate to a woman who was in every way different from his other girlfriends. For men such as Chow, male "heroism" translates into the ability to provide for and to better the lives of their female partner and her family members.

I Want to Show Her the World! New Targets of Protection
Male hierarchies of power and competition often give structure to masculinity. As illustrated so far, financial ability is perceived as one of the major stakes in any sexual or marital relationship, and it serves as a primary means of constituting masculinity. In addition to financial security, a relatively broader worldview and education enhances a man's claim to secure masculinity.

Wu, aged fifty-two, a human resources consultant, had worked in Shanghai for more than ten years. His wife and his son had moved to Shanghai to be with him. However, he had an affair with a twenty-one-year-old woman when he was forty-four and then later fell in love with one of his business associates, a woman who worked in Shanghai while her husband stayed in the United States. He said,

> It feels good to show her the ways of the world and help her establish herself in Shanghai. My wife is quite tolerant of this. She hopes that I will find what I want. (Wu)

However, Wu's wife later divorced him and returned to Hong Kong with their son after learning that Wu was serious about his relationship with this married woman. "The time has come for me to make a decision, and I do want to have a new life," Wu said.

Mak, a thirty-year-old sales promoter who lives in Shenzhen with his Mainland girlfriend from the North, described similar motivations for his cross-border relationship. Like Wu, Mak found it satisfying to teach young women and help them find their way in the world; he also derived greater status and financial power because his Hong Kong salary offered him a lifestyle in China that he could not afford in Hong Kong:

> I am doing better when compared with other guys my age who only have a secondary school education, both in terms of my financial stability and dating prospects. (Mak)

Mak emphasized that his integration into Shenzhen had provided him with a sense of personal pride and external validation because he is seen as above average in the eyes of Mainland people, rather than below average, or just average, as he would be seen in Hong Kong. He was proud that very attractive women would date him. He also felt Mainland women were much easier to handle due to their lack of education and their youth:

> I like to talk; I like to teach. I like manipulating that person to become who I want her to become. (Mak)

Over the years, Mak has dated numerous women in the Mainland. His main leverage is his financial status, which has allowed him to date his current girlfriend, who is only twenty-one, as well as his previous girlfriend, who was barely sixteen. However, his current relationship is unstable: He revealed a wound from a physical fight with his girlfriend and expressed doubt as to how much longer the relationship would last:

> Now I want to date local women because it is not as easy as it seems to handle those women from the North. They are demanding. I have begun to see how cultural differences are difficult to deal with. (Mak)

Money is also a concern for Mak because he not only supports his girlfriend but also cares for his parents, including his mentally ill mother. He wanted to be responsible both to his parents and to his girlfriends, but these expectations created financial pressures for him.

From the previous paragraphs, we see the various strategies that men use to perform gender and intimacy and how they use the popular but derogatory discourse of "Hong Kong girls" to express their dissatisfaction with Hong Kong women. Men with multiple sex partners presented themselves as having multiple roles and competing demands. They wanted to stress how they were victims of life circumstances (Ho 2006, 2012) or of personal desires (including greed and lust) that were often not fully under their control. Their desires for different forms of recognition from women and from their families, as well as their need for sex and pursuit of less boring lives, inspired them to risk new adventures, including romantic and sexual relationships outside of their marriages or primary relationships. They find themselves most valorized when they feel needed. However, these new experiences with new targets of rescue have also created personal dilemmas that call forth new justifications for their choices.

CHANGING MASCULINITY: NEW DISCOURSE OF BEING RESPONSIBLE AND WORTHY

Hong Kong men have found a variety of ways to describe and resolve the contradictions that they have experienced in trying to meet social expectations and personal desires. One of the discourses that they often use highlights the idea of being "responsible." However, the ways they define being responsible differ dramatically. It could be any one of the following: (1) admitting to mistakes and paying the price; (2) committing to not having extramarital sex even at the cost of mental health and taking pride in being able to sacrifice; (3) fooling around before marriage and settling down after; (4) being responsible providers and not telling their wives about their extramarital sex. In all of these cases, they consider themselves to be responsible. In all of these scenarios, they justify their rationale and actions as being "worthy."

I Have Done My Best to Compensate for My Mistakes!
Asking for Forgiveness

One of the ways to be a responsible guy is to admit mistakes and do whatever possible to compensate for those mistakes. Liu had been a Hong Kong civil servant, previously married to a Hong Kong woman with whom he had three daughters, now aged twenty-seven, twenty-five, and fourteen. When he was fifty, he divorced his wife and moved to Shenzhen. He applied for early retirement and now gives half of his pension to his ex-wife and uses the other half to support a new family with a twenty-eight-year-old woman from Hunan, who had been living in Dongguan but moved to Shenzhen to be with him. Liu does not call himself a good guy because he divorced his wife and left their three daughters, but he insists that he is a responsible father because he has maintained connections with his daughters even after his new wife gave birth to their son in Shenzhen:

> It is a misperception that I left my ex-wife because of my relationship with my current wife. This is not true. I argued with my wife all the time. It was a hopeless marriage, and so I decided to go. I did not run away from my family. I am still connected to them in many ways. I see my youngest daughter regularly. She is just fourteen, and she needs me. But my two older daughters are adults. One will get married soon, and the other is already a post-graduate. Why would they want me to stay with them under one roof? (Liu)

Liu said he is happy with his second life on the whole but is worried about his son's education and frequently disagrees with his second wife about child-rearing decisions. He has even considered whether it would be best to move back to Hong Kong so that his son would not have to travel across the border daily to attend school. Liu helps a friend run a business in Hong Kong and thus does not mind traveling every day to Hong Kong, but it is hard for his son. He is proud to be able to work and have an affordable home in Shenzhen while paying alimony to his ex-wife, thus fulfilling his duties to his two families as the good man that he thinks he is. However, he has some regrets about having married his new wife and admits to having thoughts about divorcing her:

> My second wife was young and beautiful when I met her. I used to argue with my ex-wife every day, but this one was very nice to me. I thought that it would be nice to have a family with her. I really wanted to settle down and be a good man. I used to gamble a lot, but slowly I got tired of the game. I did not realize that I had to take up so many responsibilities again with this new family. Rents are cheap here. I paid $600 yuan, and we can have a nice, good-sized apartment. Now she is only interested in playing mahjong every day and has little concern for our son's education. She was from a rural village, and so she did not find it important to bring our son to drawing classes or to take piano lessons. (Liu)

In his ten years in the Mainland, Liu has noticed how most cross-border marriages break up for the same reason: the education gap between Hong

Kong men and the rural Chinese women they tend to marry, which makes it difficult for them to agree on hygiene issues and how to bring up a child. Liu came to the conclusion that his ex-wife was really a good mother in the way she had brought up their three daughters and that Mainland women were "useless" in this respect. They were also liars:

> It is a big lie. All Mainland women are liars. They would be nice to you when you first meet them because they saw you as rich. They then revealed themselves to be lazy bums after marriage. They also expect you to take care of their parents and families. I don't mind doing it if I have the money. Even if I really had the money, it would be used up by these women one day. They would keep asking for more regardless of your actual financial situation. (Liu)

Liu felt it was a big burden to have to take care of two families, especially as his new wife was not helpful or understanding of his financial situation. When he talked about his suffering, it was as if he was saying that he had learned his lesson, and therefore he hoped that he would be given the freedom to live a new life without his two wives.

I Deserve a 20 Percent Discount! Bargaining for Full Acceptance

"Responsibility" carries a variety of meanings for Hong Kong men. It might mean doing the best in their social roles in order to feel more legitimate about pursuing other involvements outside their main relationship. It could also mean that they have a perception of what a "good guy" is and therefore do all they can to meet that "standard." These men always hear women say, "Are you good enough for me to marry?" and feel stressed about becoming a good guy for these pragmatic women, who desire the security offered by married status and its financial benefits. Some, like Lee, feel that, by behaving well, they earn themselves a "20 percent discount," which they want to cash in for sex with other women on the side or for some freedom to do what they want. They stressed that they could understand women's material concerns in Hong Kong society, which provides little social security, and that a lot of women need men's commitment to feel secure in their relationships. However, they felt it unfair to be judged all the time and to be found lacking:

> Because women care so much about marriage and whether their men are financially okay and socially presentable, they should also be prepared to give their men a 20 percent discount by putting up with their imperfections. As

long as she does not know about my other involvements and believes that she has got what every woman wants most, that is the best option. (Lee)

These men are well aware that their involvement in other sexual relationships will make them look "bad," and that it would cause great distress to their partners if they knew about them, including regular use of commercial sex in some cases. They know the potential risks involved yet feel the need to have these multiple spaces. Their strategy of being responsible requires that they remain "in the closet" concerning their extramarital sexual experiences:

I will lose a lot of things that are important to me; that's why I dare not tell her the truth. I am not sure if I care about being able to look like a good guy or whether I truly want to be one. (Chang)

Chow is now cohabiting with his current girlfriend, who has to travel to China and other parts of Asia for her business. He feels he is not the marrying type, but he really loves children and would not mind having a child with his girlfriend. He used to have a more active love life but now seems to want to be more settled. He used to believe that he could be more honest with his girlfriends, but now he regrets being so naïve. His experience with Tina, the Mongolian woman, was horrible—the love relationship turned sour and abusive, which changed his views on relationships:

I made many mistakes by believing that I could be honest with my girlfriend by admitting my past relationships with other women. I got myself into trouble. I was even beaten up by a jealous ex-girlfriend. She came to know that I had sex once with one of my ex-girlfriends. Women from Mongolia are fierce. I had to call the police to stop her. She harassed her love enemies by sending threatening e-mail messages. I still have bad dreams about her. Now I have changed to prefer a less exciting love life. I have also learned that I should never be honest about my other involvements. (Chow)

Chow added,

I love my girlfriend, but it is just so boring to have to eat the same thing every day. You cannot have rice every day. Sometimes, you may want to have biscuits. I still have sex with prostitutes, and I would never become emotionally involved with them. (Chow)

Chang, Lee, Liu, and Chow all express the stress that Hong Kong men undergo in facing their relationships and families. They feel that they deserve to be treated better, not in terms of love and care but that their women should turn a blind eye to their other sexual involvements and appreciate them for the thoughts and practices that they have invested in their families to be responsible.

I Don't Even Have Good Sex!
Assuming the Role of a Victim

Some men also feel that they have been victimized. They stress how they have compromised their choice of sexual possibilities across the border and the wide range of very accessible sex services in different localities in Hong Kong because of their sense of duty to their partners and their desire to be a good and responsible partner. They control themselves, as far as possible, to protect their families and relationships and otherwise might have gone further.

Choi, age forty-five, a manager, for example, feels it is important for a man to feel that he is being responsible. His way of achieving this is by adhering to the standard of no extramarital sex, doing the minimum of what his roles require of him, and becoming distant. We interviewed Choi in Shenzhen near his office. He looked depressed and kept saying that he was not happy about having to travel across the border to work every day but that he had no choice after being laid off by his company in middle age. He used to be a senior manager in an investment company. Choi said, "I have tried without success to find a good job. I could only earn one-third of what I used to earn if I were to stay in Hong Kong to take up other jobs." He felt that he could never be a "good guy" if he continued to lead such a lifestyle, but he could call himself "a responsible guy" because he did his duty:

> Good guys can make everyone in the family happy. They can bring harmony to the household. I travel everyday to Shenzhen to work, and when I arrive home I am exhausted. I have become a silent and distant husband and father. I do what I do and have also tried hard to resist the temptations to have a mistress in China only because I want to be a responsible man. It is a matter of responsibility, and I don't want to pay the price of losing my family. (Choi)

Choi said he could not afford to have any relationships outside marriage. When he was in China, his wife checked on him every night and had long telephone conversations with him to make sure that he would not have time for other women. After much struggle, Choi decided to go home every night:

> If I have a mistress or girlfriend in China, I may feel happier about life. It is not just about long hours of travel to maintain a job without much prospect, but

how long will my girlfriend stay with me? Ten years? She will dump me when I am older and without money. My wife will be with me when I am seventy years old. I am not saying that I am good at resisting temptations. I just cannot afford it when the cost is so high. I have only one aim—to pay off my mortgage in a few years. (Choi)

Choi felt that Hong Kong men working in the Mainland could make life livable for themselves by having girlfriends for sex and companionship. In most situations they would not disclose their sexual choices and lifestyles to their partners, but they would not mind admitting to having desires for multiple sexual relationships.

Chang, the thirty-three-year-old physiotherapist, said he was still on very good terms with his wife, who apparently had little idea of his extramarital relationships. When asked how he made sense of his relationship with his girlfriend, he admitted that he was just being greedy. He added that this had to do with his very strong desire for sex:

It is just painful to deal with one's own sexual desire. If I could replace my time surfing pornography online and masturbating with reading or studying, I could probably have become a professor like you! (Chang)

I Can Brag about My Past Glories!
Choosing the Least Harmful Path

One of the strategies Hong Kong men used to appear as a responsible guy is to fool around before marriage and settle down after. All the interviewees proudly affirmed that they were nicer to women than other men they know and that they cared about the impact of their sexual adventures and relationships on their partners. Interviewees like Lee, Wu, and Chu were proud to have a history of being wild, as this justified their return from adventure to a stable life with a sense of security that they need as they age. They also took pride in being good lovers. It was interesting to see young men like Lee and Wu talk as if they were middle aged or older men in the way they remembered the glorious days of their youth. Lee, age thirty, a fireman, said,

My days of being wild are so important to the stability of my present life. I fooled around from nineteen to twenty-five, and I felt as if I had seen everything and tried all sorts of sexual adventures to the point that I am not tempted anymore. Among my fireman colleagues, we have come to the conclusion that all men want to have some fun and it is just a matter of when they would have it. If a man decides to have some fun after his son has graduated from university, it would be a bad time. He messes up his life. At the age of fifty, what fun can he afford to have? That is why I think that men should be wild when they are young. (Lee)

Wu, a businessman, felt at the age of thirty that he had found he could settle down and enjoy a stable relationship:

I used to be a policeman, and I had many experiences of cracking down on the brothels. I can't tell you how dirty those places are and how dirty I found those women. I just cannot imagine having sex with prostitutes. I do business in Indonesia for half of the month. I may also find some women attractive, but my wife is my best friend, and it is just so comforting to come home to her. I had many girlfriends before. They come and go. My wife is different. She will not leave me. (Wu)

These men argued that men should have sexual adventures when they are young so that they can settle down and be "good guys" after marriage. When they settle down, they should do their best to buy an apartment and own a home. They should be nice to their in-laws, too. Wu was also proud that he was able to leave his policeman job to become a businessman because of his wife's encouragement and support.

Chu, age thirty-eight, a social welfare officer, recalled his experiment in maintaining multiple relationships when he was an undergraduate. He felt that it was very difficult to take care of more than one lover:

I could not be in two places at one time. Things got complicated. Maybe it is not a lifestyle for me. Theoretically and morally, it is not a bad thing to be able to have multiple relationships. In real life, it is just too difficult to deal with jealousy. (Chu)

Chu felt that it was unfair to look at men as if they are always the ones who benefit from marriage and have all the advantages. He felt he needed a sense of uncertainty to drive him to do good:

I can't say I am a good lover or a good husband! How can a man be sure that his wife is really as happy as she looks? If you asked my wife if she is happy, I think she would say yes. But I do not live my days with this sense of certainty. I can only do my best. (Chu)

In different ways, these men took pride in being good partners and husbands, at least by conventional standards. They pointed out how they were willing to do emotional work and perform the sexual labor needed in love and marriage, as women do. When it came to their own sexual lives, they presented themselves as pitiful beings. One could attribute such behavior to a gap between desire and reality. These men are arguing that they have also made a lot of sacrifices in terms of sexual satisfaction and possibilities in their attempt to be responsible. These "responsible" guys do not talk much about their happiness, although they do not seem to be particularly unhappy. It is as if happiness is not their main concern in the context of their desire to be seen as good or responsible.

I Can Forget about Being Happy! Asking for a New Understanding of Men's Sexuality

Among the interviewees, very few used the term *happy guy* to refer to themselves individually, the exceptions being the two single men who were very proud of having more freedom and better lives than the married men, especially concerning sex. Cheung claimed to be the happiest guy on earth because he has sex and his Hong Kong girlfriend is not a typical "Hong Kong girl":

> I have had sex with women of all nationalities and not just Mainland Chinese women. I don't think you can name one country that I don't know what their women are like. I can tell by the color, texture of their skin what their sexual tastes are like even if they have their clothes on. (Cheung)

He is proud to think that most swingers like himself are highly educated professionals who respect each other's privacy and are sensitive to other people's needs. Cheung organizes swinging parties in Hong Kong and across the border. His girlfriend is not willing to join in, but she does not mind Cheung's involvement in them: "As an independent career woman who is open about sex, she gives her boyfriend the space needed to develop his varied interests."

Yuen, aged forty, is a designer/photographer. He has had a few sexual partners, most of them long term. He claimed that he would not break up with a woman once he had involved himself in a relationship. He was very proud of his own creativity in sex and very appreciative of his partners' personalities and open attitudes toward sex and relationships. He claimed that he could help women increase their sexual pleasure. He was proudest of being able to make women have orgasms that would last for ten minutes:

One last thing I would like to point out is that I have not had sexual experience with *that many* women. I may be lucky that, with those I had, they are all very different, or maybe because I tried to squeeze the last ounce out of them. It is my experience that sex cures many physical problems, and good and frequent sex is important for good health, and physical problems are frequently caused by insufficient or bad sex. (Yuen)

When his friend pointed out to him that he "cannot conquer the world by sex," his response was, "However, the right means—by love—are still an elusive thing that I am trying to grasp." The married interviewees in the focus group could not help but look at Cheung and Yuen with admiration and envy, but they also insisted that they were exceptions, and they did not expect themselves to be so lucky to meet women with such open attitudes.

It is interesting to note how some interviewees admitted that they did not have much sex in their lives (with Hong Kong or Mainland women) after a while but wanted to stress how they were good at it in the way they valued sexual intimacy with their partners and how they would compromise their pleasure to please their wives and girlfriends. They valued sexual intimacy and were interested in helping women achieve orgasms rather than just focusing on their own pleasure. Interestingly, they did not give many details about their sexual lives with their stable partners but instead gave examples of how they were capable of pleasing their other sex partners. Chang argued that psychological satisfaction with their potency and superiority was more important than physical pleasure:

> With my wife, I focus on mutual pleasure, but with my girlfriend I want to show that I am much better than her other sex partners. I will be very satisfied if I can prove this. It's been three years, and I still have a strong desire for her, probably because I find it more challenging. Physical pleasure is less satisfying than a sense of potency and pride. (Chang)

Even in their relationships with sex workers, the men are keen to impress on the women that they are good customers. This is how Lee described his experience with sex workers:

> For ten years, I resisted the idea of paying for sex, but now I really think it is not a bad thing to do. I discovered that I perform best when I have sex with a prostitute. I feel that if I pay and I can even be nice to her, I am really happy. (Lee)

Chow finds it emotionally satisfying to tell a sex worker about his problems at work. He finds it more therapeutic to visit a sex worker at lunchtime on a frustrating working day than to share his frustrations with his girlfriend:

> The sex worker would only say, "Poor boy, it must be hard for you," but the girlfriend would ask for so much detail and make judgments about my actions. I really don't need that at the end of a long work day. I am too tired to talk. (Chow)

Apparently, these men are saying that they are very different from stereotypical men who only care about their own sexual satisfaction. They are good lovers if they want to be or if they are given the opportunity to express their tender loving care.

In all the preceding narratives, there is bitterness concerning the men's Hong Kong girlfriends, wives, and/or other partners, as well as about Hong Kong women more generally. These men feel that they are under a lot of pressure to make money and achieve goals that will meet these women's expectations. Lee and Chang talked a lot about wanting to have more exciting jobs than those of civil servants, but they knew too well the risks involved when the market is so volatile. Choi made it very explicit that he felt deprived emotionally and hinted about his sexual deprivation in talking about his struggles to resist the temptations of Mainland women. Liu talked a lot about how he had felt more comfortable having a small family and a small home when he first started his family in Shenzhen. For all that they have done, these men just hope that their women will be more considerate and less judgmental about their shortcomings. They think that, by their willingness to get married and behave responsibly to their partners, they should be able to earn the respect of their partners. They also hope that their sacrifices and inhibitions would be recognized.

CHANGING DISCOURSES OF GENDER EQUALITY: NEW WAYS OF RELATING TO WOMEN

The narratives of the interviewees reveal key features of an emerging discourse of masculinity among Hong Kong men. Believing that they have a new way of treating women (with reference to their understanding of gender equality), as well as holding new ideas of how modern men should relate to themselves (focusing on self-awareness and humility that they see as uncommon among lower-class or traditional Chinese men), these men seek to resolve the contradictions that they have experienced in trying to meet social expectations and realize their own personal desires.

When asked how they make sense of their own gender roles and values, the men in this study often compared themselves favorably to the most important men in their lives—their fathers. They strongly desired to be different from their fathers, whom they felt had little respect for women, and their grandfathers, many of whom may have had multiple wives. As the concept of "gender equality" became part of their everyday language, they used this equality discourse to define their own identity as modern men who differed from older guys with patriarchal values. Ironically, however, their own desires for multiple sexual relationships or their disinclination to marry meant that they often failed to meet the expectations of modern Hong Kong women, raising questions about their interpretation of gender equality and its connection to emerging discourses of masculinity.

I Don't Want to Be Like My Father!
Awareness of Gender Equality

Chang told us of one of his most unforgettable encounters with his father:

> My father is rude and violent. He shouted at my mother all the time, and I hated it. One time, he even beat her up. I picked up a knife from the kitchen and threatened to kill him. We almost killed each other. It is only recently that I have managed to talk to him without picking a fight. (Chang)

Most of the men said they did not want to be like their fathers, especially in the way they dealt with marriage and family, as well as in their attitudes toward women. They wanted to treat women nicely and give them what they want. Sometimes they would go so far as to marry them, even though this might not be what they themselves considered most desirable.

Chow's father married at a very young age. When Chow's younger brother was born, his mother discovered that his father was having extramarital relationships. His parents divorced when Chow was a teenager. His father later got a Taiwanese woman pregnant and married her. They now have two children. Chow felt that his father was totally unfit for marriage because he lacked the communication skills to relate to his wives and children:

> I don't want to be like my father. He spent most of his time on his business, either because he was a workaholic or because he wanted to escape from his

families. He has no respect for women and could not accept anyone challenging him as an equal. (Chow)

Chow attributed his father's behavior to his experience with his own stepmother, a British woman who had mistreated Chow's father. He felt that this was why his father would never trust a woman with money and lost interest in the women he married. Chow did not want to be like his father and indicated that the major difference between him and his father was that "I do not want women to be subservient to me. I treat them as equals."

Cheung also was keen to show that he was different from his father in every way, not because his father was a bad guy but because he felt sorry for his father's weakness in his relationship with his mother:

> I am different from my father in almost every way—the way I look at my career, money, sex—totally different. For my father, marriage is important. He will do everything for the family. He is a good father, and he treats my mother nicely. On the contrary, my mother is not that good to my father. She is the queen of the house. It is almost as if they are separated. They stay together but are separated, if you know what I mean. My mother is a businesswoman, but my father is not [a businessman]. Both of them used to be actors. My mother was a starlet turned businesswoman. My father did not try as hard. I am different from all other men I know because of one word: *understanding*. I understand women. (Cheung)

Lee is proud that he has not yet married his girlfriend, and this makes him feel morally superior to his father:

> When my mother said that I hadn't treated my girlfriend in the right way and I am exactly like my father, I would tell her that at least I have not married my girlfriend and chained her down for the rest of her life. (Lee)

However, Lee added that he was disappointed with himself for his growing resemblance to his father.

> I chased after my father with a knife in my hand. I almost killed him. He does not do things at home, and he always shouts at my mother. As I grow older, I find myself more and more like him in the way I talk to my girlfriend and boss her around. (Lee)

Chang's story provides another example:

I differ from my father in the way I treat women. I think I am very much influenced by my mother, who treated me like I was her husband. She complained a lot about my father to me. After quarreling with my father, she would tell me how she, like every woman, just wanted to be pampered by her man. I hate my father for treating his family so distantly and sometimes so violently while behaving so nicely to his own friends. I want to be nice to my wife. (Chang)

These "nice guys" thus want to be better men than their fathers in the way they treat women. As a result of their different ideals of masculinity, they aim to treat women with more respect and give women what they want, within certain bounds. In short, they desire the illusion, at least, of equality.

NEW DISCOURSE OF SELF-AWARENESS AND HUMILITY: NEW WAY OF PRESENTING ONESELF

These Hong Kong men are aware of their own inadequacies and feel pressured to live up to their own ideals, those of their partners, and/or those of society. On the one hand they acknowledge that they are not as good as people imagine them to be, or as they present themselves to be, and on the other hand they feel that being a good guy, a morally good man by conventional standards, can no longer be their goal. As a result, they invoke alternative ideals to justify themselves.

These men celebrate self-awareness and humility as constitutive of what is manly and cool. In this new definition of manhood, the refusal to admit one's inabilities is bad. If they want to have extramarital relationships, they justify it by saying, "I told them from the very beginning that I have a bad CV" (Wu). They think they should be honest about their selfish intentions. This does not mean disclosing their extramarital relationships to their wives, but it means telling their partners what they can and cannot expect from them.

Many of these men thus choose to focus on two qualities—self-awareness and acknowledging one's limitations—as the most important elements of masculinity for modern men. Apparently, they feel most strongly about their changing status and the threat posed to them by women due to changing social circumstances and that it is important to be able to adapt to the new situation:

If men are rich and have career success, they can face any woman and so have no urgent need to change. If you are not, then maybe you should at least know your own position. (Cheung)

However, there are many things that they know they cannot achieve, and so they have stepped back a little to preserve some dignity for themselves through self-awareness and the courage to acknowledge their limitations. They can then despise their fathers and others who are stuck with old patriarchal values and conduct. They are saying they are different from their fathers, who couldn't see clearly their own behavior patterns and insisted on being respected in the old ways.

Chang, for example, also noted that certain "bad guy" qualities, including flirtatiousness, passion, and competence in managing multiple relationships, are sources of sexual appeal:

> "Women love bad guys," as the saying goes! Some women think I am nice. I think I am still cool! (Chang)

Some interviewees try to put themselves in other categories than those of "nice guys" or "cool guys" to avoid judging themselves too negatively.

All the interviewees, without exception, were keen to define themselves as different from ordinary, lower-middle-class men or *lou* (佬) whom they considered undesirable and vulgar. Chu is a case in point. He felt that he had tried his best to avoid being a *lou*. He said,

> I actually wished to become a woman from childhood. It seemed to me that those traditional men were really bad, even though they may be popular among girls. I just do not want to be one of them. (Chu)

These men feel they should despise these "*lous*." "They are the most uncool thing on earth!" Chu and Chang argued repeatedly.

Being good and responsible thus does not only mean taking care of the family financially and emotionally. Many of these men stressed that being aware of their own strengths and weaknesses and being brave enough to admit their limitations should also be considered the manliest things they could achieve.

Among the interviewees, only Lee considered himself "cool" in terms of physical appearance. The others considered themselves average to above average in this respect but stressed that they did not want to be outdated and old-fashioned, like some "*lous*" they had seen.

CONCLUSION

The end of the colonial era and reintegration into the Chinese nation has repositioned Hong Kong citizens politically, economically, and socially vis-à-vis those living in Mainland China. This study draws our attention to the impact of the opening of this "intra-national" border on Hong Kong men's narratives of desire, masculinity, and intimacy with women. Hong Kong men now make their life plans, relationships, and marital choices within a context of transnational labor markets, migration regimes, and cultural maps of desirable relationships or "cartographies of desire" (Constable 2003: 28) in ways that are distinct from earlier decades.

As Hong Kong is finding an uncertain anchor for its relationship to the Mainland within the whirlwind of political and economic developments, Hong Kong men, too, reveal their own insecurities. Strongly influenced by a patriarchal conception of gender roles embedded in Confucian Chinese society, Hong Kong men face pressure from work as a symbolic representation of social power and status in family and society. Although men are actually rewarded by paid work, they also suffer from taking on the role as sole or primary breadwinner and experience conflict between family and work obligations (Leung and Chan, 2012). However, rather than attributing these pressures to structural changes in the family and the labor market, they "instead blame the rising power of women" (Leung and Chan 2012: 17), as seen in the controversial figure of the high-maintenance "Hong Kong girl."

In the interviews quoted in this chapter, we repeatedly hear these seemingly successful "good guys" asking to be judged on the basis of their long-term commitments and not just by current career success, income, or a failed marriage (Ho 2012). These middle-class Hong Kong men also take pride in being desirable targets for Mainland women and in enjoying higher status in the marriage market than Mainland men. But they are also aware that their relative "cultural superiority" may decline if they fail to maintain an economic advantage.

Faced with changing expectations, these men have redefined masculine qualities of being good, successful, responsible, and cool (Ho 2012). They stress the importance of knowing their own weaknesses as modern men (unlike their fathers or the lower-middle-class men that they despise) and admit to being unable to be "good" all the time. When challenged, many justify themselves through a critique of Hong Kong women, whose expectations seem almost impossible to fulfill given the changing economic and social circumstances. Mainland women thus offer them a convenient comparison for criticizing local women.

Hong Kong men are a fulcrum of contradictions, but they see themselves as embodying the changing times. They are not only part and parcel of new discourses of masculinity, but they also participate in the production of a new collective social and sexual culture amid Hong Kong's continuing transformations (Ho 2006, 2011). Their creative agency in exploiting the economic, social, and sexual possibilities embedded in the border enables them to imagine new options for marriage, sexual intimacies, and family forms constructed by historical and contemporary flows of capital, people, images, and material goods.

NOTE

1. The larger study funded by the Hong Kong Research Grant Council had a sample of twenty men, but only twelve are included in this chapter.

REFERENCES

Constable, Nicole. 2003. *Romance on a Global Stage: Pen Pals, Virtual Ethnography, and "Mail Order" Marriages.* Berkeley: University of California Press.

Ho, Petula Sik Ying. 2006. "The (Charmed) Circle Game: Reflections on Sexual Hierarchy through Multiple Sexual Relationships." *Sexualities* 9(5): 549–566.

———. 2011. "Politics of Iconogenesis." *Asian Journal of Women's Studies* 17(1): 7–33.

———. 2012. "Hong Kong Men's Stories of Intra-National Cross Border Romances." *Asian Pacific Journal of Social Work and Development* 22(3): 176–186.

Huang Qing Tian (黃擎天). 2010. 港男港女愛作戰 (Love and War between Kong Men and Kong Girls). Hong Kong: Yong qing wen hua you xian gong si.

Lang, Graeme, and Josephine Smart. 2002. "Migration and the 'Second Wife' in South China: Toward Cross Border Polygyny." *International Migration Review* 36: 546–549.

Leung, Lai-Ching, and Kam-Wah Chan. 2012. "Understanding the Masculinity Crisis: Implications for Men's Services in Hong Kong," *British Journal of Social Work* 42: 1–20.

Lin, Ge, and Zhong Dong Ma 2008. "Examining Cross-Border Marriages in Hong Kong since Its Return to China in 1997." *Population, Space and Place* 14: 407–418.

Newendorp, Nicole 2008. *Uneasy Reunions: Immigration, Citizenship, and Family Life in Post-1997 Hong Kong.* Stanford, CA: Stanford University Press.

So, Alvin. 2003. "Cross-Border Families in Hong Kong: The Role of Social Class and Politics." *Critical Asian Studies* 35(4): 515–534.

Yip Yat Chi (葉一知). 2008. 港男筆記 (A Memoir of a Hong Kong Man). Hong Kong: FLY Media.

8 MARRIAGE RIGHTS FOR TRANSGENDER PEOPLE IN HONG KONG

Reading the W Case

John Nguyet Erni

THIS CHAPTER ADDRESSES A CASE of a transgender person living in Hong Kong who sought to marry through the Hong Kong legal system. In 2010 and 2011, the Hong Kong Court of First Instance and Court of Appeal respectively rejected the appellant, a "Miss W," who, as a certified male-to-female transgender person, wished to marry her boyfriend, a biological male. However, with strong determination, Miss W took this case, *W v. Registrar of Marriages*, to the Court of Final Appeal (CFA), which overturned the previous judgments and declared the obstruction of a transgender person's right to marry unconstitutional. By the time the CFA issued its ruling in May 2013, this first-ever transgender marital rights case in Hong Kong's legal history had already stirred considerable debate in society and among legal circles.

W v. Registrar of Marriages has become a landmark case, legally and socially speaking, for the struggle of transgender rights in particular and for our understanding of the deinstitutionalization of normative marriage at large. I wish to use the W case to examine the powerful meanings derived from legal efforts to define "marriageability" in terms that put public ordering (in the name of "societal consensus") in conflict with autonomous private choices. Much like the regulation of cross-Strait marriages discussed by Friedman (Chapter 12), the social and legal debates surrounding this case, despite it being "victorious" in a narrow sense, seem to be at odds with the dominant social and legal trends analyzed by several other authors in this volume. Just as those authors find the analysis of "private ordering" over public command of marriage and intimacy a helpful rubric through which to show that traditional expectations about acceptable marital and sexual behaviors have weakened or even disappeared, a reading of the W case shows that the legal imagination concerning marriage rights for transgender people in Hong Kong up until the 2013 CFA ruling appeared to be moving in the opposite direction.

An analysis of the discourse that was mobilized in the lower courts to block transgender marital rights remains vital today because it can shed important light on future debates concerning sexual minority rights at large. A strong declaration made by the judges in the CFA ruling was that its judgment was to be strictly confined to transgender marriage rights and therefore was not to be applied to, or confused with, same-sex marriage rights (W, CFA, para. 2). Pitting one kind of rights against another kind, this distinction raises questions about the implications of this "exceptionalist" logic for the long-term struggle for the rights of *all* sexual minorities. It is in this spirit that this chapter largely confines itself to analyzing the W case as it was debated in the lower courts. I will, however, conclude with a coda that returns to the CFA ruling to provide readers with a summary and a critical review of its approaches.

Very little is known about Miss W directly, and even the Courts admitted that their order for nondisclosure of W's identity reflected the stigma attached to being a transgender person in Hong Kong (W, CA, para. 24). It is not my purpose to attempt to fathom W's private world.[1] Instead, this chapter focuses on the public milieu of social and legal phobia in Hong Kong toward alternative forms of private intimacy. As in Kuo's Chapter 9 in this volume, I argue here that the rejection of explicit legal rights for sexual minorities creates a climate of vulnerability while shoring up traditional understandings of marriage.

In October 2009, after being refused permission to register their marriage by the Registrar of Marriages, W and her boyfriend sought legal action to demand from the Hong Kong Court: (1) a recognition that both the Marriage Ordinance and the Matrimonial Causes Ordinance should include in the purview of the definitions of "man," "woman," "male," and "female" an "updated" inclusion of post-operative transsexual persons in their acquired sex; and (2) a declaration that a denial of such recognition constitutes a violation of the freedom and right of marriage as expressly provided by both the Basic Law and the Hong Kong Bill of Rights. A year later, on October 5, 2010, the Court of First Instance, which heard the case, squashed W's judicial challenges; the judge held that Hong Kong laws would not permit—more precisely, did not enjoy the "societal consensus" to recognize—the marriage right of a transgender person.

Disappointed but determined, W took her case to the Court of Appeal. In the appeal, her legal team raised several legal challenges to the decision of the Court of First Instance, including the latter's use of (a) an outdated 1970 court case (*Corbett v. Corbett*) as a primary statutory reference;[2] (b) a view of gender that did not keep up with advances in medical technologies; and (c) a view of marriage that was in discordance with advances in international family and marriage laws. Unfortunately, the Court of Appeal argued against these challenges and handed down a judgment on November 25, 2011, to uphold the original decision.

In what follows, I want to offer a reading of the court's legal reasoning as a case that did not challenge transsexuality as such (nowhere in the judgment was W's transsexuality mis- or unrecognized), but that forcefully exposed the historical and legal anachronism and thus discursive instability of conventional marriage itself. In the first section of this chapter, I begin by providing a brief contextual discussion of marriage laws in Hong Kong, as well as changing trends in marriage, divorce, and household formation. Next, I turn to the social and cultural realities faced by transgender people in Hong Kong. Special attention will be paid to the legal dimensions of "transphobia" both in general and as it has emerged in Hong Kong to lay the ground for a close reading of the lower courts' judgments and their ramifications for marriage rights.

SOCIOLEGAL CONTEXTS

In Hong Kong, marriage is governed by the Marriage Ordinance, which was first enacted in 1875. It remains statutorily in force today, despite vast historical, social, and medical changes since its framing. According to its preamble, the Ordinance is to provide for "the celebration of Christian marriage or the civil equivalent thereof, and for matters connected therewith." Part two of Section 40 goes on to clarify that this form of marriage "implies a formal ceremony recognized by the law as involving the voluntary union for life of one man and one woman to the exclusion of all others." Legally, the introduction of Christian marriage or its civil equivalent into Hong Kong at the time of British colonial rule (known as "registry marriage") is "particularly natural given that otherwise, in those days, marriages were mostly conducted according to Chinese customary law" (*W*, CFI, para. 114). Traditional marriage up to the early twentieth century was commonly known as "Chinese customary marriage," which was likely to be an outcome of parental arrangement and often was polygamous in nature. After the introduction of the 1931 Civil Code in the Mainland, people in Hong Kong contracted marriages by following the marriage provisions contained in the Code, and those marriages, when formalized in Hong Kong (which was, of course, outside the scope of application of the Civil Code), became known as "Chinese modern marriages." No registration was required of a Chinese modern marriage, but an open ceremony was necessary. And, unlike a Chinese customary marriage, a Chinese modern marriage was bound by the code of monogamy.

Reforms in 1970–1971 did away with both Chinese customary marriage and Chinese modern marriage in Hong Kong, and, with the enactment of the Matrimonial Causes Ordinance (a direct adoption of the United Kingdom's Nullity of Marriage Act), a marriage that took place after June 30, 1972, would be void on the grounds that "the parties are not respectively male and female" (see Pegg 1994: 8). The restriction of marriage to a heterosexual relationship (monogamous in nature) is a direct inheritance of dogmatic stipulations by the Church of England. Judge Andrew Cheung, who heard the W case, made the following forceful assertion:

> According to the doctrine of the Church of England, marriage is in its nature a union permanent and life-long, for better or for worse, till death them do part, of one man and one woman, to the exclusion of all others on either side, for the procreation and nurture of children, for the hallowing and right direction of the natural instincts and affections, and for the mutual society, help and comfort which the one ought to have of the other, both in prosperity and adversity. . . . The 19th century case of *Hyde v Hyde and Woodmansee* (1866) . . . gave a shorter definition of Christian marriage, a definition adopted in section 40(2) of the [Hong Kong] Marriage Ordinance, that is to say, "the voluntary union for life of one man and one woman, to the exclusion of all others." . . . Whilst this shorter definition does not, by comparison, expressly refer to procreation, the traditional significance of procreation in Christian marriage, when viewed in the relevant religious and historical context, cannot be doubted. And procreation is, by definition, a matter for members of the opposite biological sex. (para. 116)

A whole discursive landscape of Judeo-Christian dogma thus was laid out by the judge, in which marriage was put in lockstep with heterosexuality, monogamy, procreation, even the preferred form of intimacy. But he did acknowledge this: "There is, however, no relevant definition of 'man,' 'woman,' 'male' or 'female' in either of the Ordinances [Marriage Ordinance and Matrimonial Causes Ordinance]. The matter is therefore left to the interpretation of the court" (para. 54).

Over the years, there was no legal challenge to the restrictive gender provisions of the two marriage ordinances (that is, until the groundbreaking W case), although there have been many challenges to inheritance rights and challenges arising from disputes between traditional customary marriage and modern registry marriage (see, for example, *Leung Lai Fong v. Ho Sing Ying* [2009]). Neither has there been policy change to update those statutes to reflect changes brought about by new understandings of gender, family, and marriage, unlike Taiwan where, as Kuo shows (Chapter 9), both district courts and the grand justices of the Constitutional Court have proven receptive to implementing legal reforms that reflect some transformations in family forms and gender and sexual norms. But, in fact, vast changes have occurred in Hong Kong outside of the court.

In Hong Kong, as in Taiwan and Mainland China (see Chapter 1), age at first marriage has risen, marriage rates have declined, and the crude divorce rate has spiked upward.[3] At the same time, the percentage of households with five or more members has fallen while that with only two persons has substantially increased.[4] Changes in household size and composition raise important questions about what types of people are sharing these households and how we should characterize the relationships among household members. To date, the Hong Kong government has proven reluctant to attribute changes in marriage and household patterns to new norms of sexuality and sexual difference. For example, even when the government predicts that two-person households will be the modal household size and that the proportion of these will increase steadily over the next ten years (from 25.6 percent in 2009 to 28.3 percent in 2019), it states that "large family size ceases to be a norm owing to delay of marriage and low fertility" (Census and Statistics Department 2011: 19). The government, in other words, is unable to imagine shared household arrangements or even family patterns without marriage or fertility. The importance of Miss W's case, therefore, lies not only in challenging the established marriage laws by possibly setting a legal precedent but also in exposing underlying cultural biases against nonheterosexual and/or nonprocreative intimate relationships, including those involving transgender people.[5] Transgenderism per se pushes for a specific kind of "deinstitutional-ization" of marriage, one that goes well beyond normative gender definitions and conventional notions of marital intimacy. In the face of these alternate intimacies, how do we explain the lack of governmental and legal imagina-tion about the growing diversity of gender, family, and marriage in society at large?

LEGAL AND CULTURAL IMAGINATIONS OF TRANSSEXUALITY

Records show that the first sex change surgery for a transgender person in Hong Kong was performed in 1981 by an ad hoc group of doctors in a gov-ernment hospital. In the following years, more transgender patients came to government hospitals to ask for the surgery. To treat these patients according to consistent and internationally acceptable standards, a gender identity team (GIT), composed of psychiatrists, clinical psychologists, medical social work-ers, geneticists, gynecologists, surgeons, and lawyers from both the public and private sectors, was formed in 1986 within the sex clinic of Queen Mary Hos-pital (see Ma 1997). Between 1991 and 2001, thirty-four persons were assessed by the GIT (Cheung 2006). However, in spite of the GIT's achievements, the Hospital Authority in Hong Kong closed the unit in 2005, citing budget defi-cits. As a result, transgender patients turned to private clinics, where many of the doctors they saw had little or no experience treating transgender patients (see Cheung 2010; Ng et al. 1989).

Legal Misreadings

In the legal imagination, transgender or transsexual persons are not yet leg-ible subjects; rather, they are an abject class. U.S. transgender scholar-activists Currah and Minter have written that it is "not possible to identify any single doctrinal error or logical mistake that will account for—and thus provide a simple means of remedying—the historical exclusion of transgender people from equal protection in the Courts" (2000: 37–38). Transgender plaintiffs convey their injuries in a legal system that either does not recognize them at all or draws a line in such a way as to render them strangers to all of the laws that were supposed to protect them. Legal scholar Abby Lloyd goes so far as to say that "at a systemic level, the law fails to recognize liminal subjects; faced with a transgender person who challenges traditional categories of normalcy, the law makes his or her identity so impossible, invisible, and monstrous as to be outside of the law's protection" (2005: 152). Palpable here is the hint of legal dehumanization reminiscent of the colonial treatment of racial minorities. Lloyd cites *Ashlie v. Chester-Upland School District* (1979), a U.S. court case that held that Jenell Ashlie, a male-to-female transgender schoolteacher, may not seek protection under the privacy doctrine from a state government employer's job discrimination clause. In what that court said, there was a stunning analogy made by the judge:

> It might just as easily be argued that the right of privacy protects a person's decision to be surgically transformed into a donkey. The transformation, by its very happening, would lose the quality of privateness. Certainly, those who had known the donkey as a man would detect the change, even though those acquainted only with the donkey might never have occasion to remark upon it. In addition, the change from man to beast might be just as devoutly wished, as psychologically imperative, and as medically appropriate as the change from man to woman, but the Constitution, I fear, could not long bear the weight of such an interpretation. (*Ashlie*, 160–161)

Lloyd goes on to argue that "beastly analogies" can in fact be found in many legal judgments of the transgender person's legal personality.

More Misreadings

As an increasing number of jurisdictions worldwide have protected same-sex marriage rights, we have seen a lesser degree of explicit "transphobia" in law. Yet, for transgender persons, courts extend protections most readily *insofar* as transgender people "humanize" their identities by twisting them to fit into such recognizable legal domains as sex discrimination laws, psychiatry-supported disability laws, and sexual orientation laws. In other words, a transgender person fares better in court if she or he identifies as a natural woman (in the case of a male-to-female transsexual), a disabled person (purportedly "scarred" by surgical procedures that incapacitated some of their biological abilities), or more commonly, as a queer person (with unconventional bodily fantasies and sexual object choice). While there is no question that advancements in women's rights and same-sex anti-discrimination and equality laws have brought about many political benefits,[6] these advancements are a double-edged sword for transgender people because the transgender person's very existence defies and repudiates the gender-sexuality system as we know it (see Gordon 2009).

Another problem in the way the law reads transgender people is that typically the latter are codified by a legal discourse dominated by a psychomedical model of transsexuality. It is only recently that activists have been able to redefine the term in a more psychosocial and anthropological sense. This redefinition challenges the courts' tendency to rely on crude physiological markers and conditions of psychiatric disorder, most commonly with such medical labels as "gender dysphoria" and "gender identity disorder" as professionally defined by the psychiatric standards established in the fourth edition of the *Diagnostic and Statistical Manual of Mental Disorders* (DSM-IV).

Activists have asked the courts to adopt the more preferred word *transgender*.[7] To date, however, courts around the world continue to give preference to the psychomedical labels of "gender identity disorder" and "gender dysphoria." In other words, transgender people do not yet have a liberty interest in defining their own sex; the courts still have not officially held that they had a universal right to self-identify their own legal sex. Moreover, the switch from a restrictive biopsychiatric understanding to a more cultural one has introduced its own dilemmas as culture becomes another source of cruelty.

Transphobic Culture in Hong Kong

In Hong Kong, two primary terms commonly call forth the transgender person in public discourse: *bin tai* (變態) and *yan yiu* (人妖). The term *bin tai* is a common lexicon referring to all real or imagined perversions designated as a deviation from or subversion of reproductive, heterosexual, family-centered norms of the body, gender, and sexuality. Yet the term's basic meaning is rather innocuous: *bin* refers to change, whereas *tai* means a state of affairs, a condition, or a position. But when transposed into an insult to the cross-dresser, the pedophile, the polygamist, the same-sex lover, the masculine woman, the sissy boy, or the transgender person, *bin tai* exposes its epistemological foundation in reproductive, heterosexual, family-centered normativity. As such, it achieves cultural ubiquity in a conservative society like Hong Kong (see Erni 2013).

Arguably, diverse forms of symbolic and anatomical gender and sexual boundary crossings have produced a sweeping "trans" cultural sensibility in Chinese contexts. This is evidenced by a long history of exquisite queer performativity in the Chinese popular imagination, a tradition that makes it very difficult to distinguish among homosociality, homosexuality (同性戀), cross-dressing, and bodily alterations (see, for example, Li 2003; Lim 2006; Martin

2003). *Yiu* (妖) is possibly the unifying term that refers to the "transifying" gender and sexual economy, something that the term *queer* has always tried to approximate in more global contexts. Seen in this way, *yan yiu* (literally translated as "human ghost," "human monster," or "freak") is a term that arguably exceeds a narrow reference to transgender people. Like the term *queer*, *yan yiu* seems to gesture toward a larger realm of liminal sociosexual practices: All queerly sexed subjects are members of the "*yan yiu* family." However, in Hong Kong, no cultural celebration or political positivity is in store for queerly sexed subjects like transgender people.

Terms like *bin tai* and *yan yiu* do not usually carry with them a direct indictment of biomedical or religious pathologization. They do not need to. Rather, they command a kind of cultural ubiquity that produces a sensation of shame and humiliation strong enough to induce self-policing. Put differently, they are a language that pierces through the body, gender, and sexuality to perform a deeper social degradation of one's "personal character." This explains why *bin tai* and *yan yiu* can mortify an individual into withdrawing from sociality. In Josephine Ho's ethnographic study of transgender persons in Taiwan, she delineates how transgender people are trapped between two difficult choices: to endlessly craft a self-narrative that they hope will yield social acceptance or to withdraw into aloofness so as to preemptively block contact with other people. Ho suggests that this acute project of daily self-management is an attempt to defend one's personal character in the face of a Taiwanese social atmosphere steeped in "gender policing" as well as a general erosion of social trust (2007: 348–349).

Much of Ho's essay can apply to Hong Kong. Despite the fact that the government of Hong Kong has been providing counseling and sex reassignment surgery (SRS) since the mid-1980s, and despite the existence of a growing transgender rights movement since the early 2000s, transgender people are almost entirely invisible in Hong Kong.[8] However, as is the case in Taiwan and many other countries, transgender visibility typically arrives as a shock after the (sensationalized) death of a transgender person. In 2004, this happened in Hong Kong when, within a single week, two transgender women—Louise Chan and Sasha Moon—committed suicide. The circumstances of their deaths rehearse the cultural and political tragedy of a city plagued with routine social disregard and degradation, as well as institutional dismissal of transgender people in employment, education, housing, prison, and the media (see Winter

2009a; Winter et al. 2008). Before her suicide, Louise Chan had been stalked and outed as a transgender person by the local press, costing her her job as a hairdresser. And when Sasha Moon leaped from her high-rise apartment to her death, her plunge was captured in a morbid sequence of photographs published in the following morning's local newspapers. "The media used to treat us like a freak show. Today, we're seen as a genuinely good story," laments a friend of Sasha Moon and a member of TEAM (Transgender Equality and Acceptance Movement) (quoted in Watkins 2004: 20).

Rampant transphobia in Hong Kong has also been recorded by Mark King in his small-scale study of secondary school teachers. His study confirms a significant level of fear and pathologization of transgender people among school teachers:

> Among the 183 teachers, 54% thought that TG's are mentally ill and need treatment, 16% thought that TG's are promiscuous, also 54% thought that TG's are likely to have diseases requiring treatment. Of the sample teachers, 45% would not be happy leaving their own children alone with a GID [gender identity disorder]/TG individual, 16% thought that they should not be allowed around any children. (King 2003)

Besides attributing such biases to a general lack of sex knowledge among the populace, King further shows that transphobia in Hong Kong is in fact mixed with racial phobia, which produces a belief that transgenderism must be rare among ethnic Chinese. King (2003) writes, "The local conceptualization of transgender may also have been conflated with images and ideas of transgender from neighboring Southeast Asian nations, particularly Thailand, Malaysia, and Singapore."

It should be noted that transgender people in Hong Kong do not fully lack legal rights in the civil law domain. In Emerton's (2004) study of transgender rights in Hong Kong, she discusses the administrative concessions that the Hong Kong government offers to transgender persons in an attempt to comply with international legal trends. The concessions include a transgender person's ability to change his or her name and sex identification on his or her identity card, driver's license, passport, and education certificates once that person has provided adequate evidence of a successful transition. The reissuance of the identity card is important because Hong Kong residents are required to produce their identity card at all times, even though the card does not establish a person's sex for legal purposes. The latter can only be established by one's birth certificate. Unfortunately, current laws in Hong Kong do not allow for the alteration of the birth certificate for post-operative transgender persons, a legal restriction that has an impact on the right to marriage, custody of children, and use of public spaces (for example, a public toilet or changing facility). With this discussion of the legal and cultural contours that shape the way we understand marriage and transgenderism in mind, I now return to W's case.

THE LAW IS NOT PART OF SOCIETY: READING THE CASE OF W

Miss W's legal team, who had previously won a groundbreaking gay rights case in Hong Kong,[9] laid before the Court a two-step demand: First, provide legal recognition of transgender people in their post-operative acquired sex as a full "woman" or "man"; and second, if that fails, charge that the laws of Hong Kong, by restricting or denying Hong Kong residents the right of marriage, are unconstitutional. In the proceedings, the appellant made clear that hers was *not* a same-sex marriage right litigation, so that the very core institution of heterosexual marriage was *never* the point of the legal challenge. Rather they were determined to break open the rigidity and outdated meanings of sex and gender in the context of the institution of marriage.

In his ruling, the judge positioned his thinking on transgenderism in a middle ground between two conflicting understandings of what transgenderism is and who has the right to define it. On one side is the "expert-based stereotyping" of medical professionals that defines transsexualism as a medical condition, even a disability. On the other side is a position of total ignorance and passivity. The judge took the middle road between the two extremes, positioning the court in a space ostensibly identified by rational, scientific, and tolerant discourse. And at the heart of this space was the question of deciding who and what a transgender person is.

The law has never bothered to define such plain words as man/male and woman/female. But the Court did construct transgender people as incapable of achieving the full or complete status of "man/male" or "woman/female." The middle speaking position invented by the judge has helped to cloak him in a veneer of tolerant liberalism, but the real discursive work that his position accomplished was the sculpting of transsexuality as a wounded, less-than-complete, half- or even subhuman identity.[10] In the eyes of the court, W was reduced to something neither here nor there.

The Legal Minefield

To position the court as a civilized space, Judge Cheung dutifully examined the prevailing international views on transgender people's right to marriage. As in any similar exercise in a judicial review, this canvassing of established international practice and prevalent legal opinions was necessary to lay the foundation of a court's judgment. In the legal picture painted by the judge, we were informed of several crucial facts. First, the Hong Kong Marriage Ordinance was first enacted in 1875, following nineteenth-century UK laws of the same kind. In addition, Section 20(1) of the Matrimonial Causes Ordinance states that a marriage shall be void on the ground that "the parties are not respectively male and female" (paras. 50, 51, 62, 109, 116). Second, the imperative to nullify a marriage if the married couple is found not to be a man and a woman was derived from the landmark case of *Corbett v. Corbett* decided in 1970. In *Corbett*, the decision to nullify the marriage—a decision that amounted to a rejection of the right of transgender people to marriage— was ultimately based on the importance the Court placed on the capacity for "natural heterosexual intercourse" (paras. 58–60). Third, as influential as *Corbett* has been around the world in similar and relevant litigations, its reception has been mixed. Importantly, it was not followed in jurisdictions including Australia and New Zealand.[11] Some U.S. cases also came to a different conclusion from *Corbett*, whether after referring to *Corbett* or not (paras. 65–72).

Fourth, the landmark case decided by the European Court of Human Rights of *Goodwin v. United Kingdom* (2002), affirmed the transgender person's right to marriage. Commenting on the *Corbett* criteria, the European Court was not persuaded that, in 2002, "it [could] still be assumed that the right of a man and woman to marry must refer to a determination of gender by purely biological criteria" (para. 76–81). As a result of *Goodwin*, at least 54 percent of the Contracting States of the European Convention have permitted post-operative transgender people to marry those of the opposite sex to their assigned gender. All forty-seven Member States of the Council of Europe are now required to give full legal recognition to a change of gender and to respect the right to marry of a post-operative transgender person in his or her acquired sex (para. 96).

Fifth, in the same year as *Goodwin*, the UK case of *Bellinger v. Bellinger* (2002) held a ruling that continued to adhere to the *Corbett* criteria. The *Bell-*

inger Court pointed out that legal recognition of marriage is a matter of status and is not for the spouses alone to decide; it affected society and was a question of public policy for Parliament (para. 74). Sixth, around the world today, other countries that hold the positive view as in *Goodwin* include Canada, South Africa, Israel, the United States (except three states), and in Asia, Japan, South Korea, Malaysia, Singapore, Taiwan, and Mainland China (paras. 97–103).

What one gains most from this picture of the legal landscape is the simple realization that *marriage is a constantly evolving institution*. The biologistic restrictions of marriage of the bygone era—restrictions based on chromosomes, gonads, genes, and procreative capacities—can no longer define the contemporary shape of marriage. Sweeping medical, social, and cultural changes in marriage also abound: On the one hand, genetic engineering research, prosthetics, and artificial insemination have altered the traditional understanding of "human"; on the other hand, changing notions of family, the practice of cohabitation, childless marriage, and so on, have given us a new image of marriage as practiced in real life (see also Wan 2010). Moreover, from the facts already mentioned, there seems to be a harmonization of the scientific, sociocultural, and legal arenas to recognize the evolving nature of marriage, leaving any view that wants to remain or dwell in outdated definitions and practices less and less acceptable. Cases like *Corbett* are, therefore, seriously outdated.

In fact, the challenge of *Corbett* as a reliable reference arose in the appeal proceedings for the W case. The International Court of Justice (ICJ) issued an intervention by way of written submissions to the Court of Appeal, and argued that *Corbett* should not now be regarded as good law in Hong Kong because it had been overturned by the European Court of Human Rights in *Goodwin*. The ICJ submits,

> Internationally, there is a strong trend toward recognition of an individual's new gender by changing the gender indicated on birth certificates and other identity documents. The change of official identity documents is closely linked, in turn, with an individual's ability to marry a now opposite sex partner . . . Most Asian countries permit a transgender individual to marry in his or her acquired gender or have erected no legal barrier. (*W*, CA, paras. 147–149)

Thus, the international legal consensus clearly challenges the relevance of the *Corbett* decision to the contemporary social landscape of gender and marriage.

How to "Change" without Change

Despite the many rulings around the world that have favored transgender people's right to marriage, the judge chose to establish his judgment through the *Bellinger* case—the rare instance in the international legal landscape that adhered to the 1970 *Corbett* decision—to raise an argument that *Corbett* still represented the present state of the law. He writes: "Given the close resemblance between Hong Kong and the United Kingdom in terms of the law of marriage, and the close link between the common law in Hong Kong and the common law in England, at least prior to 1997, it is unrealistic to suggest that *Corbett* did not represent the state of Hong Kong law prior to 1997 or, that it does not represent the present state of the law here, subject to any possible change thereto" (para. 121). With regard to the "possible change thereto," the judge decided to ignore evidence of undeniable and widespread changes in marriage laws and practices and argued that "there is a limit to what an updating construction can do. What is not permitted is to alter the meaning of the words used in the enactment in ways which do not fall within the principles originally envisaged by the enactment" (para. 127), and "interpretation is ultimately a matter of construing the relevant text according to its plain meaning" (para. 134).

Two constructions by the judge regarding the need to subject an outdated legal view to "possible change" must be noted. First, his idea of "change" is, paradoxically, regressive. To him, an "updating construction," which is a legal device used to reframe a law as time passes, falls on "originally envisaged" principles. In this way, the original nineteenth-century principle of marriage-for-procreation, enshrined in *Corbett* in 1970, is used by the judge to assess the need for updating the meaning of marriage in the twenty-first century.[12] In the appeals court, the judges upheld this decision to allow the statute as "always speaking," meaning that "the court should construe it in accordance with the need to treat it as continuing to operate as current law" (W, CA, para. 73). Second, the judge's idea of "interpretation" is, paradoxically, denotative. Charging the court with the responsibility to interpret the law afresh is a primary objective of a judicial review. In essence, what was presented to the Cheung court was an opportunity to consider the legal ground for a reinterpretation of the meanings of sex, gender, and marriage. Yet the path of reasoning taken by the judge is one of searching for "plain meaning" in the face of mammoth linguistic, social, cultural, and legal changes to the words "man," "woman," and "marriage" since the drafting of the relevant marriage laws in the nine-teenth century. Again, in the appeal judgment, the Court refused to budge on this point, arguing that:

> The fact that a post-operative transsexual is generally known as a "sex-changed male/female" suggests that the person is not regarded, as a matter of ordinary language, as having truly acquired his or her post-operative sex. That this may be a prejudiced view, and one which should no way be encouraged, is not to the point. The simple fact remains that the contemporary meaning of the words "man" and "woman" has not shown to have expanded in ordinary, everyday usage to include a post-operative transsexual man or woman respectively. (*W*, CA, paras. 92, 93)

We may thus describe the various judges' "method" of adjudicating "change" as backward referencing and linguistic de-connotation. If this is a permissible and legitimate legal method, then a strict, unwavering, and dog-matic adherence to the plain words and constructions of doctrines should be tried.

"A Man and a Woman" in Marriage
Is Only Prima Facie Legal

Allow me to digress and be a little technical in this section, because, as evi-denced in Judge Cheung's methodology, technical precision matters. In prin-ciple, what is the "plain" in the "plain meanings" of sex and gender for the legal purpose of marriage?

Any linguist can attest that the vital ideological supremacy of a phrase like "union of a man and a woman" in the definition of a marriage rests on its lack of representational presence. That is to say, on the discursive plane, the scale of ideological domination of a term or phrase is often positively propor-tional to the scale of the term's or phrase's representational *invisibility*. The more powerful the ability of something to restrict our imagination, the more "natural" and taken for granted it appears. However, as espoused by Judge Cheung, it seems that the opposite is true on the legal plane: The magnitude of legal force for a "true party" (whether it is a person, an institution, or a thing) is positively proportional to the degree of precise visibility, designation, and plain enunciation of the party's identity. In this way, what concept must be present in the "plain meaning" of the phrase "union of a man and a woman" other than, plainly and precisely, "heterosexuality"? It follows that for this phrase to be validly recognized, there must somewhere or somehow be an explicit citational, statutory presence of the term or idea of heterosexuality in the requisite laws of marriage.

In the W case, the judge worried that a favorable ruling to allow her to marry would inadvertently give legal recognition to gay marriage. That is to say, he was anxious that, as far as the legal meaning of marriage is concerned, any personal business deviating from the (biological) designation of "a man and a woman" would defile it. One may ask: Isn't that phrase (and the concept of heterosexuality that underlies it) the only natural and indisputable language that would appear in any marriage law or family law? Quite rationally, one may think: Isn't it the case that gay, lesbian, and transgender people do not have the right to marry in the majority of places in the world today precisely because the laws are written in such a way that "a man and a woman" would be the only condition that enjoys solid statutory protection?

The truth is, as a question of law, whether and how heterosexuality is a wholly recognizable, codified, and defensible statutory reality in marriage and sexuality-related legal judgments remains an open question. In a legal environment, a statutory designation of a term or a phrase does two things: Statutory confirmation would supply the term with argumentative authority, and it would also enable legal dismissal of other terms that are different or excluded by the endorsed term. In the jurisprudence concerning marriage, however, the shocking discovery is that what society deems to be a taken-for-granted norm of marriage—heterosexuality—has in fact very rarely received an explicit and unambiguous statutory designation. In fact, the terms *heterosexual* and *heterosexuality* have not once appeared in any major doctrine in international public law.[13]

My point in this short digression is that because technicality does matter, we may say that other than the U.S. Defense of Marriage Act and similar legislation in other countries, heterosexuality in law is by and large *presumed* heterosexuality.[14] All claims of legitimacy and protection in the name of heterosexuality therefore rest on *implied* validity and authority. Yet, importantly, what we need to remember about presumed heterosexuality is that its shadowy legal status still works to bring about legal discrimination against nonheterosexuals. But it does not do so by formally declaring homosexuals or transgender people as the classes of people denied protection.[15] I have given much attention to nomenclature because, at a root level, naming (or the absence of it) forms a part of rights thinking and claim making.

By extension, looking at Miss W's case, one may reasonably deduce that the deceptively simple notions of "man/male" and "woman/female," like the ubiquitous term *heterosexuality*, exist only in a shadowy zone of ambiguity. In law, we may say that the universalism, the public visibility, and the majority rule of normative gender and sex in their "true form" derived from "plain meaning" are, again technically speaking, established not through absolute legal clarity but rather through invoking other corollary forms of legal power: the family order, the religious order, and the moral sanctity of children. In this way, the normative power underlying "union of a man and a woman" can only be prima facie legal.

The Law Is Not Part of Society

In his finding, Judge Cheung reiterated his commitment to public reasonableness by diverting the question of the constitutional validity of the current marriage laws in Hong Kong to the broad and difficult to define sphere of "societal consensus." Yet he proceeded to pen a statement that, nonetheless, reveals his own assumption about what that "societal consensus" in Hong Kong might be: "The all important question is, therefore, whether we have, in Hong Kong, reached a point where the type of transgender marriage under discussion is no longer regarded as repugnant to our society's understanding of the institution of marriage and its essence" (para. 206). Although it would be difficult to argue against the fact that transprejudice *is* rampant in Hong Kong, the court, by lifting itself away from the social sphere, became either complicit with the implied uneducated ethos of the masses or outright indifferent to it. Again, by positioning the court, and the fact of its power, as insufficient to effect change, the judge redirects attention away from the Court's duty:

> The versatility of the constitutional right to marry does *not* give the Courts a judicial licence to engineer a fundamental social and legal reform of the institution of marriage. In other words, what is constitutionally guaranteed is the right to participate in the institution of marriage as informed by the contemporary societal consensus, everything else being equal. Absent any compelling reasons, the constitutional guarantee does not mean that a Hong Kong resident can ask a Court to construe the right to marry in such a way that does not enjoy contemporary societal consensual support, and, in substance, to effect a fundamental social and legal reform of the current institution of marriage to accord with the resident's idea of what it ought to be. Nor does the guarantee give the Court a judicial licence to bring about a fundamental social

and legal reform by interpreting (or reinterpreting) the right to accord with the Court's own notion of what the institution of marriage ought to be. That, it must be emphasized, lies outside the Court's constitutional remit and institutional capability. It is a function that properly belongs to the Government and the Legislature, which, as mentioned, is at liberty to relax or otherwise liberalise the existing marriage law in accordance with its view of the public good. (para. 192)

Repeatedly, the judge followed the normative approach prescribed by the Department of Justice to defer responsibility to the legislature and government and assigned them the moral duty to ascertain the majority's view to determine if a restrictive or a more generous statutory interpretation of the marriage laws should be made possible.[16] Justifying this approach, the judge reasoned:

I have not forgotten that fundamental rights are an exception to the democratic principle of majority rule. Some rights are considered to be so fundamental that even the majority of a society cannot, or cannot without justification, take them away from the minority. However, one is not here concerned with determining whether a fundamental right may be restricted according to the wishes of the majority. Rather, one is here to discover the present day boundary of the social institution of marriage as is understood by society or a majority thereof, and to give the fundamental right to marry a contemporary context or meaning that conforms to the social institution as it is understood now. (para. 217)

How do we reasonably make a hairsplitting distinction between the need to discover the present-day boundary of acceptability as "understood by society or a majority thereof," on the one hand, and the necessity of "determining whether a fundamental right may be restricted according to the wishes of the majority," on the other? How is the deferment of judgment to the general public not a way to "let the majority rule in by the back door" (Emerton 2010)? How much could the right to marry possibly mean if it resorts to seeking public approval, in the denial of a person's wish to choose whom to marry? If we follow the judge's logic, in historical terms, how could a groundbreaking human rights case such as the U.S. Supreme Court case of *Loving v. Virginia* (1967) legalizing interracial marriage ever arise under the prevailing "societal consensus" of 1960s racist America? In the Court of Appeal, the judges concurred with the original ruling, adding that "a change of the law of the nature sought by the appellant raises issues of public policy and is not for the court to effect such a change by statutory interpretation. It is a task which, if it should be undertaken, should be left to the legislature" (*W*, CA, para. 112).

It is important to reiterate that W's case was not one of attacking the binary heteronormative nature of marriage, the consanguinity contract, or any of the other gatekeeping provisions of the marriage laws. Judge Andrew Cheung's inability to conceptually differentiate same-sex marriage from W's wish for a *heterosexual* marriage notwithstanding, he resorts to the fear tactic derived from erroneous inferential logic:

> One must recognise the potential breadth of the applicant's argument, which essentially downplays the significance of procreation and emphasizes on the aspect about affording mutual society, help and comfort. The same logic, and the same argument, would appear to justify also a *pre-operative* transsexual person marrying in his or her preferred sex, as well as other forms of same sex marriage and even polygamous marriages (whether same sex or heterosexual). (para. 206)

One of the rhetorical partners to the argument supporting the "tyrannical majority rule" is the "slippery slope" projection. By confirming the boundary-setting power of the majority, the argument deduces that any force that manages to chip away at the boundary of the majority would embolden, rouse, and sanction other unruly forces to do the same, leading to total social collapse. The lethal power of the majority rule, therefore, lies in its ability to produce and escalate the fear of the minoritized other.[17]

CONCLUSION

In this chapter, the critique of the lower courts' triangular defenses of marriage to the exclusion of minority rights—that is, back-referencing to outdated originary meanings of legal constructions, reliance on "plain meanings" that backfire, and divergence of judicial responsibility to the realm of "societal consensus" (a divergence plainly antithetical to the basic ethos of rights thinking)—shows how the courts were out of step with the prevailing international view that has granted recognition of transgender people's rights of marriage. Robyn Emerton (2010: 12) is correct in suggesting that "the [CA] ruling seems to have tapped into the public conscience, arguably igniting a general sense of injustice in denying W the right to marry." It is not hard to imagine that as feelings of injustice grow in the populace out of their sympathy with Miss W's plight, public debates will arise. In fact, they have (see, for example, Collett 2010, 2011; "Readers' comments" 2011; Siu 2010). Such debates may help illuminate the moral argument that recognizing the right of a transgender individual to marry another person *in a voluntary hetero-union* will not diminish the validity or dignity of conventional marriage, any more than recognizing the right of an individual to marry a person of a different race or nationality devalues the marriage of a person who marries someone of his or her own race or nationality. On the surface, marriage is reaffirmed through uncomplicated public sympathy. But, in fact, the definition of marriage, including the definition of who is worthy of getting married, has opened up considerably.

It might appear that Miss W's legal case could be traced to her own claim of normativity, that is, by positioning herself as an "ordinary" woman, she in no way challenged an "ordinary" heterosexual marriage institution. One might intuit that Miss W's case was built on gender, sexual, and institutional conservatism. Yet, when reading the politics of the case more subtly, we find that the challenges that Miss W sought represent precisely a form of political interruption *through a radical redefinition of "woman" and "heterosexual marriage."* Hers is not a simple politics of resistance-by-substitution (that is, substituting genders in a marriage act) nor is it a politics of discursive inversion (that is, claiming discursive supremacy of the term *transgender* to topple and denigrate normative gender terms in the normative ideology of marriage). Rather, the transgender challenge to marriage is the politics of subversion par excellence. It works not by substituting or inverting the centers of power but by insinuating into the discursive field an *internal reconfiguration of power itself.* In this view, the claim that Miss W's case is merely an attempt to enact a "new normal" is untenable because this linguistic configuration still retains the normativity of the normal.

CODA

How was the Miss W case "won" in the Court of Final Appeal, a judgment that was handed down on May 13, 2013? Chief Justice Ma and his colleagues on the bench did not refute the validity of *Corbett* but ruled that its approach to confine transgenderism to merely biological realities reinforced by the fulfillment of "Christian duties"—to the exclusion of social and psychological facets of transgenderism—was inadequate for the purpose of determining the marriageability of a transgender person. Supplementing this was another agreement of the court to allow for the preservation of the statutory construction of marriage as involving "a man and a woman." Yet the court rebuffed the argument that the meanings of *man* and *woman* be read merely through "ordinary, plain meanings." The court, in other words, refused to accept what I earlier called "linguistic deconnotation" for understanding those categories. In short, these two positions advanced by the CFA—affirming the applicability and legitimacy of *Corbett* to the Hong Kong situation and affirming the union of two genders in marriage—nonetheless sought to *rework* the statutory constructions of transgenderism to encompass sociopsychological and cultural-interpretive dimensions. This brought about a major blow to the statutory framework advanced in the lower courts.

But the W case was finally won not on the court's reworking of statutory constructions: The CFA ruled the position of the Registrar of Marriages unconstitutional, that is, counter to fundamental rights as guaranteed in Hong Kong's Basic Law (specifically Article 37) and in the Hong Kong Bill of Rights (specifically Article 19(2)). In other words, the Court took a legal essentialist approach, which preserved the unadulterated fundamental freedom to marry. While this essentialist approach allows for restrictions, such as the requirement of monogamy, legal age of marriage, and the like, it cannot do so by reducing that freedom to such an extent that its very essence is impaired (*W*, CFA, para. 65). In a case in which the impairment of fundamental rights has been camouflaged by the requirements to adhere to an outdated understanding of marriage, to the deconnotative meaning of a person's lived gender, and to "societal consensus," it seems that the CFA held its ground by examining closely whether those requirements went too far and threatened the rights concerned.

In doing so, the court has addressed the key criticisms advanced in this chapter:

1. That marriage has to a certain extent been deinstitutionalized (that is, answerable only to the state power of regulation) to encompass vast changes brought about by medical technologies, as well as men's and women's concepts of cohabitation, reproduction, divorce, and so on (see *W*, CFA, paras. 84–89);

2. That a post-operative transsexual woman has not only not deviated from "womanhood" as a necessary category in marriage but has also *transformed* its meaning from the inside out. Aside from the legal recognition of her female identity as bestowed by the state (for example, issuance of a new identity card, legal acceptance of her using a public

toilet for women), Miss W is a woman *in otherness.* Her lived gender asserts her womanhood as a *new sign* fit for marriage (cf. *W*, CFA, para. 99);

3. That reliance on "societal consensus"—that is, to allow the will of the majority to dictate who can and cannot enjoy fundamental freedoms—is inimical to minority rights doctrines and adjudicative responsibility (W, CFA, paras. 113–116).

By taking these positions, the court has sent a strong message of anti-discrimination to society. Yet, as indicated at the beginning of this chapter, this was accomplished, unfortunately, through an ideological divide that continues to negate same-sex couples' equal right to marriage. Nonetheless, the legal team's approach of disarticulating Miss W's case from being a gay marriage case has set in motion new legal thinking. It is hoped that the abandonment of legal anachronism, the reexamination of rigid definitions of gender and sexual intimacy, and the striking down of the tyranny of majoritarianism as seen in the CFA ruling will produce a ripple effect that will coalesce with the larger struggle for legislation against *all* forms of discrimination, a movement that is already underway in Hong Kong.[18]

NOTES

1. Journalist Nigel Collett's (2010) report was one of a small handful of media reports that gave us a glimpse of Miss W's determination to fight:

> Ms W describes herself as "a shy girl, not able to handle the pressure of the media" . . . "This case is important to me and my partner," she told me, "but it's also important for the TG [transgender] community. Everyone should have the right to marry." So she is fighting. "I don't want the Government to treat us as TG," she added. "I want the Government to treat us as male or female in our reassigned gender. There's lot of discrimination in this world, and I want to rid our society of it."

2. In the *Corbett* case, the court was asked by a husband to grant a declaration that the marriage was null and void on the ground that his "wife" was in fact a post-operative male-to-female transsexual person who was, additionally, incapable of consummating a marriage (because she had only an artificial vagina). The court, which was able to rely only on the (limited) medical evidence of the time, restricted "sex" to chromosomal, gonadal, and genital factors (to the exclusion of psychological, social, or cultural factors) and thus construed the validity of a marriage as dependent only on biological criteria.

3. As noted in Chapter 1, the standardized percentages of never-married population in Hong Kong increased steadily from 1981 to 2011, reflecting the tendency toward marriage postponement if not refusal for both men and women.

4. Between 1981 and 2011 the percentage of households with five people and above declined from 36.8 percent to 9 percent, while the percentage of two-person households rose from 15.4 percent to 25.2 percent (Census and Statistics Department 2011).

5. TEAM (Transgender Equality and Acceptance Movement) estimates that there are far more transgender persons in Hong Kong than the approximately 3,000 reported by the government, especially given that only 10 percent of those eligible for gender reassignment surgery have actually undergone the procedure (cited in Shamdasani 2004: 4; see also Winter 2009b).

6. On June 26, 2013, the U.S. Supreme Court in *United States v. Windsor* handed a judgment to overturn the 1996 Defense of Marriage Act (DOMA) that denied equal rights to same-sex couples who are legally married. The ruling means that several thousand legally married gay and lesbian couples will be able to take advantage of tax breaks, pension rights, and other federal benefits that are available to other married couples.

7. Darren Rosenblum argues that transgender

. . . reflects [a] shift away from the historical primacy of medical treatment, toward a growing awareness of the psychological element of gender identity . . . "Transgender" grew into a useful umbrella term, including and not subordinating the proliferation of transgendered people who avoid medical treatment. "Transsexual" refers to "sex" rather than "gender," a biological emphasis that excludes psychological gender identity. "Transgendered" recognizes the extrabiological nature of gender. (Rosenblum 2000: 507)

8. For a discussion of the transgender movement in Hong Kong, particularly the history and practices of the transgender rights group TEAM, see Emerton (2006).

9. Chief counsel for Miss W, Mr. Philip Dykes, had led a victory in *Leung TC William Roy v. Secretary of Justice* in Hong Kong in 2005, in which both the Court of First Instance and the Court of Appeal found sections of the Crime Ordinance specifying age of consent inconsistent with the equality and nondiscrimination provisions of the Basic Law and the Hong Kong Bill of Rights.

10. Wendy Brown argues that one of the characteristics of tolerant discourse in contemporary times is to shore up what liberalism perceives to be its own inadequacies, and this often diverted liberalism's attention from its duty to protect or promote justice:

Tolerance can function as a substitute for or as a supplement to formal liberal equality or liberty; it can also overtly block the pursuit of substantive equality and freedom. At times, tolerance shores up troubled orders of power, repairs state legitimacy, glosses troubled universalism, and provides cover for imperialism. (Brown 2006: 9–10)

To critique the judge's sympathies is not the same as saying that the sentiment was totally useless. Rather, it is to help us see through the innocence of liberal tolerance as a political practice. In a similar vein, legal scholars Morgan and Walker (1995: 206) argue that "tolerance is used as a mechanism of containment. It is portrayed as beneficial to the tolerated subject, but in fact the language of toleration is the language of subordination; it reinforces the subordination already experienced by those it claims to protect."

11. In the New Zealand case, *Attorney-General v. Otahuhu Family Court* (1995), the court refused to follow *Corbett* and argued that what mattered was not the transsexual person's ability to function sexually ("Where two persons present themselves as having the apparent genitals of a man or a woman, they should not have to establish that each can function sexually") (*W*, CFI, para. 68). Even more crucially, in an Australian case, *Kevin v. Attorney-General (Cth)* (2001) (also widely known as the "Kevin and Jennifer" case), the judge also refused to follow Corbett because he believed that sex, for the purposes of marriage, should be determined by considering all relevant matters beyond biological determinations. Ultimately, the court granted that the postoperative transsexual man involved in the case (Kevin) was indeed a "man" for the purposes of marriage and held that the marriage between the transsexual man and a woman (Jennifer) was valid. This case successfully expanded the ordinary contemporary meanings of "man" and "woman" to include post-operative transsexuals as men or women in accordance with their sexual reassignment (para. 69–71).

12. See Macnamee (2004) for a useful critique of Corbett, especially the formal construction of the judgment in this case and how legitimacy was sought for an eventual pronouncement on sexual identity, in order to lay bare the founding moment of law on transsexuality in the United Kingdom.

13. These terms are entirely absent from even the 1962 UN Convention on Consent to Marriage, Minimum Age for Marriage and Registration of Marriages. Further, in the range of treaty articles that directly underwrite the legal sanctity of family, there exists not once a definitional correlation between family and heterosexuality. Likewise, Article 10 of the International Covenant on Economic, Social, and Cultural Rights (ICESCR) mirrors Art. 23(3) of the International Covenant on Civil and Political Rights (ICCPR): "Marriage must be entered into with the free consent of the intending spouses." In these two bedrock covenants in international human rights law, neither the heterosexual *composition* of a family nor the heterosexual order of marriage has been given unambiguous legal recognition. Ambiguity did arise in Art. 23(3) of the ICCPR seen above, when the phrase "the right of men and women of marriage-

able age to marry and form a family" never says with absolute legal clarity that these parties would be doing so *with each other*. Phil Chan also argues such wording, "with both genders in plural form, does not necessarily preclude marriage between two persons of the same sex" (2007: 68). In a similar vein, Paul Rishworth (2007) suggests that it was the exclusivity of a union of two persons rather than their respective genders that gave rise to a New Zealand case concerning the prohibition of polygamous marriage. In Article 23 of the ICCPR, it is clear that the onus of the "heterosexual proof" for the sanctity of family rests in the phrase "natural and fundamental," therefore securing a religious meaning of marriage more than anything else.

14. As per note 6 above, DOMA was declared unconstitutional by the U.S. Supreme Court on June 26, 2013.

15. The bias of presumed heterosexuality often relies on the formal designation of queer behavior and desires as legal entities. So, it is queerness, not queer identity as such, that has been identified in legal judgments. For instance, *Bowers v. Hardwick* (1986), the major backlash case against queer sexual rights and privacy rights in the United States, demonstrates that naming "homosexual conduct" is a prerequisite for shoring up the presumed but all-powerful sanctity of heterosexuality. In the ruling, it is clear that the naming of homosexual conduct is far more important than defining who or what a "homosexual" is. In the long repealed criminal code in Hong Kong against gay sex, the terms *buggery* and *gross indecency* were the designated offences. Nowhere did that code mention homosexual people.

16. According to the Department of Justice's normative view of the common law tradition:

> While [the common law] is flexible and adaptable, the doctrine of precedent often makes it difficult for judges to change well-established legal doctrines. If significant, rather than incremental, changes need to be made to the law, it is usually necessary to achieve these by way of legislation. (Department of Justice, 2014)

17. In a major case of victory for privacy rights of sexual minorities delivered by the U.S. Supreme Court, *Lawrence v. Texas* (2003), Judge Scalia in his dissenting opinion deployed the same flawed "slippery slope" rhetoric by arguing that the decriminalization of homosexuality would interfere with state laws that enforced the prohibition of "bigamy, same-sex marriage, adult incest, prostitution, masturbation, adultery, fornication, bestiality, and obscenity" (Lawrence *per* Scalia J. [dissenting opinion], 2003, 533).

18. On February 28, 2014, the government gazette announced the Marriage (Amendment) Bill 2014, intended to implement the CFA ruling in the W case (available at www.legco.gov.hk/yr13-14/english/bills/brief/b201402282_brf.pdf). The bill stipulates that only fully postoperative transgender persons are eligible to marry in their acquired gender. Local transgender activists have complained that this requirement amounts to "forced sterilization."

REFERENCES

Ashlie v. Chester-Upland School District (1979) U.S. Dist. LEXIS 12516.

Attorney-General v. Otahuhu Family Court [1995] 1 NZLR 603.

Bellinger v. Bellinger (2002) Fam 150.

Bowers v. Hardwick (1986) 478 U.S. 186.

Brown, Wendy. 2006. *Regulating Aversion: Tolerance in the Age of Identity and Empire.* Princeton, NJ: Princeton University Press.

Census and Statistics Department. 2011. Hong Kong SAR Government. Available at www.census2011.gov.hk/en/census-result.html.

Chan, Phil. 2007. "Same-Sex Marriage/Constitutionalism and Their Centrality to Equality Rights in Hong Kong: A Comparative-Socio-Legal Appraisal." *The International Journal of Human Rights* 11(1–2): 33–84.

Cheung, Pui Kei Eleanor. 2006. "Transsexuals and Other Gender-Variant People in Hong Kong: An Exploration of the Spectrum of Their Gender Identity Formation and Transformation." Paper presented at the UK Postgraduate Conference in Gender Studies, June 21–22, University of Leeds, UK. Available at www.gender-studies.leeds.ac.uk/assets/files/epapers/epaper5-eleanor-cheung.pdf.

———. 2010. "GID in Hong Kong: A Critical Overview of Medical Treatments for Transexual Patients." In *As Normal as Possible: Negotiating Sexuality and Gender in Mainland China and Hong Kong*, Yau Ching, ed., pp. 75-86. Hong Kong: Hong Kong University Press.

Collett, Nigel. 2010. "Ms W vs. the Hong Kong Registrar of Marriages." August 19. Retrieved on December 7, 2011, from www.fridae.asia/newsfeatures/2010/08/19/10235 .ms-w-vs-the-hong-kong-registrar-of-marriages.

———. 2011. "Setback to Transgender Rights in Hong Kong: Ms W Loses Her Appeal for the Right to Marry." November 30. Retrieved on December 7, 2011, from www.fridae .asia/newsfeatures/2011/11/28/11351.setback-to-transgender-rights-in-hong-kong.

Corbett v. Corbett. 1970. 2 All ER 33.

Currah, Paisley, and Minter, Shannon. 2000. "Unprincipled Exclusions: The Struggle to Achieve Judicial and Legislative Equality for Transgender People." *William & Mary Journal of Women & Law* 7: 37–59.

Department of Justice. 2014. "Legal system in Hong Kong." Government of Hong Kong Special Administrative Region. Retrieved on January 16, 2014, from http:// www.doj.gov.hk/eng/legal/.

Emerton, Robyn. 2004. "Neither Here nor There: The Current Status of Transsexual and Other Transgender Persons under Hong Kong Law." *Hong Kong Law Journal* 34: 245–277.

———. 2006. "Finding a Voice, Fighting for Rights: The Emergence of the Transgender Movement in Hong Kong." *Inter-Asia Cultural Studies* 7(2): 243–269.

———. 2010. "Next, the Right to Marry," *South China Morning Post*, October 14: 12.

Erni, John N. 2013. "Legitimating Transphobia: The Legal Disavowal of Transgender Rights in Prison." *Cultural Studies* 27(1): 136–159.

Goodwin v. United Kingdom. 2002. 35 EHRR 447.

Gordon, Demoya. 2009. "Transgender Legal Advocacy: What Do Feminist Legal Theories Have to Offer?" *California Law Review* 97: 1719–1762.

Ho, Josephine. 2007. "Embodying Gender: Transgender Body/Subject Formations in Taiwan." In *The Inter-Asia Cultural Studies Reader,* Kuan-Hsing Chen and Chua Beng Huat, eds., pp. 347–363. London and New York: Routledge.

Kevin v. Attorney-General (Cth). 2001. 165 FLR 404.

King, Mark. 2003. "Research and Discussion Paper: Perceptions of MTF Transgendered Persons and Their Sexual Partners in Hong Kong: A Study of Social, Emotional, and Cognitive Sources of Biases." October 4. Retrieved on March 8, 2011, from http://web.hku.hk/~sjwinter/TransgenderASIA/paper_perceptions_of_mtf .htm.

Lawrence v. Texas (2003) 539 U.S. 558.

Leung Lai Fong v. Ho Sing Ying (2009) 12 HKCFAR 581.

Leung TC William Roy v. Secretary for Justice [2005]3 HKLRD 657, [2006] 4 HKLRD 211 (HCAL 160/2004, Court of First Instance judgment dated 24 Aug 2005 AND CACV 317/2005, Court of Appeal judgment dated 20 Sep 2006).

Li, Siu Leung. 2003. *Cross-Dressing in Chinese Opera.* Hong Kong: Hong Kong University Press.

Lim, Song Hwee. 2006. *Celluloid Comrades: Representations of Male Homosexuality in Contemporary Chinese Cinemas.* Honolulu: University of Hawai'i Press.

Lloyd, Abby. 2005. "Are Transgender People Strangers to the Law?" *Berkeley Journal of Gender Law & Justice* 20: 150–195.

Loving v. Virginia (1965) 243 F. Supp. 231; 1965 U.S. Dist. LEXIS 7370.

Ma, Joyce. 1997. "A Systems Approach to the Social Difficulties of Transsexuals in Hong Kong." *Journal of Family Therapy* 19: 71–88.

Macnamee, Eugene. 2004. "Girls and Boys." *Law and Critique* 15: 25–43.

Martin, Fran. 2003. *Situating Sexualities: Queer Representation in Taiwanese Fiction, Film and Public Culture.* Hong Kong: Hong Kong University Press.

Morgan, Wayne, and Walker, Kristen. 1995. "Tolerance and Homosex: A Policy of Control and Containment." *Melbourne University Law Review* 20: 202–214.

Ng, M. L., et al. 1989. "Transsexualism: Service and Problems in Hong Kong." *Hong Kong Practitioner* 11: 591–602.

Pegg, Leonard. 1994. *Family Law in Hong Kong,* 3rd edition. London: Butterworths.

"Readers' Comments." 2011. In Nigel Collett's "Setback to Transgender Rights in Hong Kong: Ms W Loses Her Appeal for the Right to Marry." November 30. Retrieved on December 7, 2011, from www.fridae.asia/newsfeatures/2011/11/28/11351 .setback-to-transgender-rights-in-hong-kong.

Rishworth, Paul. 2007. "Changing Times, Changing Minds, Changing Laws: Sexual Orientation and New Zealand Law." *The International Journal of Human Rights* 11(1–2): 85–108.

Rosenblum, Darren. 2000. "'Trapped' in Sing Sing: Transgendered Prisoners Caught in the Gender Binarism." *Michigan Journal of Gender & Law* 6: 499–571.

Shamdasani, Ravina. 2004. "Victory of Woman in Sex Bias Dispute," *South China Morning Post*, October 14: 4.

Siu, Wing-sum. 2010. "Transsexuals Face So Much Discrimination." *South China Morning Post*, August 23: 10.

United States v. Windsor (2013) 570 U.S. (Docket No. 12-307).

W v. Registrar of Marriages (2013) HKCFA, 39.

Wan, Marco. 2010. "A March over the Years towards Choice," *South China Morning Post*, October 20: 10.

Watkins, David. 2004. "Victories and Setbacks for Hong Kong's Transsexuals," *South China Morning Post*, October 26: 20.

Winter, Sam. 2009a. "Country Report: Hong Kong: Social and Cultural Issues." Retrieved on March 20, 2011, from http://web.hku.hk/~sjwinter/TransgenderASIA/country_report_hk_social.htm.

———. 2009b. "Lost in Transition: Transpeople, Transprejudice and Pathology in Asia." *International Journal of Human Rights* 13(2/3): 357–382.

Winter, Sam, et al. 2008. "Measuring Hong Kong Undergraduate Students' Attitudes towards Transpeople." *Sex Roles* 59(9/10): 670–683.

MARRIAGE AND SEXUALITY IN TAIWAN

Part III

9 THE ALTERNATIVE FUTURES OF MARRIAGE

A Sociolegal Analysis of Family Law Reform in Taiwan

Grace Shu-Chin Kuo

FOR SOCIOLOGIST ANDREW CHERLIN, the deinstitutionalization of marriage is an ongoing phenomenon that diversifies the possibilities for marital relationships and destigmatizes alternative forms of cohabitation. As noted by Davis and Friedman in their introduction, initially Cherlin thought that, after decades of deinstitutionalization, marriage in Europe and North America would be reinstitutionalized around new norms, but more recently he has concluded that no new normative consensus or equilibrium has emerged (Cherlin 2004). By contrast, law and society theorists focused more narrowly on changes in marriage and family law assume that as societal norms surrounding marriage and intimate relationships shift, the law in turn must relegitimize itself so as to adapt to societal changes (Fineman 1995: 18; Nader 2002). Concerned with these recalibrations of the law and legal practice, legal scholars closely study specific legal decisions or the passage of new statutes to identify key building blocks for both the deinstitutionalization and reinstitutionalization of marriage.

For legal scholar Jana Singer, as for many who write in English, the primary empirical cases are drawn from U.S. courts and statutes. But statutes and legal procedures are grounded in specific political, cultural, and societal substrata. Thus, when Singer argues that "the law governing the marriage process also reflects an increased role for private ordering" (Singer 1992: 1447), we cannot assume that this argument will hold outside the United States. In this chapter, I review changes in Taiwan statute and in a series of recent decisions by Taiwan's Constitutional Court to assess the applicability of Singer's argument about the increased private ordering of intimate relationships for a society rooted in social and cultural values very different from those of the United States. More broadly, I seek to explain how the law, through its coercive power to grant marriage certificates and define family membership, integrates societal changes with respect to marital norms and values into its legal doctrines, verdicts, and interpretations. In this way, I use a sociolegal analysis of family law as a basis for a broader discussion about the "alternative futures of marriage" by examining how Taiwanese law has responded to a range of changes in the intimate lives and material conditions of Taiwanese families.

By explicitly linking the deinstitutionalization of marriage to changing norms and definitions of families, I follow Glendon's (1989: 5–6) proposition that "families and marriages are pre-legal institutions." According to this argument, changes in marriage and family entail the transformation of family law. In particular, this chapter focuses on paradigm shifts in family law and the corresponding legal norms created by the grand justices of the Constitutional Court.[1] In so doing, it speaks to this volume's shared interest in how statutes and legal decisions increasingly privilege private preferences in civil disputes, and it debates how best to fulfill and protect human desires for intimate relationships. By reviewing how the link between marriage and family has been defined and redefined by the law, I document shifts in the larger sociolegal environment in Taiwan within which men and women create their intimate lives.

THE CHARACTER AND CHALLENGE OF FAMILY LAW

Over time, the interrelationships among the three institutions of marriage, family, and law in Taiwan have shifted dramatically, and recent recalibrations have been substantial and consequential. First, both the end of martial law in 1987 and the creation of a vibrant multiparty democracy have increased the independence of the judiciary and have made it more responsive to citizens' discontent. Second, the general rise in living standards over the past thirty years, combined with increased openness to global trends with regard to gender equality, have created additional pressure among citizens for legal change. Third, as more Taiwanese participate in global trade and commerce, marriage markets have extended beyond the island, and questions of citizenship and sovereignty now routinely enter adjudication of family disputes. Fourth, Taiwanese are deeply connected to and engaged with international precedents through their involvement in global social media and the Internet, and they mobilize these precedents in legal struggles, such as recent initiatives to protect the rights of sexual minorities and destigmatize same-sex relationships.[2] Finally, as new forms of assisted reproduction have enabled surrogacy and insemination with sperm donors, Taiwanese courts, like those in North America and Europe, have been required to reconsider familial logics that privileged bloodlines. All of these factors have had a profound impact on shifts in family law, including the substance of black-letter law and court procedures for resolving family disputes.[3]

Before analyzing these interactions between broad political and economic structural shifts and the changing definitions of marriage and family in the sociolegal context, I first clarify what *family law* refers to in the Taiwanese legal system premised on civil law. The principal laws pertaining to marriage and family are included in Part IV ("Family") and Part V ("Succession") of the Civil Code. Therefore, the term *family law* in this chapter refers to Parts IV and V of the Civil Code.[4] Part IV includes chapters on marriage, parents and children, guardianship, maintenance, household, and the family council. Part V includes chapters on heirs to property, succession to property, partition of inheritance, waiver of inheritance, and wills.

In this chapter, I focus on the changing concepts of marriage and family that have emerged over the course of Taiwan's legal transition during the past two decades, a period marked by rapid developments in women's rights and the democratization of the political system as a whole. In terms of activity of the courts, the most common cases involved application of the law to settle family and marital disputes or restore order to the lives of those whose marital quarrels enter the court and require legal intervention. During these moments, such as cases of domestic violence or long-term conflict caused by marital disharmony, people claim to be entitled to their rights and seek legal enforcement to resolve their problems. Therefore, I discuss how the law has been applied in particular disputes.[5] I also explain how legal applications, particularly constitutional interpretations, have responded to the changing trends in marriage and family in Taiwan.[6]

Unlike the character of property law or business-related regulations, the character of family law is marked by the conflicting form and substance of tradition and modernity (Chen 2005). Tradition in family law follows a doctrinal sequence whereby a man and woman first get married, then form a family and bear children within the legitimated marriage.[7] An automobile advertisement frequently broadcast on Taiwanese television portrays the "ideal family" in contemporary Taiwan, which is reflected in the family law. The advertisement shows a father behind the wheel with a smiling mother at his side, while their adorable son sits in the backseat.[8] This scene depicts the normative subject of most contemporary family law: a monogamous couple composed of one man and one woman and the children they produce within the marriage. This image of a two-generation family composed of a husband, a wife, and their children dominates legal regulations.[9]

Historically, Taiwanese applied similar traditional legal logics to marriage and family. By contrast, in recent decades, particularly in rulings by the Constitutional Court, one observes some new approaches to marriage and family. Traditional assumptions generally persist in the doctrinal structure of family law, but in rulings and interpretations of the Constitutional Court one can see the influence of the rapid societal changes that have occurred over the last few decades in Taiwan. For example, gender equality within marriage and the child's best interest have become two primary value considerations among family court judges.

In practice, the earlier conflation of marriage and family has also gradually disintegrated, and family disputes that make their way into the legal system now include an ever-greater number of nonconjugal families (Kuo 2008). These alternative family structures include families created by two same-sex partners, by a single parent and children, by stepfathers or stepmothers and their children, and by divorced homosexuals or bisexuals with children from previous marriages (Kuo 2008). Families can also consist of unmarried adult children still living with their parents or an elderly person living alone or with a companion. Households where one partner lives in Taiwan and the other lives elsewhere, most often in China, are also becoming more common (Shen Chapter 11). Among the newly married, it is not uncommon that one spouse, usually the wife, is not Taiwanese (Friedman Chapter 12).

These new family structures and new forms of cohabitation rarely build on the relational foundation of one husband and one wife or draw exclusively on blood ties or shared nationality. Instead, these diverse families in contemporary Taiwanese society are based on subjective desires and objective decisions about shared finances and how best to meet the practical needs of everyday life (Lee and Hsu 2011).[10] In the legal domain, the loosening of strict regulations on intimacy has taken place primarily with regard to heterosexual foreign spouses, even though discrimination on the basis of gender and nationality still permeates the larger realm of law and policy regulating marital immigrants (Friedman Chapter 12; Kuo 2011).[11] By contrast, activism in support of marriage rights for same-sex couples has yet to bear legal fruit, although in 2012 over 50,000 people marched in Taipei's Lesbian, Gay, Bisexual, and Transgender (LGBT) Pride Parade to support legalizing same-sex marriage (Loa 2012).[12]

RISING DIVORCE RATES AND THE SOCIOLEGAL CONTEXT OF FAMILY LAW

Over the past twenty years, the numbers of childless families and single-parent families have increased dramatically (Yang and Liu 2002). Multiple factors have contributed to this increase, but one primary driver is the upsurge in divorce. Figure 9.1 shows the rise in the crude divorce rate (CDR) between 1991 and 2003, followed by a short plateau and then a decline after 2006 to the same level as 2001. The CDR is the annual number of divorces per 1,000 persons in the total population, and it includes divorces that are either mutually or unilaterally desired and privately settled or adjudicated in court.[13] The steady rise in Taiwan's CDR over the last decade of the twentieth century and its leveling off in the new millennium reflect several major legal reforms during that period.

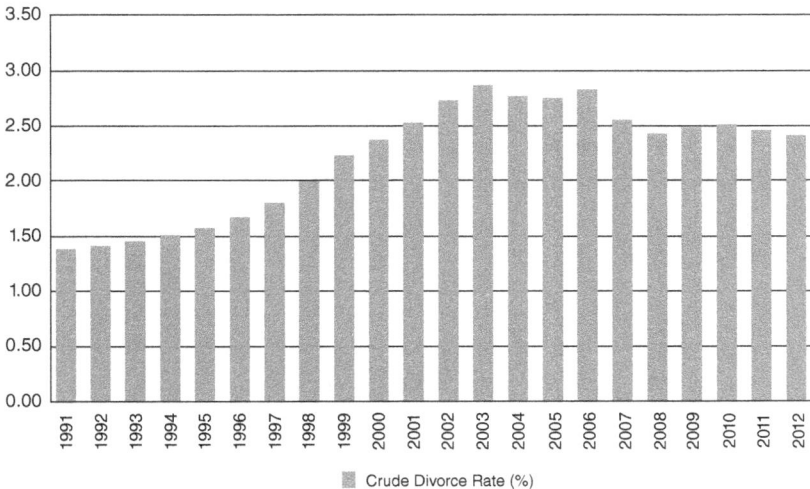

Figure 9.1. Changes in the crude divorce rate in Taiwan.

SOURCE: Taiwan Department of Household Registration, Ministry of the Interior, "Number and Rates of Birth, Death, Marriage and Divorce, 1981–2012"; available at http://sowf.moi.gov.tw/stat/month/m1-02.xls.

The steady upward slope in the CDR shown in Figure 9.1, however, obscures a longer and more contested legal history of divorce across three major periods of rule in Taiwan: Imperial China under the Qing Dynasty, Japanese colonial rule (1895–1945), and the Republic of China (1945–present) (Chen 1999; Chen 2005: 74–87). Prior to Japanese colonization in 1895, Taiwanese were subject to Qing laws, which banned a woman from petitioning for divorce on her own behalf and required a male relative to act in her stead. The Japanese colonial government introduced a Western model of civil law to Taiwan, which included women's right to divorce. Japanese colonial law listed ten reasons for filing a divorce suit. These included bigamy or consensual sex with a third party, abuse of a spouse or lineal relatives, desertion, incurable disease, disappearance, and imprisonment for a crime. In this legal context, filing for divorce was "fault based," and, if either the husband or the wife met one of the criteria, the innocent spouse could file a divorce suit. The Nationalist Civil Code brought to Taiwan in 1945 recognized many of the same forms of "fault" as the Japanese law in its divorce provisions (Chen 1999: 50–51). Both laws imposed strict limitations on who was eligible to file for divorce, and their legal definitions of fault derived from cultural traditions that did not recognize other forms of harm (Dai et al. 2007: 226–227; Lin 1994: 56–58).

Despite widespread acknowledgment of the limitations of these specific forms of fault, the divorce provisions in the Nationalist Civil Code were not revised until 1985. The impetus for reform came from a changing social environment that included greater pressure for gender equality in the face of women's mass entry into the labor market, rapid democratic reforms, and the growing economic affluence of Taiwanese society (Deng 1997: 15–16).[14] However, the 1985 reform did not revise the existing ten conditions of fault but rather simply added a new clause that allowed for an exception in cases that did not meet any of those conditions:

> Either the husband or the wife may petition for a juridical decree of divorce upon the occurrence of any gross event other than that set forth in the preceding paragraph that renders it difficult to maintain the marriage, except if either the husband or the wife is responsible for the event, only the other party may petition for the divorce. (Article 1052-II)

According to this amendment, if there is a critical event within the marriage that makes it difficult to maintain the marriage, the innocent party can file a divorce suit even if none of the previously mentioned reasons for divorce applies. The amended family law adopted the spirit of no-fault divorce but limited its effects by stating that only the "innocent" party was qualified to file for divorce.

Criticism of this limited form of no-fault divorce has continued unabated into the present, and scholars and legal professionals alike have emphasized the problems inherent in requiring judges to evaluate what kind of "gross event" makes a marriage "difficult to maintain." Moreover, the persistent framework of fault heightens contestation over which party is guilty or innocent and thereby able to initiate the divorce petition. Despite the cumbersome nature of the exception, it has become the number one reason for granting a divorce decree in Taiwan today, as indicated by the growing number of divorces granted on the basis of "other causes" (see Table 9.1).

THE REORDERING OF PRIVATE LIVES IN TAIWAN

Jana Singer (1992) asserts that the revolution in family law in the United States represents a transformation from public to private ordering of behavior. Singer also notes the disadvantages and dangers generated by the privatization of family matters and concludes that the privatization of family law may be simply a transition strategy from a legal reformer's point of view (Singer 1992). However, the privatization of family law could fail in a situation where the state shirks its social welfare duties and requires the family to serve as the caretaker in private matters, such as assuming care for dependent family members (Singer 1992; see also Fineman 2004).

Singer's and Fineman's worries are certainly valid. But can family law be characterized merely through the lens of privatization? The distinction between the public and private boundaries of family law can easily be blurred. For instance, bringing domestic disputes into the courts necessarily places private family lives in the context of public legal debates. Sociolegal studies of the dispute process have argued that bringing a suit to court is equivalent to bringing personal matters from the private area into the public domain (Merry 1990; Nader 2004). Scholars claim that disputants, especially racial and gender minorities, suffer more from the dispute process, particularly when it involves unfamiliar legal language and techniques. The language and techniques of the dispute process are infused with the patriarchal character of law (Fineman 1995; Mertz 2007). Family law involves matters of privacy and intimacy; yet from the perspective of the dispute process, particularly involving trials or public attention, it is no longer private.

Table 9.1. Primary grounds for granting divorce in Taiwan, 2000–2009.

Year	Number of divorce suits	Polygamy	Adultery	Ill treatment	Ill treatment by relative	Desertion	Attempt to murder the other party	Incurable disease	Psychological illness	Unknown whether dead or alive	Sentenced to imprisonment	Other causes
2000	4,302	1	131	1191	9	1,878	3	11	21	3	498	556
2001	4,469	3	100	970	6	2,119	2	10	10	5	365	879
2002	6,089	7	97	1,074	4	2,638	7	11	16	6	344	1,885
2003	7,744	4	117	1,089	3	3,169	0	5	5	14	358	2,980
2004	7,873	8	69	860	4	3,325	3	6	10	13	313	3,262
2005	7,623	6	35	695	5	3,201	1	3	7	7	282	3,381
2006	7,584	6	44	626	2	2,996	1	9	9	14	324	3,553
2007	6,716	5	26	558	3	2,537	1	4	5	8	159	3,410
2008	6,465	2	44	388	1	2,114	3	8	2	3	150	3,750
2009	5,619	5	18	297	1	1,793	2	3	3	5	99	3,393

SOURCE: Taiwan Judicial Yuan 2009.

Child custody disputes are a major arena where the public character of family law intersects with private concerns in ways that exceed technical legal concepts. When divorcing parents dispute child custody arrangements or neglect their parenting duties, judges may become aggressively involved in the case even when not explicitly requested to do so by the disputants. The motivating concern with the child's best interest propels the case into the public sphere and out of the hands of the divorcing parents or their own families.[15]

In this section, I address the various stages of transformation of family law in Taiwan with an eye to how societal changes manifested in domestic disputes in the court have brought private matters to public attention. Over the past thirty years, Taiwanese family law has gone through three major stages of revision in response to the reordering of private or intimate life and changes in the larger political economy. The first stage addressed growing pressures for gender equality by introducing the principle of spousal equity within marriage. The second set of revisions extended this focus on women's rights and integrated it with new attention to the best interests of the child in making custody decisions in cases of divorce. Finally, the most recent overhaul of the law in 2009 redefined guardianship by allowing family members to transfer care of their elderly to the state.[16]

These family law reforms have followed the heteronormative life cycle by focusing first on women's equal protection in marriage or in the process of marital dissolution. The subsequent revision took on the status of children in cases of divorce, endowing them with their own best interests instead of viewing them simply as the property of their parents. Most recently, legal reforms have addressed the plight of seniors or adults who are unable to care for themselves. A traditional cultural view rooted in the principle of filial piety held that adult children were responsible for supporting seniors and that the immediate family would care for any incapacitated family member. Therefore, raising children was like buying old-age security. However, in Taiwan today, some children cannot afford to pay maintenance for their senior parents, or they dispute any legal requirement do so. To address these issues, the law was amended in 2009 to empower the state to claim guardianship in cases where adult children were unable to care for elderly parents with dementia, thereby transferring filial responsibilities and care obligations from the family to the state.

There are two shared features of these changes to marriage, family, and family law. First, marriage and families in Taiwan are undergoing similar changes to those described by Cherlin (2004), who emphasized alternative forms of cohabitation, childbearing outside of marriage, and the changing division of labor and housework in domestic arrangements. This situation also pushes private matters into the public sphere. For example, as the number of single parents resulting from divorce increases, these parents encounter issues such as parental authority,[17] child care, social welfare assistance, and juggling family and career commitments. Thus, their individual private dilemmas are brought into the public sphere; this shift has accelerated political and legal reforms designed to meet their needs, as their life choices are no longer those of the nuclear, two-parent family type (Yang, Chen, and Li 2008).

The second feature is that, based on the prevalence of nontypical families, family courts do not take culture or traditional values as their ideology. They do not presume that families are created only through marriage. Instead, they seek to resolve family disputes or reorder the financial and material arrangements of families. As with the changes in the statutory treatment of divorce, a changing definition of family has emerged in several recent constitutional judgments. The next section examines four recent interpretations by the grand justices of Taiwan's Constitutional Court that addressed new needs and desires with regard to marriage, family, and children.

Unlike China's Supreme People's Court (SPC) discussed in this volume (Davis Chapter 2), the Constitutional Court is the supreme legal institution in Taiwan. It has sole authority to make constitutional interpretations and uniform interpretations of statutes and regulations and to declare the dissolution of political parties in violation of the Constitution.[18] The interpretations of the grand justices of the Constitutional Court represent the highest legal authority on the Constitution as well as Taiwan's statutes and regulations. With regard to family law matters, Taiwan's justices of the Constitutional Court deliver powerful messages combining culture, morality, and the value of marriage and family in the social order.

Most family law scholars agree that constitutional interpretations initiated two significant stages in Taiwan's family law reform process. The first stage was in the 1980s, with the introduction of the principle of gender equality. Both the constitutional interpretations and the legal enforcements of gender equality during this stage were motivated primarily by democratic and feminist movements in Taiwanese society. The second stage in the 2000s introduced the principle of the best interests of the child. The primary amendments and legal reforms during this stage were related to the protection of children's rights, including children born outside of marriage (Deng 1997: 3–48). In the following sections, I discuss four constitutional interpretations that dealt with de facto marriages, parental rights, spousal equity, and the interests of the child.

FACING UP TO "DE FACTO" MARRIAGE

Interpretation No. 242, issued in 1989, recognized that marital relationships did not exist independently of broader social and political conditions. This interpretation was the first to acknowledge how the contested political and military relationship across the Taiwan Strait had affected subsequent family formation in Taiwan. Hence, it shifted the terrain of family law away from a purely cultural domain and situated it squarely in the political realities resulting from a "divided China" by acknowledging how the political separation manifested in individual marital decisions and family formation.

At issue in this interpretation was the status of marriages made in Taiwan that involved a man born in Mainland China with a first wife from a previously contracted marriage in the Mainland from whom he had been forcefully separated as a result of the cross-Strait conflict. Was the subsequent marriage made in Taiwan bigamy? Did the second wife and her children enjoy inheritance rights? Once ties across the Strait were reinstated in 1987, these questions assumed heightened importance because a man could now reconnect with his prior spouse and children in China, and they could potentially make claims on his property in Taiwan were he to die.

The grand justices took up the questions of which marriage should be protected in this new context, who had inheritance rights, and who should be recognized as the legitimate wife. According to Interpretation No. 242, a man with a wife and children in Mainland China had little hope of reuniting with them due to the war across the Taiwan Strait following the arrival of the Kuomintang (Nationalist Party) government in Taiwan. When communication with the first wife was completely severed due to these political conditions, a "later marriage with an extended time of actual cohabitation" in Taiwan could be legitimated.

In Interpretation No. 242, the grand justices considered factors such as normal human emotions, the stability of the man's family life, and social stability, and concluded that the latter marriage would not be considered polygamous or invalid and thus would not be revoked. The law in Taiwan would legitimate this relationship, allowing the man to remarry, and would consider the children resulting from this marriage in Taiwan as legal heirs. Therefore, the property of the Taiwanese spouse and children would be upheld by law. This interpretation shows the grand justices' willingness to accommodate the controversies in family law created by social change and political factors, especially now that communication across the Strait had become possible. In other words, the grand justices of the Constitutional Court recognized de facto marriages in the special context of contentious cross-Strait relations.

EQUAL PARENTAL RIGHTS

In the past decades, Taiwan courts have confronted a variety of disputes over parental rights. For example, who has the right to make the final decision about a child's place of residence? Do the father's parental rights trump those of the mother? Article 1089 of the old Civil Code granted fathers the right to make the final decision about a child in cases where the parents disagreed, an obvious violation of the principle of gender equality. Recognizing women's increased access to education and employment, the grand justices of the Constitutional Court in 1994 claimed that such a law was out of step with the virtually equal conditions of men and women, "constitut[ing] a gross violation of gender equality, and creat[ing] a glaring discrepancy with the actual status of women in today's family" (Interpretation No. 365). Responding to growing societal attention to the issue of gender equality in Taiwanese society, the grand justices called for the amendment of Article 1089. Yet, perhaps as a sign of the still tentative acknowledgment of gender equality principles, the grand justices did not declare the article void immediately but instead imposed a two-year window for discussion and revision.

THE PRINCIPLE OF SPOUSAL EQUITY

A mere four years later, the grand justices returned to the question of gender equity within marriage, this time by addressing which spouse had the right to determine a couple's place of residence after marriage. Article 1002 of the old Civil Code had granted the husband the right to decide the place of residence in accordance with patrilineal principles that assumed a woman "married into" her husband's family and took up residence with him and possibly his extended family. Interpretation No. 452, issued in 1998, argued that the law "violate[d] the principle of equality and proportionality of the Constitution," and failed to recognize the nearly equal educational and employment opportunities of husbands and wives in the contemporary era. Therefore, the grand justices declared the law void within one year.

Why did the grand justices of the Constitutional Court care so deeply about gender equality within marriage that they rendered two articles void in a span of four years in the 1990s? The demand for gender equality presented in these two interpretations was closely related to the feminist movement launched in Taiwan during the same period. The Awakening Foundation (婦女新知), a prominent feminist organization, was established in 1982. With the end of martial law in Taiwan in 1987, the group worked tirelessly to increase awareness of women's rights. The Awakening Foundation provided legal assistance to women, especially in matters related to marriage, thereby directly influencing the broad family law reforms of the 1990s. Law, especially regulations that were unfavorable to women, became the battleground for feminist struggles. Feminist activism in this arena bore fruit in these two judicial interpretations that recognized the need to reform gender arrangements with regard to marital residence and parental rights. By rejecting the position that law should mandate the superior rights of fathers and husbands, the grand justices favored the practical, material arrangements of married couples over cultural principles that enshrined male privilege.

THE BEST INTERESTS OF THE CHILD

The principle of the best interests of the child is usually applied to determine which parent should receive parental rights following a divorce. Taiwan began to apply this standard in 1996, following a 1994 Constitutional Interpretation that declared the previous preference for fathers' parental rights a violation of equal gender rights protected by the Constitution. The two principles of gender equality and the best interests of the child have figured prominently in judicial decisions in divorce disputes involving child custody. Judges have heavily favored mothers in their rulings in child custody cases (Chen 2011; Chen and Chiu 2010; Liu 2001).[19] Yet, in cases of mutual divorce that do not involve suits, fathers have been 10 percent more likely to receive child custody than mothers (Chen 2011; Chen and Chiu 2010).[20]

More recently, the grand justices applied the principle of the best interests of the child in a new way to encompass a child's right to know his or her biological parents. Interpretation No. 587 (2004) challenged the presumption of a paternity system that recognizes the husband as the legal father when a married woman bears a child. Established legal reasoning assumed that it was not appropriate for a child to interfere in his or her parents' privacy, especially their intimate lives. If a child harbored suspicions about his or her own biological origins, that sentiment could be seen as a violation of a child's filial duty to obey his or her parents, including not questioning the mother's allegiance and purity in the marriage.

Addressing a scenario in which both of the child's legal parents had disappeared and the actual biological father had no recourse to recognition, the grand justices found that the child's rights exceeded the parents' right to privacy. According to Interpretation No. 587, "a child's right to identify his/her blood filiations and to ascertain his/her paternity is concerned with the right to personality and shall be protected by the Constitution." In so ruling, the grand justices dramatically challenged the cultural principle of filial piety and recognized the child as a person with inherent rights and needs. This interpretation has potentially opened the door to legal recognition of new family forms and new understandings of age and gender hierarchies within the family.

CONCLUSION

In this chapter, I have examined the sociolegal context of family law to illustrate how the law responds to social needs. Using the concept of deinstitutionalization of marriage and addressing the various stages of societal change in Taiwanese society, I explained the reforms in family law associated with the alternative types of contemporary marriage and families emerging in Taiwan, as well as with social movements and changes in the overall political climate.

Divorce is the end of a marriage, yet it simultaneously introduces the power of the state as manifested in laws governing domestic disputes. Therefore, I use divorce as an opportunity to discuss significant sociolegal changes in contemporary Taiwanese society. As divorce became viewed as a woman's right, existing models of fault-based divorce expanded to include a quasi–no-fault option, although no-fault divorce still is not formally recognized in Taiwanese family law.

Cherlin (2004) discusses three alternative futures of marriage and family. The first is the return to a more dominant form of heterosexual, monogamous marriage. However, this is unlikely to happen, as the division of labor, gender roles, and economic lives have changed in contemporary society. The second is marriage retaining a high symbolic status but decreasing its institutional function, and the third is marriage fading into one of many kinds of "interpersonal romantic relationships" (Cherlin 2004: 857–859). In Taiwan, however, these three alternative futures exist contemporaneously when viewed through the changing institutions of marriage, family, and law.

In this chapter, I have shown how the vivid image of the "ideal family" portrayed in the automobile advertisement dominates the structure of family law. This mainstream family ideal includes several elements identified by Cherlin as critical to the first type of marriage: heterosexual, monogamous, with clear divisions of labor and gender roles. However, recent constitutional interpretations reveal an increasing willingness to question the institutional function of this idealized model of marriage and family, as seen in the recognition of certain "de facto" marriages by the grand justices in constitutional interpretation No. 242. In other words, No. 242 weighed marriage as it existed in reality against marriage as defined in statute and found on the basis of the former. In a similar manner, the constitutional court's interpretation No. 587 emphasized the child's best interest over the sanctity of marriage and parental privacy.

The recent social movement promoting civil partnership rights in Taiwan adopts a different strategy for rethinking the future of marriage by expanding the options available for building a family through recognizing a multiperson family. This movement for same-sex partnership rights reveals the necessity of reconsidering the institutional function of marriage and family; it also reminds mainstream Taiwanese society that heterosexual marriage is only one of many kinds of interpersonal romantic relationships. These multiple possibilities coexist in contemporary Taiwan, knocking at the law's "front door" in search of formal recognition. As more disputes over nontraditional relationships come before the courts and more settlements spur constitutional interpretations, the three institutions of marriage, family, and law will continue to influence each other and recast their respective shapes and consequences. The demand for legal reform reflects the growing desire in Taiwanese society for more than a singular form of intimacy and family life.

NOTES

1. The grand justices of the Constitutional Court represent the highest legal institution in Taiwan and have sole power to interpret the Constitution. On the authority of the grand justices of the Constitutional Court, see Justices of the Constitutional Court, Judicial Yuan, R.O.C., 2004; retrieved on November 26, 2011, from www.judicial .gov.tw/constitutionalcourt/en/p01_02.asp (English version).

2. For example, the Taiwan Alliance to Promote Civil Partnership Rights (TAPCPR) released the first draft of their civil code in September 2011, which covers the civil partnership system, the system of multiperson family, and the adoption system. TAPCPR's draft declares marriage and partnership as two different systems that should be shared by people regardless of their sexuality. See Taiwan Alliance to Promote Civil Partnership Rights; retrieved December 14, 2012, from http://tapcpr .wordpress.com/關於伴侶盟/.

3. To better adapt to the character of family disputes and to expedite dispute resolution procedures, the Family Proceedings Act was released in June 2012. The text of the law is available through the Global Legal Information Network, Legislative Yuan, ROC; retrieved on December 14, 2012, from http://glin.ly.gov.tw/web/nationalLegal .do?isChinese=false&method=legalSummary&id=4973&fromWhere=legalHistory.

4. There is no unified usage of family law in Chinese in the Taiwanese context. Therefore, I use law of personal status (身分法) to illustrate how personal status has been contested or recognized, denied or approved, and dissolved or arranged in Parts IV and V of the Civil Code. I suggest that the usage of personal status law in the Chinese context is appropriate to indicate that modern family law should focus more on respect for privacy and individual life choices. See Kuo (2010).

5. I use *law* here to refer to the legislative acts of legislators, interpretations of judges, and the assessments of various interest groups in society.

6. Throughout the chapter, I use various technical Taiwanese legal terms and concepts, especially in the section where I review the interpretations made by the grand justices of the Constitutional Court. Because Chinese–English translations make the terms and categories of law more complicated, I hope that these legal technical terms and concepts will be considered data rather than just doctrines. Convinced that insights are better than data (Riles 2011), I expect that the legal technical jargon will not hinder interdisciplinary communication on the topics of marriage, family, and intimate lives.

7. The order and arrangement of Article 967 to Article 1090 of the Civil Code demonstrate the ideology of heterosexual marriage as the root of the family. See the Civil Code of Taiwan; retrieved on December 14, 2012, from http://glin.ly.gov.tw/web/ nationalLegal.do?isChinese=false&method=legalSummary&id=4973&fromWhere= legalHistory.

8. To view this automobile advertisement, "M323, a Part of Family," see www .youtube.com/watch?v=BvauCZ13_IU (retrieved January 22, 2014).

9. With regard to the nuclear family ideology in family law, see Civil Code Article 1127: "Dependents who have reached adulthood or who are minors but have already married may request a separation from the family," and Civil Code Article 1128: "Parents may order dependents who have reached adulthood or who are minors but have already married to separate from the family, but limitations due to reasonable grounds

exist." These laws confirm that modern family law is centered on individualistic family relations and considers the small family system (nuclear family model) to be the fundamental image of a family (Dai, Dai, and Dai 2007: 472–474).

10. One manifestation of the multiple forms of family in the courts are the cases of third parties involved in an intimate relationship with a married individual who have asked the courts for alimony after the end of a long-standing "de facto marriage."

11. Since 2008, the Taiwanese government has gradually eased certain restrictions for foreign spouses and Mainland spouses. See "Naturalization Rules Relaxed for Foreign Spouses," International Taiwan Service Portal, September 15, 2008; retrieved on April 1, 2012, from www.i-taiwan.nat.gov.tw/en/index.php?option=com_content&view=article&id=304:naturalization-rules-relaxed-for-foreign-spouses&catid=18:news-a-events&Itemid=69. On the financial requirement at the point of naturalization, see Enforcement of Nationality Act, Article 7 (amended on April 29, 2010).

12. A legal case promised to open the door to legal recognition of same-sex marriage, but it stalled in the courts and was finally withdrawn by the plaintiff in January 2013. See "Couple Drop Court Appeal over Gay Marriage Ban"; retrieved on June 5, 2013, from www.taipeitimes.com/News/taiwan/archives/2013/01/24/2003553311.

13. See Civil Code, Chapter IV ("Family") Article 1049: "The husband and the wife may effect a divorce by themselves with their mutual consent; but in the case of a minor, the consent of his or her statutory agent must be obtained." Article 1052 Paragraph 1: "Where either the husband or the wife meets one of the following conditions, the other party may petition the court for a juridical decree of divorce."

14. The global trend in favor of no-fault divorce also had a strong influence on the additional clause included in the revised 1985 family law (Deng 1997: 28–29).

15. See Civil Code, Chapter IV (Family) Article 1055-1:

When the court makes the jurisdiction in Article 1055, it should be decided in accordance with the best interests of the minor child, consider all the conditions and the visiting reports of the social workers, and especially consider the following: (1) The age, sex, numbers and health condition of the minor child. (2) The willingness of the minor child and personality development needs. (3) The age, occupation, character, health condition, economic ability and lifestyle of the parents. (4) The parent's willingness and attitude of protecting and educating the minor child. (5) The emotional feelings between the parents and the minor child or between the other persons living together and the minor child.

16. See Civil Code, Chapter I ("General Provisions") Article 14, Paragraph I:

With respect to any person who is not able to make declaration of intention, receive declaration of intention, or who lacks the ability to discern the outcome of the declaration of intention due to mental disability, the court may order the commencement of guardianship at the request of the person in question, his/her spouse, any relative within the fourth degree of kinship, a prosecutor, a competent authority or an organization of social welfare.

17. For information on parental authority, see Civil Code Chapter IV ("Family") Article 1084: "Children shall be filial to and respect their parents. Parents have the rights and the duties to protect, educate and maintain their minor children." Article 1085: "Parents may, within the limit of necessity, inflict punishment upon their children."

18. Aside from the Constitutional Court, there is the Supreme Court system. The system and the function of the Supreme Court in Taiwan are similar to the People's Court System in China. However, the Supreme Court in Taiwan has no authority to make interpretations of the Constitution or invalidate the law due to violation of the Constitution.

19. However, Liu (2001) argues that we should not conclude that this shift to maternal custody works to the benefit of women. He finds that judges granted custody to mothers not in accordance with principles of gender equality but in adherence to traditional norms and values that identified mothers as caregivers who had stronger affective bonds with their children. Moreover, judges' preference for "all-or-nothing" divorce settlements that did not adjudicate child support from the noncustodial parent exacerbated the double burden faced by custodial mothers by intensifying the simultaneous demands of child care and economic support.

20. Chen found that in cases of mutually agreed on divorce, the father's cultural and financial advantages granted him stronger bargaining power. As a result, mothers tended to give up their battle for child custody. In contrast, in cases of disputed divorces involving child custody, Chen found that social workers and social welfare groups provided mediation, consultation, and assistance to the disputants and detailed information to the judges. These additional resources led judges to favor mothers more heavily in adjudicated divorce settlements (Chen 2011; Chen and Chiu 2010).

REFERENCES

Chen Chao-ju (陳昭如). 1999. "權利、法律改革與本土婦運: 以台灣離婚權的發展為例" (Rights, Legal Reform and Native Women's Movement: The Development of the Right to Divorce in Taiwan [1985–1999]). 政大法學評論 (*Chengchi Law Review*) 62:25–74.

Chen Hui-Hsin (陳惠馨). 2005. 傳統個人、家庭、婚姻與國家 (*The Traditional Individual, Family, Marriage, and Nation: Research and Method in Chinese Legal History*). Taipei: Wunan Press.

Chen Jwu-Shang (陳竹上). 2011. "大台南格局下婚姻家庭課題的再思考" (Some Thoughts on the Issues of Marriage and Family in Greater Tainan). 台南市女性

權益促進會回訊 (*Bulletin of the Tainan City Women's Rights Promotion Association*), No. 29.

Chen Jwu-Shang (陳竹上), and Chiu May-Yuan (邱美月). 2010. 法院內外大不同？離婚途徑對於兒童利益之影響及我國發展家事仲裁之可行性分析 (*Why So Different Inside and Outside the Court? An Analysis of the Influence of the Divorce Path on the Child's Interests and the Potential for Family Arbitration in Taiwan*). Research project report sponsored by the Ministry of the Interior (on file with the author).

Cherlin, Andrew J. 2004. "The Deinstitutionalization of American Marriage." *Journal of Marriage and Family* 66:848–861.

"Couple Drop Court Appeal over Gay Marriage Ban." 2013. *Taipei Times*, January 24; retrieved on June 5, 2013, from www.taipeitimes.com/News/taiwan/archives/2013/01/24/2003553311.

Dai Yen–fui (戴炎輝), Dai Dong-xiong (戴東雄), and Dai Yu-ru (戴瑀如). 2007. 親屬法 (*Family Law*), revised version. Taipei: Yuan Chao.

Deng Xue-ren (鄧學仁). 1997. 親屬法變革與展望 (*Changes and Future Directions of Family Law*). Taipei: Yuedan.

Fineman, Martha. 1995. *The Neutered Mother, the Sexual Family, and Other Twentieth Century Tragedies*. New York: Routledge.

———. 2004. *The Autonomy Myth: A Theory of Dependency*. New York: The New Press.

Glendon, Mary Ann. 1989. *The Transformation of Family Law: State, Law, and Family in the United States and Western Europe*. Chicago: The University of Chicago Press.

Kuo, Shu-chin Grace (郭書琴). 2008. "身分法之法律文化分析初探: 以婚約篇為例" (A Cultural Analysis of Family Law: The Case of the Section on Matrimonial Engagement). 台北大學法學論叢 (*Taipei University Law Review*) 67:1–42.

———.2010. "從「伴侶」到「父母」論身分法規範重心之轉變: 兼評96年度養聲字第81號裁定" (From Partner to Parent: Changing Family Law and Critique of the Gay Parent Adoption Case in Taiwan). 成大法學 (*Cheng Kung Law Review*) 20:75–119.

———.2011. "A Socio-Legal Analysis of the Regulations on Foreign Spouses in Taiwan." *NTU Law Review* 6(2):495–520.

Lee, Shao-Fen, and Victoria Hsu. 2011. "Importance of Gender Education." *Taipei Times*, May 9; available at www.taipeitimes.com/News/editorials/archives/2011/05/09/2003502756/2.

Lin Hsiu-hsiung (林秀雄). 1994. 家族法論集 (三) (*Anthology of Family Law in Taiwan*, III). Taipei: Han-Hsing Publishing.

Liu, Hung-en. 2001. "Mother or Father: Who Received Custody? The Best Interests of the Child Standard and Judges' Custody Decisions in Taiwan." *International Journal of Law, Policy, and the Family* 15(2): 185–225.

Loa, Lok-sin. 2012. "Annual LGBT Pride Parade Attracts 50,000 People." *Taipei Times.* October 28; retrieved on December 14, 2012, from www.taipeitimes.com/News/front/archives/2012/10/28/2003546269/1.

Merry, Sally Engle. 1990. *Getting Justice and Getting Even: Legal Consciousness among Working-Class Americans.* Chicago: The University of Chicago Press.

Mertz, Elizabeth. 2007. *The Language of Law School: Learning to "Think Like a Lawyer."* New York: Oxford University Press.

Nader, Laura. 2002. *The Life of the Law: Anthropological Projects.* Berkeley: University of California Press.

———.2004. "The Link between Justice and International Law." *Peace and Conflict: Journal of Peace Psychology* 10(3): 297–299.

"Naturalization Rules Relaxed for Foreign Spouses." 2008. International Taiwan Service Portal, September 15; retrieved on April 1, 2012, from www.i-taiwan.nat.gov.tw/en/index.php?option=com_content&view=article&id=304:naturalization-rules-relaxed-for-foreign-spouses&catid=18:news-a-events&Itemid=69.

Riles, Annelise. 2011. "How Can We Better Harness the Insights of Different Disciplines to Address Market Reform?" Available at http://collateralknowledge.com/blog/2011/05/how- can-we-better-harness-the-insights-of-different-disciplines-to-address-market-reform/.

Singer, Jana B. 1992. "The Privatization of Family Law." *Wisconsin Law Review* 1443: 1443–1567.

Taiwan Department of Household Registration, Ministry of the Interior, "Number and Rates of Birth, Death, Marriage and Divorce, 1981–2012." Available at http://sowf.moi.gov.tw/stat/month/m1-02.xls.

Taiwan Judicial Yuan. 2009. "Causes of Divorce Cases Terminated by the District Courts—by Year." 司法統計年報 (*Judicial Statistics Yearbook*). Available at www.judicial.gov.tw/juds/year98/09/026.pdf.

Yang Jing-li (楊靜利), and Liu Yilong (劉一龍). 2002. "台灣的家庭生活歷程" (The Family Life Course in Taiwan). 台灣社會學刊 (*Taiwanese Journal of Sociology*) 27 (June): 77–105.

Yang Jing-li (楊靜利), Chen Kuan-zheng (陳寬政), and Li Da-zheng (李大正). 2008. "台灣近二十年來的家庭結構變遷: 1984–2005" (Changes in Family Structure in Taiwan in the Past Twenty Years: 1984–2005). 台灣社會變遷調查計畫第11次研討會 (*The Proceedings of the Eleventh Symposium on Societal Change in Taiwan, 1985–2005*). Institute of Sociology, Academia Sinica. March 28. Available at www.ios.sinica.edu.tw/sc/cht/files/conf11-2/A2.pdf.

10 CHANGE AND CONTINUITY IN THE EXPERIENCE OF MARRIAGE IN TAIWAN

Ruoh-rong Yu and Yu-sheng Liu

IN THE PAST THREE DECADES residents of Taiwan, like those in Hong Kong and urban China, have experienced rapid economic, political, and cultural change. Between 1980 and 2010, an already prosperous society became affluent, and an industrializing economy moved industrial production offshore and became a postindustrial service economy where the types of employment and the determinants of financial success for men and women shifted dramatically.[1] Many new colleges were established, and by 2010 more than 80 percent of those of college age went on to tertiary education.[2] Moreover, as in other affluent countries in Europe and North America, women in Taiwan are now more likely to enroll in university than men (see Figure 10.1), and recent estimates predict that for those six years old or older in 2010, females will average 16.27 years of school and males 16.11.[3] Not surprisingly, between 1981 and 2010 the ratio of men's average monthly income to that of women's steadily declined.[4]

In the realm of politics, change has been particularly momentous. After nearly forty years, martial law ended in 1987, multiparty democracy flourished, and in 1996 Taiwan held its first direct presidential election. In such a vibrant democratic society, Taiwanese elected officials became increasingly responsive to domestic and transnational social forces, even though the country lacked sovereign recognition from most other nation-states.

Simultaneous with these fundamental political and economic transformations, there have been multiple departures from what one might term the "demographic profile" of traditional marriage patterns and norms of family formation. During the 1950s and early 1960s, Taiwan along with Japan was at

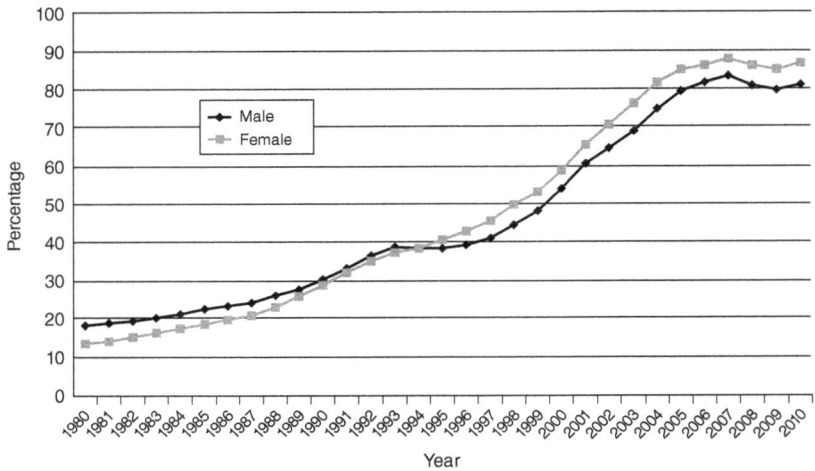

Figure 10.1. Changes in gross enrollment ratios of higher education in Taiwan.

SOURCE: Taiwan Department of Statistics, Ministry of Education. "Gross Enrollment Ratio. Tertiary - By Year & Gender." Retrieved on December 19, 2011, from https://stats.moe.gov.tw/files/gender_e/e106-10.xls.

the forefront of family planning initiatives to popularize two-child families (兩個恰恰好), but over the past few decades, without any explicit policy shifts, birth rates fell far below the two-child replacement level (see Figure 10.2), and the population began to age rapidly.[5]

As in other predominantly Chinese societies,[6] Confucian traditions defined the institution of marriage in Taiwan, and even after the island was colonized by Japan (1895–1945), family processes and relationships resembled those in China (Thornton and Lin 1994). Families were viewed as the primary societal units, and family elders were the main decision makers in their families. Marriages were early, universal, and arranged by the older generation to continue the family line, increase family labor, provide old-age security, extend social networks, and facilitate financial transfers between the bride's and the groom's families. Embedded in this multigenerational family context, marriage was rarely oriented toward satisfying individual or spousal interests or desires (Fan and Huang 1998: 229; Thornton and Lin 1994: 2).

However, as access to education expanded and Taiwanese society became more urbanized, prosperous, and integrated with global flows of trade and culture, four major departures from these Confucian traditions began to emerge. These departures have produced a trajectory of change away from

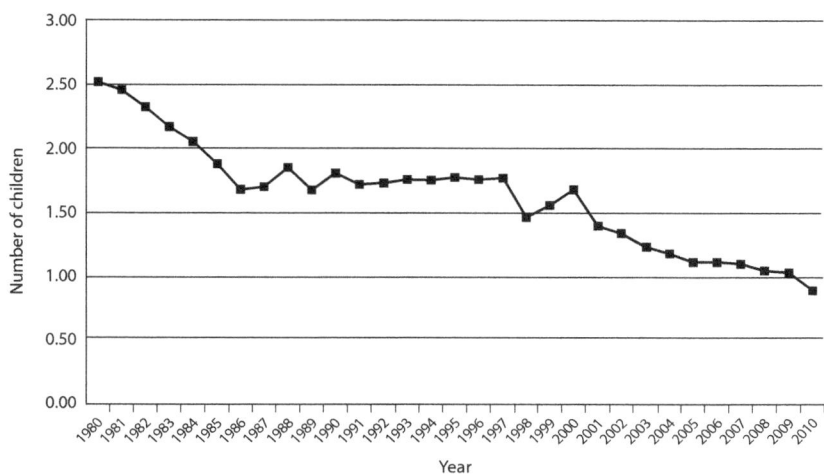

Figure 10.2. Changes in total fertility rates.

SOURCE: Taiwan Directorate-General of Budget, Accounting and Statistics (DGBAS). "Table 14. Fertility Rates for Women of Childbearing Age." Retrieved on December 19, 2011, from http://eng.stat.gov.tw/public/data/dgbas03/bs2/yearbook_eng/y014.pdf.

existing "rules of the game" that parallels in striking ways what Andrew Cherlin (2004) has defined as the deinstitutionalization of marriage. First, couples increasingly choose a mate without parental intervention. Whereas a mere 12.4 percent of couples who married before 1970 chose their own spouse, the proportion rose to 42.15 percent among those who married during the 1990s (Chu and Yu 2010: 91–92). Second, both men and women now marry at a later point in the life course. In 1970, the average age at first marriage was 28.2 for men and 22.1 for women. By 2005, the average age at first marriage had risen to 30.6 for men and 27.4 for women; although the increase was particularly marked among college-educated women, the shift appears across all levels of education (see Figure 10.3). Third, marriages in Taiwan, as in Hong Kong and Shanghai, have become more fragile. In 1980 the crude divorce rate (CDR) was 0.76; by 2010 it had jumped to 2.51. Finally, in Taiwan fewer and fewer people believe that the primary purpose of marriage is to continue the family line. In the nationally representative sample of the 2006 Taiwan Social Change Survey (TSCS),[7] only 18.8 percent of respondents agreed that "one should have at least a son to sustain the male lineage (為了傳宗接代至少要生一個兒子)," and a surprising 49.5 percent agreed that "it is not necessary to have a child after marriage (結婚後不一定要有小孩)."

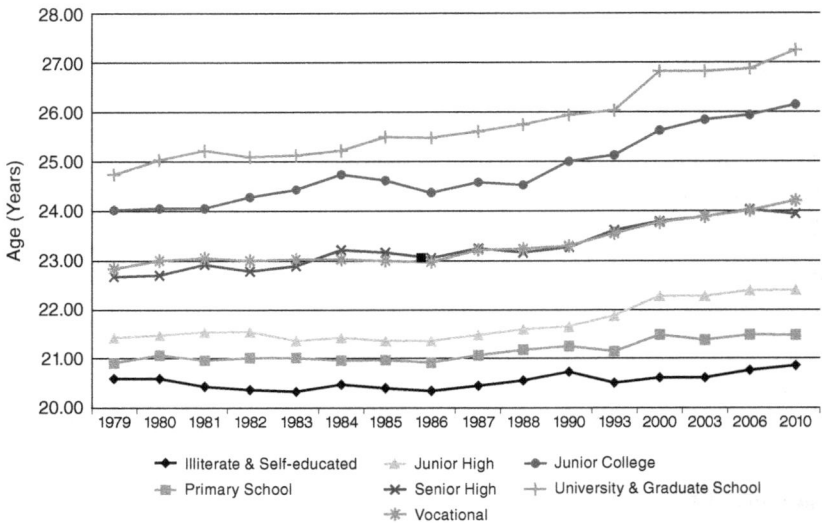

Figure 10.3. Changes in average age of first marriage of women in Taiwan.

SOURCE: Taiwan Directorate-General of Budget, Accounting and Statistics (DGBAS). "Table 1. Average Age at Entering First Marriage of Married Women Aged 15 Years and Over." Retrieved on December 19, 2011, from http://www.stat.gov.tw/public/data/dgbas04/bc4/wtable1.xls.

CONTINUITIES

Despite these many changes in the "demographic" elements of marriage, in other more subjective dimensions we see continuity. It is a common view in Taiwan that men should marry women who are younger, less educated, and of lower socioeconomic status (Chu and Yu 2010: chapter 5; Tsai 1996; Tsay 1996; Wong and Lu 1999; Yi and Hsung 1994). The 2006 Taiwan Social Change Survey (TSCS) reveals that more than half of the respondents (52 percent) agreed that a groom should be older than his bride, while only 16 percent of respondents disagreed. With regard to spousal responsibilities for family labor, respondents in the family module of the TSCS were asked whether they agreed that "the husband should be the breadwinner and the wife the homemaker (丈夫的責任就是賺錢, 妻子的責任就是照顧家庭)." This item is often used as a measure of traditional attitudes toward gender roles because it stresses the dichotomy between the husband's and wife's roles (Amato and Booth 1995). The 2006 TSCS Report revealed that 52.1 percent of the respondents agreed with the above statement, while only 37.4 percent disagreed.

Kinship loyalties and obligations in Taiwan also retain a patrilateral tilt. Chu and Yu (2010: chapter 10) found that, with respect to married couples and their parents, financial transfers flowed primarily from men (and their spouses) to the man's parents. Chu, Xie, and Yu (2011) also found that coresiding with the husband's parents was quite common in Taiwanese society, while coresiding with the wife's parents was rare. Thus, overall the surveys on Taiwanese families show neither a total break from past practices nor marriages that completely adhere to the expectations and behaviors of earlier generations. Rather, as in Hong Kong and urban China, the deinstitutionalization of marriage is not a coherent or linear process but rather an incomplete breakdown of earlier traditions with only partial reinstitutionalization around new "rules of the game." To probe deeper into this complex picture, we now turn to a multivariate analysis of several nationwide surveys to identify the characteristics of individual marital histories that document this pattern of uneven and incomplete change. We turn first to surveys of division of household labor and then to those focused on marital decision making. After reviewing the findings from these two different sets of surveys, we conclude by comparing similarities with and divergences from trends in urban China and Hong Kong.

CONTINUITIES IN DIVISION OF HOUSEWORK

We first turn our attention to the issue of how men and women divide responsibilities for housework and care of family members. When Taiwan was primarily an agricultural society anchored in small family farm enterprises, husbands and wives both actively engaged in the household economy. However, as elsewhere, these jobs were often assigned by gender. Once a woman married, she focused on unpaid domestic work, and when men became husbands they assumed greater responsibility for financially supporting the family and representing the family in the larger community. Even after most Taiwanese households had left farming, the distinction between the roles of husbands and wives persisted, and questions about how spouses divided their time on housework then became a proxy by which research calibrated and compared the changing character of marriage.

In this chapter we draw on the Panel Study of Family Dynamics (PSFD) to explore variation in division of housework between husbands and wives.[8] For PSFD, three groups of main respondents were first interviewed in 1999, 2000, and 2003, respectively, and follow-up surveys then were conducted on an annual basis. These respondents were first drawn by a stratified three-stage random sampling procedure. The data used in our regression analysis come from the information of the respondents and their spouses collected from the first-wave survey through the 2007 survey.[9] These data include 2,649 couples and 11,490 observations. Before proceeding to the analysis, we shall take a glimpse at the overall pattern of housework allocation using the 2007 data, which contain 1,172 husband and wife pairs.

According to the PSFD conducted in 2004, husbands averaged 6.2 hours of housework per week and their wives 19.8 hours (Chu and Yu 2010: 117–119). In the 2007 follow-up survey, both men and women reported slightly fewer hours, but the gap between men and women remained almost unchanged, even when we excluded couples where husbands were sixty-five or older (the cohort of men least likely to perform household labor).[10] It is noteworthy that this gender gap in division of housework is greater in Taiwan than in families interviewed in Fujian, Zhejiang, and Shanghai during the same period.[11]

Because we assumed that wives who do not work outside the home have more time to specialize in domestic housework, we hypothesized that women employed outside the home would do fewer hours of housework than women who did not work outside the home. The results for the 2007 survey reported in Table 10.1 confirm that hypothesis. However, the percentage of housework performed by wives, regardless of their work status or that of their husbands, remains virtually the same across the two groups. When neither spouse works, wives contribute 74.7 percent; when both work, wives contribute 72.9 percent; and when husbands do not work, but wives do, wives still contribute over 70 percent (see Table 10.1). Moreover, as we demonstrate in the following pages, this pattern of a heavier housework burden for wives is most pronounced among the youngest cohorts. Before moving through the multivari-

Table 10.1. Average hours and share of housework: By husband's and wife's working statuses.

| | Husband full-time work or not/wife full-time work or not | | | |
	Husband yes/ wife yes	Husband yes/ wife not	Husband not/ wife yes	Husband not/ wife not
Wife's housework (in hours)	14.72	22.52	12.90	20.69
Husband's housework (in hours)	5.17	5.54	6.85	5.49
Wife's housework share (percent)	72.87	73.06	71.32	74.70
Number of observations (N)	454	334	133	251

SOURCE: Authors' own calculations from the 2007 Panel Study of Family Dynamics data.

ate results in Table 10.2, however, we first discuss our choice of variables and the central hypotheses in greater detail.

Because of Taiwan's multiethnic history, ethnic identity is often used as a variable that sheds light on attitudes toward gender roles in the household, specifically with regard to division of housework between men and women. Mainlanders who came to Taiwan with the Nationalist government and army between 1946 and 1950 are often assumed to hold less traditional views on gender role divisions, in part because of long-standing occupational or educational advantages over native Taiwanese or because they experienced unconventional marriage and family histories due to social marginalization in Taiwan. By contrast, native Taiwanese, and especially Hakka families, are presumed to display a greater commitment to gendered divisions of labor in the household, often enforced by the older generation. Although social distinctions between Mainlanders and Taiwanese have narrowed over time, especially with intermarriage, we nonetheless presume that all else being equal those of Mainlander background will hold less traditional views on the division of housework. In our analysis, therefore, we note whether the wife and the husband come from Mainlander families (1 = Mainlander; 0 = not Mainlander) to assess the impact of ethnicity on gender role expectations.

The economic conditions of one's childhood, or what sociologists term *family of origin*, are also presumed to shape how husbands and wives behave in their own marriages. In particular, it is presumed that the higher the education of the wife's father, the more her husband will contribute to the housework. In our analysis we simply indicate whether or not the wife's father had a junior high school education or higher (1 = junior high or higher; 0 = less than junior high). We also are interested in the couple's relative resources. In our analysis, we adopt two measures for the couple's relative resources. One is the spousal educational difference, which is defined by the husband's schooling (in years) minus the wife's. The other is the difference between the husband's and wife's income. The spousal income is retrieved from the respondent's answers to monthly labor income (in thousands of new Taiwan dollars, NTD). According to the relative resources hypothesis (Bianchi et al. 2000; Blood and Wolfe 1960; Knudsen and Wærness 2008; Mannino and Deutsch 2007; Pinto and Coltrane 2009), an increase in a spouse's relative resources, either in terms of income or education, is expected to lower his or her burden of household chores.

We also look explicitly at the impact of the time people spend working outside the home. As expected by the time availability hypothesis (Bartley, Blanton, and Gillard 2005; Cunningham 2007; Davis, Greenstein, and Marks 2007), a spouse's own market work time has negative effects on his or her housework time. In addition to the already mentioned variables, we also assess several aspects of the couple, namely length of marriage, health condition of each spouse, whether or not they have young children in the home, and whether they coreside with the husband's or wife's parents. The husband's and wife's health condition dummies are constructed using the self-reported information provided by the respondent. If a spouse's health condition is fair or good, he or she is expected to take on more of the housework load. Having a child aged six or under is expected to increase the housework load for both spouses. Coresidence with the spouses' parents may exert several influences. First, the coresiding parents may share the household labor and lessen the housework load of the couple. Second, coresiding with a spouse's parents may exert pressure on the other partner to behave well in front of coresiding parents, especially in a more traditional family. Because coresidence with the husband's parents conforms to traditional norms of patrilineality and patriarchy, such a practice is expected to result in a heavier housework load for the wife.

Finally we look at attitudes toward gender roles, assuming that the more liberal the attitudes toward gender roles the greater will be the husband's contribution. The gender ideology variable is measured by the respondent's answer to the "husband breadwinner–wife homemaker" question. In terms of a 1 to 5 scale, a larger value indicates stronger traditional attitudes.[12] The gender ideology hypothesis predicts that more traditional attitudes induce a less egalitarian division of housework (Cunningham 2001; Davis et al. 2007; Knudsen and Wærness 2008; Parkman 2004).

Given the rapid and dramatic changes in the social and economic profiles of the Taiwan population in the past thirty years, we explicitly examine the impact of variation in birth cohort; in the models of Table 10.2 we have divided the respondents into six groups by husband's year of birth.[13] Overall we expect that couples from more recent cohorts will exhibit more equal division of household labor.

We confine our sample to married couples with husbands aged below sixty-five and delete the observations with missing variables. The sample used in our regression models is panel data retrieved from the first wave up to the

Table 10.2. Division of housework between spouses: Random effects model.

	Wife's housework (in hours)	Husband's housework (in hours)	Wife's housework share (percentage)
Wife's ethnicity (1 = Mainlander)	0.304	0.174	−0.010
	(0.759)	(0.448)	(0.017)
Husband's ethnicity (1 = Mainlander)	−1.403*	0.668	−0.031*
	(0.743)	(0.438)	(0.017)
Wife's father's education being junior high or above (1 = yes)	−1.329**	0.367	−0.007
	(0.655)	(0.386)	(0.015)
Husband's father's education being junior high or above (1 = yes)	−0.278	0.184	−0.018
	(0.652)	(0.385)	(0.015)
Age difference between spouses (in years)	−0.038	0.012	−0.001
	(0.056)	(0.033)	(0.001)
Education difference between spouses (in years)	−0.008	−0.003	−0.001
	(0.064)	(0.037)	(0.001)
Income difference between spouses (in thousand NTD)	0.012***	−4.357E-04	0.843E-04**
	(0.002)	(0.001)	(0.380E-04)
Sum of spouses' income (in thousand NTD)	−0.010***	−0.983E-04	−0.526E-04
	(0.002)	(0.001)	(0.372E-04)
Wife's working time (in hours)	−0.100***	0.011***	−4.160E-04***
	(0.006)	(0.003)	(1.080E-04)
Husband's working time (in hours)	0.006	−0.024***	4.556E-04***
	(0.006)	(0.003)	(1.03E-04)
Wife's health being fair or good (1 = yes)	−0.121	0.042	4.290E-06
	(0.465)	(0.266)	(0.008)
Husband's health being fair or good (1 = yes)	−0.820*	0.465*	−0.020**
	(0.481)	(0.276)	(0.009)
Any child aged six or below (1 = yes)	1.425***	0.441**	−0.011*
	(0.323)	(0.186)	(0.006)
Coresiding with wife's parent (1 = yes)	−1.703*	−1.622***	0.027
	(0.901)	(0.519)	(0.017)
Coresiding with husband's parent (1 = yes)	0.554	−0.152	−0.005
	(0.383)	(0.221)	(0.007)
Residential areas (other areas being reference group)			
Living in metropolitan cities (1 = yes)	−1.510***	−0.626**	0.005
	(0.491)	(0.288)	(0.011)
Living in provincial cities (1 = yes)	0.646	−0.252	0.016
	(0.579)	(0.340)	(0.013)
Gender role ideology (1–5)	0.977***	−0.116	0.013***
	(0.160)	(0.094)	(0.004)
Years of marriage (in years)	0.339***	0.093***	0.005***
	(0.044)	(0.026)	(0.001)
Years of marriage squared	−0.005***	−0.002**	−0.742E-04***
	(0.001)	(0.001)	(0.253E-04)
Husband's birth cohort dummies (> = 1966 being reference group)			
< 1945	0.435	0.831*	−0.068***
	(0.852)	(0.497)	(0.018)
1946–1950	0.456	0.787	−0.057***
	(0.830)	(0.486)	(0.018)
1951–1955	0.771	0.299	−0.038**
	(0.735)	(0.431)	(0.016)
1956–1960	0.608	0.190	−0.042**
	(0.796)	(0.468)	(0.018)
1961–1965	−0.414	−0.557	0.006
	(0.714)	(0.420)	(0.016)
Wald statistics for overall significance	760.68***	152.46***	167.69***
	(d.f. = 25)	(d.f. = 25)	(d.f. = 25)
Test statistics for joint significance of birth cohort dummies	3.27	10.18*	23.51***
Number of families/observations	2,649/11,490	2,649/11,490	2,649/11,490

NOTES: (1) Standard errors are in parentheses. ***, ** and * denote 1 percent, 5 percent, and 10 percent levels of significance.
(2) The intercept terms are omitted for brevity.

2007 surveys of the PSFD, which consists of 11,490 observations pertaining to 2,649 families. For the ith married couple at time t, consider the following housework time (h) equation:[14]

$$h_{it} = \beta_0 + \sum_k \beta_k \cdot X_{k,it} + \sum_l \beta_l \cdot Z_{l,i} + \beta_{d1} \cdot DUR_{it} + \beta_{d2} \cdot DUR_{it}^2$$
$$+ \sum_c \beta_c \cdot COHORT_{c,it} + v_i + u_{it}. \qquad (1)$$

Three variables are adopted to measure the absolute and relative housework load (h) of the spouses: (1) the wife's housework time, (2) the husband's housework time, and (3) the wife's housework share. The first two variables were constructed using the respondent's report of his or her own and the spouse's housework hours per week. The wife's housework share is defined by the ratio of the wife's housework time to the sum of the spouses' housework time. The results for the random-effects models are listed in Table 10.2.[15]

The years of marriage exhibit nonlinear effects. The housework load and share first increase with the duration of marriage; then they decline after a certain point. As predicted by the relative resources hypothesis, we find that, when the wives have relatively higher income, they are more likely to lighten their housework load, either in absolute terms or by relative share. However, educational differences do not exhibit significant effects. It seems that the relative resources hypothesis is only partly supported by the evidence. On the other hand, more liberal attitudes toward gender roles do significantly affect the wife's absolute and relative housework equations. This indicates that when women hold more traditional attitudes about gender roles there is a less egalitarian division of housework. However, it can be seen from the husband's housework equation that neither relative resources nor gender role attitudes are significant. In short, for men but not women, the earnings and gender ideology have little impact.

As for family background variables, our initial hypotheses hold true. Women married to Mainlander men engage in less housework time, which leads to less housework share accordingly. Similarly, having a better-educated father reduces the hours a wife spends on domestic work. As predicted, if the couple has a child aged six or younger, the housework load of both of the spouses will become heavier, although eventually the wife's housework share will decrease slightly. Coresiding with the wife's parents tends to lessen both the wife's and the husband's housework load. For couples residing in more urbanized areas, both of the spouses' housework hours are reduced.

In terms of cohort effect, however, our predictions did not hold up. Overall there is no significant variation by cohort, and, in the one case where there is, estimates reveal that the wife's housework share (the last column of the table) is significantly lower for the older cohorts than the younger ones. This implies that the wife's relative housework burden is heavier in families formed by younger cohorts. One possible explanation for this counter-intuitive finding is the effect of self-selection. That is, women who self-select into marriage at a younger age might also be those who were most likely to adopt existing norms of marital allocation and thus prone to assume relatively more housework responsibilities.

As previously mentioned, the allocation of housework between spouses does not change much across birth cohorts in Taiwan. This result parallels Ting's finding (Chapter 6 in this volume) that Hong Kong women's perceptions of the quality of their marriages have remained unchanged among cohorts. Even though the educational and employment opportunities of women have improved significantly during the past few decades, the housework load and marital satisfaction of married women have remained almost intact from cohort to cohort, as indicated by the findings of the PSFD. However, because the PSFD was initiated only in 1999, the panel is not long enough for us to make inferences about long-term patterns. What we illustrate in the preceding discussion can be interpreted only as evidence for prevailing trends during the early to mid-2000s.

CONTINUITIES IN MARITAL POWER

Unequal division of housework in part reflects opportunity and opportunity costs, but it does not necessarily predict unequal marital power. In theory wives could do more than 70 percent of all housework and still be equally "powerful" in terms of making critical decisions.[16] In fact, they might even have more power over those decisions that directly affect management and maintenance of the family residence. We thus turn from our analysis of determinants of division of housework to look directly at the question of marital power. Studies on marital power in North America and Europe suggest that as women's incomes increase their control over money in the marital relationship also increases (Blumstein and Schwartz 1983; Pahl 1989; Whyte 1990). However, others find that men's power and privileges within the home have largely been preserved (Tichenor 1999, 2005). It is also observed that women's employment only slightly increases their control over family finances and decision making, and women still bear a disproportionate burden of domestic labor and child care (Coltrane 2000; Pyke 1994). In addition, others have found that, even when women are able to use their resources to enhance their power, both spouses may feel more comfortable adhering to traditional decision-making patterns (Coltrane 1996). Such a gender display may override the role of spousal resources in marital power (Bittman et al. 2003; Greenstein 2000).

The results on division of housework suggest that Taiwanese couples may also experience similar patterns of persistent male dominance in spite of a wife's larger financial contribution to the household budget. Whether the same pattern pertains for marital power in Taiwan is an interesting issue. Using data from the late 1980s through early 2000s, Yi and Yang (1995) found a gradual shift toward greater egalitarianism, and Yi, Lu, and Pan (2000) and Xu and Lai (2002) found support for norms of gender equality that were significantly associated with the sharing of marital power. Chu and Yu (2010: chapter 6), who focused on the impact of relative resources, found that the wife's relative resources (measured by her share of income) significantly increased her relative power with regard to decisions involving savings and investment, housing and moving, and purchasing high-priced commodities but oddly enough not those involving daily expenditures.

For our analysis of marital power we use the Taiwan Social Change Surveys (TSCS) conducted in 1996 and 2006. The TSCS is a repeated cross-sectional survey that was started in 1985. This survey has been conducted jointly by the Institute of Sociology and the Center for Survey Research, Academia Sinica. The target population is individuals aged twenty and above, with the sample randomly selected using the stratified multistage random sampling method. Similar to the design of the General Social Survey (GSS), the survey topics of TSCS are rotated every five years. "Family module" is one of the rotating topics. However, only the 1996 and 2006 questionnaires contained questions related to marital power. As in the previous analysis of housework, we are particularly interested in whether attitudes and reported behaviors vary by birth cohort, the relative resources of each spouse, and attitudes toward gender equality.

In the 1996 and 2006 TSCS surveys, the question related to marital power contains three different types of decision making: (1) the allocation of daily expenditures (家用支出的分配); (2) the purchasing of high-priced commodi-

Table 10.3. Distribution of marital power: By husband's and wife's working statuses (percentage).

Type of decision/ whose decision	Husband full-time work or not/wife full-time work or not			
	Husband yes/ wife yes	Husband yes/ wife not	Husband not/ wife yes	Husband not/ wife not
Daily expenditure				
Husband	20.44	31.44	18.04	29.46
Jointly	39.88	27.42	37.70	37.50
Wife	39.68	41.14	44.26	33.04
Sum	100.00	100.00	100.00	100.00
Number of observations (N)	(499)	(299)	(61)	(112)
High-priced commodities				
Husband	32.73	40.34	27.86	30.36
Jointly	47.59	40.67	47.54	53.57
Wife	19.68	19.00	24.59	16.07
Sum	100.00	100.00	100.00	100.00
Number of observations (N)	(498)	(300)	(61)	(112)
Child discipline				
Husband	16.77	12.32	20.34	16.66
Jointly	49.04	50.68	47.46	48.15
Wife	34.18	36.98	32.20	35.18
Sum	100.00	100.00	100.00	100.00
Number of observations (N)	(471)	(292)	(59)	(108)

SOURCE: Authors' own calculations from the 2006 Taiwan Social Change Survey data.

ties (買高消費物品); and (3) disciplining children (子女的教養). The respondents were asked to identify the main decision maker in each case.

In Table 10.3 we summarize the descriptive results for 2006. Here we observe that, regardless of spousal working statuses or the type of decisions, joint decision making is the modal type. Moreover, men only rarely make decisions unilaterally, and wives usually have more say except when purchasing high-priced commodities. Because daily expenditures and child discipline are in the domestic domain and high-priced commodities may involve extradomestic decisions, the figures presented in Table 10.3 may simply reflect the dichotomy of gender roles within marriage.

We turn now to the multivariate analysis of results in both 1996 and 2006 to move beyond descriptive summaries. Here responses to the three questions have been rescaled into ordered measures ("husband" = 1, "jointly decided by husband and wife" = 2, "wife" = 3). A larger value indicates a higher degree of power on the wife's side, and the following model is specified for marital power:[17]

$$P^*_{it} = \gamma_0 + \sum_k \gamma_k X_{k,it} + \gamma_{d1} \cdot DUR_{it} + \gamma_{d2} \cdot DUR^2_{it} + \sum_c \gamma_c \cdot COHORT_{c,it}$$
$$+ \gamma_y \cdot YEAR_{it} + \varepsilon_{it}. \tag{2}$$

To make our analysis comparable with the discussion of housework sharing, we adopt the same meanings for most explanatory variables here, as in Table 10.2. For brevity, we discuss only the variables with different definitions. First, the economic statuses of the spouses in the original families are used instead of parental education. The main reason is that not all the TSCS surveys contain questions about parental education. The original families' economic statuses are composed of three dummies, with the spousal families being similar in terms of their economic situation to the reference group. Second, the spousal working statuses are used in place of the working hours. This is because the 1996 and 2006 survey data do not contain the number of hours worked. Third, the total family income is defined by the household's total income. Unlike the sum of spousal income used in Table 10.2, the variable used here is not confined to the spouses. In addition, both labor and nonlabor incomes are included in the income variable.

The estimation results for the ordered probit models are listed in Table 10.4. The birth cohort dummies exhibit only minor effects in the daily expenditure and child discipline equations.[18] Compared to the couples where husbands were in the youngest cohort, those with husbands in the eldest cohort possessed significantly less power with respect to daily financial decisions. However, as indicated by the test statistics for the joint significance of the cohort effects (see the bottom of Table 10.4), the overall influence of the birth cohort dummies, as in the previous analysis of division of housework, is insignificant.

The significance of the survey year dummy in the child discipline equation illustrates that the wife's power in child discipline in 2006 is higher than it had been in 1996. However, because there are only two survey years in our sample, the robustness of this finding may be questionable. With respect to marital duration, the inverted-U relationship between power and marital duration in the daily expenditure equation is similar to the findings in the housework equations. The similarity might reflect the close connection between the sharing of housework and marital power in the domestic sphere.

Table 10.4. Wife's relative marital power: Ordered probit regressions (3-point scale).

	Daily Expenditure	High-priced Commodities	Child Discipline
Wife's ethnicity (1 = Mainlander)	−0.088	0.008	0.017
	(0.087)	(0.088)	(0.089)
Husband's ethnicity (1 = Mainlander)	0.221***	0.003	0.140*
	(0.083)	(0.082)	(0.084)
Original families' economic status ("similar" being reference group)			
Wife's family being better off (1 = yes)	0.179**	0.110	−0.054
	(0.071)	(0.070)	(0.072)
Husband's family being better off (1 = yes)	−0.036	−0.112	−0.084
	(0.073)	(0.073)	(0.074)
Age difference between spouses (in years)	0.005	−0.006	−0.004
	(0.008)	(0.008)	(0.008)
Education difference between spouses (in years)	−0.020**	−0.024***	−0.039***
	(0.009)	(0.009)	(0.009)
Wife working (1 = yes)	0.124**	0.085	−0.074
	(0.055)	(0.055)	(0.056)
Husband working (1 = yes)	−0.095	−0.137	−0.017
	(0.100)	(0.100)	(0.102)
Total family income (in thousand NTD)	1.507E-04	−0.001**	−3.390E-04
	(2.821E-04)	(0.000)	(2.848E-04)
Having at least one son (1 = yes)	0.007	0.137*	−0.309***
	(0.070)	(0.071)	(0.073)
Having at least one daughter (1 = yes)	0.027	0.119*	−0.053
	(0.061)	(0.061)	(0.062)
Coresiding with wife's parent (1 = yes)	0.272	0.480**	−0.003
	(0.198)	(0.194)	(0.198)
Coresiding with husband's parent (1 = yes)	−0.221***	−0.073	−0.046
	(0.061)	(0.062)	(0.063)
Residential areas (other areas being reference group)			
Metropolitan cities	−0.096	−0.004	−0.055
	(0.070)	(0.070)	(0.071)
Provincial cities	0.002	0.129	0.039
	(0.081)	(0.081)	(0.083)
Gender role ideology (1–5)	−0.011	−0.035	0.006
	(0.023)	(0.023)	(0.023)
Years of marriage	0.034***	−0.001	−0.010
	(0.011)	(0.011)	(0.011)
Years of marriage squared	−4.606E-04**	1.342E-04	1.095E-04
	(1.891E-04)	(1.989E-04)	(1.957E-04)
Husband's birth cohort dummies (> = 1966 being reference group)			
< 1945	−0.482**	0.083	−0.061
	(0.202)	(0.204)	(0.207)
1946–1950	−0.221	0.132	−0.076
	(0.166)	(0.167)	(0.170)
1951–1955	−0.192	0.110	−0.226
	(0.139)	(0.141)	(0.143)
1956–1960	−0.110	0.143	−0.166
	(0.118)	(0.119)	(0.121)
1961–1965	−0.128	0.030	−0.203*
	(0.103)	(0.104)	(0.106)
Survey year being 2006 (1 = yes)	−0.108	−0.026	0.245***
	(0.074)	(0.075)	(0.076)
Log likelihood	−2,055.531	−1,894.942	−1,766.9101
Likelihood ratio statistics for overall significance	71.18	62.48	103.70
	(d.f. = 24)***	(d.f. = 24)***	(d.f. = 24)***
Test statistics for joint significance of birth cohort dummies	8.35	2.57	8.59
Number of observations (N)	1,956	1,956	1,956

NOTES: (1) Standard errors are in parentheses. ***, ** and * denote 1 percent, 5 percent, and 10 percent levels of significance.
(2) The two intercept terms are omitted for brevity.

Resource theory can be examined in several ways. First, the significantly negative effects of educational differences in all three columns imply that higher education for the husband leads to a decrease in the wife's power in all aspects. Second, the better the economic condition of the wife's original family, the greater the wife's power over daily expenditures. Both of these findings are consistent with the predictions of the resource theory. The gender ideology variable is insignificant in all the equations, which is not consistent with the expectation of the gender role hypothesis.

As for the other explanatory variables, having a Mainlander husband or holding a market job tends to enhance the wife's power regarding daily expenditures (column 1). Higher family income is detrimental for the wife's power concerning high-priced commodities, but the presence of a child is beneficial. The existence of a son tends to reduce the wife's power in terms of child discipline. As one would expect, coresiding with the wife's parents tends to enhance the wife's power (column 2), but coresiding with the husband's parents has the opposite effect (column 1).

The previously mentioned finding on the insignificant effects of birth cohort is very similar to what we found for the housework allocation of married couples. This indicates that, though in many respects norms and experience of marriage have changed, the roles of husband and wife by and large have remained intact across cohorts. Men and women of younger generations are similar to those in older generations in terms of the sharing of housework load and marital power. In addition, the traditional expectation of man as breadwinner and woman as homemaker has not changed much from cohort to cohort. However, it should be mentioned again that only two years of survey data were used in the analysis. When interpreting the cohort effects, such a limitation should be kept in mind. Nevertheless, this finding is consistent with Shen's (Chapter 11) observations about the marital arrangements of Taiwanese businessmen in China. Even though most married businessmen did not take their families with them when they worked in China, they strove to sustain their marriage by sending remittances back to their families.

CONCLUSIONS

Government statistics document dramatic changes in the demographic profile of marriage in Taiwan. Crude marriage rates have fallen, and crude divorce rates have risen. Late or no marriage is becoming the norm among highly educated women and men, and, since the late 1990s, between 15 and 28 percent of men have married a non-Taiwanese woman.[19]

Yet, as we have shown when we looked closely at the determinants of variation in how couples divide housework or share marital decision making, there are also substantial continuities with a traditional patrilineal Confucian family model. Most striking and unexpected was that we found no significant variation when we compared couples according to the birth cohort of the husband. Furthermore, contrary to our conjecture, the wife's relative housework share is heavier among the younger cohorts than the older cohorts. One explanation we noted is that women who choose to marry young might be those who are most likely to adopt traditional gender norms and thus are willing to take on more household labor. But, overall, the significantly heavier housework burden among women speaks to resistance among men from a wide range of educational and economic backgrounds to share housework equally. Thus, regardless of the wife's characteristics, traditional norms still dominate among married couples of all birth cohorts.

At first glance, the coexistence of rising divorce, falling fertility, and a higher percentage of college-educated men and women postponing (or even eschewing) marriage with persistence of a traditional division of household labor and marital power may seem anomalous. However, we would argue that, rather than seeing Taiwan as anomalous, what we find is the general unevenness of deinstitutionalization as observed in Hong Kong and China. In addition, it is also possible that what is emerging in Taiwan and perhaps elsewhere is a split in marital experiences and desires by gender and at times by education. Those who remain comfortable with the traditional division of labor and marital power are more likely to marry and remain married, while the never-married or unmarried, who were not included in our surveys, would behave very differently and espouse different views. In short, traditional behaviors endure without drastic changes in marriage per se, but the institution of heterosexual marriage begins to encompass an ever-smaller proportion of the adult population.

NOTES

1. For example, in 1999 Taiwan's gross domestic product (GDP) per capita in terms of purchasing power parity (PPP) was 16,100; by 2010 it had more than doubled to 35,700. Retrieved on January 21, 2012, from the website of Index Mundi (www .indexmundi.com/g/g.aspx?c=tw&v=67).

2. According to Chen and Chang (2010), there were in total 105 colleges and universities in 1986. In 2010, the number had increased to 163.

3. According to the statistics from the Ministry of Education of Taiwan, the years of school-life expectancy are calculated based on the progression rates and schooling years of various education tiers.

4. The decline was from 1.56 in 1981 to 1.25 in 2010. The figures are calculated by the authors based on the statistics published by the Directorate-General of Budget, Accounting and Statistics, Taiwan.

5. The percentage of the population aged 65 and over rose from 4.6 percent in 1982 to 10.7 percent in 2010, as indicated in Table 10 of the 2010 Statistical Yearbook published the Directorate-General of Budget, Accounting and Statistics, Taiwan.

6. The majority of Taiwan's population is composed of four ethnic groups. Except for the Aborigines, each of the other three ethnic groups is made up of immigrants from Mainland China. Mainlanders immigrated from Mainland China during the Chinese Civil War (1945–1949), while the Hoklo and Hakka came from Fujian and Guangdong provinces beginning in the seventeenth century. The Hoklo, Hakka, Mainlanders, and Aboriginal communities now constitute 73 percent, 12 percent, 13 percent, and 2 percent of the population of Taiwan, respectively (Scott and Tiun 2007).

7. The Report on the 2006 Taiwan Social Change Survey (in Chinese) can be downloaded from the website of the survey project (www.ios.sinica.edu.tw/sc/cht/datafile/tscs06.pdf).

8. The main respondents of the PSFD come from three birth cohorts drawn by a stratified three-stage random sampling procedure: (1) the cohort born 1935–1954, (2) the cohort born 1953–1964, and (3) the cohort born 1964–1976. The cohorts are listed according to the calendar year of their first contact. The 1953–1964 cohort is first interviewed in year 1999; the 1935–1954 and 1964–1976 cohorts are first contacted in years 2000 and 2003 respectively. As a result, the birth cohorts have some overlap with respect to their birth years. However, the overall distribution of the combined sample is similar to that of the population in terms of birth year, gender, and education.

9. We exclude data for the year 2003 from our analysis. The questionnaire for the year 2003 is mainly based on the individual's life-event history, with its contents differing from counterparts in other surveys.

10. In 2007 the average weekly hours of household tasks for husbands and wives were 5.7 and 18.0, respectively. After deleting those couples where husbands were aged sixty-five or above, the estimates are basically unchanged at 5.4 for men and 18.0 for women.

11. The survey conducted in China was designed in parallel to the PSFD survey of Taiwan. The targeted respondents and the contents of the questionnaire are almost identical to those of the Taiwan counterpart.

12. Although some scholars have noticed that spouses may espouse divergent attitudes toward gender roles (Amato and Booth 1995), we temporally put aside this problem in our analysis.

13. For the 1953–1964 birth cohort first interviewed in the year 1999, a panel is obtained by merging data files using the respondents' serial numbers. Panels for respondents born in 1935–1954 (first interviewed in 2000) and 1964–1976 (first interviewed in 2003) are obtained likewise. Because positive assortative matching in spousal ages at marriage is a common practice in Taiwan, the wife's birth cohort dummies are dropped from the equations to avoid possible multicollinearity.

14. In the equation, h_{it} denotes the dependent variable. The $X_{k,it}$'s and $Z_{l,i}$'s denote time-varying and time-invariant explanatory variables, respectively. DUR_{it} represents the years of marriage for the couple. The $COHORT_{c,it}$'s are birth cohort dummies. The β's are the corresponding coefficients. v_i and u_{it} are assumed to be random errors satisfying the required assumptions of a random-effects model (Wooldridge 2010: chapter 10). Thus, the generalized least squares method can be applied to estimate equation (1). In the earlier model, the $X_{k,it}$'s and $Z_{l,i}$'s contain the variables relevant to the spousal relative resources, time availability, and gender ideology. The corresponding variables are spousal income and educational differences, wife's and husband's working hours, and gender role attitudes, respectively. Within these variables, spousal educational differences and gender role attitudes are time invariant in the data set, while others are time variant. In addition to these variables, the $X_{k,it}$ include the sum of the husband's and wife's incomes, the wife's and husband's health condition, whether there are any children aged six or below, whether coresiding with the wife's or husband's parent(s), and residential area. In addition, the $Z_{l,i}$'s contain the wife's/husband's ethnicity, wife's/husband's father's education, and the spousal age difference.

15. Even though both cohort dummies and duration of marriage were controlled in the model, multicollinearity may not constitute a serious problem because panel data were used in the analysis.

16. Marital power is defined as one spouse's ability to enforce his or her will and to overcome the marital partner's resistance in the decision-making process (Blood and Wolfe 1960; Rodman 1967; Thompson 1993; Xu and Lai 2004).

17. Similar to equation (1), the subscripts i and t in this equation denote the ith couple from the tth-year (t = 1996, 2006) survey. DUR denotes the years of marriage (marital duration), and DUR^2 is its squared term. The $COHORT_c$'s represent the birth cohort dummies, $YEAR$ is the survey year dummies (1 = year 2006, 0 = year 1996), and the X_k's denote other explanatory variables. The γ's are the corresponding coefficients. The error term ε is assumed to be standardized normally distributed. We further assume that the latent variable P^* has certain relationships with the observed ordered response P (= 1, 2, 3). Equation (2) is estimated using the ordered probit method (see Wooldridge 2010: 655).

18. Because the 1996 and 2006 survey data were combined to analyze the model, the correlation between birth cohorts and marriage duration should not be a serious problem.

19. Detailed figures were retrieved on March 31, 2011, from the website of the Ministry of the Interior, Taiwan (www.moi.gov.tw/stat/gender.aspx, Table 04).

REFERENCES

Amato, Paul R., and Alan Booth. 1995. "Changes in Gender Role Attitudes and Perceived Marital Quality." *American Sociological Review* 60: 58–66.

Bartley, Sharon J., Priscilla W. Blanton, and Jennifer L. Gillard. 2005. "Husbands and Wives in Dual-Earner Marriages: Decision-Making, Gender Role Attitudes, Division of Household Labor, and Equity." *Marriage and Family Review* 37: 69–74.

Bianchi, Suzanne M., Melissa A. Milkie, Liana C. Sayer, and John P. Robinson. 2000. "Is Anyone Doing the Housework? Trends in the Gender Division of Household Labor." *Social Forces* 79: 191–228.

Bittman, M., Paula England, Liana Sayer, Nancy Folbre, and George Matheson. 2003. "When Does Gender Trump Money? Bargaining and Time in Household Work." *American Journal of Sociology* 109: 186–214.

Blood, Robert O., and Donald M. Wolfe. 1960. *Husbands and Wives*. Glencoe, IL: The Free Press.

Blumstein, Philip, and Pepper Schwartz. 1983. *American Couples: Money, Work, Sex.* New York: Morrow.

Chen, Dung-Sheng, and Mau-Kuei Chang. 2010. "Higher Education in Taiwan: The Crisis of Rapid Expansion." Retrieved on June 1, 2011, from the Blog of the International Sociological Association: www.isa-sociology.org/universities-in-crisis/?p=417.

Cherlin, Andrew J. 2004. "The Deinstitutionalization of American Marriage." *Journal of Marriage and Family* 66: 848–861.

Chu, Cyrus C. Y., and Ruoh-Rong Yu. 2010. *Understanding Chinese Families: A Comparative Study of Taiwan and Southeast China*. Oxford, UK: Oxford University Press.

Chu, Cyrus C. Y., Yu Xie, and Ruoh-Rong Yu. 2011. "Coresidence with Elderly Parents: A Comparative Study of Southeast China and Taiwan." *Journal of Marriage and the Family* 73: 120–135.

Coltrane, Scott. 1996. *Family Man: Fatherhood, Housework, and Gender Equity*. New York: Oxford University Press.

———. 2000. "Research on Household Labor: Modeling and Measuring the Social Embeddedness of Routine Family Work." *Journal of Marriage and the Family* 62: 1208–1233.

Cunningham, Mick. 2001. "Parental Influences on the Gendered Division of House-work." *American Sociological Review* 66: 184–203.

———. 2007. "Influences of Women's Employment on the Gendered Division of Household Labor over the Life Course: Evidence from a 31-Year Panel Study." *Journal of Family Issues* 28: 422–444.

Davis, Shannon N., Theodore N. Greenstein, and Jennifer P. G. Marks. 2007. "Effects of Union Type on Division of Household Labor: Do Cohabiting Men Really Perform More Housework?" *Journal of Family Issues* 28: 1246–1272.

Fan, C. Cindy, and Youqin Huang. 1998. "Waves of Rural Brides: Female Marriage Migration in China." *Annals of the Association of American Geographers* 88: 227–251.

Greenstein, Theodore N. 2000. "Economic Dependence, Gender, and the Division of Labor in the Home: A Replication and Extension." *Journal of Marriage and the Family* 62: 322–335.

Knudsen, Knud, and Kari Wærness. 2008. "National Context and Spouses' Housework in 34 Countries." *European Sociological Review* 24: 97–113.

Mannino, Clelia Anna, and Francine M. Deutsch. 2007. "Changing the Division of Household Labor: A Negotiated Process between Partners." *Sex Roles* 56: 309–324.

Pahl, Jan. 1989. *Money and Marriage*. New York: St. Martin's Press.

Parkman, Allen M. 2004. "Bargaining Over Housework: The Frustrating Situation of Secondary Wage Earners." *American Journal of Economics and Sociology* 63: 765–794.

Pinto, Katy M., and Scott Coltrane. 2009. "Divisions of Labor in Mexican Origin and Anglo Families: Structure and Culture." *Sex Roles* 60: 482–495.

Pyke, Karen D. 1994. "Women's Employment as a Gift or Burden? Marital Power across Marriage, Divorce, and Remarriage." *Gender & Society* 8: 73–91.

Rodman, Hyman. 1967. "Marital Power in France, Greece, Yugoslavia, and the United States: A Cross-National Discussion." *Journal of Marriage and the Family* 29: 320–324.

Scott, Mandy, and Hak-khiam Tiun. 2007. "Mandarin-Only to Mandarin-Plus: Taiwan." *Language Policy* 6: 53–72.

Taiwan Department of Statistics, Ministry of Education. "Appendix 2: School Life Expectancy for Age 6 and Above by Gender." Retrieved on June, 30, 2012, from http://stats.moe.gov.tw/files/ebook/International_Comparison/2012/i2012_a-2.xls.

———. "Gross Enrollment Ratio. Tertiary - By Year & Gender." Retrieved on December 19, 2011, from https://stats.moe.gov.tw/files/gender_e/e106-10.xls.

Taiwan Department of Statistics, Ministry of the Interior. "Number and Rates of Birth, Death, Marriage and Divorce, 1981–2012." Retrieved on February 13, 2013, from http://sowf.moi.gov.tw/stat/month/m1-02.xls.

Taiwan Directorate-General of Budget, Accounting and Statistics (DGBAS). 1981. *Report on the 1981 Manpower Utilization Survey Report*. Taipei: DGBAS.

———. 2010. *Report on the 2010 Manpower Utilization Survey Report*. Taipei: DGBAS.

———. 2011. "Table 10. Age-specific Distribution of Population, Dependency Ratio, Index of Aging and Median Age." *2010 Statistical Yearbook*. Taipei: DGBAS. Available at http://ebook.dgbas.gov.tw/public/Data/33716301153.pdf.

———. "Table 14. Fertility Rates for Women of Childbearing Age." Retrieved on December 19, 2011, from http://eng.stat.gov.tw/public/data/dgbas03/bs2/yearbook_eng/y014.pdf.

———. "Table 1. Average Age at Entering First Marriage of Married Women Aged 15 Years and Over." Retrieved on December 19, 2011, from www.stat.gov.tw/public/data/dgbas04/bc4/wtable1.xls.

Taiwan Social Change Survey. 2006. *Report on the 2006 Taiwan Social Change Survey: Year 5 of Cycle 2* (台灣社會變遷基本調查第五期第二次調查計畫執行報告). Retrieved on December 1, 2011, from www.ios.sinica.edu.tw/sc/cht/datafile/tscs06.pdf.

Tichenor, Veronica. 1999. "Status and Income as Gendered Resources: The Case of Marital Power." *Journal of Marriage and the Family* 61: 638–650.

———. 2005. "Maintaining Men's Dominance: Negotiating Identity and Power when She Earns More." *Sex Roles* 53: 191–205.

Thompson, Linda. 1993. "Conceptualizing Gender in Marriage: The Case of Marital Care." *Journal of Marriage and the Family* 55: 557–570.

Thornton, Arland, and Hui-Sheng Lin. 1994. *Social Change and the Family in Taiwan*. Chicago: University of Chicago Press.

Tsai, Shu-Ling. 1996. "The Relative Importance of Ethnicity and Education in Taiwan's Changing Marriage Market." *Proceedings of the NSC, Part C: Humanities and Social Sciences* (國科會研究彙刊: 人文與社會科學) 6: 301–315.

Tsay, Ruey-Ming. 1996. "Who Marries Whom? The Associations between Wives' and Husbands' Educational Attainment and Class in Taiwan." *Proceedings of the NSC, Part C: Humanities and Social Sciences* (國科會研究彙刊: 人文與社會科學) 6: 258–277.

Whyte, Martin King. 1990. *Dating, Mating, and Marriage*. New York: Aldine de Gruyter.

Wong, Raymond Sin-Kwok, and Hsien-Hen Lu. 1999. "Assortative Mating in Taiwan: Cohorts Trends in Educational and Ethnic Intermarriages." U.C. Santa Barbara mimeo.

Wooldridge, Jeffrey M. 2010. *Econometric Analysis of Cross Section and Panel Data*, 2nd ed. Cambridge, MA: The MIT Press.

Xu, Xiaohe, and Shu-Chuan Lai. 2002. "Resources, Gender Ideologies, and Marital Power: The Case of Taiwan." *Journal of Family Issues* 23: 209–245.

———. 2004. "Gender Ideologies, Marital Roles, and Marital Quality in Taiwan." *Journal of Family Issues* 25: 318–355.

Yi, Chin-Chun, and Ray-May Hsung. 1994. "Network and Marriage Connections in the Process of Mate-Searching." *ISSP Essays on Humanities and Social Sciences* 6: 135–177.

Yi, Chin-Chun, and Wen-Shan Yang. 1995. "The Perceived Conflict and Decision-Making Patterns among Husbands and Wives in Taiwan." In *Family Formation and Dissolution: Perspectives from East and West*, C. Yi and W. Yang, eds., pp. 129–168. Taipei: Sun Yat-Sen Institute for Social Sciences and Philosophy, Academia Sinica.

Yi, Chin-Chun, Yu-Hsia Lu, and Yun-Kang Pan. 2000. "Women's Family Status: A Comparison of the Family Power Structure in Taiwan and China." In *Walking a Tight Rope: Meeting the Challenges of Work and Family*, C. D. H. Harvey, ed., pp. 91–116. Aldershot, UK: Ashgate.

11 STAYING IN MARRIAGE ACROSS THE TAIWAN STRAIT

Gender, Migration, and Transnational Family

Hsiu-hua Shen

MR. HU MOVED FROM TAIWAN to Guangdong, China in the early 1990s to open a textile factory with his siblings. Before relocating to China, Hu's family had owned a textile factory in Taiwan, but rising operational costs, an abundant and cheap labor supply across the Strait, and the departure of many of the family's business associates for China finally encouraged the family to move their factory to southern China. Hu's decision to go to China was mainly a family decision to continue his extended family's business in hopes of improving his nuclear family's economic situation.

At that time, the factory's future in China was too uncertain for Hu to consider bringing the whole family along, and Hu's wife, Ai-ling, did not want to leave Taiwan to live in Guangdong. As a result, when Hu left for China, Ai-ling and their two children, a boy in second grade and a girl in kindergarten, stayed in Taiwan. Today, twenty years later, the son teaches at a tutorial school for junior high and high school students, the daughter just graduated from university in Taiwan, and Ai-ling operates a small clothing shop in Taipei. Hu is still in China, managing a restaurant with friends after closing down his textile factory several years ago.

During the couple's two decades of separation, Ai-ling relied on the help of her natal family in Taiwan to care for her two children and keep her shop running. Over the same period, Hu sent home money regularly, with the exception of periods when his business floundered. To stay connected, he also made conjugal visits back to Taiwan every two to three months, with each trip lasting roughly one week. After twenty years, Hu's absence from his family has become the norm.

Hu's family situation is not unique in Taiwan today. The recent emergence of large numbers of transnational families in Taiwan has to do with the formation of a "Greater China economy" across Taiwan, Hong Kong, and China beginning in the late 1980s (see the special issue of *China Quarterly* on this subject, December 1993; Harding 1993; Kemenade 1997; Shambaugh 1995) and the rise in China's economic power. To take advantage of China's cheap labor and huge domestic market, thousands of Taiwanese business owners and managers, mainly married men, have worked and lived in China for extended periods of time. Due to various reasons—such as children's education, spouse's job, the need to care for elderly family members, or living preferences—many of their spouses and children have stayed in Taiwan. As a result, transnational families that maintain one household in Taiwan and another in China have become a recognized family form in Taiwanese society (Kuo 2006; Sha 2006; Wang 2001). The popular Taiwanese magazine *Education, Parenting, Family Lifestyle* featured "Family, Changed" as its April 2011 cover story, and transnational Taiwanese business families across the Taiwan Strait were selected to illustrate the changing family structure and marital relations in contemporary Taiwan.

As in other parts of the world, the rise of regional economies, a growing reliance on international contract labor, and new communication networks have increased the likelihood of both short-term and longer-term transnational migrations. The ease and frequency of the moves vary according to the characteristics of the individuals involved, the specific conditions of sending and receiving societies, and the increasingly restrictive and differential entry regulations in many countries. But, overall, the current global environment can be characterized by its fluidity "in the form of circular movements, multiple sojourns, unexpected displacements and periodic homecomings" (Yeoh, Huang, and Lam 2005: 309; see also Lorente, Piper, and Shen 2005; Shen 2005).

To enable this fluidity, the organization and culture of family and intimate relations also have become more flexible. Family is no longer primarily signified by members residing together physically but by the kinship ties that provide flexibility in dispersing members and in renegotiating the meaning of intimate ties to maximize social mobility and the economic role of the family unit as a whole (Bryceson and Vuorela 2002; Burholt 2004; Dreby 2007; Ley and Kobayashi 2005; Ong 1999; Shen 2008b; Waters 2002). Such transnational family forms are by no means limited to families like that of Mr. Hu, where men use family capital to establish new businesses overseas while women remain in the home country. In fact, globally, the majority of transnational families include women as well as men who migrate to perform low-wage work as domestics, nannies, nurses, or factory and construction workers. And faced with restrictive labor immigration policies in receiving countries that limit their length of stay and rights to family reunification, these migrants have little choice but to live apart from their families for months or even years (Gambaurd 2000; Hochschild 2003; Lan 2006; Parreñas 2001). Their spouses and children may stay behind at home, or they may migrate to another country for employment or education, but the family endures across vast geographic distances (Hondagneu-Sotelo and Avila 1997; Lima 2001; Ong 1999; Parreñas 2001, 2005; Shen 2005, 2008b; Wilding 2006; Yeoh and Wills 2004).

As Mr. Hu's experience demonstrates, migration is often adopted by a family as a strategy to maximize economic and cultural resources; simultaneously, and often unintentionally, migration processes reshape marital and family structures and relationships (Freeman 2011). Given the important role of gender as an organizing principle of migration (Grasmuck and Pessar 1991; Hirsch 2003; Hondagneu-Sotelo 1994; Hondagneu-Sotelo and Avila 1997; Parreñas 2001, 2005), the transnational families that emerge from migrations also depend on and produce specific gender orders of their own. In this chapter, focused on the experiences of married couples divided by the Taiwan Strait, I examine how commitments to the centrality of the gendered family roles of wife, husband, mother, father, daughter, and son provide the "glue" that holds these marriages together despite years, or even decades, of transnational separation and long-term sojourning. In particular, I am concerned with couples who have children but experience long separations during which they act as "situational singles" (Shen 2003) and take a "gendered break" from marriage.

By *situational singles*, I refer to those married Taiwanese women and men who are somehow free from the daily tasks and responsibilities related to their spouses and/or families and from the social and moral constraints imposed by their marital status. By a "gendered break" from marriage, I point to the ways that gender roles and expectations condition how "situationally single" women and men temporarily escape specific marital tasks, responsibilities, and moralities. In this context, Taiwanese businessmen act as situational singles by being freed from a monogamous sexual and even emotional contract with their wife and from daily care work for their family. They affirm a traditionally polygamous culture and patriarchal division of labor that privileges their own private desires over those of their spouse and other family members.

Their wives, by contrast, act as situational singles by being liberated from patriarchal expectations that they provide daily care and attention to their husband. These gendered practices of break taking from marriage are not about individual choices and actions but are structured by the larger economic, cultural, and gender contexts in which couples are situated. The specific "breaks" that Taiwanese businessmen and their wives take reinforce their conventional gendered roles as financial supporters and familial caregivers. In other words, transnational migration may not directly end Taiwanese marriages, but such marriages endure in part by reaffirming traditional gender role expectations for husbands and wives within the familial context.

Kuo (Chapter 9) and Yu and Liu (Chapter 10) have shown that marriage patterns in contemporary Taiwan have undergone significant transformations or "deinstitutionalization" (Cherlin 2004) that include rapidly increasing rates of divorce and nonmarriage. At the same time, however, the internal dynamics of marriages—from distribution of household tasks to family decision making—have not changed as much as one might expect. The split couples discussed in this chapter support this pattern insofar as they remain in their marriages in part by adhering to traditional gender expectations. Taiwanese men who relocate to China for employment are better able to fulfill their expected role as financial supporter who enhances the economic welfare of the family. Similarly, Taiwanese wives who stay behind take responsibility for the daily care of children and family elders, including the husband's parents. A couple's extended time apart reinforces the interdependence of these distinctly gendered roles and responsibilities. In other words, by fulfilling traditional gender roles as husbands and wives, separated couples create the material and moral grounds that enable them to keep the marriage and family together even as they take a gendered break from other dimensions of their marital responsibilities.

Although some aspects of the internal dynamics of marriages remain the same, other rules of the game in the marriage are redefined by the experience of marital separation. An intriguing dimension of this process of marital renegotiation is the commitment of the Taiwanese wife to keeping "a family of her own." Unlike the "private money" (私房錢) of the past that a wife accumulated to use as she pleased, Taiwanese wives in split marriages emphasize the freedom to keep and manage a family of their own, without daily "meddling" from their husband. As long as the husband continues to provide the financial support that makes this "family of her own" possible, a wife may be willing to overlook her husband's dalliances in China and remain in a marriage that allows her considerable agency even in a broadly patriarchal context. In other words, these marriages and families survive, despite long periods of separation, precisely because couples adhere to a conventional gender order in ways that permit both men's sexual freedom and women's ability to maneuver around patriarchal influences. The institution of the Taiwanese family remains strong despite the partial deinstitutionalization of Taiwanese marriages and the emergence of new marital norms among split couples.

GENDER AND TRANSNATIONAL CONJUGAL RELATIONS

The phenomenon of families living far apart is not new. Historically, colonial bureaucrats or travelers were likely to leave their families behind when they sought political and economic opportunities. Chinese migrants to North America or Southeast Asia during the nineteenth and twentieth centuries were usually individual male sojourners who aspired to return to their families in China as wealthy men (Chen 1940; Chu and Chu 1967; Lee 1965; Shen 2012; Wang 2000; Watson 1975). Transnational families during the colonial era or among prior generations of Chinese migrants therefore were organized mainly around the pattern of men leaving and women staying behind.

Recent migration waves, by contrast, have witnessed a growing number of female migrants that has changed the gender organization of contemporary transnational families. Studies of contemporary female migration also help us to see how the processes of keeping families together across national borders are not gender neutral. For instance, studies have found that, when women are migrants themselves, they are more likely than their male counterparts to engage in day-to-day long distance communication with and care work for their families, particularly their children (Hondagneu-Sotelo 1994; Kibria 1993; Parreñas 2005, 2008). My research on Taiwanese businessmen has also found that men's definition of being a good parent and spouse from afar has less to do with the frequency of their long-distance communication and care work and more with their continuing financial support to their families (Shen 2005), a crucial factor in defining responsible masculinity that we also see in Ho's study (Chapter 7) of Hong Kong men's intimate life.

Whether among nineteenth and early twentieth-century Chinese migrants to North America and Southeast Asia or more contemporary transnational labor and professional migrants, gendered divisions of labor in the family (regardless of whether men or women act as financial providers or caregivers) have played an important role in keeping marriages and families together across borders (Menjívar and Agadjanian 2007; Pribilsky 2004; Shen 2012; Shen 2008b; Siu 1987). Husbands and wives signal their continuing commitment to marriage and family in gender-specific ways by regularly remitting earnings or providing care work. In this chapter, I argue that this particular gender division of labor in split households is more than simply a traditional holdover; it also determines who migrates and who stays at home, and it becomes a crucial factor holding marriages and families together by creating interdependent roles and moral expectations for women and men in their marriage.

Social ideologies and practices of intimate and sexual relations in marital life constitute other critical pieces of the gender orders that shape conjugal relations in transnational families. In many migration contexts, sexual infidelity and the threat of divorce loom large. Across Asia we have seen considerable tolerance for men's extramarital affairs, regardless of whether these take the form of casual sexual liaisons or the formation of a second family. Earlier generations of Chinese men who migrated to the West or Southeast Asia were well known for patronizing prostitutes or even marrying second wives from among the local population (Shen 2012; Siu 1987). In the contemporary context, with their economic capacity and internationally mobile status, transnational businessmen and professionals are seen as attractive and competitive candidates in the local dating and sexual scenes of less-developed host societies. It is not uncommon for foreign businessmen in China, whether they hail from Hong Kong, as shown in Ho's study, or from Singapore, North America, or Taiwan, to engage in a variety of sexual liaisons, from casual sexual transactions to comparatively stable relationships, including taking local women as temporary wives or long-term mistresses (包二奶) (Farrer 2010; Kung 2004; Lang and Smart 2000; Shen 2003, 2005, 2008a, 2008b; Tam 2004; Yeoh and Wills 2004).

Societal tolerance of men's extramarital sexuality is a key cultural reference that wives of migrant men draw on to interpret their marital situation. As a consequence, many wives from Asian countries do not view divorce because of a husband's extramarital affair as a viable option, especially in societies where divorce is still considered a stigma for women (Lang and Smart 2000; Shen 2005, 2008b; Shen 2012). Extramarital sexual relations on the part of "left behind" wives, however, incite a very different kind of response from husbands and society more generally.

Hui-fen Shen's (2012) study of the wives of Chinese migrant men who remained at home when their spouses left for Southeast Asia in the first half of the twentieth century shows that these generations of women who stayed behind were closely controlled by their extended conjugal families. Women were expected to remain faithful to their husbands by adhering to codes of chastity, even while their husbands were likely having affairs abroad. When adultery with local men did occur, news of affairs circulated quickly, and women were forced to divorce (Shen 2012). Although wives in contemporary Taiwan enjoy greater autonomy than previous generations of Chinese women, a patriarchal double standard for female and male sexuality still influences the ability of marriages to survive within transnational migration contexts. One wonders, nevertheless, whether transnational marriages continue even with men's extramarital affairs simply because wives decide to bear their husband's betrayal and stay in the marriage. The answer, I suggest, is not so simple.

We should not treat a split couple's decision to stay married and connected as merely a personal or conjugal matter; it is a family and even community affair. When a migrant man decides to abandon or divorce his left-behind wife because of his new intimate relationship in the receiving society, he may also decrease or discontinue his economic contributions and emotional attachments to his children and extended family. For this reason, although the extramarital sexuality of early Chinese migrant men was tolerated, their marriages to local women in Southeast Asia were actively discouraged by their families, at least until the outbreak of the Pacific War, which made movement between China and Southeast Asia difficult and attenuated migrants' ties with family back home (Shen 2012).

Staying married within the context of extramarital relationships can also be in the interest of migrant men. My previous study of Taiwanese businessmen's sexual liaisons with Chinese women in China showed that Taiwanese businessmen thought it was in their best interest to stay married, and they clearly distinguished their roles in their relationships with their Taiwanese wives from those with their Chinese lovers (Shen 2005). Although the marriages of contemporary split couples may resemble those of earlier generations of migrants, they display significant differences in marital quality and role negotiation that were not possible in earlier eras.

Feminist scholarship has long shown that women are not passive actors in transnational families. Many women feel unsettled and suffer from loneliness when their spouses first leave them behind (Pribilsky 2004; Shen 2012;

Shen 2008a). At the same time, women face a greater household burden as they must take on tasks formerly performed by their husband, especially given contemporary nuclear family arrangements. Compared to early generations of wives of migrant men, many married women today work and have their own social circles aside from their family. Their husband's migration gives them opportunities to grow and develop along trajectories that are distinct from the patriarchal influences represented by husbands or in-laws, and married women gain a sense of independence and autonomy when leading a separate conjugal life from their spouse (Petrozziello 2011; Pribilsky 2004; Shen 2008b). The independence and agency of migrant men's wives create new marital dynamics even in the face of broader structural features and gendered roles that conform more closely to traditional marriage patterns.

In this chapter, I build from other studies of gendered transnational family dynamics that have focused either on women's or men's experiences to address the importance of simultaneously taking both spouses' experiences into account to better understand the material, cultural, and gender grounds for maintaining long-distance marriages. The next section describes the methodology behind the study. I then explore how the constitution of gender in the formation of situational singlehood among transnational Taiwanese businessmen and their spouses across the Taiwan Strait shapes family and intimate relations in Taiwan.

METHODS AND DATA

This chapter is largely based on a decade of research between 1999 and 2012 on the creation of Taiwanese business expatriate communities in China and the formation of transnational Taiwanese families across the Taiwan Strait. By transnational Taiwanese businesspeople in China, I refer to the investors and managers working for Taiwanese-owned companies in China and residing in China but making conjugal visits to Taiwan. My interviews with Taiwanese businessmen were conducted between 1999 and 2012 in Kunshan (located in the Shanghai–Nanjing Economic Corridor), Shanghai, Xiamen (Fujian Province), and Dongguan (Guangdong Province), where most Taiwanese companies are located.

For the purpose of this chapter, I focus on those married Taiwanese business investors and managers who were in their thirties to sixties at the time of our interviews and who had maintained a transnational family arrangement across the Taiwan Strait for at least five years. My interviews with Taiwanese wives in Taiwan were mainly conducted in 2011 and 2012. These women were in their late twenties to late fifties and had educational levels of vocational school or above. The majority of them held a formal job outside the home. All women lived in nuclear families with one to three children at the time of the interview, but a few had previously lived with in-laws. Many of my interviewees had been living apart from their spouse for an extended period of time, ranging from less than ten years to more than twenty. However, the women and men I interviewed were not matched as couples. I asked my interviewees, often Taiwanese businessmen, to introduce their spouses to me for interviews, and many of them did, but their spouses tended to reject my requests. The usual reasons for rejecting my interview request were that they were too busy with work and family and/or did not want to share their personal life with a stranger. The reason I asked Taiwanese businessmen, not Taiwanese women, to introduce their spouses for interviews was because it was geographically easier for me to interview Taiwanese women in Taiwan than to interview Taiwanese businessmen located in different parts of China. Because I shared a similar Taiwanese background with businessmen in China, they were more willing to talk to me as a fellow compatriot in a strange place, and they generally felt more relaxed about discussing their personal life in a setting far from their family and members of their close social circle. Each interview I conducted lasted two to four hours. In addition to interview data, I have supplemented my findings with newspaper articles and other secondary sources.

To understand how Taiwanese businesspeople and their spouses maintain transnational intimacy, I asked Taiwanese businessmen and their wives how they stayed connected to their dispersed family members, how they led their separated lives in their respective locations, and how their relationship with their spouse had changed over the years. While the majority of married Taiwanese businesspeople in China have been men, the number of married women working and living alone in China while their husbands and/or children reside in Taiwan has increased in recent years. During my research trips to China in 2010, I met three married Taiwanese female managers: one with elementary-school-aged children, one with adult children, and one who was childless. What was unusual about them was that they left for China alone while their families remained in Taiwan. However, I have not been able to interview men who have stayed behind in Taiwan while their spouse worked in China. Thus, my conceptualization of what it means to be a "situational single" and to take "a gendered break from marriage" is largely based on the division between Taiwanese men as mobile subjects across the Taiwan Strait and Taiwanese women as left-behind spouses.

STAYING CONNECTED BY TRANSNATIONAL COMMUNICATION AND REMITTANCES

Like other split families, transnational Taiwanese families stay connected between Taiwan and China through phone calls, Internet communication, remittances, and conjugal trips. Many Taiwanese companies in China provide free Internet phone connections in their offices. To save on phone bills for the family, it makes more sense for men in China to call home to Taiwan. However, the increasing accessibility of Internet communication and cheaper international telephone fees also make it easier for families in Taiwan to contact their family members in China. Couples' communication frequency ranges from phone or Internet contact once a week to several times a day. For younger couples (roughly those born after 1975) the frequency of communication is higher than among older couples. Older couples discuss family affairs such as issues related to children or extended kin, whereas younger couples also focus on their own relationship. The mobile Taiwanese fathers tend not to engage in direct long-distance communication or exchanges with their children but to go through their spouse to learn about their children's lives, particularly when their children are young. This practice of long-distance fatherhood reinforces the role of the mother as the center of the children's life in transnational families.

Regular remittances are a critical, if not the only factor keeping families connected across the Taiwan Strait. To avoid the troubles imposed by China's foreign currency exchange restrictions and to avoid paying high taxes in China, the majority of Taiwanese companies in China transfer a large part of an employee's monthly salary directly from the Taiwan office into the employee's bank account in Taiwan. What Taiwanese managers and professionals receive in China is so-called pocket money, often a few thousand Chinese yuan that they use to cover their own local expenses. The direct salary deposit in Taiwan becomes an important mechanism for stabilizing male Taiwanese managers' and professionals' financial support for their families back home. It also grants a great degree of financial autonomy and security to wives who do not need to ask for money or wait for their absent spouse to transfer funds. According to my research, some of the banking accounts are in the husband's name, some are existing family accounts, and some are in the wife's name.

All the Taiwanese wives I interviewed had direct access to the bank accounts where their husband's salary was transferred, and they also enjoyed a certain degree of freedom in using the money, especially for daily family expenses. When it comes to large expenditures for furniture or other goods, Taiwanese wives might first discuss the purchases with their spouse in China.

It is fair to say that a central characteristic of the Taiwanese transnational families that have survived through an extended period of separation is stable financial support from the husband/father in China. In fact, this support is the defining feature of these men's contribution to their families. In 2003, I talked to two Taiwanese investors who operated small-scale farms in Southern China and who had already lost contact with their former spouses and children in Taiwan. They claimed that a major cause of their disconnection from their families in Taiwan was their inability to send money home, coupled with their repeated requests to use family savings to build their businesses in China.[1]

Compared to other Taiwanese business personnel in China, owners of small businesses who control their own finances and assume considerable business risk in China are more likely to have economic conflicts with their families in Taiwan. For instance, in the account of Mr. Hu that I described in the introduction, Hu's family factory did not flourish, and Hu's wife was forced to sell their only family home in Taipei city to support the family and his business in China. Hu finally had to shut down his factory to avoid burdening his family in Taiwan with more debt. Although Hu was able to maintain his marriage and family despite his temporary failure to provide financial support, his wife and children did speak openly about the financial difficulties Hu had created for them in separate conversations.

Until several years ago, Taiwanese managers and professionals were able to receive expatriate packages for working in China in which they earned one and half to two times their previous salary in Taiwan. In recent years, with more competition for jobs from locals in China and limited job opportunities in Taiwan, expatriate packages for Taiwanese managers and professionals are not as generous as in the past. However, working in China still is considered a major path to future economic gain. This enhanced job opportunity and income create an important economic base that enables families back home to lead a better material life. In addition, because of Taiwanese expatriates' long absence from their spouse and children, their ability to support their family financially becomes a major source of connection with family members. The ultimate result of this conceptualization of family connection and contribution is the reinforcement of men's gendered family role as economic provider.

STAYING MARRIED WHEN TAKING A GENDERED
BREAK FROM MARRIAGE

In this section I discuss how male Taiwanese business migrants in China and their wives in Taiwan stay married when both act as situational singles by taking gendered breaks from marriage. My conceptualization of gendered situational singlehood starts from my observations of how married Taiwanese men act as situational singles by establishing intimate liaisons with Chinese women in China while they are temporarily freed from the sexual loyalty expectations of the marriage contract. By contrast, their spouses at home literally become heads of single families and are encumbered by the duty of daily family labor. These Taiwanese women retain their married status, but in practice they are more like singles or single parents with an unclear family arrangement. However, I later observed that Taiwanese women are not merely victims reduced to serving as solo caregivers for their families and silently bearing their spouse's infidelity. They also enjoy their own breaks from patriarchal marriage arrangements by leading a life separate from their husband's, but with his financial support, and enjoying the freedom of meeting their own needs.

Taiwanese Businessmen: Sexual Play as a
Break from Marriage

In her popular book, *Against Love*, Laura Kipnis (2003) argues that monogamous love-marriage as our fundamental social structure organizes our desires in an exclusive fashion and constantly demands more labor to make it work. Ultimately, she contends, this model of marriage imprisons our sexuality and soul. Infidelity, according to Kipnis, serves as a break and an escape for both men and women, at least temporarily, from this marriage "prison." Taiwanese businessmen's extramarital affairs in China can be seen as an example of this very "break" from the institution of monogamous marriage as they take advantage of distance from familiar social relations and close social policing in Taiwan. Sexual freedom is the primary component of the breaks they take from the institution of marriage, and it is generally condoned by the masculine communities of Taiwanese business expatriates in China (Shen 2008a). Serious romantic involvements with Chinese women, however, for instance in the form of long-term mistresses, are seen by businessmen and their wives alike as violating the accepted boundaries of the "break" from marriage because such involvements can turn a "break from" into an "end to" marriage.

Taiwanese businessmen's intimate relations with Chinese women often take place in karaoke bars and other entertainment settings where men pay hostesses to flirt with them and provide sexual favors. Such relations are categorized by Taiwanese businessmen as "sexual play" that establishes and expresses their transnational gender and class status and identity as members of the transnational capitalist class in China (Shen 2008a). I found that six major justifications are commonly articulated by Taiwanese businessmen in China for their "sexual play" with Chinese women (Shen 2008a: 62–69): sexual play as a part of normal business operations; sexual play as fulfilling men's biological needs and emotional loneliness while away from home; sexual play as expressing men's economic power and their objectification of Chinese women as sexual and class Others; sexual play as an accepted practice by transnational, privileged men; sexual play as performing charity for Chinese women; and, finally, sexual play as a result of peer pressure.

Some of these justifications resonate with statements by Hong Kong men who engage in sexual liaisons with Chinese women (Ho Chapter 7). At the same time, these explanations also enable Taiwanese businessmen to sexually commodify Chinese women without subjecting themselves to moral judgment. But these justifications of sexual play do not in themselves define such play as a break from marriage. More work is required to define the type, content, and scope of sexual play to transform it into a "break from" as opposed to an "end to" marriage.

For married Taiwanese businessmen in China, taking a break from marriage means that they are free from providing daily care for their family due to their physical absence and that they are liberated from sexual constraints imposed by their marriage contract with their spouse in Taiwan. But why do married Taiwanese businessmen take breaks from marriage instead of breaking off the marriage by establishing intimate relations with Chinese women? According to my study, unless they seek to marry a Chinese woman, the majority of Taiwanese businessmen have no intention of divorcing their wife even though they form relationships with Chinese women. A major reason for this is because they tend not to consider Chinese women good marriage potential (Shen 2008a). For instance, a high-ranking manager in a shoemaking factory in Dongguan firmly believed that, in Taiwanese businessmen's relationships with Chinese women, "it is because of the man's money, not because of him as a person, that a Chinese woman is with a Taiwanese businessman" (interview with author, November 13, 2009). Images of Chinese women as gold diggers and sexually loose Others compare unfavorably with images of Taiwanese wives as dutiful wives and mothers (Shen 2005). These attitudes toward Chinese women set social limitations on the preference for private over public ordering of intimate relationships and keep sexual liaisons on the safe terrain of masculine, sexual "play" that does not threaten Taiwanese marriages and families.

Accordingly, various "rules" and "insights" circulate within Taiwanese business communities in China that teach men how to maintain intimate relations with Chinese women strictly as forms of sexual play that provide a break from the sexual exclusivity of marriage. For instance, Taiwanese businessmen are advised not to "get seasick," meaning to fall in love with a Chinese woman. Married Taiwanese men who fall in love with Chinese women are teased as being inexperienced and lost in the sea of Chinese women's traps. The debates between "purchasing a cup of milk" or "bringing a cow home" also illustrate efforts to create boundaries around sexual play and its complementary relationship to marriage. For those who consider the economic and health costs of multiple sexual partners, taking in a Chinese woman as a temporary wife or mistress (the bringing a cow home theory) seems to make more sense than developing casual sexual relations with different Chinese women each time (the purchasing a cup of milk theory). However, taking a mistress or temporary wife is also seen as dangerous to a man's marital status because that relationship may become more emotionally involved over time. A married Taiwanese businessman in Xiamen illustrated this point:

> It is as if you are hungry; you should purchase a cup of milk to drink but not bring a cow home just for the sake of a cup of milk. It is less complicated and creates fewer ties between people if sex is done by monetary deals. (interview with author, April 12, 1999)

Thus, those Taiwanese businessmen who establish a more stable relationship with a Chinese woman are advised by other Taiwanese men to make clear the condition of their financial support as an exchange for sexual favors. "Play, but not keeping (mistresses)" and "keeping (a mistress), but not making her pregnant" are valuable rules advocated by Taiwanese businessmen to protect themselves from troubles caused by intimate associations with Chinese women (Hsieh 2001: 166–167).

Extramarital sex is portrayed as play and as a break from marriage so that it interferes as little as possible with regular marital practices and relations. Conventional wisdom among Taiwanese business communities in China advises married Taiwanese men to act as responsible husbands and fathers by maintaining regular communication, making conjugal visits, and providing financial support to their families in Taiwan despite their intimate relations with Chinese women. In contrast to men's negative representations of Chinese women, they view Taiwanese wives as devoted caregivers for their children and even parents. Hence, "How can a man abandon his devoted wife? If he does, he is not a real man" is a common piece of moral advice passed from man to man in the expatriate Taiwanese community. This saying also recognizes that it is in a Taiwanese businessman's best interests to stay married because his wife performs necessary care work for his family and because the marriage enables him to remain connected with his children back in Taiwan.

Taiwanese Wives: Autonomy and Independence as a Break from Patriarchal Marriage

Although many Taiwanese businessmen in China use sexual play as a break from marriage, I found that many of their wives in Taiwan view daily autonomy and independence in organizing their time, space, social networks, and lives as a break from patriarchal marriage. The majority of the Taiwanese wives I have interviewed to date are in their late forties to early sixties. Most of them have lived a separated marital life for more than ten years. During the course of living apart from their husbands, they have gone through at least three stages of separation.

The first stage is the period when their husbands first leave for China. They often characterized this stage as defined by uncertainty, anxiety, and worry. Ailing, mentioned earlier in the chapter, described her tumultuous emotions during the first few years of separation from her husband:

> During the first years of his absence, I wondered what was the use of getting married. I had to take care of my children on my own and operate a household alone. I felt that getting married seemed not to make any difference. In addition, my classmates or even my own mother would say to me, "How could you let him go to China? Don't you worry that he may have a mistress in China?" How could my emotions not be influenced by those disruptions? Thus, by then my husband and I easily got into fights over the smallest things. (interview with author, March 29, 2011, Taipei)

The burden of being the primary caregiver for their children and in some cases even for their parents-in-law, acclimating to their husband's absence from home, and the insecurity produced by their husband's possible infidelity and business failure generated considerable anxieties for wives who remained in Taiwan.

The second stage for Taiwanese wives is often categorized as a time of seeking strength and balance in response to the uncertainties and insecurities of the first stage of their husband's daily absence. Mei, a Taiwanese wife in her late forties, told me that she didn't like how insecure she felt about being separated from her husband, especially with regard to his possible infidelity in China. One day, after her husband was in China for more than two years, she saw an ad recruiting people to participate in a reading group organized by the residents of her apartment complex. She joined the group, read various self-help books, engaged in self-reflection, and finally achieved peace of mind as she coped with her husband's absence. The possibility that their husbands might act as situational singles by developing intimate liaisons with Chinese women worries Taiwanese wives the most, at least during the first few years of a split-household arrangement. To enable them to move on with their daily lives in Taiwan, they told me in interviews, they had to trust their husbands and let go of their worries as much as possible.

These women tended to focus their lives on their children and their own jobs. By drawing support mainly from their own parents and siblings, not from their in-laws, Taiwanese wives found themselves not only gradually adjusting to their husband's absence but actually enjoying their autonomy in arranging their own lives without having to be attentive to their husband's daily needs or the demands of conjugal kin.

The third stage Taiwanese wives go through in the context of transnational family life is enjoying and celebrating their autonomy and independence from their husbands. Lan, a sixty-year-old Taiwanese wife living in a southern city, described her current state of a break from marriage:

> I feel that I am rather free. I can go anywhere I want. My husband's absence does have a positive effect. Once he is home, I feel that I am tied down by him and cannot move freely. I have to rush to get groceries and cook the dishes he likes. So every time after I send him off to the airport, I feel liberated. When he is not around, if I don't want to cook, I don't need to cook. Although I cook for myself most of the time, when he is around I have to pay special attention

to his needs. What a relief when he is gone! (interview with author, May 19, 2011, Tainan)

By this stage, some of my interviewees' children were already in university or had entered the job market. The wives had been liberated from some daily care work and had more free time to themselves. They could also enjoy a better family financial situation that had improved over the years through the accumulation of their husband's and their own incomes. As Ching mentioned, "If I feel like learning Japanese, I can just go without having to discuss it with anyone. I have many good female friends. When they invite me to drive up to the mountains to enjoy the night scenery, I just go. I have lots of good women friends" (interview with author, April 2, 2011). It is very common for the women I talked to to join afternoon teas, frequent karaoke bars, or engage in other leisure activities with their female friends.

Taiwanese women's celebration of their autonomy and independence becomes more visible when they discuss their concerns about their husbands returning home to live with them after retirement. They worry that the different lifestyles and even values that each spouse has developed over the years of separation will create conflicts between them. Moreover, they do not relish the fact that they will have to provide day-to-day care in response their husband's needs. These women, by contrast, hope that their break from marriage can last a little longer.

DISCUSSION AND CONCLUSION

In this chapter, I use emerging transnational family arrangements among Taiwanese businesspeople across the Taiwan Strait as the starting point for exploring changing sexual and marital relations in contemporary Taiwan. I found that long-distance communication and remittances have become significant features keeping Taiwanese families together across transnational space. However, my analysis also shows that, even though they remain married, many Taiwanese businessmen in China and their wives in Taiwan act as situational singles in relation to the institution of monogamous marriage by taking gendered breaks from marriage. These gendered breaks follow different rules, moreover, as a result of gender-distinct roles within marriage and societal expectations about wives' and husbands' own needs and desires.

Over the past two decades, some Taiwanese men have hypersexualized their roles as situational singles by viewing sex with Chinese women mainly as a form of personal play and a site for collective pleasure among Taiwanese businessmen resident in China. The waves of Taiwanese men who travel to China as sex tourists feed this perception of an intensely sexualized Taiwanese male subjectivity. As Ho finds in Hong Kong, moreover, the counterpart of a sexualized Taiwanese male enactment of situational singledom is the construction of Chinese women across the Taiwan Strait as erotic Others readily available for men's sexual pleasure.

Although the open display of sexual desire is central to Taiwanese businessmen's performance as situational singles, the sexuality of their Taiwanese wives remains hidden and ambiguous. When I asked women how they dealt with their sexual desires and needs when their husbands were away, most of them either replied that sex was not very important to them (and a few were actually happy to be free from their sexual obligations during their husband's absences) or that they used their husband's conjugal visits to make up for the lack of sex during periods of separation. Only a few of them, most of whom were on the younger end of my sample, admitted that they sometimes called their husbands in China to express their feelings and desires when they felt sexual drives.

Compared to the rather quick and direct process through which Taiwanese businessmen take breaks from their marriage, Taiwanese wives require a longer period of adaptation to make sense of their break from the patriarchal institution of marriage. Over the years, transnational family arrangements have provided space for many married Taiwanese women to establish and strengthen friend and kin networks, draw family boundaries, and arrange lifestyles and living spaces centered on their own needs without direct intervention from their husband or in-laws. Living apart from their husband, particularly in a transnational space, gives some women the opportunity to cultivate a gendered sense of agency even while remaining in the institution of marriage.

Let me return to the question of why Taiwanese businessmen and their wives stay married despite extended periods of transnational separation. Of course, some of these couples do divorce, and some Taiwanese businessmen do marry Chinese women (see Friedman Chapter 12). Based on my own research findings and media reports, the two major causes commonly cited for divorce are a husband's infidelity and/or his business failure in China. However, most marriages continue, despite affairs and growing differences between the couple. I argue that the practice of situational singledom and the gendered breaks that each party takes from marriage ultimately enable these long-distance marriages and families to survive over time. Hence, the persistence of distinct gender roles within Taiwanese marriages may provide resources for couples as they adapt to extended separations and create new lives for themselves apart from their spouse.

The importance of Taiwanese businessmen's role as family financial providers is reinforced by their long absence from daily caregiving. In short, if what they can give to their families is not affection and care, then it must at least be financial support. But financial support is not merely about material welfare. As Zelizer (2005) argues, intimate activities cannot be separated from economic activities. Stable financial support from Taiwanese men conveys their continued commitment to the marriage and the family. In turn, it secures their membership in the marriage and the family, especially in the context of a tolerant attitude toward men's extramarital sexuality, as long as it does not lead to marital dissolution. On the other hand, performing their role as a situationally single parent to their children on a daily basis gives Taiwanese women moral legitimacy in their marriages and protects them as moral superiors vis-à-vis Chinese women whose only recognized role is as sexualized Other. After Taiwanese wives go through the hard work of caring for their children and resolving their anxieties about their husband's absence, many finally enjoy a sense of financial security and gender autonomy that enhances their commitment to their marriage.

Contrary to the argument that the institution of marriage has been weakened by transnational flows of people and ideas, many Taiwanese transnational couples appear to have survived the dramas of extramarital affairs and long-term separations. In short, marriage as an institution for distributing material resources, caring for family members, and creating intimacy remains surprisingly strong and flexible, even when other features of traditional marriage in contemporary Taiwan are undergoing fundamental changes. Perhaps more surprising is the recognition that this strength derives both from the persistence of traditional gender role expectations in marriage and from the flexibility enabled by marital separations that allows a reworking of those roles within certain limits. It is simultaneously the reinforcement of some established norms and the deinstitutionalization of others that keep transnational Taiwanese businessmen's marriages and families together. Davis and Friedman point out in their introduction that the deinstitutionalization of marriage does not necessarily lead to the deinstitutionalization of family. The institution of the Taiwanese family remains strong even when the emotional ties between married couples may have eroded in a context of long-term separation. By the end, many Taiwanese marriages survive because of the strength of Taiwanese families. As this preliminary study suggests, the elephant in the room, so to speak, is Taiwanese wives' own sexual needs and desires. Whether this kind of marriage can survive a wife's extramarital affair remains a topic for future research.

NOTE

1. In addition, one of the men had developed a stable extramarital relationship with a local woman.

REFERENCES

Bryceson, Deborah F., and Ulla Vuorela, eds. 2002. *The Transnational Family: New European Frontiers and Global Networks*. Oxford, UK: Berg.

Burholt, Vanessa. 2004. "Transnationalism, Economic Transfers and Families' Ties: Intercontinental Contacts of older Gujuratis, Punjabis and Sylhetis in Birmingham with Families Abroad." *Ethnic and Racial Studies* 27(5): 800–829.

Chen, Ta. 1940. *Emigrant Communities in South China*. New York: Institute of Pacific Relations.

Cherlin, Andrew J. 2004. "The Deinstitutionalization of American Marriage." *Journal of Marriage and Family* 66 (November): 848–861.

China Quarterly. 1993. Special Issue on The Emergence of Greater China. 136 (December): 653-983.

Chu, Daniel, and Samuel Chu. 1967. *Passage to the Golden Gate: A History of the Chinese in America until 1910*. New York: Doubleday.

Dreby, Joanna. 2007. "Children and Power in Mexican Transnational Families." *Journal of Marriage and Family* 69: 1050–1064.

Farrer, James. 2010. "A Foreign Adventurer's Paradise? Interracial Sexuality and Alien Sexual Capital in Reform Era Shanghai." *Journal of Sexualities* 13(1): 69–95.

Freeman, Caren. 2011. *Making and Faking Kinship: Marriage and Labor Migration between China and South Korea*. Ithaca, NY: Cornell University Press.

Gambaurd, Michele R. 2000. *The Kitchen Spoon's Handle: Transnationalism and Sri Lanka's Migrant Housemaids*. Ithaca, NY: Cornell University Press.

Grasmuck, Sherri, and Patricia R. Pessar. 1991. *Between Two Islands: Dominican International Migration*. Berkeley: University of California Press.

Harding, Harry. 1993. "The Concept of 'Greater China': Themes, Variations and Reservations." *China Quarterly* 136 (December): 660–686.

Hirsch, Jennifer S. 2003. *A Courtship after Marriage: Sexuality and Love in Mexican Transnational Families*. Berkeley: University of California Press.

Hondagneu-Sotelo, Pierrette. 1994. *Gendered Transitions: Mexican Experiences of Immigration*. Berkeley: University of California Press.

Hondagneu-Sotelo, Pierrette, and Ernestine Avila. 1997. "'I'm Here, but I'm There': The Meanings of Latina Transnational Motherhood." *Gender and Society* 11(5): 548–571.

Hochschild, Arlie R. 2003. "Love and Gold." In *Global Woman: Nannies, Maids and Sex Workers in the New Economy*, Barbara Ehrenreich and Arlie R. Hochschild, eds., pp. 15–30. London: Granta Books.

Hsieh Guo-hua (謝國華). 2001. 都是二奶惹的禍 (*It's All Provoked by the Calamity of a Mistress*). Taipei: Hai Ge Publishing.

Kemenade, Willem van. 1997. *China, Hong Kong, Taiwan INC*. Diane Webb, trans. New York: Vintage Books.

Kibria, Nazli. 1993. *Family Tightrope: The Changing Lives of Vietnamese Americans*. Princeton, NJ: Princeton University Press.

Kipnis, Laura. 2003. *Against Love: A Polemic*. New York: Vintage Books.

Kung I-chun (龔宜君). 2004. "跨國資本的性別政治: 越南台商與在地女性的交換關係" (The Sexual Politics of Foreign Capital: Exchange Relations between Taiwanese Capital and Local Women in Vietnam). 台灣社會研究季刊 (*Taiwan: A Radical Quarterly in Social Science*) 55: 101–140.

Kuo Jeng-Jeng (郭姃姃). 2006. "分偶家庭: 大陸台商配偶婚姻生活經驗之研究" (Divided Spouse Households: A Study of the Marital Life Experiences of Spouses of Taiwanese Businessmen in the Mainland). Unpublished MA thesis, Family Education Research Institute, National Chia-yi University.

Lan, Pei-chia. 2006. *Global Cinderellas: Migrant Domestics and Newly Rich Employers in Taiwan*. Durham, NC: Duke University Press.

Lang, Graeme, and Josephine Smart. 2000. "Migration and the Second Wife in South China: Toward Cross-Border Polygyny." *International Migration Review* 36: 546–569.

Lee, Calvin. 1965. *Chinatown, U.S.A.* Garden City, NY: Doubleday.

Ley, David, and Audrey Kobayashi. 2005. "Back to Hong Kong: Return Migration or Transnational Sojourn?" *Global Networks* 5(2): 111–127.

Lima, Fernando H. 2001. "Transnational Families: Institutions of Transnational Social Space." In *New Transnational Social Spaces: International Migration and Transnational Companies in the Early Twenty-First Century*, Lugger Pries, ed., pp. 77–93. London: Routledge.

Lorente, Bretriz P., Nicola Piper, and Hsiu-hua Shen, eds. 2005. *Asian Migrations: Sojourning, Displacement, Homecoming and Other Travels*. Singapore: National Singapore University Press.

Menjívar, Cecilia, and Victor Agadjanian. 2007. "Men's Migration and Women's Lives: Views from Rural Armenia and Guatemala." *Social Science Quarterly* 88: 1243–1262.

Ong, Aihwa. 1999. *Flexible Citizenship: The Cultural Logics of Transnationality.* Durham, NC: Duke University Press.

Parreñas, Rhacel S. 2001. *Servants of Globalization: Women, Migration, and Domestic Work.* Palo Alto, CA: Stanford University Press.

———. 2005. "Long Distance Intimacy: Class, Gender, and Intergenerational Relations between Mothers and Children in Filipino Transnational Families." *Global Networks* 5(4): 317–336.

———. 2008. "Transnational Fathering: Gendered Conflicts, Distant Disciplining, and Emotional Gaps." *Journal of Ethnic and Migration Studies* 34(7): 1057–1072.

Petrozziell, Allison J. 2011. "Feminised Financial Flows: How Gender Affects Remittances in Honduran–US Transnational Families." *Gender and Development* 19(1): 53–67.

Pribilsky, Jason. 2004. "Aprendemos a convivir: Conjugal Relations, Co-Parenting, and Family Life among Ecuadorian Transnational Migrants in New York City and the Ecuadorian Andes." *Global Networks* 4(3): 313–334.

Sha Li-ling (沙儷伶). 2006. "轉變的家—兩岸分偶家庭之初探" (Changing Family: A Preliminary Investigation of Households with Spouses Separated across the Strait). Unpublished MA Thesis, Social Transformation Research Institute, Shih Hsin University, Taipei.

Shambaugh, David. 1995. *Greater China.* Oxford, UK: Oxford University Press.

Shen, Hui-fen. 2012. *China's Left-Behind Wives: Families of Migrants from Fujian to Southeast Asia, 1930s–1950s.* Singapore: NUS Press, co-published by The University of Hawaii Press and Hong Kong University Press.

Shen, Hsiu-hua. 2003. *Crossing the Taiwan Strait: Global Disjunctures and Multiple Hegemonies of Class, Politics, Gender, and Sexuality.* PhD Dissertation, Department of Sociology, University of Kansas, Lawrence.

———. 2005. "'The First Taiwanese Wives' and 'the Chinese Mistresses': The International Division of Labour in Familial and Intimate Relations across the Taiwan Strait." *Global Networks* 5(4): 419–437.

———. 2008a. "The Purchase of Transnational Intimacy: Women's Bodies, Transnational Masculine Privileges in Chinese Economic Zones." *Asian Studies Review* 32: 57–75.

———. 2008b. "Becoming 'the First Wives': Gender, Intimacy, and Regional Economy between Taiwan and China." In *East Asian Sexualities: Modernity, Gender and New Sexual Cultures*, Liu Jieyu and Stevi Jackson, eds., with Woo Juhyun, pp. 216–235. London: Zed Books.

Siu, Paul C. P. (John Kuo Wei Tchen, ed.). 1987. *The Chinese Laundryman: A Study of Social Isolation*. New York: New York University Press.

Tam, Siumi Maria. 2004. "Imaginations and Realities of Femininity: Polygyny across the Hongkong–China Border." *Journal of Guangxi University for Nationalities* 26(6): 18–25.

Wang, Gungwu. 2000. *The Chinese Overseas: From Earth-Bound China to the Quest for Autonomy*. Cambridge, MA: Harvard University Press.

Wang Jun-lin (王君琳). 2001. "流動的家:大陸台商女性配偶的家生活與認同" (Flowing Home: The Home Life and Identity of the Wives of the Taiwanese Businessmen in China). Unpublished MA thesis, Architecture and Urban Planning Research Institute, National Taiwan University, Taipei.

Waters, James L. 2002. "Flexible Families? 'Astronaut' Households and the Experiences of Lone Mothers in Vancouver, British Columbia." *Social and Cultural Geography* 3: 117–134.

Watson, James L. 1975. *Emigration and the Chinese Lineage: The Mans in Hong Kong and London*. Berkeley: University of California Press.

Wilding, Raelene. 2006. "'Virtual' Intimacies? Families Communicating across Transnational Contexts." *Global Networks* 6(2): 125–142.

Yeoh, Brenda, and Katie Wills. 2004. "Constructing Masculinities in Transnational Space: Singapore Men on the 'Regional Beat.'" In *Transnational Spaces*, Peter Jackson, Phil Crang, and Claire Dwyer, eds., pp. 147–163. London and New York: Routledge.

Yeoh, Brenda S. A., Shirlena Huang, and Theodora Lam. 2005. "Transnationalizing the 'Asian' Family: Imaginaries, Intimacies and Strategic Intents." *Global Networks* (Special Issue on Asian Transnational Families) 5(4): 307–315.

Zelizer, Viviana. 2005. *The Purchase of Intimacy*. Princeton, NJ: Princeton University Press.

12 MARITAL BORDERS

Gender, Population, and Sovereignty across the
Taiwan Strait

Sara L. Friedman

THE INSTITUTION OF MARRIAGE IN TAIWAN today is changing rapidly as seen by a
rising age at first marriage, soaring divorce rates, and a growing disinclination
among young people to marry at all. These domestic patterns of marital deinstitutionalization are coupled with the now two-decade-long phenomenon
of cross-border marriages that typically pair Taiwanese men with Southeast
Asian and Mainland Chinese women. These cross-border unions feed a variety of very public anxieties in Taiwan concerning racial and cultural integration, the fate of mixed-race and mixed-heritage children, immigrant spouses'
futures as Taiwanese citizens, and the potential for a silent invasion of Mainland Chinese through family reunification. Marriage, in short, has become a
nexus linking gender, population, and national sovereignty.

This chapter examines how marriages between Taiwanese and Mainland
Chinese both reinforce and perturb this nexus of gender, population, and
sovereignty in contemporary Taiwan. With regard to the first two terms, we
might say that gender norms organize how states categorize and regulate their
populations. I use the case of cross-Strait marriages to show how Taiwanese
immigration policies produce a gendered ideal of authentic marriage that af-
firms traditional gender roles and, in so doing, mitigates anxieties stemming
from the population's rapid aging and low rates of reproduction. Although
marital immigration inspires its own complex set of demographic concerns,
those concerns may be balanced by the perception that cross-border marriages help remedy the "care deficit" and "shortage of children" produced by
the changing composition of the Taiwanese national body. To successfully

actualize this promise of demographic salvation, however, immigrant spouses must conform to the gendered role expectations that define cross-border marital authenticity.

Sovereignty, the third term in the nexus, is less commonly linked to kinship ties or to the emotional, economic, social, and legal entanglements that characterize marriage. Through a detailed analysis of how the Taiwanese state regulates cross-Strait marriages and how those regulations affect Chinese spouses in Taiwan, I show how new forms of state power directed at recent changes in marriage and population may generate sovereignty effects for a country that has struggled to claim an independent national status, especially in relation to China. Cross-border marriages broaden the frame of reference for marriage from a union of citizens who form families and reproduce the nation to a bond that legally joins citizens to noncitizens, carving out new immigration pathways that expand the scope of border control and immigration regulation, the latter both critical markers of sovereign status (Newendorp 2008; Surkis 2010). At the same time, however, cross-Strait family reunification also generates new concerns about national identification directed at both Chinese spouses and their children that deepen anxieties about immigrants' and citizens' national commitments and potentially undermine the sovereignty effects produced by an increasingly robust immigration regime.[1]

Taiwan is not alone in regulating the entry of foreign spouses or in monitoring their path toward naturalization, nor is it unique in evaluating the nature and quality of its citizens' transnational marriages (Constable 2003; Surkis 2010). Border inspections and consular interviews have long been used by governments around the world to produce categories of people deemed desirable and undesirable from the perspective of family stability, the health and uniformity of the population, and national reproduction.[2] Whereas domestic couples in Taiwan benefit from the turn to private ordering that increasingly characterizes the stance of Taiwanese courts (Kuo Chapter 9), cross-border couples face persistent pressure to conform to public ordering of their marriages. This public ordering is produced through immigration policies, techniques of border control, and state regulatory practices designed to police Chinese marital immigrants and evaluate the authenticity and quality of their marriages. But such public ordering also generates effects that extend beyond disciplining the scope of recognized intimate relationships. Precisely because of Taiwan's uncertain sovereign status and its contested political ties with China, the regulation of Chinese marital immigrants and cross-Strait marriages acquires added significance as a critical—albeit contested—mechanism for asserting Taiwanese sovereignty.[3]

This chapter is based on research conducted between 2003 and 2011 with cross-Strait couples in Taiwan and China; Taiwanese governmental entities charged with immigrant policing, monitoring, and service support; and NGOs that provide assistance to Chinese spouses in Taiwan or work as activists for immigrant rights.[4] Over these eight years, I conducted over 150 interviews with Chinese spouses, some of which included their Taiwanese partners and in-laws. I joined social gatherings in homes and leisure sites and participated in a wide array of government- and NGO-sponsored events, training classes, and public demonstrations. In addition, I completed in-depth interviews and participant observation with immigration bureaucrats and officials in sites ranging from the National Immigration Agency (NIA) headquarters in Taipei to the control zone of Taoyuan International Airport, where I observed border interviews with cross-Strait couples. This wide array of sources and perspectives informs my ethnographically based analysis of the gendered nature of cross-border marital regulation, the disciplinary power of the category "sham marriage," and the association of cross-Strait marriages with key demographic concerns in Taiwan today. In the final section, I show how cross-Strait marriages have enabled Taiwan's sovereignty claims by expanding practices of border control and immigrant regulation. Here I supplement my ethnographic material with a close reading of the video art production *Empire's Borders I* (帝國邊界一), produced by Taiwanese artist Chen Chieh-jen. Chen's insightful critique of global border regimes speaks to the broader consequences of asserting sovereignty through marital regulation.

MARITAL BORDERS

The most recent wave of marriages between Taiwanese and Mainland Chinese began in 1987 with the reinstatement of cross-Strait ties after nearly forty years of military and political conflict. Among the first Taiwanese to cross the Strait were retired veterans and men exploring business opportunities in China, some of whom used this opportunity to seek a Chinese spouse. Veterans were more likely to marry divorced or widowed middle-aged women, while businessmen found partners among the never-married and previously married alike. Over time, cross-Strait marriages diversified to include a wider array of spouses with different class and ethnic backgrounds and prior marital histories. Taiwanese partners range from members of the working class to white-collar professionals, although more are concentrated in the lower income ranges, and they include those marrying for the first time (often in middle age) as well as divorcees and widowers. Chinese spouses also span a broad spectrum of ages, places of origin, educational and professional backgrounds, and previous marital and romantic histories. Although popular stereotypes of cross-Strait marriages depict both spouses as poor or otherwise disadvantaged (and thus unable or unwilling to marry domestically), in fact these unions increasingly join better-educated, never-married individuals from both sides of the Strait, and a small minority pair Chinese men with Taiwanese women.

As these marriages grew in number throughout the 1990s and into the new millennium, cross-Strait couples faced a confusing array of policies that dictated where they lived and what rights were available to the noncitizen partner. Most couples resided in Taiwan in accordance with patrilocal residence norms, except in cases where the Taiwanese partner worked in China. But Chinese spouses occupied an ambiguous status in Taiwan as neither foreigners nor natives: designated as "people of the Mainland area," they faced immigration and citizenship procedures that differed in substance and degree from those directed at "foreign" spouses, primarily women from Southeast Asian countries.[5] Thus, although cross-Strait marriages are part of a changing landscape of intimacy in Taiwan that includes same-sex unions, marriages with Southeast Asian wives, and Taiwanese couples who live apart (Kuo Chapter 9; Shen Chapter 11), they occupy an unusual niche in this marital field precisely because the status of Chinese spouses in Taiwan is tainted by the contested political ties across the Strait.

In brief, for much of the past two decades Chinese spouses have waited twice as long as other foreign spouses before becoming eligible for citizenship. This time frame of eight years was often extended, moreover, due to backlogs created by quotas imposed initially at the residency stage and later at the point of granting citizenship. Efforts to equalize the waiting period for Chinese and foreign spouses produced a slight reduction in 2009, from eight years to six. Furthermore, unlike foreign spouses who receive residency status and work rights immediately on arrival in Taiwan, prior to 2009 Chinese spouses faced a delay of several years in obtaining residency, and legal work rights could take from two to six years, depending on individual circumstances.

Bureaucrats and officials have justified these delays as necessary to prevent "sham marriages" (假結婚) contracted merely for economic motives, whether

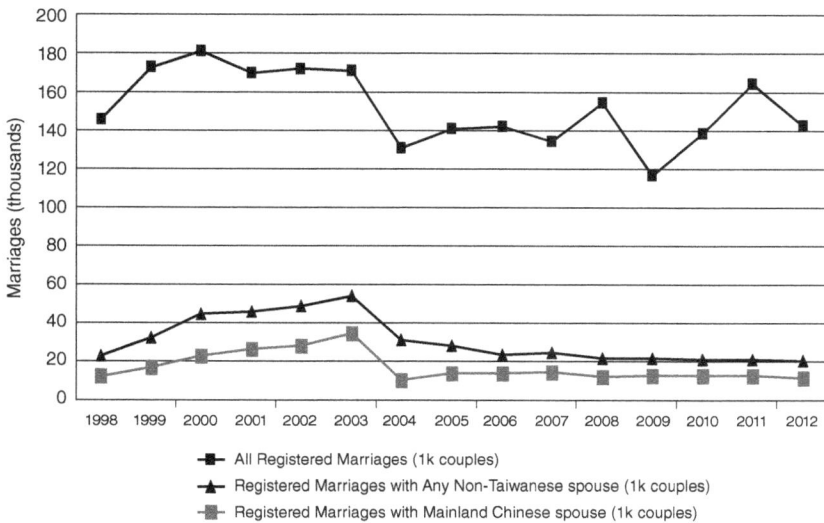

Figure 12.1. Registered marriages in Taiwan, 1998–2012.
SOURCE: Taiwan Department of Household Registration, Ministry of the Interior, "Statistics on Marriages between Nationals and Foreigners."

through legal or illegal channels. The main bureaucratic procedure put in place to block the entry of "sham" Chinese spouses was the border interview, a system implemented in late 2003–2004 at the peak of marital immigration from China to Taiwan. In 2003 alone, 32 percent of all registered marriages included a noncitizen spouse, and 20 percent involved a Chinese spouse specifically. Although the number of cross-border marriages has declined since that peak, these unions continue to represent 10–15 percent of all annual registered marriages in Taiwan (Figure 12.1). Chinese spouses have outnumbered their other foreign counterparts by a factor of more than two to one, but their longer wait to citizenship has meant that fewer have acquired Taiwanese citizenship. By the end of 2012, 306,514 Chinese spouses had applied for entry to Taiwan and 100,337 had become Taiwanese citizens.[6]

Marital immigration, coupled with the influx of temporary migrant workers from Southeast Asia, has spawned a robust regulatory regime in Taiwan that integrates prevailing policing and national security goals with welfare and other social services that promote immigrant adjustment and familial stability. The regulation of cross-border marriages thus fosters an expansion of governmental power now directed internationally as well as domestically.

New marriage practices in Taiwan have transformed the terrain on which state regulation encounters intimate life, pairing marital decisions with sovereign decisions and deepening the reach and scope of state power.

ENGENDERING CROSS-BORDER MARITAL REGULATION

The regulatory system that has emerged in response to cross-border marriages is inherently gendered. By this I mean that it both rests on and reproduces specifically gendered expectations for proper marital roles and behaviors on the part of immigrant spouses, what elsewhere I have called "a dependency model" of marital immigration (Friedman 2013). This model ties a Chinese wife's or husband's legal standing in Taiwan to family and marital status alone, providing no independent basis for residency or citizenship claims. At the same time, restrictions on Chinese spouses' work rights (in place prior to August 2009) and regular government monitoring of cross-Strait marital relationships affirmed a presumed norm of feminized domesticity for immigrant women and men alike by valuing Chinese spouses' reproductive contributions to their Taiwanese families and defining the desire to engage in nondomestic labor and remunerated employment as suspect, a potential sign of questionable marital motives. This regulatory regime has created gendered standards for cross-border mobility and naturalized citizenship that make marital immigrants dependent on their citizen-spouse for legal and economic support.

Domestic marriage trends in Taiwan show Taiwanese women increasingly delaying marriage, with some rejecting it altogether.[7] As the analyses by Yu and Liu (Chapter 10) and Shen (Chapter 11) demonstrate, despite broad social, economic, and political challenges to traditional models of marriage and family in Taiwan, gendered expectations for marital roles and responsibilities have not changed dramatically for those who opt in to marriage.[8] Immigrant wives thus find themselves caught in the intersection of traditional social expectations and changing legal regulations (Kuo Chapter 9). Their citizen-partner and in-laws often expect them to perform housework, bear and raise children (their own or those from a Taiwanese spouse's previous marriage), and care for elderly or sick family members. Even Chinese husbands in Taiwan face a similar domestic orientation because of delays in acquiring legal work rights and difficulties finding employment commensurate with their education and previous work experience (Friedman 2013).[9] As a result, Chinese spouses may find they have no choice but to conform to these domestic orientations, especially because refusing to do so may cast doubt on their own immigration intentions and interrupt their trajectory toward citizenship (Friedman 2013). In short, public ordering often trumps their own private desires when it comes to the opportunities and expectations Chinese spouses face as marital immigrants in Taiwan.

Lu Jingjing's marital experiences in Taiwan exemplify some of the conundrums produced by this dependency model. I first met Jingjing at a 2007 government-sponsored life skills course held for Chinese spouses who lived in an eastern district of Taipei city. A quiet, serious woman whose glasses and ponytail made her look more like a student than a married woman in her early thirties, Jingjing rarely spoke out during the class sessions except to offer the occasional, sardonic comment about the poor prospects many of them, including herself, faced on both sides of the Strait. Jingjing was forced to drop out of the class halfway through to care for her sick father-in-law. Aware of the care expectations faced by many of the Chinese women I had met in Taiwan, I did not think much of the situation until Jingjing contacted me in late October to ask whether I would be willing to meet with her.

"Even on the day we registered our marriage, I didn't believe it," Jingjing professed as we took our seats in a coffee shop near the working-class neighborhood where she lived with her husband, his parents, and his two divorced sisters. "I never thought I would marry someone from outside [of China]. Taiwan is a very distant place." Jingjing shed the reticent demeanor she had adopted in the classroom and launched into a nonstop narrative until the shop closed, at which point we moved to a bench in the park across the street and continued our conversation until nearly midnight. Jingjing traced her current circumstances back to the Cultural Revolution when her father, a teacher at Nanjing University, was sent down to the Jiangsu countryside where he met and married her mother, a peasant woman twelve years his junior. Although her father had successfully shifted the family's household registration back to Nanjing after the Cultural Revolution, his premature death in 1980 left her mother to fend for herself with two young children. Unable to cope, her mother returned to her native village in the southern Jiangsu countryside.

This move initiated what Jingjing went on to describe as over two decades of personal disappointments and struggles: testing into university but lacking the resources to pay for tuition; struggling as a migrant worker in Shenzhen without an identification card (身分證); following her mother to Shanghai, then back to their rural township in Jiangsu, and later to Anhui, all moves sparked by her mother's relationships with different men or efforts to find

Jingjing a suitable husband. In her late twenties, Jingjing ended up back in Nanjing where she used the engagement money given to her by a prospective suitor (a disabled man whom she had no intention of marrying) to enroll in a computer course and later a training school to become a foot masseuse. While working in a foot massage clinic she read a newspaper article about a rural lecturer from Henan who had married a European man after meeting him online. Inspired by this woman's success story, Jingjing began to correspond with foreign men via the Internet, ultimately meeting her Taiwanese husband online in June 2006.

After corresponding with her husband for one month, Jingjing agreed when he proposed to meet her in person in Shanghai. He asked her to marry him on the second day of the visit, and six weeks later they registered their marriage in her hometown. Her husband was thirteen years her senior and, like her, was a never-married high school graduate. Jingjing admitted that she had lowered her standards to find a stable partner, and she knew that being from the Mainland put her at a disadvantage in Taiwan. At the same time, she clearly recognized that, without connections in China, she had no hope of "turning over" (翻不了身) and improving her life circumstances were she to remain.

Full of hope for a better future, Jingjing arrived in Taiwan in January 2007, only to discover that Taiwanese ways of thinking differed dramatically from Mainland Chinese, and she was surprised by the discrimination she faced from her husband's family. Because she had not yet borne them a child and could not work legally outside the home, she was viewed with suspicion as an outsider who made no contributions to the family. Moreover, two of her four sisters-in-law had divorced, and their husbands had either had an affair with a Chinese woman or married one after the divorce. As a result, the extended family was predisposed to distrust her motives, and her husband tended to side with his mother and sisters in any family disputes.

Jingjing spent her days caring for her father-in-law who was bedridden after a stroke—feeding him, changing his diapers, and doing other house-work—freeing her mother-in-law from these tasks. She chafed at the restrictions her care responsibilities placed on her movement, and she resented the fact that she had been forced to drop out of the life-skills class even though it met only three days a week for a few hours. She described her mother-in-law as a traditional woman from the southern Taiwan countryside who believed Jingjing should remain obediently at home to avoid being influenced by other

Chinese women. In Jingjing's case, government regulations that prohibited her from working legally outside the home dovetailed with family care work expectations to make her, as she put it, a prisoner in her husband's house. If she were to challenge these restrictions on her mobility and employment opportunities, she ran the risk of being accused of harboring inauthentic marital motives and undermining her authorized immigration status.

THE SPECTER OF SHAM MARRIAGE

The tension Jingjing faced between familial care work demands and her own desire to seek employment was not unusual. For her and other Chinese spouses, the consequences of this conflict were intensified by the disciplinary category of "sham marriage" and the way the category sutured together marital and migration intentions. Constructed through border interview decisions, bureaucrats' evaluations of Chinese spouses' residency and citizenship applications, media representations of cross-border marriages, and societal distrust of Chinese wives, the category of sham marriage created a powerful disciplinary field that subjected all Chinese spouses to potentially severe consequences, including the threat of deportation.

Initially, sham marriage stood in for the intention to engage in illegal employment such as sex work, but in the last decade its scope has expanded to encompass migration goals that exceed a commitment to the marriage itself. Immigration bureaucrats typically identify these nonmarital intentions as the desire to work and earn money, even in occupations that are not themselves illegal. As one immigration officer described to me, in such cases the Chinese spouse is merely "using marriage to enter the country" to gain access to more lucrative employment opportunities than those available in the Mainland.[10] This focus on intentions as the cornerstone of a sham marriage makes the category notoriously difficult to define, however, and the bureaucratic procedures put in place to evaluate marital authenticity (such as the border interview) often reinforce the fuzziness of the category itself, even as they empower bureaucrats to deport immigrant spouses whom they suspect of inauthentic marital motives (Friedman 2010a).

Although most Chinese spouses pass through the border interview system and subsequent bureaucratic encounters relatively uneventfully, their experiences educate them about the power of the category of sham marriage and its ability to determine their own opportunities and status in Taiwan. As stories and accusations of sham marriage circulate among communities of Chinese spouses, those narratives do important work by shoring up claims of marital authenticity and assertions that one deserves better treatment as a result. Some of this discourse is directed at the government, but equally pertinent and powerful interlocutors are other Chinese women and men who readily judge their compatriots. Some of my earliest conversations with Chinese wives in Taiwan drove home for me the salience of the category of sham marriage in the lives of all Chinese marital immigrants.

When Pan first walked into the Taipei café where we had arranged to meet one August night in 2003 after she got off work, I did not recognize her as being from China. She was tall and thin, with dark hair that she wore loose around her shoulders. She had on red-rimmed glasses with stylish frames and was dressed casually in a shirt and jeans, a look that belied the fact that she was already in her forties. Pan spoke with virtually no Mainland accent, and the only thing that might reveal her origins was her direct style of speech.

Pan hailed from a coastal area of Zhejiang Province and had first married a Taiwanese in 1995 when she was thirty-two years old. After a few years she divorced her husband because of his infidelities and in 1998 married her current husband, with whom she had a daughter a year later. Because both Pan and her husband worked long hours in restaurants, they could not care for their daughter, and Pan had sent the child to live with her parents in China. As Pan continued to talk about her life in Taiwan, it became clear that she was unhappy in her marriage and despised her husband, whom she described as lazy and unmotivated. Yet, for her daughter's sake, she was not willing to divorce him, although she talked frequently of moving back to Zhejiang once she became a citizen.

For Pan, the authenticity of her marriage stemmed both from the fact that she had borne a child with her husband and from her commitment to hard work and maintaining legal status in Taiwan. By contrast, she claimed, Chinese women in sham marriages wanted only to make money; they did not care about becoming citizens or receiving legal work rights. Having a child tied Pan to Taiwan in a way that differed from those in ostensibly sham marriages; they simply wanted to earn as much money as possible and then leave. Moreover, her money was "clean." Pan emphasized time and again how hard she worked for the $25,000 NT she earned each month. If she was like the women in sham marriages, she would simply find a man and live with him for a monthly fee. Her commitment to working hard for "clean money," coupled with her good family background and willingness to remain in an unhappy marriage, distinguished her from those who, she argued, viewed marriage simply as a means to improve their material circumstances.[11]

Yet despite Pan's efforts to draw clear lines between herself and women in sham marriages, her narrative constantly traversed those boundaries as she spoke in greater detail about her life and aspirations. Although the money she earned was not tainted by sex work, she remained in Taiwan for a reason not terribly different from the one she attributed to those in sham marriages: the ability to earn more money than she could in China. And although she claimed to have a stronger tie to Taiwan because of her marriage and her child, she nonetheless talked repeatedly about returning to China, with or without her husband, to start up a business there. In short, her decisions to date and her plans for the future looked in many ways like those she described for women in sham relationships, the major difference being the type of work she performed and how that work enabled her to assert a sense of familial responsibility and personal respectability.

Many cross-Strait couples claimed the mantle of authentic marriage to demand that immigration officials do a better job of weeding out sham marriages instead of punishing all with harsher immigration policies. Like Pan, however, they, too, struggled to define the slippery contours of the category itself. In 2009, I attended a government-sponsored immigration policy education forum held for cross-Strait couples residing in southern Taiwan. A Taiwanese man in his forties stood up with a small child in his arms and addressed the National Immigration Agency (NIA) representative with an accusatory question about the border interview system. He described the system as a rude interference in personal privacy and an obstruction of marital freedom, as evidenced by the fact that his wife twice flew to Taiwan only to be sent back after failing to pass the border interview:

> I don't know what our government is safeguarding us from. My wife went through two interviews before she passed. And we now have a child. I'm really suspicious about what kind of reason was used for deporting her; was it sham marriage? If it was sham marriage, then is this child sitting here today also a sham? I feel that the problems with the interview should have been eliminated long ago. We have basic freedom of marriage. Whatever country I want to marry someone from, that is my own personal affair. The government absolutely has no right to interfere. (Chia-yi, Taiwan, June 7, 2009)

The NIA representative's reply was polite and apologetic, and he repeatedly stressed that, as far as he knew, interviewers were now trained not to ask the kinds of personal questions that the gentleman found so offensive. Although he agreed with the man's assertion of marital freedom, the representative failed to address the man's other major critique, namely the questionable status of the category of sham marriage itself and its deployment as a rationale for border control.

The audience of several hundred men and women listened attentively to this man's critique and those that followed. Virtually every Chinese immigrant I interviewed claimed to know someone in a sham marriage, an assertion through which they simultaneously identified themselves with the category of authentic marriage. Widespread dissatisfaction with the policies and procedures in place to discourage sham marriages, coupled with recognition of those policies' obvious failures, led some to demand more effective government intervention, while others wanted the government to stop regulating cross-border unions altogether. Regardless of their position on governmental involvement, however, few challenged the notion that one could distinguish categories of real and sham. Only on rare occasions, such as in the husband's outburst at the policy education session, did individuals comment on the ontological ambiguities created by the concept of sham marriage, including the status of the children who might result from such unions.[12] By underscoring the fluidity of the boundaries between these categories, such challenges articulated the difficulties of defining the essence of a real marriage and the obstacles this categorical uncertainty generated for bureaucrats and immigrants alike.

POPULATION

Concerns about the quality and composition of contemporary Taiwanese marriages raise broader questions about national population that have preoccupied the government over the past decade. Marriage cuts across the three areas of concern described in the Population Policy White Paper of 2007: population aging, declining fertility, and immigration. Cross-Strait marriages traverse this population terrain and link marriage to the construction and management of population as a focus of governmental attention.

So-called caretaking marriages (照顧式的婚姻) directly link immigration flows to growing elder care needs in a society with ever-fewer young people available to support an aging population. Caretaking marriages typically pair middle-aged Chinese women with elderly veterans, former soldiers who retreated to Taiwan with the Nationalist army in the late 1940s and formed a marginalized community of single men largely ostracized from local Taiwanese society and its marital opportunities.[13] By the time cross-Strait ties resumed in the late 1980s, these men were in their fifties and sixties, facing old age without family support (and most with only a meager pension as veterans). In China, they looked for wives who would return with them to Taiwan and provide care as they aged. Most of these women hailed from the veterans' home provinces and were middle-aged and divorced or widowed, with teenage or adult children of their own.[14] Many had been pressured to retire or "step down" (下崗) from collective and state-sector jobs with the onset of China's market reforms, and they found themselves increasingly disadvantaged in a job market that favored youth and higher education. They imagined that Taiwan would offer them better employment opportunities, and many were attracted by the promise of companionship and their husbands' (often exaggerated) portrayals of comfortable living environments and substantial financial resources.

Once they arrived in Taiwan, however, these women often found themselves living in dismal conditions, struggling to make ends meet on extremely tight budgets. As veterans grew older, moreover, many suffered strokes or other debilitating illnesses that required constant care from their wives. Hence, on the one hand, Chinese women relieved the burden on the state by providing care for aging veterans; on the other hand, these caretaking expectations came to define the authenticity of marriages that were otherwise deemed suspect due to significant age gaps between spouses and assumptions that older women's "real" migration goals were material, not relational. Wives who were perceived as not fulfilling their care responsibilities, either because they went out to work or because their husbands were so ill that they had to move to a nursing home, faced accusations of sham marriage and potential deportation.

Immigration bureaucrats have relied heavily on this caretaking paradigm to adjudicate marital authenticity in veteran marriages. The NIA often turns to the Veterans Affairs Administration to conduct investigations when the Chinese wife of a veteran applies for citizenship. On a warm September day in 2007, I found myself in a car with Mr. Liu, a Veterans Affairs officer, hurtling through traffic en route to a northern Taipei suburb to investigate a case where the eighty-year-old veteran-husband resided in a nursing home and his thirty-something Fujianese wife lived downtown near the restaurant where she worked. As we parked outside the small, single-story building that housed the care facility, Mr. Liu commented to me that the wife's application would probably be rejected, not merely because of the couple's age difference (forty-two years) but, more important, because the wife had not been caring for her husband. The VA had a network of district-level volunteer representatives who provided support services to veterans and completed background research in cases such as this one. The local representative already had informed Mr. Liu that the wife rarely visited her husband in the four years he had lived in the nursing home, and Mr. Liu clearly was inclined to recommend that her application be denied.

The wife had been awaiting our arrival, and we walked quickly through the waiting area to a back room where the husband lay listlessly on a hospital bed. The group gathered around him, and Mr. Liu, shouting to counteract the man's deafness, asked whether he knew why we were there. Receiving no answer, other than a forceful shaking of the head, Mr. Liu casually reminded me that I had wanted to chat with the wife, thereby providing him an opportunity to speak privately with the husband. She and I retreated to the waiting room and, with the television blaring in the background, she described quite matter-of-factly the chain of events that had led her to marry her elderly husband. They had lived together in Taiwan for three years, she added, until two car accidents and a stroke forced him to move to the nursing home.

Walking back to the car after Mr. Liu had finished his inquiry, I asked the local representative what she thought about the case, and she responded drily that the wife merely wanted an identification card (that is, citizenship) and, according to the nursing home staff, had rarely visited her husband over the years. As the driver guided the car down the narrow alley that connected the nursing home to the main road, Mr. Liu pointed to a middle-aged man leaning against the wall next to a moped. "That is her boyfriend," Liu told me, information they had received from the staff who confirmed that he had brought her there on other occasions. I wondered how they knew for certain that he was her boyfriend, recalling that the wife had described him to me as a co-worker's husband. The details, it seemed, were irrelevant at this point, and the VA personnel were much more inclined to believe the staff at the nursing home than the wife's own claims that she cared for her husband even after he moved to the nursing facility. The final straw in her case was the testimony of her husband, who evidently had instructed Mr. Liu not to grant her citizenship out of fear that she then would leave him.

In the end, Mr. Liu recommended to the NIA that the wife's application for citizenship be denied. He explained to me that when couples live apart, as in this case, the Chinese wife "must show that she has continued to care for her husband. [She must] visit him often, on her own initiative, [to show] definitively that she is caring for this 'uncle.'" In this and other cases, the caretaking paradigm defined the outcome of bureaucratic evaluations of marital authenticity. Because a Chinese wife's citizenship application rests on her status as the spouse of a citizen, the evaluation of her application assesses the nature of her marriage as part of determining her future in Taiwan. The irony of this process, of course, is that despite the VA's professed commitment to protecting veterans' interests, Mr. Liu's negative assessment of the wife's application likely produced the very outcome that the husband had hoped to avoid: his wife's inability to continue to care for him—not because she had left him for another man but because the government had deported her for being in a "sham marriage."

If caretaking serves as the measure of marital authenticity for women married to elderly men, then childbearing performs this function for Chinese spouses with younger partners. As with elder care, immigrant childbearing also helps resolve critical population problems, in this case by offsetting low birth rates among Taiwanese women and "filling the gap" produced by a rapid decline in national fertility.[15] On several occasions, I heard government officials herald this procreative contribution during public events targeting Chinese spouses (see also the 2007 white paper section on fertility, Li 2007: 232). Of course, the opposite sentiment also featured prominently in government statements and media accounts that criticized the additional resources that had to be spent on these children as compared to their native counterparts to ensure their future educational and employment success (Lin and Hu 2010).[16] Yet, as Taiwan's birth rate tumbled to one (or even fewer) children per woman by the end of the first decade of the new millennium, the government seemed increasingly willing to expend these resources as part of efforts to encourage all married women, citizen and immigrant alike, to bear more children.[17]

For Chinese spouses who face sustained suspicion about their migration motives, childbearing enables them to assert marital authenticity and to benefit from preferential treatment that moves them more rapidly through the sequence of immigration stages toward citizenship and offers some security if their marriage fails. As they learn the intricacies of immigration policies, Chinese spouses quickly become aware of the personal and legal benefits of childbearing and the protections it provides them. At the same time, those who cannot or who choose not to procreate experience greater anxiety about their prospects for citizenship and societal acceptance.

Although immigrant childbearing is widely identified by bureaucrats as a sign that the marriage is not a sham, it also raises questions about what kind of Taiwanese children these will be. Ethnic and cultural similarities across the Strait, combined with the nearly universal choice of Taiwanese citizenship for these children, mean that procreative Chinese spouses contribute to reproducing an ethnically Chinese Taiwanese nation.[18] At the same time, however, concerns that ethnic similarities might mask differences in political views and national identification also extend to the second generation, who, so it is feared, may be unduly influenced by their Mainland Chinese parent or, like Pan's daughter, may even be raised and educated in China.

For many of the bureaucrats and officials I interviewed in Taiwan, the primary means of insuring that a child of a cross-Strait marriage would become Taiwanese in orientation and commitment was to raise and educate that child in Taiwan. Although bureaucrats had no right to monitor a child's place of residence while a cross-Strait marriage was intact, they could and did regulate those arrangements when a Taiwanese child became the basis for a Chinese parent's residency status. In 2008, during revisions to the policy permitting continued legal residence for a divorced Chinese spouse who had received child custody, bureaucrats added a clause specifying that the child in question had to reside in Taiwan for more than 183 days per year; otherwise the Chinese parent's residency status would be revoked. One NIA bureaucrat in the residency division spelled out two rationales for this restriction aimed at preventing Chinese spouses with child custody from sending their children back to China: One, the practice made immigration officials suspicious that the Chinese spouse demanded custody after a divorce only as a means of obtaining citizenship; and two, it created an undesirable custody situation for the child "because we all know that it is best for children to be cared for by their parents." Dismissing the validity of any pragmatic arguments regarding how best to support that child, the bureaucrat then admitted:

> Actually, the primary [reason] for this requirement is that [we] want her to care for our Taiwanese children [台灣之子]. To be frank, we don't want Taiwanese children receiving a Mainland education. Once the child is older and is brought back to Taiwan, that accent [and] way of thinking will cause adjustment difficulties and will create another wave of societal problems.[19]

This bureaucrat's frank comments on motivations behind these policy changes reflect the complex position of Chinese spouses who bear children for their Taiwanese families. On the one hand, childbearing attests to the authenticity of the marriage (or, presumably, at least its consummation) and the Chinese spouse's willingness to reproduce a multigenerational Taiwanese family. On the other hand, however, the government is concerned about protecting those children from becoming too tainted by their parent's Mainland origins, especially in divorce cases where the Taiwanese parent might not actively participate in childrearing. As a result, what is often a practical decision on the part of a divorced Chinese spouse—sending a small child to live with parents or siblings so that she can work long hours to support the child—is transformed into the strategic "use" of child custody for purposes ostensibly unrelated to her parental status, with the undesirable result of making a Taiwanese child into a Mainland child through the force of family socialization and exposure to the Chinese education system.

SOVEREIGNTY

Government concerns about national identification, whether directed at Chinese spouses or at their children, situate cross-Strait marriages squarely in the contested political terrain of China–Taiwan relations and Taiwan's own uncertain sovereign standing. Marital regulation is not typically considered a sovereign act, but in a world increasingly defined by cross-border mobility and international legal norms, it has become a site for enacting sovereign power through literal and figurative control over national borders (Dailey 2009; Surkis 2010). When marriage to a citizen constitutes grounds for entry or naturalized citizenship or when cross-border marriages are viewed as potential threats to the desired composition of the national body, marital immigration laws and regulations may enact sovereign claims by policing the boundaries of national inclusion. In cases such as Taiwan where other modes of sovereign assertion are foreclosed by the lack of international recognition, the government's ability to regulate cross-border marriages and marital immigrants powerfully substantiates Taiwan's sovereign aspirations, and no more so than when the foreign spouse hails from Mainland China.

Taiwanese artist Chen Chieh-jen's video art production *Empire's Borders I* integrates marriage and sovereignty in a single representational frame as it contrasts the fate of young unmarried Taiwanese women denied visas to the United States with the experiences of the Chinese wives of Taiwanese citizens who face similar obstacles in their efforts to enter Taiwan or establish residency and citizenship. Created in response to Chen's own humiliating treatment by a visa processing officer at the American Institute in Taiwan (AIT), the U.S. consular office in Taipei, *Empire's Borders I* employs a stripped down, quasi-documentary style in which the eight women in each section impassively narrate their own encounters with bureaucratic representatives of sovereign power.[20] Their accounts starkly depict the arbitrary nature of border control decisions that enact sovereignty through marital evaluations. Chen's choice to pair Taiwanese with Chinese border crossers and the AIT with the NIA powerfully situates Taiwan and its sovereignty dilemmas at the borders of both the United States and China.

Empire's Borders I enacts the gendered features of border regulation through its focus on marital status as the common bond linking unmarried Taiwanese women applying for U.S. visas to Mainland Chinese women seeking entry to and citizenship in Taiwan on the basis of their marriage to a Taiwanese citizen. The first part of the video shows how the motives of the eight young Taiwanese women are rendered suspect precisely because the women's unmarried status suggests to AIT interviewers that there is nothing tying them to Taiwan, a suspicion that assumes marriage is an inevitable, even necessary, stage in a Taiwanese woman's life course. As a result of their single status, the young women are viewed as likely candidates for illegally overstaying their visas or seeking permanent residence in the United States.

The video depicts how gendered expectations for marital roles and behaviors undergird border decision making (just as they inform subsequent immigration decisions made after entry, as previously described); as a result, women who seek to cross borders find their marital lives scrutinized closely by immigration officials. The Mainland Chinese wives in the second part of *Empire's Borders I* come under the Taiwanese state's investigative and regulatory gaze precisely because of their marriage to a citizen. Their unions generate suspicions about their border-crossing motives that derive from gendered assumptions about proper marital roles and behaviors that reaffirm many of the gender continuities in Taiwanese marriages described by Yu and Liu (Chapter 10).

The eight Mainland Chinese women featured in the video represent different kinds of cross-Strait unions, from younger women who have borne children with their Taiwanese partners to middle-aged women in "caretaking marriages" with elderly veteran-husbands. Portrayed standing in the control zone of Taiwan's main international airport, facing away from immigration with their luggage carts in front of them (as if they are being sent back to their place of origin), the women read from notes jotted on the back of official forms. Speaking in Mandarin and various dialects, they, like their Taiwanese counterparts in the first segment of the video, recount experiences of bureaucratic suspicion and heartlessness, the arbitrary nature of sovereign power, fears of deportation, and painful separations from children and other family members. Running throughout their narratives is an indictment of their harsher treatment in comparison to other foreign spouses and the societal discrimination they have faced while resident in Taiwan.

Chen portrays the U.S. visa system (here enacted by AIT interviewers) as the international standard of border regulation, a status confirmed through its modeling by Taiwanese immigration bureaucrats in the second part of the video. The narratives in both sections affirm the arbitrary nature of bureaucratic decision making and the indiscriminate sovereign power that stands behind it; at the same time, the women's stories depict the marital foundations of sovereign assertions as they underscore how assessments of marital status and quality pervade bureaucrats' exercise of discretionary power. One middle-aged Chinese woman whose husband was in a nursing home recounted a tale that paralleled my encounter with the Veteran's Affairs Administration described in the previous section. In a trembling voice, the woman narrated how she had fought to obtain citizenship after nursing home workers reported to an investigator that she and her husband argued frequently, misinterpreting her raised voice as anger instead of as a response to her husband's growing deafness. As a result, her application for citizenship was denied, and only after her husband wrote a letter to the NIA testifying to her attentive care over the years did she finally receive citizenship.

The arbitrary nature of decisions about whom to admit, deny entry to, or bestow citizenship on does not point to an exceptional form of governance that deviates from rational administrative procedures. Instead, this very arbitrariness (as seen in the exercise of bureaucratic discretion) undergirds a mode of sovereign power that reconstitutes itself through constructing an ever-changing legal threshold where inclusion and exclusion, approval and denial, meet (Agamben 1998, 2005). For many countries, border control practices have spread beyond the physical site of the border to ports of embarkation and government offices overseas, thereby extending the reach of sovereign decision making through the spatial extension of specific bureaucratic and policing practices (Bigo and Guild 2005; Coutin 2003; Mountz 2004; Ong 2000; Pratt 2005; Rajaram and Grundy-Warr 2007; Salter 2006; Sassen 2006). Chen's pairing of Taiwanese women's U.S. visa application failures with Chinese women's immigration obstacles in Taiwan shows how Taiwan has adopted these bureaucratic procedures to assert its own sovereignty, even in the face of a contracted space of national governance that prevents it from projecting those sovereign practices across the border into China.

Given Taiwan's limited international recognition, the border interview system best exemplifies the kind of bureaucratic practice that produces sovereignty effects (Friedman 2010a). Applied only to Mainland Chinese spouses and their Taiwanese partners, the border interview requires a face-to-face encounter between Chinese immigrants and Taiwanese state actors during which the state representative is empowered to make a sovereign decision about whether to admit the Chinese spouse. The effect of this decision is not lost on the couple or the interviewer. For Chinese spouses, the interview is the first in a series of evaluations they face during their long wait to citizenship, and it confirms their differential treatment as compared to other foreign spouses. "Why is it only Mainland Chinese spouses who have to suffer endless scrutiny in Taiwan?" asks a young woman in the second half of *Empire's Borders I*. "Can't we just be treated the same as other people?"

This question—why must Chinese spouses be treated differently from all other foreigners?—speaks directly to the contestations over sovereignty that infuse cross-Strait relations more generally and that shape cross-Strait marital regulation specifically. Because Taiwanese bureaucrats are unable to interview potential immigrants on Chinese soil (as they do with foreign spouses in their home countries), their border decisions assume heightened importance by repeatedly invoking the specter of deportation. At the same time, their very decision-making power also reaffirms Taiwan's de facto sovereignty, especially when it is enacted in response to Chinese border crossers who stand in for China's refusal to recognize Taiwan as an independent nation-state.

The substance of this sovereign power is not just any kind of border control, however, but specifically the decision about whether to recognize the marriage of a Taiwanese citizen to a Mainland Chinese. Cross-Strait marriages, in this sense, create the foundation for sovereignty by enabling family reunification claims that require governmental evaluation of the authenticity of such marriages, in part through assessing whether Chinese spouses perform expected gender roles defined by a traditional model of culturally Chinese marriage.

Whether this immigration apparatus actually makes Taiwan more sovereign or whether it merely reaffirms the violence of border control is the question that animates *Empire's Borders I* and its undisguised critique of Taiwan's efforts to imitate the United States through its policing of Chinese spouses.

CONCLUSION

The key place of marital regulation in Taiwan's sovereignty project is perhaps unexpected, and yet, seen from another perspective, the marriage–sovereignty nexus merely broadens the role of marriage as a relationship that normalizes diverse forms of intimacy by weaving them into the fabric of a national body politic (Berlant 1997; Cott 2000; Friedman 2006). Through evaluating marital roles and migration intentions, immigration bureaucrats create a gendered ideal of authentic marriage that channels Chinese spouses into care work, household labor, and childbearing. These expectations subsequently affirm both traditional Taiwanese gender norms and definitions of "real marriage" that are incorporated into immigration policies designed to block "sham marriages." As a result, Chinese spouses may find that the decision to marry a Taiwanese does not enable them to "develop" (發展), as many desire, so much as it relegates them to domestic spaces and the unremunerated (and largely unrecognized) work of caring for others.

Current Taiwan government concerns with a rapidly aging population and below-replacement birth rates offer some possibilities for integrating Chinese spouses into the national body. As caretakers of elderly husbands or in-laws and as bearers of new Taiwanese children, Chinese spouses reduce the burden these population pressures place on the state. Hence, marital immigration—although deemed a population concern in its own right—nonetheless cuts across these other demographic domains to offer redemptive possibilities for the nation and the immigrant spouse. But this redemption rests on the condition that an immigrant spouse conform to expectations that she place her marital commitments above all other interests, lest the shadow of material motives darken her migration intentions.

By linking care for the elderly and childbearing with the influx of immigrant Chinese spouses, cross-Strait marriages provoke a wide array of regulatory policies aimed at limiting access to national inclusion, cultivating the health and competitiveness of the population, and maximizing identification with the Taiwanese nation. Precisely because Taiwan faces its greatest sovereign threat from China, the entry of Chinese marital immigrants provokes heightened governmental and societal anxiety about the future national identification of these immigrants and even that of their children. The labyrinthine immigration and residency system that regulates Chinese spouses speaks to the depths of this anxiety and its contested management across the complex terrain of cross-Strait relations. At the same time, however, the myriad decisions Taiwanese bureaucrats and officials make on a daily basis about the fate of Chinese spouses also enable them to enact national sovereignty both at the border and domestically as they assess marital immigrants' entry, residency, and citizenship claims through evaluating marital authenticity and the performance of expected spousal roles. These bureaucratic practices reaffirm public investments in the state of Taiwanese marriages, especially those that enable sovereign claims by uniting spouses across the fluid borders of the Taiwan Strait.

NOTES

1. On the relation of marriage to nation, see Berlant (1997), Borneman (1992), Chao (2004), Constable (2003, 2009), Cott (2000), Friedman (2006), Glosser (2003), and Somerville (2005).

2. For a sample of this literature, see Canaday (2009), Chen (2009), Gardner (2005), Luibhéid (2002), McKeown (2008), and Yue (2008).

3. In her analysis of marriage annulment as a governmental tactic in France, Surkis also shows how "the regulation of marriage produces and protects French sovereignty." Although France certainly enjoys secure sovereignty in comparison to Taiwan, its efforts to combat "fake" and "forced" marriages involving Muslim immigrants invoke a need to uphold the sanctity of French law and public order that reflects "a perceived crisis of the French state" (Surkis 2010: 537).

4. Over the years, this research has been supported by the National Science Foundation (#BCS-0612679), the Wenner-Gren Foundation for Anthropological Research, and the Chiang Ching-kuo Foundation. I am grateful to the many people in Taiwan and China—immigrants, citizens, bureaucrats, officials, NGO workers, and activists—who gave generously of their time and energy to educate me about their experiences, concerns, and aspirations.

5. Only in 1992 were Chinese spouses granted rights to enter, obtain residency, and gain citizenship in Taiwan with passage of the Act Governing Relations between Peoples of the Taiwan Area and the Mainland Area (台灣地區與大陸地區人民關係條例).

6. By comparison, 153,858 foreign spouses had entered Taiwan by the end of 2012, and 101,679 had become naturalized citizens (Taiwan National Immigration Agency and Department of Household Registration, "Number of Foreign and Mainland

Spouses in Each County and City by Documented Status, 1987-2012"; retrieved on August 13, 2013, from www.immigration.gov.tw/public/Attachment/31241924454.xls).

7. For instance, based on surveys conducted between 1999 and 2006, Chu and Yu (2010: 98–99) found that approximately 31 percent of women who first married after 1990 were age twenty-nine or older, and approximately 40 percent were in the twenty-five to twenty-eight age range. In 2012, the average age at first marriage for women was 29.5 years, up from 27.8 in 2006 (Taiwan Department of Household Registration, Ministry of the Interior, "Median and Average Age at Marriage," updated May 30, 2013; retrieved on January 22, 2014, from www.ris.gov.tw/346).

8. A 2010 survey on gender equality conducted by the government-affiliated Research, Development and Evaluation Commission found, however, that roughly 60 percent of respondents did not agree with the statement: "Men should bear the responsibility of making money to support their families, while women's work is handling household chores and caring for the family" ("Taiwanese Believe" 2010). These findings recognize women's high rates of workforce participation but may not indicate actual changes in the gender division of household work, as Yu and Liu (Chapter 10) suggest.

9. Men are certainly a minority among Chinese spouses in Taiwan, constituting approximately 5 percent or less of those who enter the country. Wealthier and better-educated Chinese men tend to expect their Taiwanese wives to relocate to China. I interviewed approximately ten Chinese husbands in Taiwan and China, together with several Taiwanese women married to Chinese men.

10. Interview with author at National Immigration Agency Headquarters in Taipei, February 4, 2008. Another factor that informs this formulation of sham marriage is the inability of Mainland Chinese to enter Taiwan purely for employment unless they are skilled white-collar workers.

11. Pan emphasized her parents' respectability by describing how they worked for reputable work units and raised three daughters, of whom she was the youngest. Pan claimed she had fallen only a few points short of testing into college and, as a result, worked for eighteen years in a state-owned foodstuffs company before marrying her first Taiwanese husband. Although she had had a boyfriend in China, she had never wed prior to this marriage, itself a sign of changing marriage practices in the Mainland.

12. This categorical ambiguity was also recognized by bureaucrats at the other end of the system, such as those who arrested and investigated Chinese spouses suspected of sham marriages and prepared them for deportation. See Chao (2010: 174–175) for a similar commentary by a Mainland affairs policeman about the fluidity between categories of sham and authentic marriages.

13. Not only were these men separated from civilian society in military camps and communities, but military regulations in force in the 1950s barred them from

marriage while they remained in the service. I did interview some couples where the elderly husband was native Taiwanese, typically divorced or widowed, and also seeking a caregiver in old age.

14. I also interviewed veterans who had married younger, never-married women, some of whom bore them children. The risk faced by all wives of elderly veterans was that their husbands might die before they obtained Taiwan citizenship. Prior to 2004, widowed Chinese spouses without minor children in Taiwan enjoyed no protections against deportation if they had not yet become Taiwanese citizens.

15. In both 2009 and 2010, Taiwan's total fertility rate was 1.0, one of the lowest in the world (Population Reference Bureau 2010). By 2011, it had dropped below 1.0. Of the roughly 190,000 babies born in Taiwan in 2009, some 17,000 were born to Chinese and foreign mothers, or 8.7 percent of all births. From 2004 until 2009, children born to foreign and Chinese spouses grew from 1.6 percent of primary and middle-school children to 6.1 percent. By 2009, this meant that 1 in every 8.4 children in the first year of primary school had a parent who was not Taiwanese, and 1 in 24 had a Chinese parent specifically (Lin and Hu 2010).

16. Concerns about the "quality" of children born to cross-border couples feature more prominently in assessments of childbearing by Southeast Asian spouses, and public figures have been taken to task for openly expressing racist attitudes about mixed-race Taiwanese children (Hsia 2009: 34–35).

17. During follow-up interviews I conducted in the summer of 2011, several Chinese women who already had children reported to me that they had been contacted as part of a government survey to assess their future childbearing plans and to learn what kinds of assistance would encourage them to have another child.

18. This is in contrast to Southeast Asian wives who are marked as racially different and, hence, who are seen as producing mixed-race Taiwanese children.

19. Interview at National Immigration Agency headquarters, Taipei, Taiwan, May 18, 2008. There was a year and a half period during which this restriction on the length of time a child could spend outside of Taiwan also applied to divorced Chinese spouses who had acquired citizenship within the past three years. In other words, NIA bureaucrats saw fit to regulate the childrearing arrangements made by a single Chinese parent even after she or he had become a Taiwanese citizen. Elsewhere, I have argued that this regulation was part of a broader array of policies that created a graduated citizenship structure in Taiwan that denied full citizenship rights to Taiwanese citizens who recently hailed from Mainland China (Friedman 2010b).

20. The women in the first part of the video are actresses from a local theater troupe who recite narratives culled from public responses to a blog that Chen established in the aftermath of his humiliating experience at AIT. The second section features Chinese wives narrating their own experiences.

REFERENCES

Agamben, Giorgio. 1998. *Homo Sacer: Sovereign Power and Bare Life*, Daniel Heller-Roazen, trans. Palo Alto, CA: Stanford University Press.

———. 2005. *State of Exception*, Kevin Attell, trans. Chicago: The University of Chicago Press.

Berlant, Lauren. 1997. *The Queen of America Goes to Washington City: Essays on Sex and Citizenship*. Durham, NC: Duke University Press.

Bigo, Didier, and Elspeth Guild. 2005. *Controlling Frontiers: Free Movement into and within Europe*. Aldershot, UK: Ashgate Publishing.

Borneman, John. 1992. *Belonging in the Two Berlins: Kin, State, Nation*. Cambridge, UK: Cambridge University Press.

Canaday, Margot. 2009. *The Straight State: Sexuality and Citizenship in Twentieth-Century America*. Princeton, NJ: Princeton University Press.

Chao Yen-ning (趙彥寧). 2004. "公民身分, 現代國家與親密生活: 以老單身榮民與 '大陸新娘'的婚姻為研究案例" (Citizenship Status, the Modern Nation and Intimate Life: A Case Study of Marriages between Veterans and Mainland Brides). 台灣社會學 (*Taiwan Sociology*) 8: 1–41.

———. 2010. "跨境母制公民身分: 變遷中的中國閩北國境邊區道德經濟" (Transnational Maternal Citizenship: Changing Moral Economy on State Margins). 台灣社會學刊 (*Taiwanese Journal of Sociology*) 44: 155–212.

Chen, Chao-ju. 2009. "Gendered Borders: The Historical Formation of Women's Nationality under Law in Taiwan." *Positions* 17(2): 289–314.

Chu, C. Y. Cyrus, and Ruoh-Rong Yu. 2010. *Understanding Chinese Families: A Comparative Study of Taiwan and Southeast China*. Oxford, UK: Oxford University Press.

Constable, Nicole. 2003. *Romance on a Global Stage: Pen Pals, Virtual Ethnography, and "Mail Order" Marriages*. Berkeley: University of California Press.

———. 2009. "The Commodification of Intimacy: Marriage, Sex, and Reproductive Labor." *Annual Review of Anthropology* 38: 49–64.

Cott, Nancy F. 2000. *Public Vows: A History of Marriage and the Nation*. Cambridge, MA: Harvard University Press.

Coutin, Susan. 2003. "Cultural Logics of Belonging and Movement: Transnationalism, Naturalization, and U.S. Immigration Politics." *American Ethnologist* 30(4): 508–526.

Dailey, Jane. 2009. "Race, Marriage, and Sovereignty in the New World Order." *Theoretical Inquiries in Law* 10(2): 511–533.

Friedman, Sara L. 2006. *Intimate Politics: Marriage, the Market, and State Power in Southeastern China*. Cambridge, MA: Harvard University Asia Center, Harvard University Press.

———. 2010a. "Determining 'Truth' at the Border: Immigration Interviews, Chinese Marital Migrants, and Taiwan's Sovereignty Dilemmas." *Citizenship Studies* 14(2): 167–183.

———. 2010b. "Marital Immigration and Graduated Citizenship: Post-Naturalization Restrictions on Mainland Chinese Spouses in Taiwan." *Pacific Affairs* 83(1): 73–93.

———. 2013. "Mobilizing Gender in Cross-Strait Marriages: Patrilineal Tensions, Care Work Expectations, and a Dependency Model of Marital Immigration." In *Mobile Horizons: Dynamics across the Taiwan Strait*, Wen-hsin Yeh, ed., pp. 147–177. Berkeley: Institute of East Asian Studies Publications, University of California.

Gardner, Martha. 2005. *The Qualities of a Citizen: Women, Immigration, and Citizenship, 1870–1965*. Princeton, NJ: Princeton University Press.

Glosser, Susan L. 2003. *Chinese Visions of Family and State, 1915–1953*. Berkeley: University of California Press.

Hsia, Hsiao-chuan. 2009. "Foreign Brides, Multiple Citizenship and the Immigrant Movement in Taiwan." *Asian and Pacific Migration Journal* 18(1): 17–46.

Li Mei-ling (李美玲). 2007. 人口政策白皮書及實施計畫之研究: 子計畫一 '因應我國少子女化社會對策之研究' 期末報告 (Population Policy White Paper and Implementation Plan Study: Sub-Plan 1 "Study of Societal Counter-Measures to Address Our Nation's Declining Birthrate," Final Report). Commissioned by the Taiwan Ministry of the Interior, Taipei.

Lin Xiaoyun (林曉雲) and Hu Qinghui (胡清暉). 2010. "外配子女激增, 小一生8個就一個" (Children of Foreign Spouses Soar in Number, One in Eight among First-Year Primary School Students). 自由時報 (*Liberty Times*), March 31. Available at www.libertytimes.com.tw/2010/new/mar/31/today-life10.htm.

Luibhéid, Eithne. 2002. *Entry Denied: Controlling Sexuality at the Border*. Minneapolis: University of Minnesota Press.

McKeown, Adam M. 2008. *Melancholy Order: Asian Migration and the Globalization of Borders*. New York: Columbia University Press.

Mountz, Alison. 2004. "Embodying the Nation-State: Canada's Response to Human Smuggling." *Political Geography* 23(3): 323–345.

Newendorp, Nicole DeJong. 2008. *Uneasy Reunions: Immigration, Citizenship, and Family Life in Post-1997 Hong Kong*. Palo Alto, CA: Stanford University Press.

Ong, Aihwa. 2000. "Graduated Sovereignty in South-East Asia." *Theory, Culture and Society* 17(4): 55–75.

Population Reference Bureau. 2010. World Population Data Sheet. Available at www.prb.org/pdf10/10wpds_eng.pdf.

Pratt, Anna. 2005. *Securing Borders: Detention and Deportation in Canada*. Vancouver, BC: UBC Press.

Rajaram, Prem Kumar, and Carl Grundy-Warr. 2007. *Borderscapes: Hidden Geographies and Politics at Territory's Edge*. Minneapolis: University of Minnesota Press.

Salter, Mark B. 2006. "The Global Visa Regime and the Political Technologies of the International Self: Borders, Bodies, Biopolitics." *Alternatives* 31(2): 167–189.

Sassen, Saskia. 2006. *Territory, Authority, Rights: From Medieval to Global Assemblages*. Princeton, NJ: Princeton University Press.

Somerville, Siobhan B. 2005. "Queer *Loving*." *GLQ* 11(3): 335–370.

Surkis, Judith. 2010. "Hymenal Politics: Marriage, Secularism, and French Sovereignty." *Public Culture* 22(3): 531–556.

Taiwan Department of Household Registration, Ministry of the Interior, "Median and Average Age at Marriage," updated May 30, 2013; retrieved on January 22, 2014, from www.ris.gov.tw/346.

———. "Statistics on Marriages between Nationals and Foreigners," February 28, 2013; retrieved on May 17, 2013, from www.immigration.gov.tw/public/Attachment/33261451333.xls.

Taiwan National Immigration Agency and Department of Household Registration, "Number of Foreign and Mainland Spouses in Each County and City by Documented Status, 1987–2012"; retrieved on August 13, 2013, from www.immigration.gov.tw/public/Attachment/31241924454.xls.

"Taiwanese Believe Men and Women Should Share Work." *Taipei Times*, August 15, 2010: 2.

Yue, Audrey. 2008. "Same-Sex Migration in Australia: From Interdependency to Intimacy." *GLQ* 14(2–3): 239–262.

INDEX

Europe: age at first marriage in, 97, 98; education of women in, 239; extramarital births in, 21, 28n1; fertility rates in, 23; marriage in, 3–4, 147–48, 219; mate choice in, 98; OECD, 21, 97; SDT in, 3, 23; transgender marriage in, 200

European Court of Human Rights: *Goodwin v. United Kingdom*, 200, 201

Evans, Harriet, 15, 126, 127

extramarital births, 5, 228; in Europe, 21, 28n1; in Hong Kong, 22, 28n4, 147; in Mexico, 21; in PRC, 28n4, 41, 43; in Taiwan, 22, 28n4

extramarital sexual relationships, 3, 138, 177–80, 181; cohabitation, 16, 23, 42–43, 46, 50, 52, 53, 62–63, 68, 113, 114, 147, 159n, 176, 201, 228; concubinage, 11, 14, 17, 42, 56n3; gender differences regarding, 10, 14, 15, 16–17, 25, 45, 63, 64, 73, 76–77, 79, 81, 82–83, 90, 267–68; marital infidelity, 1, 10, 14, 15, 26, 46, 47, 49, 51–53, 55, 56n3, 78, 92, 171–72, 175–76, 177–78, 183, 185, 266, 267, 273–76, 277, 278–79; in transnational families, 266, 267, 273–76, 277, 278–79, 280, 281. *See also* love relationships; premarital sexual relationships; prostitution

failed dog, 125, 140n9

family formation: in Confucianism, 2, 5, 6, 25–26, 91, 113, 240–41, 255; deinstitutionalization of, 5, 26–27, 281; nuclear family ideology, 221–22, 228, 233, 234n9; as patrilineal, 2, 25–26, 42, 230, 241, 242–43, 246, 255. *See also* childbearing; one-child policy; parenthood

Family Planning Association of Hong Kong, 154

Fan, C. Cindy, 240

Fan Shuwei, 53

Farquhar, Judith, 89

Farrer, James, 16, 45, 112, 124, 133, 138, 140n2, 150, 267

Feeney, Griffith, 100

feminism, 12, 30n13, 228, 231, 268–69

fertility rates: in Hong Kong, 3, 6, 21–22, 31nn27,29, 147; in PRC, 21–22, 31nn27,29; as subreplacement, 6, 22, 23, 97, 147, 240, 299, 305, 308n15; in Taiwan, 21, 22, 31nn27,29, 239–40, 241, 255,

256n5, 296, 299, 305, 308n15. *See also* marital fertility; one-child policy

Fienberg, Stephen, 161n11

filial obligation, 6, 27, 138, 227, 232, 236n17

Fincham, Frank, 161n11

Finder, Susan, 48

Fineman, Martha, 219, 225

Fong, Vanessa L., 122

Foucault, Michel, 99

France: marriage annulment in, 306n3

Franck, Jens-Uwe, 55n1

Freeman, Caren, 25, 264

Friedman, Sara L., 43, 44, 45, 48, 50, 119, 138, 189, 219, 222, 223, 279, 280–81

Fu, Hualing, 48, 54–55

Fujian, 244

Gagnon, John H., 66

Gambaurd, Michele R., 264

Gao Heping, 65

Gao, Lu, 45

Gardner, Martha, 306n2

Garner, Paul, 65

gay men, 18, 27

gender differences: regarding age at first marriage, 98, 99, 100, 101, 102, 103–9, 114nn1,3,6–8, 115n9, 152, 241; regarding cross-border marriages, 24–25, 149, 160n5, 174–75, 288; regarding dating, 150–51, 155, 156, 157, 160n7; regarding education, 122, 140nn5,6, 149–50, 151, 154–55, 156, 159, 167, 239, 240, 252, 254, 257n14; regarding employment, 155, 156, 157–58, 160n2, 239, 244, 250–51, 252; regarding expectations of marriage, 10, 154, 167, 168; regarding extramarital sexual relationships, 10, 14, 15, 16–17, 25, 45, 63, 64, 73, 76–77, 79, 81, 82–83, 90, 267–68; regarding income, 80, 121, 132, 154, 156, 157, 239, 245, 247, 248, 249, 250, 256n4, 257n14; regarding love relationships, 71–72, 73, 74, 76–78, 79–80, 81, 82–83, 90, 92n5; regarding premarital sexual relationships, 14, 63, 64, 73, 76–77, 79, 81, 82–83, 90; regarding rejection of marriage, 107–11, 115n12, 123, 125, 148–49, 159; regarding satisfaction with marriage, 9–10, 153–54, 155, 156, 157, 158–59; regarding sexual norms, 14–15, 16, 18, 65–66, 89, 90, 267–68. *See also* division of housework; gender roles; marital power

Hong Kong (*continued*)
Legislative Council, 19; marital satisfaction in, 9–10, 152–58, 160n10, 161nn11,12, 249; Marriage Ordinance, 190, 191–93, 200; Matrimonial Causes Ordinance, 190, 192–94, 200; men's attitudes regarding gender equality, 182–85; men's attitudes regarding Hong Kong women, 165–66, 167, 168–70, 173, 175–77, 180, 182, 187; men's attitudes regarding Mainland women, 172, 174–75, 176, 177, 187, 279; migration to, 148; Miss W case, 19, 20, 189–91, 192, 193–94, 199–210, 210n1; vs. PRC, 1–2, 4, 7–9, 11, 12–13, 15–16, 17, 19, 20–21, 22, 23, 26–27, 28, 30n14, 31nn27,29, 41, 55, 74, 125; rejection of marriage in, 147, 148–50, 159, 160n6, 211n3; same-sex relationships in, 17, 19, 20–21, 31n22, 32n32; sexual norms in, 15–16, 63; as Special Administrative Region (SAR) of PRC, 2, 165, 166, 186–87; vs. Taiwan, 1–2, 4, 7–10, 11, 12–13, 15, 17, 20–21, 22, 23, 25, 26–27, 28, 30n14, 31nn27,29, 193, 197, 239, 241, 243, 274; transgender people in, 19, 20, 159, 189–210, 210n1, 211nn5,8
Hong Kong Council of Social Services: Social Development Index, 160n3
Hong Kong Family Life Survey, 152, 160n9
Honig, Emily, 125
hookups, 66, 67, 89
housework. *See* division of housework
Hsia, Hsiao-chuan, 308n16
Hsieh Guo-hua, 275
Hsu, Jenny W., 20
Hsu, Victoria, 222
Hsung, Ray-May, 242
Hu Qinghui, 299, 308n15
Hu, Xiaoling, 140n3
Hu, Yu-Ying, 20, 27
Huang, Chieh-shan, 29n7, 98
Huang, Hans Tao-Ming, 15, 20
Huang, Philip C. C., 29n12, 43
Huang, Qing Tian, 167
Huang, Shirlena, 263
Huang Yingying, 63, 65, 66, 92n3
Huang, Youqin, 240
Human Rights Watch, 31n24
humility, 167, 182–83, 185–86, 187
hypergamy. *See* marriage

Imperial China: divorce in, 10–11, 29n10, 224; Ming dynasty, 17; polygamous marriages in, 30n17; vs. PRC, 10–11, 17, 136; Qing Dynasty, 11, 14, 17, 29n10, 224; same-sex relationships in, 17, 30n17
income, 56n10, 125, 131, 133, 134, 168, 187, 288; gender differences regarding, 80, 121, 132, 154, 156, 157, 239, 245, 247, 248, 249, 250, 256n4, 257n14; relationship to division of housework, 245, 247, 248, 249, 257n14; relationship to marital power, 252, 253, 254
International Court of Justice (ICJ), 201
International Covenant on Civil and Political Rights (ICCPR): Article 23(3), 212n13
International Covenant on Economic, Social, and Cultural Rights (ICESCR): Article 10, 212n13
Internet, 85, 86, 271; social media, 1, 4, 69, 70, 220–21
Israel: transgender marriage in, 201

Jankowiak, William R., 62, 63, 64, 66, 68, 77, 81
Japan: cohabitation in, 23, 112, 114; family planning in, 239–40; Taiwan as colony of, 15, 224, 240; transgender marriage in, 201
Jeffreys, Elaine, 18
Jia Mingjun, 52, 53
Jiang Yongping, 126
Jin Yihong, 125
Johnson, David R., 161n11
Jones, Gavin, 7, 23, 97, 109

Kalmijn, Mathew, 151
Kang, Wenqing, 17, 18, 30nn18,19
Kemenade, Willem van, 263
Kenney, Catherin T., 152
Kevin v. Attorney-General (Cth), 212n11
Khan, Aziz, 45
Kibria, Nazli, 266
King, Mark, 198
Kipnis, Laura: *Against Love*, 273
Knudsen, Knud, 245, 246
Kobayashi, Audrey, 263
Ko, Dorothy, 126
Kong, Travis S. K., 20, 27
Koo, Anita C., 159n
Kung I-chun, 267
Kunshan, 269

Tsay, Ruey-Ming, 242
Tsuchiya, Haruka, 68
Tsuya, Noriko O., 97, 109
Tu, Ping, 31n27
Tuma, Nancy, 99, 111

Unger, Jonathan, 64
United Kingdom: *Bellinger v. Bellinger*,
    200–201; *Corbett v. Corbett*, 191,
    200–201, 202, 208, 209, 210n2,
    212nn11,12; Nullity of Marriage Act,
    192; transgender marriage in, 200–201
United Nations, 123; Convention on Consent
    to Marry, Minimum Age for Marriage
    and Registration of Marriages, 212n13
United States: cohabitation in, 114;
    contraception in, 55n1; dating
    relationships in, 62–63; Defense of
    Marriage Act, 204, 211n6, 213n14;
    divorce in, 56n2; education of women
    in, 239; extramarital births in, 5, 28n4;
    family law in, 225; "hooking up" in,
    89; interracial marriage in, 56n1, 206;
    marriage in, 3–4, 5, 113, 114, 147–48,
    201, 219; mythic code of love in, 70–71;
    transgender people in, 195, 201; visa
    policies in, 301–2, 303–4
United States Supreme Court: *Bowers
    v. Hardwick*, 213n15; *Griswold v.
    Connecticut*, 55n1; *Lawrence v. Texas*,
    213n17; *Loving v. Virginia*, 56n1, 206;
    United States v. Windsor, 211n6

Van Laningham, Jody, 161n11
Ventrone, Nicole A., 66
Voigt, Kevin, 19
Vuorela, Ulla, 263

Walker, Kristen, 212n10
Waller, Willard, 64
Wan, Marco, 201
Wang, Annie Y., 45, 50, 56n9
Wang Baoan, 45
Wang, Chieh-shan, 6
Wang Feng, 6, 7, 21, 65, 89, 122, 123, 138,
    140n8
Wang, Gungwu, 266
Wang, Jun-lin, 263
Wang Xiaodong, 28n4
Waters, James L., 263
Watson, James L., 266
Watson, Rubie S., 24, 42

Weiss, Robert: on issue-based grounded
    theory, 92n2
Wærness, Kari, 245, 246
Whyte, Martin King, 65, 119, 121, 129, 137,
    249; on marital change in China, 64, 99,
    112, 113–14
widowed/widows, 14, 42,108, 287, 288, 297,
    308nn13,14
Wilding, Raelene, 264
Wills, Katie, 264, 267
Wilson, James Q., 148
Winter, Sam, 197–98, 211n5
Wolf, Arthur, 6, 29n7, 98
Wolfe, Donald M., 245, 257n16
Wong, Raymond Sin-Kwok, 242
Wong, Thomas W. P., 159n
Wooldridge, Jeffrey M., 257nn14,17
Woo, Margaret, 46, 53
World Bank, 31nn27,29
World Trade Organization (WTO), 47
Wouters, Cas, 63, 64, 68
Wu, H. Laura, 17, 30n17
Wu, Juanjuan, 125
W v. Registrar of Marriages, 19, 20, 189–91,
    192, 193–94, 199–210, 210n1

Xia Feng, 135–36
Xiamen (Fujian Province), 269, 275
Xie, Yu, 243
Xu Anqi, 46, 63, 64, 65, 69, 70, 76, 77, 81, 84
Xu Hua, 53
Xu, Xiaohe, 64, 65, 250, 257n16
Xu Xu, 44

Yan, Yunxiang, 16, 44, 45, 63, 64, 66, 89, 119,
    133
Yang, C. K., 98
Yang Fan, 122
Yang, Feng, 126, 127
Yang, Jing-li, 223, 228
Yang Quanhe, 104
Yang, Wen-Shan, 250
Yang Xiong, 66, 80, 92n3
yan yiu, 196–97
Yao Peikuan, 80
Ye, Wenzhen, 127
Yeh, Anthony G. O., 44
Yeoh, Brenda, 263, 264, 267
Yi, Chin-Chun, 242, 250
Yi, Chuizhi, 140n6
Yip, Yat Chi, 167
Yongchun, 126

The authorized representative in the EU for product safety and compliance is:
Mare Nostrum Group
B.V Doelen 72
4831 GR Breda
The Netherlands

www.ingramcontent.com/pod-product-compliance
Lightning Source LLC
Chambersburg PA
CBHW031726280326
41926CB00098B/620